ROYAL HISTORICAL SOCIETY
STUDIES IN HISTORY
SERIES
No. 15

GUNS AND GOVERNMENT

The Ordnance Office under the later Stuarts

Other volumes in this series

Copies obtainable on order from
Swift Printers, (Sales) Ltd, 1-7 Albion Place, Britton Street, London EC1M 5RE

GUNS AND GOVERNMENT

The Ordnance Office under the later Stuarts

H. C. Tomlinson

LONDON
ROYAL HISTORICAL SOCIETY
1979

The Society records its gratitude to the following, whose generosity made possible the initiation of this series: The British Academy; The Pilgrim Trust; The Twenty-Seven Foundation; The United States Embassy's bicentennial funds; The Wolfson Trust; several private donors.

This volume is published with the help of a grant from the late Isobel Thornley's Bequest to the University of London.

Printed in England
by Swift Printers Ltd
London, E.C.1.

To my parents

Within the Tower is kept the Office of her majesty's Ordnance, which hath been always an Office of great account and importance, as being the only standing and grand magazine of the principal preparatives, habiliaments, utensils and instruments of war, as well by sea as land, for the defence and safety of the kingdom. And consequently hath influence in the navies, forts, castles and armies thereof, having the superintendence, ordering and disposing as well of the grand magazine lodged in the Tower as at the Minories, Woolwich, Chatham, Windsor, Portsmouth, Plymouth, Hull and elsewhere, wherein is ammunition at all times for as many land and sea forces as may not only defend England but be formidable to all our neighbours. (Edward Chamberlayne, *The . . . Present State of England . . .* , 4th edn., 1673, p. 224.)

CONTENTS

TABLES

ABBREVIATIONS

Acts PCCol.	*Acts of the Privy Council, Colonial*
Add. MS. or Charter	Additional Manuscript or Charter, British Library
Adm.	Admiralty Document, Public Record Office
AO	Audit Office Roll, Public Record Office
Blenheim	Manuscript at Blenheim Palace, Oxfordshire
Bodl.	Bodleian Library, Oxford
BL	British Library, London
BIHR	*Bulletin of the Institute of Historical Research*
Burnet	Burnet, *History of . . . Own Time,* 6 vols. (2nd edn., Oxford, 1933)
Cal. SP Col. Am. & W. Indies	*Calendar of State Papers Colonial, America and West Indies*
Cal. SP Dom.	*Calendar of State Papers, Domestic*
Cal. Treas. Books	*Calendar of Treasury Books*
Cal. Treas. Papers	*Calendar of Treasury Papers*
Cat. Pepys	*Catalogue of Pepys Manuscripts at Magdalene College, Cambridge*
C.	Chancery Document, Public Record Office
(C.) RO	(County) Record Office
Chandler	Chandler, Richard, *History of the Proceedings of the House of Commons . . . ,* 14 vols. (1742-44)
Cobbett	Cobbett, William, *Parliamentary History of England . . . ,* 36 vols. (1806-20)
CJ	*Journals of the House of Commons*
Corbett	Corbett Manuscript, Admiralty Library, London
D.	Dartmouth Collection, Staffordshire County Record Office, Stafford
DNB	Dictionary of National Biography
EHR	*English Historical Review*

Egerton	Egerton Manuscript, British Library
Erle	Erle Manuscript, Churchill College, Cambridge
Harl.	Harleian Manuscript, British Library
HMC	*Historical Manuscripts Commission*
King's	King's Manuscript, British Library
Lansdowne	Lansdowne Manuscript, British Library
LJ	*Journals of the House of Lords*
Luttrell	N. Luttrell, *A Brief Historical Relation of State Affairs from September 1678 to April 1714* (6 vols. Oxford, 1857)
Luttrell Diary	*The Parliamentary Diary of Narcissus Luttrell, 1691-93,* ed. H. Horwitz, (Oxford, 1972)
NMM	National Maritime Museum, Greenwich
Naval Minutes	*Samuel Pepys Naval Minutes,* ed. J.R. Tanner, Navy Records Society 60 (1926)
O.b.	Ordnance board
Own Life	*The Life of Edward, Earl of Clarendon . . . by Himself,* 3 vols. (3rd edn., Oxford, 1761)
Parl. Papers	*Parliamentary Papers.* (British Library pagination)
Pepys Diary	*The Diary of Samuel Pepys,* ed. H.B. Wheatley, 8 vols. (1904-05)
PL	Pepys Library Manuscript, Magdalene College, Cambridge
Prob.	Probate Document Public Record Office
PC	Privy Council Record, Public Record Office
PRO	Public Record Office, London
Rawl.	Rawlinson Manuscript, Bodleian Library
Sloane	Sloane Manuscript, British Library
SP	State Papers, Public Record Office
Stowe	Stowe Manuscript, British Library
TRHS	*Transactions of the Royal Historical Society*
T.	Treasury Document, Public Record Office
VCH	*Victoria County Histories.*
WO	War Office Document, Public Record Office

Note on dates, spelling etc.

All dates are given in the English Old Style (that is the Julian Calendar). The new year, however, has been taken to start on 1 January rather than 25 March.

Spelling and punctuation have been modernised.

Place of publication is London unless otherwise stated.

A full bibliography can be consulted in the bound Reading University Library copy of my Ph. D. dissertation on which this book is based. ('The Organisation and Activities of the English Ordnance Office, 1660-1714', University of Reading, 1974).

References to the Marlborough MSS. (now at the British Library) relate to the system of classification that was in use before the collection was transferred from Blenheim Palace.

PREFACE

No administrative historian of the modern period can truthfully claim to have written a fully comprehensive account of his subject. This is especially true of the historian of the later Stuart Ordnance Office. For quite apart from the density of his sources, which necessitates a vigorous selection of material, the vast range of the responsibilities of the department obliges him to limit the scope of his study. (If, in the words of Napoleon's nephew, 'l'histoire de l'artillerie est l'histoire du progrès des sciences et partant de la civilisation',[1] the history of the department that administers 'l'artillerie' is no less all-embracing.) There is nothing in the following pages, therefore, about the military activities of the department on campaign[2]; there is only a passing mention of Ordnance technology; there is little on the building activities of the department.[3] This study, moreover, is confined to the English Ordnance Office and does not deal with the Scottish and Irish departments, which were separately administered until the Unions of 1707 and 1801. This book, then, is essentially a home-based account of the personnel and organisation of the later Stuart Ordnance Office. In the introduction, the origins of the Office prior to 1660 are briefly traced and the importance of the period in the department's development is discussed. Chapter 1 places the department in relation to other organs of central government. Chapter 2 examines the office-holders themselves — their background, their duties and how seriously these were undertaken; their methods of appointment, promotion and dismissal; and the rewards of an Ordnance place. The following two chapters are concerned with the department in action — the contracting system for various Ordnance stores, the problems of storage and the efficiency of distribution, as well as the organisation of artillery trains. The fifth chapter deals with the key to efficient administration — finances. In the final chapter an attempt is made to place the Ordnance reforms of the period in the context of the advances that were made in

---

1 Cited by F. Duncan, *History of the Royal Regiment of Artillery*, 2 vols. (2nd, edn. 1874), I, titlepage.

2 For an excellent recent study on this, see David Chandler, *The Art of War in the Age of Marlborough* (1976), pp. 141 ff.

3 It is hoped that this will form the subject of a later book on the re-fortification of Restoration England. For an interim survey see my 'The Ordnance Office and the King's, Forts, 1660-1714', *Architectural History* 16 (1973), 5-25. My chapter in a forthcoming book on Forts and Fortification (ed. R.H. Whitworth) will be devoted to an examination of the growth and development of the department's control over fortifications in the 300 years of its existence.

late seventeenth-century central government in general. This book, then, examines, within the broad context of central government, the performance, as well as the organisation, composition and development of an important and hitherto neglected department of state in a formative period of English administrative history.

The book is based on a doctoral thesis, which has been completely revised for publication. Chapter 2 has been re-written and all the other chapters have been substantially modified. I therefore wish to thank all those who have helped me in the preparation of both works.

The initial research for the thesis was undertaken during the years 1970-4, when I was a postgraduate student at Reading University and Bedford College, London. The transition from thesis to book was undertaken intermittently during my tenure of a University of Wales fellowship at University College, Cardiff. I am grateful to all these bodies for having financed my research. I am also indebted to numerous scholars for assistance in the preparation of this work but I would especially like to acknowledge the help of the following: Professor G.E. Aylmer, who examined my thesis and made innumerable suggestions as to how it might be improved; Dr J. Mordaunt Crook, my former tutor, who originally suggested that the Ordnance records would be worth investigating; Mr E.C.L. Mullins for allowing me to make use of the History of Parliament draft biographies in his custody; Dr Ian Roy, who kindly agreed to read my thesis before it was re-written for publication; Mr E.A. Smith, my former supervisor, who read my thesis in draft form and skilfully guided me over the Ph. D. degree hurdle; and Mr J.C. Sainty, who read an earlier version of the Office-Holders chapter and generously provided me with many references. I should also like to thank the staffs of the libraries and record offices where I have worked, especially those at the Public Record Office, the British Library and the Institute of Historical Research. My typists, Mrs C. Johnson, Mrs Dobie and Mrs Sansom, have also coped magnificently with my badly mutilated pencil scripts. My greatest debt, however, is due to my wife, who gave unfailingly of her time at a hectic period of her own research and who has been a constant source of encouragement throughout. It scarcely needs saying that I alone as author am responsible for any sins of omission or commission.

H. C. TOMLINSON

INTRODUCTION

The ancestry of the Ordnance Office may be traced back to the early part of the reign of Edward I when the Privy Wardrobe began to act as an itinerant armoury for the Household forces during the Welsh Wars. The Privy Wardrobe continued its peripatetic existence throughout the reign of Edward I and Edward II, even though it existed as a permanent storehouse with a permanent staff, and was strictly subordinate to the king's Chamber and the Great Wardrobe. A decisive chapter in the history of the Privy Wardrobe coincided with the keepership of John Fleet, 1323-44, who presided over a settled Institution, situated at the Tower of London — an institution that was still bound up with the other arms of the Household but which had a permanent base from which to operate. Fleet was succeeded by Robert Mildenhall, who became the first person appointed by patent to take charge of 'keeping the king's Wardrobe within the Tower of London'. Mildenhall drew up separate accounts of his own which were strictly limited to his Privy Wardrobe functions in the Tower, and accounted directly to the Exchequer, even though he was still a clerk and receiver of the Chamber and Keeper of the Mint. In 1348 the Chamber operated from Westminster rather than the Tower and from c.1355 the Privy Wardrobe was largely independent of its existence, the greater parts of its receipts from this time onwards coming from the Exchequer, which maintained a tight control of its finances and its activities. With the retirement of Rothwell as keeper in 1360 the independence of the Privy Wardrobe at the Tower was emphasised when the offices of keeper of the Mint and the Wardrobe were separated.

From c.1360-1500 the Privy Wardrobe consolidated its position at the expense of the Chamber and gradually emancipated itself from the active control of the Great Wardrobe. At the same time the stock of equipment at the Tower increased. The accounts of Henry Snaith from June 1360 mark the beginning of the continuous testimony to the existence of firearms as a regular part of the Tower stores, which greatly increased during the following war years. The king's artiller, his smith and carpenter, moreover, constituted a small permanent staff at the Tower to repair these stores. The gradual separation of the Privy Wardrobe at the Tower and its consequent expansion as a permanent arms store with a small ancillary staff thus occurred during the Hundred Years War when it became far more convenient for the Tower to be a central depository. Whereas the English border wars at the end of the thirteenth and the beginning of the fourteenth centuries had encouraged an itinerant organisation away from the capital.[1]

The process by which the Privy Wardrobe was replaced by an Ordnance Office is not entirely clear and the crucial change, the patenting of a master of Ordnance, cannot be precisely dated. The keepers of the Privy Wardrobe were continuously appointed until 1476 and held the additional title of keepers of the artillery within the Tower, but many of their responsibilities had disappeared before this. By 1423 they had ceased to receive funds for artillery, armour or the wages of the keeper of armour. In 1427 the keeper of armour took charge of the artillery and other military equipment in the Tower and nine years later he was receiving his wages from an independent source. The earliest surviving patented commissions mentioning the word 'ordnance' were made out in 1414 to Nicholas Merbury to be 'master of our works, engines, cannon and other kinds of ordnance for war' and to John Louth as clerk to provide workmen on account of the works of the engines, guns and ordnance. But it is likely that these men were professional soldiers who were given commissions for particular campaigns, rather than permanent administrators at the Tower, and that the title of 'master of our . . . Ordnance' was transferred from the field to the Tower at a later date. All that can be said with any certainty is that some time during the second quarter of the fifteenth century the keepers of the Privy Wardrobe became pensioners with no funds at their disposal, whilst the Armoury and Ordnance developed as offshoots of the Privy Wardrobe and became separated organisations which took over its responsibilities, just as the Privy Wardrobe itself had stemmed from the organs of the Household.

The Armoury and the Ordnance initially developed in similar ways and were established on an equal footing in the fifteenth century. In 1438 a yeoman and groom were added to the offices of keeper of armour and sergeant, which official was elevated to the rank of master in 1462. The patent appointing the master of the Ordnance in 1461 also made provision for a yeoman and a clerk, although the first appointments of these offices by patent did not occur until 1484. The masters of the Ordnance, who can be traced after 1450 without break in the patent rolls, were the administrative working heads of the Office. The yeomen and clerks had no fixed duties but performed any

1   The medieval origins of the department may be traced in T.F. Tout, *Chapters in Medieval Administrative History*, 4 vols. (Manchester, 1928), IV, 439 ff. Also see T.F. Tout, 'Firearms in England in the Fourteenth Century', *Collected Papers of T.F. Tout* (Manchester, 1924), pp. 242 ff. for the increase in Tower Stores.

miscellaneous tasks which might be necessary for the smooth running of the Office. Alongside these three officials worked a group of craftsmen who were retained by patent but were not responsible to them. By the beginning of the Tudor period, therefore, the embryo of the future Ordnance Office had emerged from the depths of the king's Household.[1]

It was in the early Tudor period that the major developments took place within the Office, so that by the middle of the sixteenth century the master, clerk and yeoman had given way to something resembling the later Ordnance board. The clerk and yeoman of the Ordnance declined in importance in relation to other Ordnance officials. The clerk became a sinecure in the 1540s when John Rogers, the engineer, held the office. After this period, the clerk simply became the one board member concerned with internal book-keeping. The office of yeoman declined more completely under the tenure of Leonard and Thomas Skeffington. Although it still existed in 1560 it had disappeared by 1584 and was not revived. A number of new offices were created. The master gunner was added to the senior staff between 1485 and 1506, but his duty of inspecting stores was taken over in c.1537 when a surveyor was appointed. The most dramatic change, however, occurred in 1544 when Thomas Seymour, the king's brother-in-law, was made master with a vastly increased fee, and Christopher Morris, the master since 1536, was given the new rank of lieutenant of the Ordnance. The new lieutenant took over the functions of the old master and became the working head of the Office. His control of the Office treasury with the surveyor after 1547 and his presentation of the annual account further increased his importance.[2] From 1544 the mastership of the Ordnance was generally held by a great man of state.

These changes were paralleled by contemporaneous developments in naval administration. By 1545 the composition of the Navy Board was remarkably similar to that of the Ordnance.[3] Ordnance and naval

1 For the above see J.H. Leslie, 'The Honourable Board of Ordnance, 1299-1855', *Journal of the Society for Army Historical Research* 4 (1925) 103; O.F.G. Hogg, *The Royal Arsenal*, (2 vols., (Oxford, 1963), I, 27; C.S.L. Davies, 'Supply Services of English Armed Forces, 1509-50' (unpublished Oxford D. Phil. thesis, 1963), pp. 120-1; R. Ashley, 'The Organisation and Administration of the Tudor Office of Ordnance', (unpublished Oxford B. Litt. thesis, 1973), pp. 27 ff.

2 These and other changes relating to the increase in the gunners and artificers establishments and the gradual definition of their responsibilities in the first half of the sixteenth century are detailed in Davies, pp. 121 ff. and Ashley, pp. 36, 38-40, 57 ff.

3 The emergence of both institutions may have been the result of Cromwell's

finances, moreover, were similarly regularised at this time. In the early years of the sixteenth century Ordnance officials had controlled only part of the money spent on supplies. Departmental creditors could be paid directly from the Chamber treasury, by the Treasury of Wars, by a special treasurer for military equipment or the master of the Ordnance himself. With the ending of these special accounts Ordnance finance became less complicated, and by the 1540s payments were beginning to be made through Ordnance treasurers, although many artificers continued to be paid direct from the central treasury. By 1546 the practice had also begun to be adopted of lump sums being issued to the Ordnance in advance of requirements. This corresponded to naval procedure but the naval officials had far greater control over the disposal of their cash than the Ordnance officers of the period.[1]

The major change in the constitution of the Office thus took place between 1537 and 1547 in a time of threatened invasion, general rearmament and major military undertakings. A separate accounting system had emerged in this period and the Office establishment had been given the form it was to keep until the civil war.

The later developments of the sixteenth century were simply a regularisation of existing procedures. The financial crisis of 1552 and the enquiry to determine the amount of money due to the government produced the first of a long series of declared accounts, which were to remain the basis of Ordnance accounting throughout much of its existence. The process of centralisation of Ordnance finances which had been tentatively set in motion in the 1540s, moreover, was continued. In the 1540s individual Ordnance debts had often been paid by particular grants of money from the Exchequer. By 1587 the situation had changed: a yearly warrant of £6,000 had been instituted to cover Office expenditure, and payments were now invariably made through the Ordnance without any interference from the Exchequer.[2] The changes that had taken place in the membership of the Ordnance board in the 1540s were also re-emphasised when two officials − the storekeeper and clerk of deliveries − whose offices probably existed in the Henrician period, were recognised as principal members of the board in Elizabeth's reign.[3]

---

reorganisations of the 1530s, although there is no direct evidence linking Cromwell with the naval and Ordnance reforms. C.S.L. Davies, 'The Administration of the Royal Navy under Henry VIII: The Origins of the Navy Board', *EHR* 80 (1965), 279, 287.

1 *Ibid.* pp. 279, 287. Davies, 'Supply Services', pp. 122, 127-30.

2 Ashley, 'Tudor Office of Ordnance', pp. 47-8, 52.

3 By 1558 the office of storekeeper had been patented, although the original

The duties of the Ordnance officers were spelled out in a series of instructions in the Elizabethan period. The first Elizabethan Ordnance regulations, which made provision for the meeting of Ordnance officers at least once a month 'to consider the state of the stores, and to draw up supply lists', were probably simply a codification of practices adopted in the 1540s.[1] More comprehensive Ordnance instructions, however, were issued in the following years. A commission for 1567-8, for example, suggested that a detailed annual report should be made out in the name of the lieutenant of the Ordnance. A commission of 1582-3, whose orders were published in the Office by the master of the Ordnance the following year, instructed that records were to be kept in duplicate, indentures were to be signed by three officers, and receipts and issues were to be annually examined. All private purchases of goods were also strictly forbidden, except on warrant from the queen or council. In 1589-in the light of the poor provision of ammunition for the fleet in the Armada campaign[2] – regulations were tightened. Each storekeeper was to keep an inventory of the Office's equipment in two books and to make out three books of receipts and issues, which were to be kept in the custody of the lieutenant, the surveyor and the master's clerks. The years transactions were to be summarised in two ledgers, the original documents having been carefully preserved. Later in 1589 the master was given his own instructions governing the bi-weekly meeting of chief officers and the regular keeping of journals of proceedings. Six years later the Council decreed that all items accounted for should be clearly distinguished, and that the annual ledgers should be properly audited.[3] These regulations, despite their intricacy, appear to have been ineffective both in limiting the gross financial malpractices of some Ordnance officers and in preventing squabbles for precedency amongst them.[4]

date of appointment of the first storekeeper was probably 1544. A similar doubt exists as to the exact dating of the office of the clerk of the deliveries. The first patent to survive was granted to Bryan Hogg for forty years service in the office, but the surveyor writing in 1602 backdated the creation of the office to 1527. *Ibid.* pp. 41, 42. Davies, 'Supply Services', pp. 131-3. Also see Ashley, 'Tudor Office of Ordnance', pp. 16, 43, 75-6, for the increase in the number of Ordnance under ministers in the late sixteenth century.

1　Davies, 'The Administration of the Royal Navy', p. 287.

2　See L. Stone, 'The Armada Campaign of 1588', *History* 19 n.s. (1944), 131 ff.

3　For further details of the various Elizabethan orders see Ashley, 'Tudor Office of Ordnance', pp. 101 ff.

4　John Lynewray, a principal Ordnance officer at the beginning of the seventeenth century, drew up an exaggerated account of abuses in the Office in this period (See, for example, his charge that two storekeepers were responsible for embezzling £60,000 and £12,000 worth of stores. Sloane 871). But there is

6

In the early years of the seventeenth century the importance of the Ordnance Office as a department of state was recognised when the titles of the master and lieutenant were re-styled master-general and lieutenant-general,[1] but there seemed to have been no major changes in the internal organisation of the Office. Indeed, with the close of the war against Spain there were few external pressures which might have resulted in an imposition of reforms and there was little need for vigilance among the Ordnance officers.[2]

That there was something seriously amiss with Ordnance administration at this time is suggested by the appointment of commissions in 1618 and 1620 to investigate the department's activities. In one of the extant reports[3] the commissioners put forward a series of wide ranging proposals to lessen the annual charge, which had grown to over £14,000 in that year. They reckoned that if the Office establishment could be severely reduced and the prices of contracted goods brought to their proper market rates, over £10,000 could be saved annually.

The effect of these reforms on the Office's efficiency — if indeed the measures were ever instituted — was negligible. The war preparations of 1625-9 revealed serious faults in the running of the Office: supplies were often inadequate and late in arriving and this was partly why the Cadiz and the Isle of Rhé expeditions were such fiascos; the prices of such supplies were excessive and payments to contractors were invariably months in arrears; Ordnance accounts were incomplete and at variance with other records. An even more extensive series of inquiries into the Office's organisation were made in the late 1620s and early 1630s as these deficiences came to light,[4] but again they appear to have been of little lasting consequence. For many of the problems of the 1625-9 operations occurred again in the preparation for the first bishop's war of 1638-9.[5]

little doubt that a number of grave deceptions were practised by Ordnance officers at this time. For a discussion of this and for examples of the vigorous internal dissensions within the department in the later years of Elizabeth I's reign, see Ashley, Tudor Office of Ordnance', pp. 129 ff.

1   Hogg, *Royal Arsenal* I, 57.

2   For Sir Roger Dallison's misappropriations and malpractices as master-general see M. Prestwich, *Cranfield: Politics and Profits under the Early Stuarts,* (Oxford, 1968), pp. 218, 221, 392, ff.

3   Add. MS.36777, fos. 14 ff., (1619?).

4   The problems of Ordnance administration and the work of the commissions of inquiry in this period have been fully documented by Professor G.E. Aylmer in 'Studies in the Institutions and Personnel of English Central Administration 1625-42' (unpublished Oxford D. Phil. thesis, 1954), pp. 49 ff. and in 'Attempts at Administrative Reform, 1625-40', *EHR* 72 (1957), 240-6. Also see Harl. 429, for the office journal book, 1626-36.

5   Although the second attempt to subdue the Scots, after a Council committee

From September 1642, after the capture of the Ordnance stores in the Tower and the dispossession of the principal Ordnance officers of their places,[1] there were two Ordnance Offices – one Royalist and the other parliamentarian. The majority of the board members, unlike their counterparts in the Navy, were Royalist or at least neutral in sympathy.[2] It is quite likely that many of the Ordnance clerks in ordinary, who were all personal appointees of the principal officers,[3] were also Royalists. It is probable, however, that many other junior officials and the majority of Ordnance craftsmen were not sufficiently committed to leave their homes and places of work in London. Indeed the location of the industries of the Ordnance contractors was probably the main factor in determining their loyalty.[4]

The Royalists, therefore, gained most of the expert Ordnance administrators but few of the existing stocks of arms and ammunition in 1642. An *ad hoc* Ordnance organisation was established at Oxford in the first few months of the civil war. The Oxford Ordnance Office, however, was not an exact replica of its pre-war counterpart, despite the fact that it was staffed by many of the same officers. The transplantation from London, and the Office's multiple functions as organiser of artillery, armaments manufacturer, and supplier and transporter to the Royalist Army south of the Trent, meant that it had to adapt to suit the prevailing circumstances. The organisation of manufacture and reception of arms into the store remained largely in the hands of civilian commissioners, the post of surveyor disappeared, and the senior officers, Heydon, Marsh and Sherburne, were all indiscriminately concerned with the keeping, issuing and transporting of supplies.[5]

had been put in charge of Ordnance affairs, and the Irish campaign of 1641-2 do not seem to have been as disastrous as the fitting out of the 1625 expedition. Aylmer, 'Attempts at Administrative Reform', pp. 244-5.

1   The best account of this is that written by the dispossessed officers, Edward Sherburne and Richard Marsh, at the Restoration, when they were petitioning for the restitution of their places. See PRO, SP 29 [State Papers Charles II] /6, fo. 158, petition, June? 1660.

2   The lieutenant-general, the clerk and the storekeeper were active royalists; the sympathies of the surveyor and clerk of deliveries are unknown. Aylmer, 'Attempts at Administrative Reform', p. 246, n. 2. For the naval officers, see G.E. Aylmer, *The King's Servants: the Civil Service of Charles I, 1625-42* (1973), (2nd edn. 1974), pp. 405-6, 408.

3   Edward Stephens, the lieutenant-general's clerk, for instance, went with him to Oxford. Some Ordnance workmen also left London and joined the king. I. Roy, 'The Royalist Army in the First Civil War' (unpublished Oxford D. Phil. thesis, 1963), p. 276, n. 1.

4   *Ibid.* pp. 276-7.

5   The organisation of the royalist office in this period has been well described by Dr. Roy, *ibid.* pp. 278 ff.

The Ordnance Office at Oxford and other similar Royalist institutions at Bristol, Reading and Worcester were temporary organisations, existing only for the duration of the first civil war. These organisations, therefore, could have had little influence on the evolution of Ordnance administration. This was not only because they were ephemeral. The prevailing circumstances also necessitated ingenuity and adaptation rather than the adoption of a settled course of procedure which could be looked upon as a precedent by future generations of administrators. More important in the long-term, then, was the parliamentary Ordnance Office, which had inherited the central magazine at the Tower from the king and which was to be established there until the Restoration.

Little is known about the parliamentary Ordnance Office during the civil war period. At the beginning of the war the efficiency of its organisation must have been hampered by the lack of expertise among the principal officers, for when the senior officials of the Ordnance defected to the king the Committee of Safety had to fill their places by the promotion of an army paymaster and the appointment of a 'late citizen and hosier of London'.[1] There does not seem to have been any fundamental change, however, in the Office establishment during the early months of the civil war.[2] It is quite likely, then, that during the civil war period the parliamentary Ordnance officers took over the existing Royalist organisation and made little change in the Office's constitution, although its procedure may have been adapted by the new administrators to suit the unprecedented circumstances of civil war.

But changes in the Office's organisation certainly occurred after the civil war had ended. On 16 January 1649 the Commonwealth Parliament passed an Act to promote the more efficient and less corrupt organisation of a number of important departments of state, including the Ordnance Office, and a commission was set up to co-operate with the commissioners of the Navy in examining the past record and suitability for employment of every officer under the jurisdiction of the Navy, the Customs and the supply departments in or near the Tower.[3] A major task of the sixteen commissioners nominated by the Act was to purge the Ordnance Office of its

---

1 *Ibid.* p. 277.

2 A 1643 list of officers shows that the establishment consisted of the principal officers, seven clerks, a keeper of small guns, a keeper of rich weapons, eleven artificers, twenty labourers and a master gunner. Hogg, *Royal Arsenal,* I, 63.

3 The extensive terms of reference of the commission are detailed by W. Reid, 'Commonwealth Supply Departments within the Tower and the Committee of London Merchants', *Guildhall Miscellany,* II, no. 8, (Sept. 1966), 320-2.

negligent personnel. Charges were made against a number of Ordnance officials, several of whom were dismissed. The reconstitution of the department was a complementary process to the dismissal of officials. The duties which had been formerly exercised by the master-general had already been given to a committee of the Council,[1] but now other fundamental changes were proposed. Among other reforms, the commission suggested that three principal officers and a number of other officials and artificers should be disestablished; that a new officer should be appointed for keeping account of stores, and that travelling expenses and other allowances should be discontinued. The retrenchment in offices and reduction in expenses was intended to save the state £3,694.18s. per annum.[2] Many of the recommendations of the committee of sixteen — with the important exception of the disestablishment of the surveyor — were accepted by its parent body, the 1642 naval committee,[3] but the extent to which the proposals were put into immediate practice is not entirely clear. Certainly it is not until 1652 that there is evidence in the Office quarter books of radical changes in the Ordnance establishment.[4]

There is also evidence from internal records of changes having been made to the routine administration of the Ordnance Office in the Commonwealth period. This again seems to have stemmed from the activities of the sixteen commissioners, who formulated extensive instructions detailing the corporate duties of the board and the individual responsibilities of each type of Ordnance officer.[5] It is difficult to determine whether their instructions were fully implemented, but a departmental minute of 1 November 1654 suggests that an attempt was made in the 1650s to limit fee taking and to regularise departmental procedures.[6] An important aspect of this regularisation was the subordination of the Ordnance Office to the

---

1 Hogg, *Royal Arsenal,* I, 64.

2 Reid, 'Commonwealth Supply Departments', pp. 323, 326-8.

3 *Ibid.* pp. 328-9.

4 The office of lieutenant-general (and that of his clerks) appears to have been the first to have been abolished early in 1652. G.E. Aylmer, *The State's Servants: The Civil Service of the English Republic, 1649-60* (1973), pp. 39, 357-8, n. 6. Thereafter, at the end of that year the positions of the keeper of rich weapons (previously held by the storekeeper in addition to his principal office) and those of all the artificers, except for the two furbishers, were reduced. The salaries of the members of the new establishment were increased to compensate for the loss of income from other sources. WO 54 (Ordnance quarter books)/18. I am indebted to Mr David Lewis of Loughborough University for this information.

5 Reid, 'Commonwealth Supply Departments', pp. 329-30.

6 See WO 47 [Ordnance minutes books]/3, pp. 139-40, minute 1 Nov. 1654.

Navy in the provision of naval ordnance.[1] Many such reforms were short-lived, for the Restoration of Charles II necessarily meant the restoration of some of the pre-war royalist Ordnance officers and a return to some of the old methods of Ordnance administration. But the influence of the Commonwealth Ordnance Office was not entirely lost on its late Stuart counterpart, and the increase in salaries of the Ordnance officials after the Restoration and the imposition of the 1683 instructions may well have been derived in part from the reforms of the late 1640s and 1650s.[2]

At the Restoration, then, the Ordnance Office had been established as a major department of state for well over a century. Its origins may be found in the Household department of the Court of the medieval kings of England, but it was essentially a product of early Tudor England. The major transformation had taken place in the last years of the reign of Henry VIII when a formal board and a separate accounting system were established. In the early years of Elizabeth I detailed instructions were instituted and the board's constitution was settled. In the later years of Elizabeth's reign and the first two quarters of the seventeenth century, however, the extant evidence suggests a deterioration in the standards of Ordnance administration.[3] And although there were periods of reform in 1618 it was not until the Commonwealth that a systematic, sustained and partially successful attempt was made to alter the Office's constitution.[4]

As may be appreciated from this brief outline of its origins, the early history of the Ordnance Office has been well documented in a number

1 Professor Aylmer remains sceptical about this (*State's Servants*, p. 358, n. 10). But the appointment of the Ordnance surveyor as a navy commissioner, (*Cal. SP Dom. 1654*, p. 76, Council of State's proceedings, 5 Apr. 1654) and correspondence between the Admiralty commissioners and Ordnance board in the state papers e.g., *Cal. SP Dom. 1654*, pp. 555, 562, letters 25 Sept., 18 Oct. 1654; *Ibid.* 1655-6, p. 517, letter 26 Mar. 1656; *Ibid.* 1656-7, p. 321, letter 28 Mar. 1657), suggest that the Admiralty had direct jurisdiction over the Ordnance board in the late 1650s. It would seem that in January 1654 Admiralty commissioners had been empowered to contract for Ordnance stores, and that in January 1655 they were empowered to issue warrants for the payment of the salaries of Ordnance officers. See Wayne Neil Hammond, 'The Administration of the English Navy, 1649-60', (unpublished University of British Columbia Ph. D. thesis, 1974), pp. 271-2.

2 For this see below, p. 87.

3 This does not necessarily mean, of course, that Ordnance administration was any less troubled in the mid sixteenth century. Ordnance administration in the late sixteenth and early seventeenth centuries may simply seem more inefficient than the earlier period because of the comparative wealth of the documentation for the later Elizabethan/early Stuart Office.

4 For a rather inaccurate and brief general history of the Office see *Historical Notes on the Ancient and Present Constitution of the Ordnance . . . c.*1780. Printed in C.M. Clode, *The Military Forces of the Crown*, 2 vols. (1869), II, 683 ff.

of important monographs. Its fortunes in the late seventeenth and early eighteenth centuries, however, have escaped the detailed attention of historians. Clode, Walton and Fortescue in their massive histories of the British Army were more interested in the fighting of campaigns than the seemingly dull routine of administration and paid scant attention to the Ordnance Office.[1] Specialist works by Forbes, Hogg, Scouller and Skentelbery contain more information but they neither place the Office in the context of the government of the period nor consider the full implications of Ordnance administration.[2] This lack of a suitable study on the Office and its activities has inevitably resulted in superficial judgements being passed on its efficiency.[3]

The failure of historians to consider the department in depth in the late seventeenth and early eighteenth centuries is surprising. For in this period of intermittent, if not incessant, warfare, the Ordnance Office had a vital role to play in the defence of the kingdom. Although the department was very much the poor relation of the other forces, in terms of money expended, the Army and Navy depended on its co-operation. The supply of munitions and a host of other stores, the organisation of artillery trains, and the maintenance of garrisons and coastal defences all lay within its province. Lord Dartmouth was not exaggerating when he urged King James II in the critical weeks before the 1688 invasion to look into the affairs of the Ordnance Office and its officials, as much of his service by sea and land depended upon the 'well ordering and management of their business'. This opinion was shared by the future William III, who in December 1688 – at least according to Sir Edward Sherburne - was more concerned in securing the Tower than establishing a free Parliament.[4]

But quite apart from the importance of the Office in relation to the nation's security, and the inherent interest of administrative history, the raw materials of which have been characterised by one historian as possessing a 'corporate personality' expressing 'individual neuroses',[5] the

1 *Ibid.* J.W. Fortescue, *A History of the British Army*, 14 vols. and 6 vols. of maps (1910-30). C. Walton, *History of the British Standing Army, 1660-1700* (1894).

2 A. Forbes, *A History of the Army Ordnance Services*, 3 vols. (1929); Hogg, *Royal Arsenal;* R.E. Scouller, *The Armies of Queen Anne* (Oxford, 1966); N. Skentelbery, *A History of the Ordnance Board; idem, Arrows to Atom Bombs: A History of the Ordnance Board* (1975).

3 See below, p. 144

4 *HMC* 20, 11 Rep. V, *Dartmouth* I, p. 259, 17 Oct. 1688. Bodl. Wood F 44, fo. 285, Sherburne to Wood, 4 Dec. 1688.

5 H.G. Roseveare, *The Treasury: The Evolution of a British Institution* (1969), p. 12.

Ordnance Office presents a formidable challenge to the historian because of the wealth of its records. Various instructions issued in this period enjoined each member of the Ordnance board to keep a meticulous account of his own as well as his colleagues' proceedings,[1] and this resulted in a proliferation of book-keeping. A sizeable quantity of paper and other materials was regularly bought from the Office stationer for this purpose.[2] By the end of the period these materials, which when expended constituted the records of the Office, had grown so voluminous that they were transferred from the custody of the departmental officers to the sword room within the White Tower, which was fitted up as a central record repository. Shortly afterwards an archivist was appointed to arrange the documents.[3] Not all of these records, of course, survive. Many Ordnance records were either sold or destroyed before their removal to the Public Record Office in 1855.[4] Other records did not even reach the collection in the Tower for officials frequently kept papers in their own possession and were very reluctant to return them, as evidenced by the reiteration of orders disavowing the practice of record hoarding.[5] The majority of these private records have been lost to posterity and the only important sources of this nature to have been traced are the Dartmouth, Erle, Lonsdale (Lowther) and Marlborough manuscripts, although there are numerous miscellaneous Ordnance items in the Pepys Library and among private collections in the British Library. Nevertheless, a sufficient quantity of official Ordnance papers, both manuscript and printed,[6] are extant in the public records to enable a detailed

---

1 WO 55 [Ordnance miscellaneous series]/332, pp. 100-1, warrant 24 Jan. 1667, for a more orderly accounting of stores. WO 47/5, p. 97; WO 47/6, fos. 51, 82, 122, 127, 132, 133; WO 47/7, fo. 18, minutes Sept. 1663 - Feb. 1665. Also see below, pp. 51-2, for the injunctions in the 1683 instructions relating to book-keeping (the keeping of check ledgers, etc.).

2 E.g. the following payments to Captain Richard Cawthorne: WO 48 [Ordnance Treasury Ledgers]/20, 2 May 1682; WO 48/21, 12 Sept. 1682, 15 Mar. 1683; WO 48/22, 30 June 1684; WO 48/23, 12 Dec. 1684, 29 June 1685; WO 48/24, 5 Aug. 1685.

3 WO 47/29, p. 47, minute 23 Feb. 1716; WO 47/30, p. 183, minute 5 July 1717; WO 47/32, p. 141, minute 7 Apr. 1719.

4 E.g. WO 47/27, p. 109, minute 17 Dec. 1714. Also see Sarah E. Barter, 'The Board of Ordnance: Some Records Recently Acquired for the Tower of London', *Journal of the Society of Archivists* 8 (1966), 195-8.

5 E.g. WO 47/5, p. 77, minute 16 July 1663; WO 47/9 fos. 51, 74, 111, minutes 14, 31 Aug., 9 Dec. 1680; *Cal. SP Dom. 1685*, p. 274, Sunderland to Chicheley, 24 July; King's 70, fo. 46 instructions 4 Feb. 1686.

6 Printed lists of remains of stores and printed indentures and instructions were used from the early part of the period. E.g. PRO 30 37 [Private Collection Pritchett MSS.]/7 *passim;* SP 63 [State Papers Ireland]/333, no. 103;

reconstruction of the organisation and activities of the Office to be made for the later Stuart period. Complete series of treasurer's ledgers, bill books and quarter books survive, as well as many of the minute books for the period. In addition there are scattered letters to and from the Ordnance board and numerous miscellaneous reports, estimates and warrants.[1] Few departments can boast of such a mass of material to document its early history. But it is not simply the quantity of Ordnance records that is impressive. Pepys, when he visited the Office in October 1666, gave testimony that its accounts and books were 'kept in mighty good order',[2] and the surviving papers bear witness to the regularity of Ordnance book keeping and accounting methods.

The mass of extant Ordnance papers from 1660-1714 makes the Office an attractive subject to the administrative historian but it is necessary to further justify the period chosen for study. After all, the late seventeenth and early eighteenth centuries were not the only fertile periods in the department's history. As we have observed, the Office had been firmly established in the sixteenth century. The Ordnance Office, moreover, was to undergo strict examination and reconstruction by various parliamentary committees and reforming master-generals in the late eighteenth and early nineteenth centuries,[3] before it was abolished as a separate department in 1855. Why, then, was the later Stuart period of particular importance in its evolution?

The terminal dates themselves are not of great significance as far as the Ordnance Office was concerned, although reasons might be advanced in favour of starting the study in 1660 and ending it in 1714. The pre-civil war Ordnance establishment, for instance, was reimposed at the Restoration, after it had been severely curtailed by the 1649 reforms, there was almost a complete change among the principal

---

WO 51 [Ordnance bill books] /4, p. 71, payment to Grismond, printer, 1 July 1664; WO 55/1650 *passim;* WO 55/1708 *passim.*

1 For a bibliographical note on these sources, see below, pp. 240-1.

2 *Pepys Diary,* VI, 7; 6 Oct. 1666. Although he could not find out the charge of (naval?) ordnance per man per month.

3 The major parliamentary inquiries were those of 1784, 1797, 1811, 1828 and 1848. For a brief synopsis of the financial aspects of these reports see *Parl. Papers, 1868-9,* XXXV (366), pp. 1153 ff. Some of the earlier proposals are discussed in J.E.D. Binney, *British Public Finance and Administration, 1774-9* (Oxford, 1958), pp. 159 ff. Also see A.G. Olson, *The Radical Duke: Career and Correspondence of Charles Lennox, third Duke of Richmond* (Oxford, 1961), p. 74, and Richard Glover, *Peninsular Preparations: The Reform of the British Army, 1795-1809* (Cambridge, 1963), p. 38, for Richmond's Ordnance reforms, which would repay further study.

officers in 1660 and 1714, and in the last year of the period Office expenditure was re-established on a peace-time footing after more than a decade of war.[1] Of far greater importance than the dates themselves, however, was the development in the size, activities and character of the Office, which took place within the boundaries encompassed by the years 1660 to 1714.

The most obvious manifestation of the Office's growth in stature was the increase in its permanent staff. There were no great changes among the highest rank of Ordnance administrators in this period. The only addition to the place of principal officer was the appointment of a treasurer in 1670, who took over financial duties from the lieutenant-general after the death of William Legge. The number of principal officers' clerks, however, was to increase dramatically. Payments were made only to nine clerks in ordinary for the September quarter of 1660, but by 1703 there were seventeen permanent clerks and twenty-one extraordinary clerks in the Office. The numbers of storekeepers, artificers and labourers also increased rapidly after the Restoration, and a regular establishment of fireworkers was soon created. But perhaps the most remarkable expansion occurred among the military personnel of the Office. In 1660 the offices of master gunner and chief engineer were in existence, but in the following years a great change was to occur in the establishment of gunners and engineers under their control. The feed gunners were completely reorganised in 1682 when sixty practitioners and three mates to the master gunner were brought together in a more disciplined organisation. A separate body of engineers, moreover, gradually emerged in the place of a select band appointed randomly by the Crown. Although it is anachronistic to speak of a separate military as opposed to a civil Ordnance establishment until the formation of two regimental companies of gunners in 1716, the beginnings of this development were foreshadowed in this period.[2]

The expansion in the size of the Office may perhaps be more readily appreciated in numerical terms.[3] In August 1667, there were

---

1 See below, pp. 173, 177.

2 For these developments see appendix, pp. 223-39, and Chandler, *The Art of War*, pp. 160-1, 222.

3 The figures have been calculated from these lists: SP 29/213, fos. 118-21, 12 Aug. 1667; Stowe 315, fos. 1-2, list made at the time of the 1679-81 commissioners; WO 54/682, list of old establishment, 25 July 1683 and extraordinary additional allowances by warrants of 27 Feb. 1682 and 15 July 1683; *HMC* 17, 14 Rep. VI, *House of Lords*, pp. 188-91, 1 Dec. 1692. *CJ* XIV, pp. 420-1, 15 Nov. 1704. All officials have been included whether they were paid on the quarter books or by extraordinary allowance. If an official held

about 175 officers attached to the Ordnance. A list compiled during the tenure of the master-general commissioners, 1679-81, suggests that the number had increased to around 237. It had been reduced by about sixty by the time of the reformation of the Office in 1683, but by 1692 the Ordnance establishment had increased again to something like 268 men. In November 1704, towards the beginning of the War of Spanish Succession, nearly 450 men were included as members of the Office in a list presented to the House of Commons. During the same period the quarter book salaries and additional extraordinary allowances of the Ordnance officers had increased almost fourfold.[1] In addition to these officials, towards the end of the period there were nearly forty men on the North Britain establishment,[2] as well as those on the Ordnance establishments at Gibraltar, Newfoundland, Jamaica, Barbados and New York.[3] Permanent offices were now beginning to be formed in the localities both at home and abroad.[4]

A parallel development to the increasing size of the Ordnance establishment was the increase in scope of the activities of the Office: the separate Armoury and Tents and Toils departments were merged with the Ordnance in 1670 and 1685; Woolwich was established as a premier royal arsenal, and other magazines were developed at the major ports and garrisons, reflecting the great expansion in the stocks of Ordnance stores; and the building of fortifications became more strictly regulated under the control of the Ordnance Office.[5]

---

more than one office he has only been counted once. The Nov. 1704 list does not include the numbers of extraordinary clerks employed but they have been determined by reference to a list compiled in the following year. See Stowe 470, fos. 4-11.

1 From £5,754 p.a. in 1667 to £22,260 p.a. in 1704. Every list shows an increase except the one for 1683.

2 At a cost of £368. 19s. 8¼d. per quarter. See WO 48/48-52, lists 11 May 1710 - 27 Apr. 1714.

3 Stowe 470, fos. 21-30, lists 1705. At the end of the war there was also an Ordnance presence at Port Mahon, Placentia and Annapolis, although not, it appears, in the West Indies, where the establishment was probably reduced, as had occurred at the end of the 1689-97 war. See *Acts of PC Col. 1680-1720*, pp. 318-20; Whitworth Porter, *History of the Corps of Royal Engineers*, 2 vols (1889), I, 140; Francis Duncan, *History of the Royal Regiment of Artillery*, 2 vols (2nd edn. 1874), I, 70.

4 Unfortunately no cache of documents relating to these regional outposts survives for this period. The earliest set of records date from 1717 and concern the Portsmouth office. See WO 55/1985 ff.

5 For the merger with the Armoury and Tents and Toils offices and developments of the arsenal, see below, pp. 105-6, 121-3. The key reforms in relation to the regulation of Ordnance control over fortifications were the warrants of 27 March and 26 April 1667, empowering the master-general commissioners to direct the building of Portsmouth and Plymouth

As important were the reforms that were initiated in an attempt to remodel the old pre-civil war methods of the department. Some of the most significant changes were made during the tenure of the first master-general commissioners from 1664 to 1670. The orders issued on 13 February 1665 for the government of the Office were of fundamental importance in the attempt to limit corruption within the Ordnance. The lieutenant's poundage fee was to be abolished and an independent salaried treasurer established after the death of William Legge, an additional salary being awarded to the succeeding lieutenant in compensation; the salaries of the master commissioners, the clerk of the Ordnance and certain clerks in ordinary were to be immediately increased; the fees of other clerks were to be limited; and debentures were to be passed within one month after the delivery of goods into the Office and the payment of these bills was to proceed in course 'to prevent the unnecessary soliciting for money and the undue preference in payments'.[1] The commissioners tenure of Office was so effective that the Duke of York considered that the experiment should be repeated at the Treasury after the death of Lord Treasurer Southampton; and despite Clarendon's fervent protestations that 'the Ordnance was conversant only with smiths and carpenters and other artificers and handicraftsmen . . . whereas the Treasury had much to do with the nobility and chief gentry of the kingdom' the king decided to put the Treasury into commission and include as one of its members Sir John Duncomb, who had served so successfully as an Ordnance commissioner.[2] The Ordnance commissioners' reforms did not by any means eliminate corruption, but they were the first of many attempts made after the Restoration to diminish the attraction of 'undue means formerly practised' by the institution of realistic salaries for some of the principal office holders, and by regularising debenture payments.

The most lasting achievement of the period, however, were the instructions of July 1683, when Lord Dartmouth was master-general, which streamlined the Ordnance establishment and minutely detailed the duties of each individual officer. The importance of these instructions did not lie in their novelty — they were based on previous

---

fortifications, and to be accountable for any repairs that had been made to the fortifications since the Restoration. (WO 55/332, pp. 134-5, 157-8, warrants 27 Mar., 26 Apr. 1667). These changes will be discussed elsewhere.

[1] SP 29/112, fos. 166-8, warrant 13 Feb. 1665. The provisions also included the order for the union of the Armoury with the Ordnance after the death of William Legge, who was also master of the Armouries.

[2] *Own Life* III, pp. 790-1. For the appointment and work of the Treasury Commission see H.G. Roseveare, *The Treasury 1660-1870: the Foundations of Control* (1973), pp. 19-22.

rules formulated for the government of the Office in the late sixteenth and early seventeenth centuries — but in the fact that they defined existing procedures, which definitions became the basis for the future constitution of the Office. Various amendments were made to the 1683 instructions in 1686, but after this date they were confirmed by every sovereign from William III to George II. As late as the first decade of the nineteenth century the public accounts commissioners could still regard these seventeenth century instructions as the basic rules that governed the conduct of the Ordnance officers.[1]

The later Stuart Ordnance Office, therefore, grew in both size and stature. But even more importantly a new spirit of public service was emerging among its officers. At the Restoration office was still a freehold to be enjoyed with a permanent tenure. By the end of the period office could no longer be looked on as a piece of property; trade in offices had disappeared and life tenures had been abolished. The older notions of medieval bureaucracy were being replaced by newer concepts; a rudimentary salaried structure of allowances had been implemented in the place of some of the more extravagent fees. A permanent civil service of clerks was also taking root under the principal officers.[2]

These changes were of obvious importance in the history of Ordnance administration, but they were far too fragmented to be termed 'revolutionary'. The growth in the Ordnance establishment, the increase in its responsibilities and the reforms instituted to heighten its efficiency, simply represent one stage in the growth of modern government.

---

1 *Parl. Papers 1810,* IX (81), p. 460. A number of copies of the original instructions and the 1686 amendments exist. See King's 70; Stowe 442, 444 (fos. 27-51), 445; Lansdowne 201; Egerton 2607; Harl 1286, 6334; Add. MSS 22876, 30152; PL 2827; NMM Sergison 120; WO 55/536, 1789, 1790.

2 See below, pp. 70 ff.

1

THE CENTRAL ADMINISTRATION

Before a detailed examination is made of the Ordnance Office it is necessary to study the relationship between that Office and the central organs of government, for it is not possible to isolate any departmental body without reference to other superior agencies which initiate policies and delegate orders so that those policies may be carried out. It is only when the connections between the Ordnance Office, the Privy Council, the secretaries of state, the Admiralty and the Treasury and other departments of state are established that the full significance of Ordnance administration can be determined.

The Privy Council

The decline of the Privy Council in the running of the affairs of state in the late seventeenth century can be over stressed, as the departments of modern government which eventually superseded that body were as yet in their infancy. The Treasury did not emerge as a separate entity in government before the appointment of the commissioners in 1667 and the Treasury's relationship with the Privy Council was not fully defined until the following year. Even then matters which were 'of such a nature as they [the Treasury commissioners] cannot or would not willingly give their determination therein' were to be referred back to the Council.[1] The Home Office and Foreign Office, moreover, were not organised on modern lines until the end of the eighteenth century, and although the Admiralty had attained departmental status by 1660, for a part of the following period it was still governed by a Lord High Admiral and not by commission, thus delaying the expansion of the Admiralty secretariat.[2] The Privy Council, therefore, to a large extent carried out the work to be done, although in the last years of the seventeenth and early years of the eighteenth century policy was ceasing to be framed in the Privy Council and beginning to be initiated by the Cabinet.[3] But for much of this

---

1 Roseveare, *Treasury, 1660-1870*, p. 115, no. 2c, order, 12 Feb. 1668. Much of Roseveare's introduction (pp. 18 ff.) is an indictment of Baxter's argument that the Treasury did not reach maturity until 1676. For a summary of Baxter's argument see S.B. Baxter, *The Development of the Treasury, 1660-1702* (1957), p. 262.

2 J. Carter, 'The Administrative Work of the English Privy Council' (unpublished London Ph.D. thesis, 1958), p. 2. A commission, of course, needed a fixed time and place of meeting and a formal method of doing business.

3 Carter, 'English Privy Council', p. 3; J.H. Plumb, 'The Organisation of the Cabinet in the Reign of Queen Anne', *TRHS* 5th ser. 7 (1957), 137-57.

period, the Privy Council was the 'central clearing house of the administration'.[1] Administrative affairs were sorted by the central Council and channelled into their proper courses and this is reflected by the relationship between that Council and the Ordnance Office.

The Privy Council acted as an intermediary between the various governmental offices and the Ordnance Office. It was contrary to the instructions of the Office for another board, apart from the Admiralty, to give directions directly to the Ordnance for a supply of stores, and before any demand was accepted it had to be laid before the King or Queen in Council for their direction. The Privy Council then considered the order and either caused an estimate to be made of the cost of the stores and at a later meeting ordered the request, or immediately demanded that the stores were sent.[2]

The nascent Council of Trade, the Treasury and the Admiralty may be taken as examples to illustrate the way the Privy Council acted as the centre of communication between the Ordnance board and other departments. The Council of Trade had no independent authority to summon Ordnance personnel to the Council board and all matters requiring official sanction were directed through the central Council, although occasionally the Council of Trade enclosed the order in council within their letter to the Ordnance board, with a request for the stores to be delivered to plantations.[3] The Treasury's authority was, of course, far greater than that of the Council of Trade and it is a mistake to over-emphasise the control of the Privy Council in financial matters. In the early part of the period, the Privy Council might order a privy seal to be sent to the Lord High Treasurer to enable him to issue money from the Exchequer to the Ordnance treasurer, but as the Treasury increased in stature as an independent department the Privy Council seems to have been by-passed in this procedure.[4] Towards the end of the period the Treasury's status was such that they would be asked by the Privy Council to report their opinion as to the feasibility of financing an Ordnance operation or settling a dispute between the

1 D. Ogg, *England in the Reigns of James II and William III* (Oxford, 1955), p. 333. Quoted by Carter, p. 240.

2 PC 2 [Privy Council Registers] /75, p. 347, 15 Feb. 1694, p. 371, 8 Mar. 1694; PC 6 [Privy Council Order Books] /18, pp. 154-5, 9, 23 May 1677.

3 *Cal. SP Col. Am. & W. Indies 1677-80*, p. 93, 23 May 1677; *ibid. 1702.* p. 537; *ibid. 1710-11*, pp. 443-4; *Acts PC Col. 1680-1720*, pp. 318-20. 13 Jan. 1698; PC 2/72, p. 132, 15 June 1688; PC 2/77, p. 81, 17 Feb. 1698; p. 87, 31 Mar. 1698.

4 PC 2/55, pp. 26-7, 21 Nov. 1660, p. 41, 14 Dec. 1660. PC 6/18, p. 19, 10 June 1661, p. 36, 3 Sept. 1662. The latest reference I have for this procedure is PC 6/18, pp. 161-2, 18 June 1679.

Ordnance and the Navy.[1] The Admiralty's authority in 1660 was far greater than that of the Treasury and it is equally misleading to exaggerate the control of the Council over naval affairs. The administration of the Navy was largely in the hands of the Admiralty itself and the secretaries of state. Yet as Mr. Ehrman observed 'many of the decisions on which the Admiralty was required to act continued to be conveyed on its [the Privy Council's] authority'.[2] The Admiralty could not sanction the extraordinary use of Ordnance stores by sea captains without a specific Privy Council order. Similarly, the alteration of the gun establishment of a ship or an increase of its stores required the consent of the Privy Council.[3] A memorial from the Admiralty for the building of defence works at a port or a proposal by the Ordnance board for a new gun wharf would pass firstly through the Privy Council rather than being directed immediately to the department concerned, and a report would be returned to the Council before the decision was reached.[4] The Privy Council was also concerned in settling such disputes between the Ordnance Office and the Admiralty as to the form of warrant used in communications between them and whether guns were to be proved at the places at which they were cast, but at times even their arbitration was insufficient for determining a long standing disagreement.[5]

The Privy Council, therefore, was a vital link in the complex relationships between departments of state and the Ordnance Office, but it was also a court of appeal for those wanting to draw official attention to a particular problem. Governors who wished to indicate the condition of their garrisons to the Ordnance Office often did so through the medium of the Council.[6] The lord lieutenant of Ireland informed the Council board when Ordnance stores were required, and mayors, aldermen and inhabitants of sea ports made representations to

1   PC 2/74, p. 96, 23 Feb. 1693; PC 2/83, p. 250, 14 June 1711.

2   J. Ehrman, *The Navy in the War of William III* (Cambridge, 1953), p. 300; Carter, English Privy Council, p. 308.

3   *Acts of PC Col. 1680-1720*, pp. 570-71, 643-45; PC 2/74, p. 330, 11 Feb. 1692; PC 2/79, p. 423, 11 July 1703; PC 2/80, p. 90, 7 Feb. 1706, pp. 150-1, 25 Mar. 1706, pp. 262-3, 18 Jan. 1705; PC 2/82, p. 80, 20 May 1708; PC 2/83, p. 375, 31 Jan. 1712.

4   PC 4 [Privy Council Minute Books]/1, pp. 151-2; PC 2/80, pp. 280-1, 22 Feb. 1705, p. 326, 23 Apr. 1705.

5   PC 6/18, p. 163, 10 July 1679; PC 2/74, p. 199, 24 Aug. 1693, p. 205, 31 Aug. 1693. For examples of the Council attempting to settle the differences between the Ordnance Office and the Admiralty see Carter, 'English Privy Council', p. 342.

6   PC 2/55, p. 46, 28 Dec. 1660; PC 2/61, p. 340, 28 June 1669; PC 2/68, p. 116, 13 June 1679; PC 6/18, pp. 4, 20, 42, 54, 62, 107, 146-7, orders 12 Oct. 1660-27 Mar. 1674.

the Council about the inadequacy of coastal defences or the danger of gunpowder magazines.[1] Ordnance artificers petitioned the Council for exemption from the onerous duties of city offices, for licence to import saltpetre and export iron guns, or for the payment of 'just' debts and salaries.[2]

The importance of the Privy Council in Ordnance affairs may be gauged by the number and the different types of orders which were transmitted to that Office. Orders relating to the Navy and the Ordnance were entered in separate copy books as well as in the daily record of Council meetings.[3] Only one Ordnance subject register appears to have survived,[4] and although not all orders were entered into this volume from the main series, an impression may be obtained from this source of the amount of business conducted by the Privy Council with one department. Such a subject register defies classification and is evidence of the multifarious nature of the Privy Council orders to the Ordnance Office.

It should not be implied, however, that the Privy Council was the instigator of all the business conducted through its channels. Many of the orders issued were of a routine character and Privy Council sanction in these cases was nothing more than a matter of course.[5] The majority of orders issued to the Ordnance Office, moreover, were simply in response to a memorial from another department or in reply to an initiative from the Ordnance officers themselves.[6] Nevertheless, it is clear that specialist Privy Council committees had considerable powers. There is evidence, especially in the years immediately after the Restoration, that many spheres of Ordnance activity were decided in committee. In the 1660s *ad hoc* committees reported on the state of the Tower, the estimates of charges necessary for repairing and supplying various garrisons and the condition of coastal fortifications. In 1663 a committee was established to consider an Ordnance paper regarding the exportation of powder and ordnance. A few months later another

1 PC 2/74, p. 252, 19 Sept. 1692; PC 2/79, pp. 138-9, 31 May 1702; PC 2/82, p. 528, 26 Jan. 1710; PC 2/83, p. 164, 13 Dec. 1710, p. 238, 19 Apr. 1711.

2 PC 6/18, p. 39, 13 Feb. 1663, p. 128, 18 Sept. 1668, p. 225, 14 Oct. 1687; PC 2/55, p. 80, 4 Mar. 1661, p. 315, 2 Aug. 1661; PC 2/69, p. 23, 14 July 1680; PC 2/73, p. 421, 10 Apr. 1690; PC 2/74, p. 102, 2 Mar. 1692; PC 2/74, p. 462, 18 Nov. 1703; PC 6/18, p. 183, 30 Nov. 1681.

3 PC 2/72, p. 604, 3 Feb. 1688.

4 PC 6/18, May 1660-3 Feb. 1688.

5 See PC 6/18, pp. 74-5 and *passim* for orders concerning the supply of stores to garrisons.

6 PC 2/73, p. 221, 2 Sept. 1689; PC 2/82, p. 51, 15 Apr. 1708; PC 6/18, p. 79, 11 Jan. 1665, p. 197, 8 Nov. 1682.

committee was formed to examine the business of fraudulently buying and selling gunpowder.[1] Ordnance matters were also discussed in the Privy Council committee dealing with the affairs of Ireland, Jersey and Guernsey, and the plantations before the formation of the Council of Trade,[2] although these standing committees should be distinguished from the other temporary committees that were appointed simply to deal with a particular problem.[3]

It is difficult to determine the extent to which Ordnance business was decided in the permanent committees rather than in the Privy Council. There are no formal committee minutes surviving and little evidence of the inner workings of a committee, though Pepys's diary occasionally reveals disputes in the Tangier Committee.[4] To a large extent, however, the Privy Council registers are the only source for committee activities and these are necessarily incomplete. Only one order from the Committee of Intelligence which related to the Ordnance Office has been found[5] and none from the Committee of Foreign Affairs. It is more likely that Ordnance business would be debated in temporary committees, such as those already cited, and in the Navy Committee established on 12 February 1668 to discuss 'matters as concern the Admiralty and Navy, as also all military matters, fortifications etc'.[6] There is a danger, however, in stressing too heavily the importance of such committees in the administration of the country. Danby observed to William III that committees were badly attended and that those that did attend acted 'like pioneers for pay rather than by inclination'.[7] Moreover, committees were constantly changing in character. If Turner has established anything it is that committees were *ad hoc* appointments of the monarch who was seemingly able to alter their nature at will. Such reorganisations could hardly have provided the force for continuity which was so necessary in any administrative system.[8]

---

1 PC 2/55, pp. 61, 74, 80-1, orders 25 Jan. - 4 Mar. 1661; PC 6/18, p. 33, 15 June 1662, p. 58, 30 Dec. 1663, p. 88, 14 June 1665, p. 117, 22 Jan. 1668.

2 *Acts of PC Col. 1613-80,* p. 324, 12 Mar. 1662, p. 704, 9 May 1677; PC 2/74, p. 98, 23 Feb. 1693; PC 6/18, p. 151, 13 Oct. 1675.

3 For temporary and standing committees see E.R. Turner, *The Privy Council of England in the Seventeenth and Eighteenth Centuries, 1603-1784,* 2 vols. (Baltimore 1927-8), II, 369.

4 *Pepys Diary,* IV, 234, 24 Sept. 1664.

5 Concerning the gunners in the Tower. PC 6/18, p. 167, 3 Dec. 1679.

6 Turner, *The Privy Council of England,* II, 268.

7 A. Browning, *Thomas Osborne Earl of Danby and Duke of Leeds,* 3 vols. (Glasgow, 1944-51), II, 197, 20 Feb. 1691.

8 For the reconstitution of committees of the Privy Council in the years after the Restoration see Turner, *The Privy Council of England,* II, 263-92.

The exact nature of the role of the Cabinet or the lords justices in the administration of the Ordnance Office at the turn of the century is even more difficult to assess. The memoranda of Cabinet meetings made by various secretaries of state in the 1690s and the reign of Anne have not been consulted,[1] but it is unlikely that these sources would reveal a significant amount of new material on the workings of the Ordnance Office. War affairs were the main consideration of these Cabinet meetings, but diplomacy and the strategy and tactics of war seemed to have been discussed rather than routine war administration.[2] On occasions, however, Ordnance officers were called to Cabinet meetings.[3] There is also evidence of the lords justices, who from their appointment in May 1695 gave Cabinet meetings a status they formerly lacked, issuing orders to the Ordnance board.[4] The Ordnance board also applied to the lords justices for authority to act during the absence of the master-general of the Ordnance or in order that they might settle disputes with the Admiralty.[5]

Although the significance of Privy Council committees and the Cabinet in the running of the Ordnance Office is not easy to establish, it is clear that the administrative work of the Privy Council itself declined in the later part of the period. The Privy Council registers after the 1660s and 1670s reveal that the number of orders emanating from the Privy Council to the Ordnance Office markedly decreased.[6] The diminution of the importance of the Privy Council in the government of the realm, however, was not only a result of the formation of Privy Council committees and a rudimentary Cabinet but also a consequence of the growth of departmental administration. As has been shown, it is probable that little administrative work was done in the Cabinet. Committees, moreover, were not able to interfere too much in departmental routine. The order which formed one of the four great standing committees of the Privy Council in February 1668 stated that the committee was only to deal with military and naval matters 'so far as they are fit to be brought to the Council

---

1   For these sources see J. Carter, 'Cabinet Records for the Reign of William III', *EHR* 78, (1963), 95-114, and Plumb, 'The Organisation of the Cabinet in the Reign of Queen Anne'.

2   Carter, 'Cabinet Records', pp. 99-100, 108; Plumb, 'Organisation of the Cabinet', p. 147.

3   *Ibid.* p. 138, Sunderland's memo., 26 Mar. 1710.

4   *Acts of PC Col. 1680-1720*, p. 371, 12 Aug. 1701; *Cal. SP Col. Am. & W. Indies 1701*, pp. 383-4, 31 July, pp. 460-1, 21 Aug. 1701.

5   *Cal. SP Dom. 1695*, pp. 74-5, minutes of the proceedings of the lords justice, 2, 3 Oct. 1695; S.P. 32 [State Papers William and Mary]/11, fos. 312-3, 29 July 1699, fo. 324, 3 Oct. 1699.

6   See PC 6/18, *passim.*

Board, without intermeddling with what concerns the proper officers unless it shall by them be so desired'.[1] Much of the work that in an earlier age had been conducted by the Privy Council was now being dealt with by the developing departments of state. It is to the departments of state rather than the Privy Council that we must turn if a proper evaluation of late seventeenth century government is to be made.

It is, nevertheless, as dangerous to minimise the standing of the Privy Council as it is to exaggerate it. Clarendon saw the Privy Council as a 'most sacred' body which:

> hath the greatest authority in the government next to the person of the king himself to whom all other powers are equally subject; and no king of England can so well secure his own prerogative or preserve it from violation as by a strict defending and supporting the dignity of his Privy Council.[2]

and during the 1660s, especially when he was lord chancellor, the Privy Council and its dependent committees were an elemental force in the government of the realm. At various times after Clarendon's death the Privy Council was refurbished as an important instrument of government. In 1679 the Council was reduced in size and remodelled in an attempt to restore its primacy in the discussion of business at the expense of its committees.[3] Nine years later when James II left the kingdom, it was the Privy Council, meeting on 11 December at the Guildhall, that guaranteed to secure the peace in London. This Council secured the keys of the Tower and directly impinged on the government of the Ordnance Office by the removal of Sir Edward Sherburne from his post as clerk of the Ordnance because he was a Roman Catholic.[4] Whilst the influence of the Privy Council on the administration of the Ordnance Office was rarely as direct as this, that influence should not be neglected simply because the Privy Council was ceasing to exercise control over routine matters of government. It was the Privy Council which acted as a central depository from which orders were transferred to the appropriate department, and it was that agency which gave the formal confirmation to administrative policies which had been determined in the departments. Before instructions to prevent the wastage of stores could be sent by the Ordnance board to the various garrison commanders, for example, they had to be presented to the

---

1 Turner, *The Privy Council of England,* II, 268.
2 Quoted in G.A. Jacobson, *William Blathwayt: A Late Seventeenth Century English Administrator* (Yale Historical Publications, XXI, 1932), p. 11.
3 Turner, *The Privy Council of England,* I, 414.
4 *Luttrell,* I, 485; *Cal. SP Dom., 1698,* p. 53, 27 Jan. 1698.

Privy Council for their official endorsement.[1] Similarly it was the Privy Council that both ordered the publication of proclamations concerning the embezzlement of arms, and authorised the import or export of ordnance.[2] Thus whilst the direct impact of the Privy Council on the ordinary practice of government was declining, its influence on affairs was considerable throughout the period because of its powers of ratification. As Turner has written 'in respect of this formal sanction the Privy Council was never superseded and its work was indispensable'.[3]

The Secretaries of State

The secretaries of state had perhaps a more direct influence over administrative matters than the Privy Council. Whilst their standing and their relationship with the other officials depended on their own character, the inclinations of the sovereign and the importance of the business in hand, their prominence in the management of affairs should be stressed because of their executive function. For the secretaries, as keepers of the king's private seal, were concerned in the initial stages of the process of obtaining the royal signature and affixing the seal of the signet. They were also the instigators of the less formal letters issued under the authority of the signet alone. Indeed, next to the king, the secretaries of state, as the instrument of the royal prerogative, the channel of communication with the queen, and the lieutenant of the Privy Council, were the fountain head of seventeenth century government.[4]

The Ordnance board acted in responce to warrants from the Crown under the royal sign manual, which were counter-signed by a secretary of state.[5] Such warrants might be in the form of a general command authorising the Ordnance Office to supply garrisons with stores from time to time as was necessary, or they might be specific single orders requesting the arming of regiments or the provision of gunpowder for ships.[6] The notification of the Crown's pleasure had to be in a written form to justify the issuing of stores by the Ordnance Office, and

1 PC 6/18, pp. 44-6, 137-8, 193-5, orders 1 July 1663 - 10 June 1682; PC 2/72, pp. 740-2, 20 Sept. 1688; PC 2/73, pp. 406-8, 13 Mar. 1690.

2 PC 2/73, p. 24, 28 Feb. 1669; PC 6/18, p. 124, 12 June 1668, p. 152, 13 May 1676; PC 2/77, p. 134, 5 Feb. 1701.

3 Turner, *The Privy Council of England*, II, 74.

4 F.M.G. Evans, *The Principal Secretary of State, 1558-1680* (Manchester, 1923), pp. 1-2, 6. The Secretary also had numerous parliamentary and diplomatic duties. *Ibid.* pp. 7-9.

5 M.A. Thomson, *The Secretaries of State, 1681-1782* (1932), p. 75.

6 For the various types of warrant see WO 55/394, p. 53, 16 Nov. 1679; WO 55/338, fo. 53, 22 Apr. 1690; SP 44 [Secretaries' Domestic Entry Books]/106,

although warrants could be issued retrospectively after stores had been delivered by the monarch's verbal command, the board usually insisted on a prior written order.[1] The secretaries had no power by themselves, however, to order stores to be issued. In a letter to Secretary Nottingham the Ordnance board pointed out that they could only act by warrant from the Crown, the Privy Council or the lord high admiral, and although stores had been supplied previously during the Crown's absence on receipt of a letter from Nottingham, the officers hoped that for the future all demands would 'come so regular that our instructions may justify our proceedings'.[2] Clearly the secretaries' authority was derived from that of the king, and their power to act on their own initiative was limited in this period.

Yet there is no doubting their power as executive agents. They were influential privy councillors, and though they might be excluded from the ranks of the lords justices in Cabinet they were usually invited to assist at Council meetings.[3] A great deal of the secretaries' business was conducted in relation to the Privy Council, especially in the years 1660-79 when no lord president was appointed. Numerous Council papers and petitions passed through their hands and these still remain in the secretaries' letter books. Such papers were delivered to the king or Council and directions were given by the secretary in accordance with their wishes.[4] The secretary was, therefore, a vital intermediary connecting the Privy Council and the Ordnance Office. The Privy Council would order the secretary to prepare a warrant for the monarch's signature to contract for arms, after representation had been made to that board by the Ordnance master-general. The warrant would then subsequently be transmitted by the secretaries to the Ordnance Office. A demand for an estimate of the cost of stores was communicated to the Ordnance board in a similar way.[5] If the estimate needed some further explanation or if a complication arose the Ordnance officers would be requested to attend the Lords of the Council, which meetings occasionally took place at the secretaries' office.[6]

23, 19 Feb. 1707; SP 44/110, fos. 107, 121, 127 and *passim*; SP 44/171, fos. 104-5, 30 Dec. 1702.

[1] *Cal. SP Col. Am. & W. Indies 1704-5*, p. 602, no. 1302, Harley to O.b., 11 Aug. 1705; WO 55/333, warrant 18 Dec. 1672; SP 41 [State papers military] /34, no. 6, O.b. to Hedges, 15 July 1704.

[2] WO 55/342, p. 287, 21 Oct. 1702.

[3] Evans, p. 7; Carter, 'Cabinet Records', p. 107.

[4] Turner, *The Privy Council of England*, I, 401-2.

[5] E.g. PC 2/80, pp. 90-1, 7 Feb. 1706; *Cal. SP Col. Am. & W. Indies 1704-5*, p. 602, 11 Aug. 1705; SP 44/105, p. 88, 5 July 1704.

[6] E.g. SP 44/105, fo. 91, Hedges to O.b., 8 July 1704; SP 44/110, fo. 324,

The secretaries of state did not always act through the Privy Council. Their more important function was as an executive arm of the Crown, although this might mean that they worked through the king in Council, or that they brought a Privy Council order to the attention of the Crown.[1] A large part of the correspondence between the Ordnance board and the Crown which was conducted through one of the secretaries of state was independent of the Privy Council. The secretary, for example, intimated the Crown's wishes to the Ordnance Office, in response to a parliamentary address for estimates to be prepared and laid before the House of Commons or the House of Lords.[2] If there were any doubts about the estimate the secretary of state resolved them by signifying whether a particular item should be included, but no demand could be made in Parliament until the board had been informed of the Crown's wishes.[3]

Other letters between secretaries and the Ordnance board reveal the extent to which the secretary was involved in the most ordinary matters of Ordnance business as direct intermediary between Crown and department. Officials could be appointed and given directions through the secretaries of state; artillery trains were altered after they had signified the monarch's command; arms were dispersed on their order.[4] The secretaries, moreover, were informed about a host of issues which reflected on every aspect of Ordnance administration, such as the arms to be spent on fortifications in North Britain, the accounts of artillery trains in Spain or the quantities of stores aboard ships of war.[5]

This dual position of the secretaries of state as the servant of the Privy Council or Cabinet and the executor of the Crown meant that they occupied the focal point in the administration of the state. They were the key figures in the tortuous chain of command between the

---

Dartmouth to O.b., 1 Mar. 1711; SP 44/113, fo. 450, Dartmouth to O.b., 9 June 1713; SP 41/34, Bolingbroke to O.b., 25 May 1714.

1 PC 2/54, p. 78, 8 Aug. 1660; *Cal. SP Col. Am. & W. Indies 1702-03,* p. 394, 1 May 1703.

2 SP 44/108, fo. 30, Sunderland to Marlborough, 2 Mar. 1709; SP 44/109, St John to O.b., 3 Dec. 1710; SP 44/111, St John to Marlborough, 12 Dec. 1711; SP 44/112, fo. 405, Dartmouth to Marlborough, 29 Nov. 1711; SP 44/114, Bolingbroke to O.b., 12 Jan. 1714; SP 44/115, fo. 191, Bromley to O.b., 12 Mar. 1714.

3 SP 44/113, fo. 413, Dartmouth to O.b., 6 May 1713; SP 41/34, Rivers to Dartmouth, 20 Jan. 1712.

4 SP 44/105, fo. 139, Hedges to O.b., Oct. 1704; SP 41/34, O.b. to Hedges, 10 July 1704, O.b. to Dartmouth, 23 Oct. 1711, 11 Apr., 16 June 1713, 20 May 1714.

5 *Ibid.* Bridges to Hedges, 5 May 1706, O.b. to Sunderland, 12 Apr. 1707, O.b. to Dartmouth, 17 Mar. 1711, 21 Mar. 1712.

Crown, Privy Council and department, as well as the link between the departments themselves. Memorials for supply or for an improvement in the state of a garrison were delegated to Ordnance officers who in turn reported back an appropriate course of action.[1] The secretaries transmitted accounts of garrison stores, which had been sent to them from the Ordnance Office, to commanders for their information and they forwarded information from the Council of Trade about the condition of the plantations.[2]

The relationship between the secretaries, the Treasury and the Admiralty with regard to Ordnance matters was less well defined, for all three Offices had direct jurisdictional powers over the Ordnance Office. Occasionally, however, Ordnance letters about extraordinary costs, or an order from committee lords that the Ordnance should be reimbursed for stores, were transmitted to the Treasury via one of the secretaries.[3] The secretaries acted in a similar way with the Admiralty. The Admiralty had power to order stores directly from the Ordnance Office, but sometimes an instance is found of an Admiralty order being passed to the Ordnance by one of the secretaries.[4] More usually they would be consulted only to arbitrate on disagreements between the two Offices.[5]

The connection between the secretaries of state and the secretary at war was far more important to the Ordnance Office than the relatively slight contact between the secretaries and the Admiralty. The office of secretary at war was of much more recent origin than many positions within the Ordnance Office. It was not firmly established until 1676 with the tenure of Matthew Locke, who had succeeded in usurping many of the secretary of state's functions connected with the quartering and movement of troops. A similar

1 SP 41/34, O.b. to Hedges, 24 Jan., 25 June 1706; O.b. to Boyle, 14 Aug. 1708; SP 44/107, fo. 165, Boyle to O.b., 25 Jan. 1709; SP 44/111, St John to O.b., 20 July 1711.

2 SP 44/110, fo. 336, Dartmouth to Argyll, 10 Mar. 1712; *Cal. SP Col. Am. & W. Indies 1701*, pp. 42-3, Vernon to Council of Trade; SP 44/112, fo. 390, Dartmouth to Marlborough, 23 Nov. 1711, fo. 416, Same to Same, 11 Dec. 1711.

3 SP 44/110, fo. 311, Dartmouth to Treasury, 27 Feb. 1711, fo. 495, Same to Same, 11 May 1711; SP 44/112, fo. 385, Same to lord treasurer, 7 Apr. 1713.

4 WO 55/338, fos. 83-4, Admiralty to Nottingham, 9 July 1690, Nottingham to Goodricke of same date. In this case the request was for arms for Chatham dockyard rather than a naval vessel which perhaps explains Nottingham's endorsement of the order.

5 SP 44/105, fo. 134, 30 Sept. 1704; SP 44/110, fo. 498, Dartmouth to O.b., 14 May 1711; SP 44/113, fo. 82, Same to Same, 5 May 1712. The matters in contention were the sending of an engineer to Newfoundland, the provision of junk for wadding and the existence of naval buildings near Ordnance fortifications.

attempt by Blathwayt to increase his authority as secretary at war at the expense of the Ordnance Office had ended in failure. As a result the secretary at war had little control over the issue of Ordnance stores, which could only be requested through one of the secretaries of state. Occasional Ordnance entry books bear the signature of Locke for the issue of minor stores, but the great majority are signed by the secretary of state. The regular procedure for issue of Army stores was for the secretary at war to acquaint the secretaries of state with the needs of the Army; they would then obtain and counter-sign a sign manual warrant which gave the master-general of the Ordnance the authority to act.[1] The secretaries were thus the hub of the whole operation.

It is difficult to over-estimate the extent to which the secretaries were involved in the conduct of war operations. From their central station on the crossroads of the administrative plain they were able to survey the landscape and authorise the appropriate measures necessary to be undertaken. Their power was to some extent shared with the secretary at war and the lord high admiral, but in a combined naval and military expedition they were the only ministers in a sufficiently central vantage point and with sufficient authority to control both the naval and military side of the operation.[2] When stores were demanded for artillery trains on the continent the secretaries were required to co-ordinate the commander in chief, the supply departments, and the Admiralty and the Transport Office that were to provide the shipping and convoy. Correspondence between the secretaries and the Ordnance Office in the War of Spanish Succession reveals the extent of their control in the planning stages of operations. The secretaries were kept informed by the Ordnance Office at all stages of the proceedings: as to the state of stores, the cost of the new assignment, the time estimated for despatch, the tons of shipping required for transports and the victuals needed for Ordnance personnel. The Navy victuallers and the secretary at war were similarly called on to state what progress had been made in the things provided by their Offices.[3] Ultimately, however, it was the secretaries who were responsible for signifying to the respective departments when the stores were to be put on board ship and the expedition should set sail.[4] The observation of William

1 For the above see Evans, p. 324; Jacobson, p. 222; Thomson, pp. 66, 76.

2 *Ibid.* pp. 67-70, 78-80, 86-8.

3 SP 41/34, Vernon to Romney, 26 Mar. 1702, O.b. to Hedges, 8 July 1704, O.b. to Hedges, 14 Apr. 1705, O.b. to Hedges, 15 Jan. 1706, 20 May 1706, O.b. to Dartmouth, 23 Mar. 1711; SP 44/105, fo. 91, Hedges to O.b., 8 July 1704, fos. 202-3, Hedges to O.b., Navy victuallers and secretary at war, 18 Apr. 1705.

4 SP 44/109, St John to Marlborough, 18 Jan. 1711, Same to O.b., 16 Feb. 2, 6, 26 Mar. 1711; SP 44/114, Bolingbroke to O.b., 24 Feb. 1714.

Knox, an under-secretary in the Colonial department during the American War, that 'all warlike preparations, every military operation, and every naval equipment must be directed by a secretary of state before they can be undertaken,'[1] holds good for the earlier part of the century.

It is anachronistic, however, to draw general conclusions for one period from evidence which has been drawn from a later one, and the second part of Knox's remarks that 'neither the Admiralty, Treasury, Ordnance nor Victualling Boards can move a step without the king's command so signified [by a secretary of state]' would certainly not apply for the 1660-1714 period. For, as has been shown, the Ordnance board were quite at liberty to act in response to an order in council which could be transmitted independently of a secretary of state. The secretaries were important privy councillors at this time, but their claim to a central position in the government of the nation could not be realised until the Privy Council had declined completely as an administrative agent, and they had been established as key ministers in the Cabinet. As late as William III's reign their appointment as lords justices was by no means automatic, although William clearly considered the two secretaries of state to be among the great offices of the Crown and their inclusion in Anne's Cabinet was a matter of course.[2]

The position of the secretaries of state was thus secure by 1714, but it was by no means certain in 1660 they would reach such heights in the running of state affairs. The period 1660-1714 was, therefore, a transitional phase for the office of secretary of state. It is interesting to note that there was an expansion of the secretariat between these dates,[3] which clearly reflects an increase in the business conducted by the secretary of state's office, and emphasises the increasing importance of the secretaries as a channel of communication between the departments. This pattern of administrative communication from the secretaries' office, however, was only in the process of being formalised. Indeed, by relying on material drawn mainly from the early eighteenth century when the process was more settled, this account may have been too precise. For in the late seventeenth century the secretaries were still instruments of the king's pleasure, as may be seen by the appointment of Blathwayt as a third secretary to King William whilst

1   Quoted in Thomson, p. 65.
2   Carter, 'Cabinet Records', pp. 103, 107; Plumb, 'Organisation of the Cabinet', p. 145.
3   J.C. Sainty, *Officials of the Secretaries of State, 1660-1782 : Office-Holders in Modern Britain II* (1973), *passim.*

he was away overseas.[1] The division of duties between them, moreover, was purely a matter of convenience regulated by the king, and the northern or southern secretaries could pass on orders for stores to the Ordnance irrespective of the place of consignment.[2] The indefinite and personal nature of administrative history at this time must be emphasised and nowhere is it more in evidence than in the office of secretary of state. The over-centralised character of the position meant that results of the planning of naval and military expeditions were successful only when the secretary had great competence. The extent to which the secretaries of state were instigators in administrative affairs, then, remains an open question in this period, but what is certain is that by 1714 they were the linchpin of government, without whose cooperation the efficient despatch of the king's business might be seriously impeded.

The Admiralty

The lord high admiral or Admiralty commission was the other authority, with the Crown and Privy Council, that had power to order the Ordnance Office to issue stores, although this power was strictly limited to naval stores.[3] The extent of Admiralty control, however, was not as great as that of the Privy Council. An Admiralty command could be counter-manded by an order in Council, which authority was also needed if any alteration was to be made to a ship's gun establishment, or if extraordinary expenses incurred by sea captains were to be justified.[4] An Admiralty warrant, indeed, could not in itself justify the activities of the Ordnance Office. This is illustrated by the Admiralty commissioners' firm rebuttal of the Ordnance board's request for permission to break into sets of ships' guns – a request that was dismissed, because 'the whole affair of gunning their Majesty's ships and vessels [was] . . . under the care and management of the master general and officers of the Ordnance'.[5] If the Admiralty was unable to resolve a dispute between the Navy Board and the Ordnance Office, moreover, it was passed on to a higher authority.[6] Similarly, the

1 Thomson, p. 67.

2 *Ibid.* p. 1. Both Dartmouth (southern secretary) and St John (northern secretary) ordered stores for one expedition. SP 44/109, St John to O.b., 2 Mar. 1711. St John's reference to Lord Dartmouth's indisposition in a letter to Marlborough, however, clearly indicates that the north-south division was recognised even though it was not always adhered to. SP 41/34, 13 Feb. 1711.

3 King's 70, fo. 14, 1683 instructions; WO 55/342, p. 287, O.b. to Nottingham, 21 Oct. 1702.

4 Adm. 3 [Admiralty minutes]/17, 12 Dec. 1702. Above, p. 20.

5 WO 55/1792, fo. 35, Southerne to O.b., 20 Mar. 1690.

6 A protracted quarrel over the provision by the Navy of junk for gun wadding

Admiralty was not powerful enough to give orders to other departments that were not under its immediate jurisdiction.[1]

Nevertheless, despite these restrictions on the autonomy of the Admiralty, the lord high admiral or Admiralty commissioners did have direct control over naval Ordnance business, which was exercised independently without interference from the Privy Council or any other body. The lord high admiral's warrants were usually issued for an individual ship to be supplied, but in times of emergency a general order was made for the fitting out of ships.[2] There was, however, some degree of flexibility in the system, for the lord high admiral was able to delegate authority to Navy commissioners, or in their absence master attendants of the yards, for ships to be supplied. Wartime measures also enabled flag officers to order munitions for ships.[3]

Admiralty authority or delegated authority was not simply confined to the ordering of munitions to be put on board ship. The Admiralty exercised control either directly or indirectly over the whole spectrum of naval affairs. The lord high admiral or Admiralty commission was directly answerable for carrying out orders for the movement of ships, court martials and the appointment of officers, and indirectly responsible through the Navy Board and later the Sick and Wounded Commission and Victualling and Transport Boards, for the great mass of naval administrative work conducted by these bodies.[4] Correspondence between the Ordnance Office and the Admiralty, therefore, ranged over many aspects of naval affairs: the provision of convoys to safeguard Ordnance shipping; the victualling of Ordnance bomb vessels; the supply of the Ordnance yacht; the building of victualling sheds near Ordnance fortifications; the extravagances of naval captains in expending stores abroad; and the changing of a ship's gun establishment.[5] In these matters the Admiralty board, like the Privy

was finally settled by the lord treasurer. Adm. 3/17, 18 June 1702; WO 55/345, pp. 282, 287; *Cal. Treas. Papers 1711*, pp. 315, 366, orders 20 June, 13 July 1711. Also see above, p. 28, n 5.

1 Adm. 3/3, fo. 91, 17 Mar. 1690.

2 E.g. WO 55/330, p. 2, warrant for the *Assistance,* 24 July 1660; WO 47/5, p. 232, minute of warrant, 23 May 1664; WO 47/7, fo. 99, minute of warrant, 21 June 1665.

3 WO 47/6, fo. 103, 28 Dec. 1664; WO 47/7, Duke of York's warrant, 8 Feb. 1666; PC 6/18, p. 124, 6 Apr. 1668; WO 46/3, p. 124, letter to Romney, 20 July 1695; Adm. 3/1, fo. 177, 2 Aug. 1689; Adm. 3/3, 9 July 1690; Adm. 3/19, 3 May 1704.

4 Sir Oswyn A.R. Murray, 'The Admiralty' III, *Mariner's Mirror* 23 (1937), 320; P.K. Watson, 'The Commission for Victualling the Navy, the Commission for Sick and Wounded Seamen and Prisoners of War, and the Commission for Transport, 1702-1714' (unpublished London Ph.D. thesis, 1965), abstract.

5 Adm. 1 [Admiralty In Letters] 3999-4005, *passim*, letters from the O.b. to

Council in routine governmental matters, acted as the central clearing house for naval business.

The Admiralty provided the formal channel of communication between the Ordnance Office and the dependent navy boards, as only the Admiralty had executive power over all the departments. The Navy Board pressed the Admiralty when the Ordnance failed to deliver arms, or when some other difficulty arose which required the Admiralty's executive authority to resolve.[1] Sea captains, similarly, used the Admiralty when they made complaints about the quality of stores or there being delays in the shipping of those stores.[2] But this was by no means a one way process and the Ordnance Office made inquiries to the Navy Board and requests to captains via the Admiralty.[3]

If the lord high admiral or Admiralty commission acted the part of the Privy Council in distributing naval business to the appropriate department, the naval aspect of the secretary of state's role was played by the secretary to the Admiralty. Pepys had direct access to the king, and he was the official conveyor of the king's wishes through warrants issued on his behalf.[4] The Ordnance Office was not officially empowered to act without this official sanction, but Pepys adapted the system to suit the particular circumstance. One of his favourite devices was to inform the Ordnance Office of the necessity of furnishing a certain ship if the king's warrant could not be immediately obtained and later to send on the authorisation, or even to crave the acceptance of the king's pleasure on his own authority.[5] Pepys's position was in many respects unrepresentative because of his intimate relationship with the king. This at times gave him the authority to act independently, like Blathwayt did when third secretary of state in the 1690s. Burchett, as secretary to the Admiralty after Pepys, did not have immediate access to the king. Consequently,

the Admiralty, c.1703-18.

1 PL 2858, p. 129, Pepys to Dartmouth, 7 July 1685, p. 166, Same to Same, 18 July 1685; Adm. 3/1, fo. 28, 13 Apr. 1689; Adm. 3/24, 21 Dec. 1709, 24 Mar. 1710.

2 PL 2861, p. 417, Pepys to O.b., 11 Sept. 1688; WO 55/1792, fo. 52, Southerne to O.b., 15 July 1690; Adm. 3/3, fo. 239, 15 July 1690; Adm. 3/5, fo. 253, 1 May 1691; Adm. 3/16, 8 Mar. 1701.

3 PL 2860, p. 20, Pepys to O.b., 19 Mar. 1687; Adm. 3/1, fos. 121-2, 21 June 1689; Adm. 3/7, 19 Sept. 1692; Adm. 3/18, 18 May 1703; Adm. 3/23, 21 Nov. 26 Dec. 1707; Adm. 3/24, 21 Jan. 1710.

4 PL 2858, p. 567, Pepys to Dartmouth, 4 Feb. 1686; PL 2861, p. 231, Pepys to Navy Board.

5 *Cal. Pepys.* II, ed. J.R. Tanner, Navy Records Society 27 (1904), 88-9, Pepys to London, 11 Oct. 1674, p. 291, Pepys to O.b., 13 Apr. 1674, p. 372, Pepys to Chicheley, 6 Oct. 1674; PL 2861, p. 209, Pepys to Cheltenham, 4 June 1688.

he was less of an executive officer and more of an administrator. The Ordnance board's retort, which pointed out Burchett's remissness 'in not mentioning by whose commands he transmitted the said account [for stores]'[1] would not have been made when Pepys was Admiralty secretary in the late 1680s.

The Admiralty, then, served as a unifying central agency which could co-ordinate the activities of the different naval bodies. Orders were thus sent by the Admiralty to the Navy Board and Offices of Ordnance, Victualling, and Transportation, for them to give preference to certain ships in the provision of stores, or for them to provide particulars of any men subject to impressment.[2] The trouble lay in the fact that the Admiralty had executive powers over all the subordinate boards and coercive powers over all of them except the Ordnance. The Admiralty, therefore, did not have the authority to compel that Office to obey the executive order which it administered.[3]

The Treasury

Whereas the Privy Council, the secretaries of state and the Admiralty exercised direct jurisdiction over the issue of Ordnance stores, the Treasury exercised control over the Ordnance Office through its power of granting money so that those stores might be supplied. The period 1660-1714 witnessed the gradual growth of this power.

The lord treasurer, unlike a secretary of state, had little initiative in directing the Ordnance Office to issue stores. In 1703 when the Treasury's control over departmental expenditure was fully established, Godolphin as lord treasurer reported to Secretary Nottingham that he had just received a 'flat refusal' from the Ordnance board about the provision of a boom for service in Newfoundland. He continued:

> I ask pardon of your lordship for presuming I had any credit with them, and transmit their answer to your lordship that you may please to send for the Navy Board and them together and acquaint them both with her majesty's pleasure in that matter.[4]

It does seem, however, that the Treasury exercised some jurisdiction over the disposal of certain Ordnance stores and the distribution of prize guns.[5] The Treasury also possessed detailed knowledge of the

1   WO 47/22, p. 200, 14 June 1705.

2   Adm. 3/6, p. 497, 12 Apr. 1692; Adm. 3/21, 11 Mar. 1706.

3   As Sir Charles Wagner pointed out in the notes he made for Lord Torrington as first sea lord (c.1727). Corbett XIV, fo. 129.

4   *Cal. SP Col. Am. & W. Indies 1702-3*, no. 713, pp. 428-9, 19 May 1703.

5   *Cal. Treas. Books 1681-5*, p. 321, Guy to Ordnance commissioners, 1 Dec. 1681; *Ibid. 1685-9*, p. 83, Guy to Dartmouth, 24 Mar. 1685; *Ibid. 1704-5*,

condition of Ordnance stores. A Treasury minute of 16 November 1669 moved the king to direct the officers of the Navy and Ordnance to give an account every Christmas of their stores, and whilst this instruction may not always have been complied with the Treasury did receive such papers from the Ordnance Office.[1] These accounts were supplemented by weekly abstracts of all contracts made in the Ordnance Office.[2] In the case of salt-petre contracts the Treasury took an active part in negotiations between the Ordnance Office and the East India Company.[3] It could also arbitrate when petitioned by an Ordnance contractor for remuneration.[4]

The power of arbitration meant that the Treasury, like the Privy Council, could act as a court of appeal. It was not always successful — in the case cited involving the provision of a boom for Newfoundland the Treasury failed to impose its will on the Ordnance board — but it was usually able to accommodate the contending departments. It was the Treasury which finally settled the long standing conflict between the Ordnance and Navy regarding the provision of junk for wadding in exchange for broken ordnance for ballast, after the dispute had been referred from the Privy Council to the Treasury. The Treasury also interceded in another dispute between the two Offices over naval captains drawing bills of exchange on the Ordnance when abroad.[5] The Treasury's powers were even stronger when dealing with Customs commissioners, or officers of the Works or Mint. Such disagreements between these officers and the Ordnance board as to the imposition of fees on exported ordnance,[6] or the exact jurisdiction of each Office,[7] were settled by the direct intervention of the Treasury.

p. 56, 31 Oct. 1704; T.I [Treasury Minutes] /92, fo. 91, 30 Oct. 1704; T.I/93, fo. 54, 20 Jan. 1705.

1 *Cal. Treas. Books 1669-72*, p. 159; *Ibid. 1685-9*, p. 1463, Guy to Dartmouth, 15 July 1687; T.I/92, no. 36, fos. 193, 197, accounts of the state of small arms and gunpowder brought in, 13 Nov. 1704.

2 *Cal. Treas. Books 1689-92*, p. 1234, Guy to O.b., 18 July 1691.

3 Baxter, p. 74; *Cal. Treas. Books 1693-6*, p. 1279, 9 Jan. 1696; *Ibid. 1696-7*, p. 63, 16 Oct. 1696; *Ibid. 1697-8*, p. 101, 12 July 1698, pp. 71-2, 12 April 1699; *Ibid. 1700-1*, p. 44, 11 Feb. 1701.

4 *Cal. Treas. Books 1681-5*, p. 1099, 16 Apr. 1684.

5 *Cal. Treas. Books 1711*, p. 101, 2 Oct. 1711, p. 108, 30 Oct. 1711. See above, p. 31, n. 6, for the dispute over the provision of wadding for junk.

6 *Cal. Treas. Books 1676-9*, p. 1167, Bertie to Customs commissioners, 19 Nov. 1678; *Ibid. 1689-92*, p. 832, 27 Sept. 1690, p. 1392, Guy to Customs commissioners, 30 Nov. 1691; *Ibid. 1698-9*, p. 67, 17 Mar. 1699; *Ibid. 1700-1*, p. 227, 18 Mar. 1701, p. 237, 31 Mar. 1701; WO 55/470, p. 285, Dartmouth's warrant, 15 Jan. 1685.

7 T.I/67, fos. 181 ff.; *Cal. Treas. Books 1705-6*, p. 290, 12 June 1705; *Ibid. 1685-9*, p. 679, Guy to Dartmouth, 30 Mar. 1686.

Far more important than the Treasury's role as an arbitrator was the part it played as the watchdog of departmental finances. But it was only gradually that the Treasury established financial control over the Ordnance Office. Lord Treasurer Southampton in the early 1660s had little superintendance of payments out of the Receipt of the Exchequer or issues to departmental treasurers.[1] In August 1662, however, an attempt was made by the Treasury to regulate the price of naval and Ordnance stores by a system of itemised estimates.[2] The scheme broke down under the pressures of the Dutch War of 1665, and it was not until the establishment of the Treasury Commission of 1667 that the Treasury attempted to establish a closer control of Ordnance expenditure. A Treasury warrant of May 1667 directed the Ordnance commissioners to send an accurate statement of current Ordnance expenditure, a table of financial disbursements since the Restoration, and an account of whatever else they might think fit to forward for the 'better information' of the Treasury. Some days later on 15 June a Treasury minute ordered the lieutenant of the Ordnance and other departmental treasurers to send weekly certificates of their receipts, disbursements and cash remains.[3] Thus the Treasury was theoretically able to give at any moment an account of every branch of the revenue and expenditure, although, in order to do this, it was dependent on the co-operation from the departmental treasurers. These series of measures firmly established the weekly cash distributions to departments, after consultation between the king and Treasury lords, as the fundamental method of Treasury business.[4] Other attempts were made to establish Treasury supremacy. An order in council of 17 June 1667, at the time of the Medway raid, laid down that the Treasury had the power to regulate expenditure in detail, even though a formal general authorisation had been given. Shortly afterwards an attempt was made through another order in council to ensure that the Ordnance Office, as well as the other departments, applied to the Treasury for their money. A further order of April 1676 decreed that every department must have Treasury permission before it spent any money it had received.[5]

In the later part of the period Ordnance credit was firmly under Treasury supervision. The Office was required to gain Treasury approval

---

1 D.M. Gill, 'The Treasury, 1660-1714', *EHR* 46 (1931), 601.

2 See Baxter, pp. 71-2.

3 WO 55/426, no. 176, 25 May 1667; WO 55/388, p. 182, 30 May 1667; *Cal. Treas. Papers 1667-8*, p. 12, 15 June 1667.

4 Gill, p. 603; Baxter, p. 44. For weekly distributions to the Ordnance in 1684 see *Cal. Treas. Books 1681-5*, pp. 1085, 1091, 1098, and *passim*.

5 Roseveare, *Treasury, 1660-1870*, p. 37; Baxter, p. 68.

before tallies were discounted. The Treasury similarly directed that care was to be taken for interest to be saved on Exchequer bills, which were to be accounted for each month at the Treasury.[1] Ordnance estimates were also rigidly controlled. An estimate of expenditure could be summarily dismissed if the Treasury thought that it was excessive, and in the period after the Revolution, when estimates or schemes for half pay for officers were presented to the House of Commons for approval, the Treasury lords were consulted before the final estimate was submitted.[2] The Treasury lords, moreover, had absolute control over the general distribution of funds once the estimates had been granted, although the Ordnance officers were sometimes asked to proffer their advice as to whether the money might be applied to sea or land service.[3]

Why did the Treasury enjoy such a measure of control over the Ordnance Office? The presence of the Crown at Treasury meetings undoubtedly gave additional authority to its orders. The Treasury could thus give directions to the Ordnance on matters which the king had determined in Treasury meetings,[4] which directions would have had almost the same force as a warrant from the king through a secretary of state. The secretary to the Treasury, who had been brought into direct and continuing contact with the king after gaining control of the dispersal of secret service funds in 1676,[5] sometimes indeed acted as a secretary in conveying the king's pleasure.[6] The gradual growth of an independent Treasury free from domination by the Privy Council and secretaries of state must also have increased its authority in relation to the spending departments. The 1667 appointment of Treasury commissioners who were not all members of the Privy Council, the order in council of 31 January 1668 strengthening the powers of the lord treasurer over the secretaries, and the 1676 retrenchment scheme authorised by a simple sign manual warrant from the king direct to the lord treasurer and not

---

1 *Cal. Treas. Books 1709,* p. 26, 29 July 1709, p. 214, 22 June 1709; *Ibid. 1711,* p. 17, 17 Feb. 1711.

2 *Cal. Treas. Books 1681-5,* p. 1394, Guy to Dartmouth, 12 Nov. 1684; *Ibid. 1697-8,* p. 281, Lowndes to Ranelagh, 24 Mar. 1698; *Ibid. 1703,* p. 298, Lowndes to O.b., 9 June 1703.

3 *Cal. Treas. Books 1689-92,* p. 1047, 6 Mar. 1691; *Ibid. 1693-6,* p. 944, 8 Mar. 1695; *Ibid. 1706-7,* p. 3, 30 Oct. 1706; *Ibid. 1711,* p. 227, Lowndes to O.b., 29 Mar. 1711.

4 *Cal. Treas. Books 1697-8,* p. 95, 25 May 1698; *Ibid. 1698-9,* p. 86, 24 May 1699.

5 Baxter, pp. 187-8.

6 *Cal. Treas. Books 1685-9,* p. 679, Guy to Dartmouth, 30 Mar. 1686.

by Privy Council order, were important landmarks in this respect.[1] The basis of Treasury power over the departments, however, lay in the signing of the Office establishment. Any deviations from this establishment, or application for remission of taxes, or requests for additions of salary from individual officers, had to receive Treasury authorisation.[2]

It is possible, however, to exaggerate the influence of the Treasury by drawing evidence from a single department. The extent of Treasury influence was by no means constant and differed in each office — the power of the lord treasurer would be greater in the Customs Office where the Treasury had extensive powers of patronage, than in another office where it had minimal influence. It is also dangerous to generalise about the effectiveness of Treasury orders. That the 1667 Treasury commission, for instance, was important in establishing a theoretical Treasury supremacy over the departments, who were obliged to send in periodic returns on the nature of stores and the state of cash under their control, is not to be doubted. What is in doubt, however, is the readiness or ability of the departments to obey these instructions. In the case of the Ordnance, their officers were frequently charged to send in their weekly abstracts of remains and contracts,[3] yet Ordnance accounts were usually submitted only after constant Treasury badgering.[4] Nor, despite Treasury supervision of Ordnance estimates and Exchequer funds, was there an absolute guarantee that expenditure could be rigidly controlled. The failure of the retrenchment schemes in 1668 and 1676 shows the limitations of Treasury power in this respect.[5]

The effectiveness of Treasury control on the Ordnance Office might be questioned, but the extent of that control cannot be denied. By the 1670s the Treasury had gained some influence over Ordnance contracts and more extensive control over Exchequer issues. From this time numerous instructions emanated from the lord treasurer to the Ordnance governing the regulating of accounts, the ordering of imprest payments, and even the conduct of the Ordnance officers themselves, for there is

1   Gill, p. 602; Baxter, pp. 12-13, 62.
2   *Ibid.* For such requests by Ordnance officers see *Cal. Treas. Books 1702,* p. 97, 8 Dec. 1702; *Ibid. 1703,* pp. 75-6, 18 Aug. 1703.
3   *Cal. Treas. Books 1685-9,* p. 1181, Guy to Bertie, 7 Feb. 1687; *Ibid. 1689-92,* pp. 1234, 1267, 1691, Guy to O.b., 18 July, 17 Aug. 1691, 21 June 1692.
4   *Cal. Treas. Books 1669-72,* pp. 356, 409, 467-8, 1 Feb., 19 Apr., 29 June 1670; *Ibid. 1705-6,* p. 753, Taylor to Mordaunt, 31 Aug. 1706.
5   See below, pp. 175, 178. On Treasury control of departmental expenditure in general see C.D. Chandaman, *The English Public Revenue, 1660-88* (Oxford, 1975), pp. 213-15, 251-2.

good reason to believe that the proposal to alter the instructions of the Office in the early 1680s was moved by the Treasury lords.[1] The authority of the Treasury over the Ordnance Office may thus have been established at an earlier date than over other spending departments. By the early eighteenth century, however, its credit with all the war departments was such that the Ordnance board, the Navy commissioners and lesser boards could be summoned at will to appear before the Treasury lords.[2]

The Ordnance Office and Other Departments and Conclusion

The Privy Council, the secretaries, the Admiralty and the Treasury all had the power to transmit orders to the Ordnance board, although the nature and the authority of these orders varied considerably. The Treasury's sphere of responsibility was limited to financial matters and it could not order any stores to be issued, though it had limited surveillance over their contracting. The Admiralty could not direct the issue of military stores, whereas the secretaries on behalf of the monarch could give orders for military and, indirectly through the Admiralty, naval ordnance to be issued. The Privy Council or the lords justices held primacy over the Admiralty, and that Council was consulted for a ruling if a dispute arose between the Ordnance and the Admiralty or its subordinate boards. The power of the Privy Council over the Treasury, however, declined in this period and the Treasury itself was able to act as a council of appeal for financial matters. The role of the Privy Council was again duplicated by the Admiralty for both bodies acted as central clearing houses for business: the Admiralty specifically for naval affairs and the Privy Council generally for all matters of administrative routine. The functions of the Privy Council were also matched to some extent by those of the secretary of state, who ensured that orders reached the appropriate body, thereby providing a link, in the same manner as the Council, between the Ordnance Office and the other departments of state.

Many of the orders received by Ordnance officers were delegated to them by the secretaries of state, Privy Council, Admiralty or Treasury, as has been shown, but this did not mean that they had no direct relation with other departments and officials. The Council for Trade

1 *Cal. Treas. Papers 1672-5,* p. 478; T.27 [Treasury Out Letters, General]/5, pp. 249-51; WO 49/111. For the Treasury attempts to reform the Office in the early 1680s see T.27/6, p. 68, Guy to Ordnance commissioners, 4 Aug. 1680, p. 300, Lowndes to Same, 27 Aug. 1681, p. 349, Guy to Same, 6 Dec. 1681, p. 405, Guy to master-general, 7 Feb. 1682. Dartmouth's outline instructions (D.1778/V86) seem to have been drafted as a corrective to ones that were biased towards Treasury interference within the department.

2 *Cal. Treas. Books 1710,* p. 34, 12 Aug. 1710.

and Plantations wrote straight to the Ordnance board to enquire about stores sent to the plantations, to speed up a consignment of arms for a colony, or to ask permission to remove an engineer from one plantation to another.[1] The Navy Board, the Transport commissioners and other offices also communicated with the Ordnance board, without leave of a central agency, on matters of administrative routine or if an expedition was being planned.[2] And the secretary at war directly informed the principal Ordnance officers about such matters as the necessity of their attending a meeting of Army personnel, the amount of bedding required by soldiers being sent overseas, or the method of disbanding an artillery train.[3] The official channel of communication, however, ran between the department, the central bodies of the administration and the Ordnance Office. It was only when the Office received directions from a higher authority that it was empowered to act. When that authority had been obtained an estimate could then be laid before the Council or sent directly to the Treasury for money to be assigned.[4]

The Ordnance Office was anxious to preserve its privileges from encroachment by other officials or departments. Blathwayt as secretary at war occasionally sent orders to the Ordnance on behalf of the king, or demands on his own authority for economy in the provision of stores. But he sometimes over-reached himself and on such occasions the Ordnance Office was quick to uphold its rights.[5] The secretaries of state also sometimes invaded the board's prerogatives and they, too, were rebuked. Secretary Hedges mistakenly signified the deputy-governor of the Tower to fire the guns upon the news of the taking of Landau and received this tart reply from the principal officers:

> We think ourselves obliged in duty to the Earl of Marlborough, our master-general, to endeavour to prevent any of the powers and privileges of this Office to be lessened during his absence. Therefore hope you will give us leave to acquaint you that the power of ordering the guns in the Tower has always been lodged in the master-general or in his absence in the principal officers. And that no further dispute may be herein, we desire you to send your commands to us upon all such occasions.[6]

1 *Cal. SP Col. Am. & W. Indies 1701*, p. 611, 14 Nov. 1701; *Ibid. 1702-3*, p. 134, p. 810, 13 Nov. 1703.
2 Adm. 106 [Navy Board minutes]/2886, 19 Sept. 1672; Adm. 106/2887, 28 Mar. 1673; Add. MS. 28876, fos. 299, 302.
3 WO 55/335, fo. 75, Blathwayt to Sherburne, 25 Sept. 1688; SP 44/105, fo. 317, Hedges to O.b., 15 Dec. 1705; *Cal. Treas. Books 1713*, p. 23, 30 Mar. 1713.
4 *Cal. SP Col. Am. & W. Indies 1693-6*, p. 241, Sidney to Blathwayt, 22 Jan. 1694; SP 41/34, O.B. to Dartmouth, 2 Apr. 1713.
5 WO 55/338, fo. 71, 4 June 1690; WO 55/339, p. 9; Jacobson, p. 222, n. 67.
6 WO 55/342, p. 273, 3 Sept. 1702.

Similar jurisdictional disputes occurred between the Ordnance Office and the Mint over the rights of the Ordnance smith in the Tower, and the Office and the Navy Board over the provision of certain types of stores, and these produced acrimonious and protracted debates.[1]

The normal exchanges between the departments were a good deal more formal. There was a correct mode of address and procedure for all warrants and communications and these had to be strictly adhered to. A warrant from the Privy Council was to be signed by at least six of the counsellors. All directives from the Admiralty to the Ordnance commissioners had to be made by way of a letter signed by all the Admiralty commissioners or a quorum of them. The style to be used in such letters was to be 'pray and desire', and they were to be obeyed as if the king by royal sign manual had signified the request. If the order was not made in the correct manner the unusual style was commented upon.[2] The departments usually expected to act on an original order under seal of office rather than on a copy, the sending of which was considered very irregular. A specific order was also required rather than a vague general missive.[3] The Ordnance Office sometimes obeyed the king's verbal order but this was usually certified by the retrospective grant of a formal warrant.[4]

The formality of the official mode of address, however, belied the general fluidity of the system. The great difficulty about tracing a general pattern of administrative communication in this period, is that as soon as the pattern has been traced, exceptions are found to the general rule. Thus the Ordnance Office might act in response to a direct order from the commander in chief for supply for the forces, rather than one obtained via the secretary at war and the secretary of state.[5] Blathwayt when secretary at war could also act like a secretary of state by sending orders to the Ordnance for information about aspects of military administration in response to a directive from the king himself, and Pepys at the Admiralty acted for the king in a similar way.[6] It was this access to the king's person which was one

1 Above, pp. 28, 31, 35.

2 PL 2867, pp. 224-5, 10 July 1679; Adm. 3/3, fo. 272, 5 Aug. 1690; WO 55/338, fo. 19, Southerne to O.b., 19 Mar. 1690.

3 *Cal. SP Col. Am. & W. Indies 1710-11*, pp. 443-4, Council of Trade to Dartmouth, 4 Apr. 1711; *Acts of PC Col. 1613-80*, pp. 471-2, 8 July 1668.

4 WO 55/333, warrant, 18 Dec. 1672; *Cal. SP Dom. 1679-80*, p. 283, 16 Nov. 1679.

5 E.g. *Cal. SP Col. Am. & W. Indies 1677-80*, p. 412, Monmouth to Ordnance commissioners, 9 Sept. 1679.

6 WO 55/338, fo. 71, 4 June 1690. For Pepys see above, p. 33.

of the most vital factors in the growth of the importance of the offices of secretary to the Admiralty and secretary at war under Pepys and Blathwayt. Both Pepys and Blathwayt were in effect third secretaries of state, but once they had relinquished their posts the importance of their offices declined and the real secretaries of state resumed their powers.[1] It is impossible to be too definite about administrative procedures when the personality of the king — and indeed that of the office holder — played such a greater part in determining the nature of those procedures. Not until the king's interest had lessened could the routine channels of communication be developed on more settled lines.

Yet the Crown was vitally interested in aspects of government in the late seventeenth century, when the administration of the realm was conducted not only in the name of the monarch as it is today, but also to some extent by his person. The king chaired Privy Council meetings, and this was no mere formality as he was occasionally required to act as arbiter on involved questions of the right of law. The monarch took an active part in Treasury meetings, arbitrating between an ever stringent Treasury and other departments, and in the latter part of the period the Crown supervised Cabinet meetings.[2] The king also had control over the appointment of his officials. It was Charles II, on prompting from the Duke of York but in direct contradiction to the wishes of Clarendon, who decided that the Treasury should be put into commission in 1667.[3] The same monarch reorganised the membership of the Privy Council in 1679, although Temple claimed credit for the scheme.[4] James II controlled appointments to the great officers of state even more rigorously than his brother, and his successor exercised similar rights. A correspondent to Dartmouth at the very beginning of his reign claimed that the Prince of Orange was 'inclined to put the management of the great offices into commission, so that he could provide for the more of his friends'.[5] At a lower level the king was sometimes directly involved in the appointment of Ordnance officers.[6]

---

1 For the position of the secretary at war see Olive Anderson, 'The Constitutional Position of the Secretary at War, 1642-1855', *Journal of the Society for Army Historical Research* 36 (1958), 165-9.

2 D. Ogg., *England in the Reign of Charles II* (Oxford, 1963), I, 190; Baxter, pp. 42-3.

3 *Own Life,* III, 790-4.

4 Turner, *Privy Council,* I, 439.

5 D.1778/I i 1749, Bowles to Dartmouth, 28 Dec. 1688.

6 See below, p. 73.

The king's concern even extended to the lower reaches of Ordnance administration. All the later Stuart kings were greatly interested in the science of fortification and its practical implementation by the Ordnance board. Charles II devised new types of fortification, and Clarendon himself noted that he supervised the initial building operations at Sheerness Fort.[1] Both Charles and his brother made periodic visits to coastal fortifications, and William III signified his approval of schemes of fortification.[2] The Crown was also concerned with other aspects of Ordnance business. The king did not attend board meetings as he did at the Treasury, but officers did have access to his presence. Sir Henry Sheer, for instance, observed that when he was in service under Charles II (although before he became an Ordnance officer) he had 'frequent occasions of privacy with his majesty in his closet'.[3] Nor was this an isolated instance. Lord Dartmouth's exhortation to James in the last months of his reign 'to look into that Office [the Ordnance] when they wait on you' and 'to go to your Admiralty, Navy, Victualling and Tower Offices at this time when you have any leisure',[4] shows that the king was expected to take an active interest in the administration of the realm. 'I believe it may be of service to your majesty a little to inspect them', continued Dartmouth, 'and it would satisfy the world of your general care of all your great concerns, though it were but by your appearing'. William III also gave directions to an Ordnance officer who had been summoned to appear before him, and even when he was abroad he made his wishes evident via the secretary of state.[5]

It should not be imagined, however, that the Crown's influence was a constant factor in late seventeenth century and early eighteenth century administration. Charles II took a lively interest in aspects of government business — his 'great sagacity' on naval matters caught the attention of no less an authority than Sir Henry Sheer[6] — but it is unlikely that he regularly applied himself to administration, though a scholar has observed that contacts with the Treasury became quite frequent after the appointment of the Treasury commission in

1 *The Correspondence of Henry Oldenburg*, ed. A.R. and M.B. Hall, 6 vols. (Wisconsin, 1965-9), IV, 207, Oldenburg to Boyle. 25 Feb. 1667, p. 545. Justel to Oldenburg, 25 July 1668; *Own Life*, III, 751-2.

2 *The Bulstrode Papers : A collection formed by Alfred Morrison* (1897), pp. 63, 183; *HMC* 11 Rep. V, *Dartmouth* I, p. 93, Musgrave to Dartmouth, 24 Sept. 1683; King's Top. Coll. XIV, 44.

3 Sloane 3828, fo. 185.

4 *HMC* 20, 11 Rep. V, *Dartmouth* I, p. 259, 17 Oct. 1688.

5 WO 55/337, fo. 34, Goodricke to O.b., 29 Oct. 1689; WO 55/339, p. 25, extract of a letter from Nottingham to Sidney, 17/27 Feb. 1691.

6 Sloane 3828, fo. 185.

1667.[1] James II and William III were probably more effective as administrators. Both had far more experience of government when they came to the throne, and both were by temperament more suited to the drudgeries of administrative routine. William, for instance, during the nine years of his reign for which minutes are extant, attended the Treasury about 176 times — an average of three times a month when he was at home. When he was abroad, moreover, he regularly received reports about financial matters from the Treasury lords.[2] There seems little evidence for James II's attendance at the Treasury, though considering his concern at the Admiralty, it would be surprising to find that he was not in constant communication with the Treasury lords. It is possible to speak in the same breath about the abilities of James and William as administrators, but it is difficult to declaim with such certainty that the control of the Crown over governmental affairs was as great after the Revolution as it was before it, for after 1689 the administration lacked the monarch's continual guidance. William might have received extensive reports about the state of affairs in England, but he could not gain complete control over government because of his frequent absences abroad. It was during his reign that a Cabinet first came into existence to provide a central focus for war administration and policy, and from 1694 onwards this body met without the king's presence. Under Anne the decline in the control of the Crown continued. It was not that she was completely withdrawn from the business of government for she attended more Cabinet meetings than any other monarch in our history. This particular distinction, however, is a result more of the age in which she lived, than her suitability to business. The instability of her emotions and her addiction to intrigue could hardly have made her an efficient administrator.[3] It is significant that during the twelve years of her reign she attended Treasury meetings only twenty-two times,[4] and that no record has been traced of her interest in Ordnance affairs.

The years 1660-1714, therefore, were a period of great flux and uncertainty in the government of England. Professor Plumb has traced the growth of political stability in England between 1675-1725, but this implies that stability was only gradually being imposed on a fundamentally unstable system. One of the reasons for this state of affairs was the fluctuating leadership of the Crown but there were also other reasons for the lack of cohesion in the central administration.

1 Baxter, p. 38.
2 Gill, 'The Treasury', pp. 607-8.
3 J.H. Plumb, *The Growth of Political Stability, 1675-1725* (1967), pp. 105-6.
4 Gill, 'The Treasury', p. 608.

The old unifying force of the Privy Council was breaking down the new centralising power of the Cabinet had not fully emerged to take its place, and the lines of communication between the central agencies and the departments was only in the process of development. Was the Ordnance Office to act on a letter from Blathwayt signifying the king's pleasure, when he was supposedly secretary at war and not secretary of state?[1] And were naval matters the province of the southern or northern secretary of state?[2] In such a state of uncertainty it is not to be wondered that only tentative guidelines to procedure can be drawn.

1   E.g. WO 55/339, p. 58, O.b. to Nottingham, 25 Apr. 1691.
2   *Cal. SP Dom. 1693*, pp. 141-2, Romney to Blathwayt. Quoted in Jacobson, p. 222, n. 68. William tried to force naval matters into the hands of Nottingham the southern secretary, who contended that the Army was his province and the Navy that of his colleague, Trenchard.

2

OFFICE—HOLDERS

Their Status, Function and Responsibility

Ordnance office-holders of this period came from a cross-section of late seventeenth century society.[1] For the department was comprised of many different types of civil and military officer, from the master-general at the top of the social hierarchy to the clerk in the middle and to the labourer at the lower end of the social scale.

The office of master-general was not considered one of great prestige in seventeenth century England and was inferior to the highest positions in the Army, Navy or state. James, Duke of York, for example, thought that the governor of Portsmouth garrison made 'a better figure in the world' and would 'always be more considered' than the master-general. Later a warrant from James as king stated that the master-general should hold only the equivalent rank to that of the youngest lieutenant-general in a garrison; in the field he was not entitled to such a rank without a special commission. The master-general had no greater authority in naval counsels — at least in the early seventeenth century, when he was a member of the lord high admiral's Council under Buckingham, and occupied a place junior to the vice and rear admiral of England. Nor did the master-general hold a central place in the counsels of the realm. He was an *ex officio* member of neither the Privy Council nor the rudimentary Cabinet formed under William III and Anne.[2] More important, however, than the actual position of the master-general *vis à vis* other officers of state was the fact that the office was invariably filled by 'a person of great eminence and integrity'[3] and usually by a member of the aristocracy. Fourteen men held the position from the Restoration to the death of Anne. Many of these officers, like Dartmouth, Schomberg, Romney and Marlborough, were important national figures, and eight of this number were either peers on appointment or elevated to the peerage soon after they had

---

[1] Detailed references to *DNB* and to the draft biographies in the possession of the History of Parliament Trust have generally not been given. For a list of some of the office-holders of the period, see appendix, pp. 223-39. For other names see the Ordnance treasury ledgers and quarter books (WO 48 and 54).

[2] For the above see *HMC* 20, 11 Rep. V, *Dartmouth I*, p. 67, York to Dartmouth, 11 Sept. 1681; WO 55/134, fo. 56, warrant 13 May 1686. *Naval Minutes*, p. 131; H.C. Tomlinson, 'The Organisation and Activities of the English Ordnance Office, 1660-1714' (unpublished Reading Ph.D. thesis, 1974), pp.105-9.

[3] Chamberlayne (4th edn, 1673), p. 244.

been made master-general. It was the man who made the office rather than the office that made the man.

The principal officers — the lieutenant-general, the surveyor-general, the clerk of the Ordnance, the storekeeper, the clerk of the deliveries and the treasurer — were not as important politically or socially as the master-generals. Only a few principal officers were influential courtiers — notably the lieutenants, at least four of whom (Goodricke, Granville, Erle and Hill) were privy councillors — and of the fifty or so appointments made to this rank from 1660 to 1714, only one, Lord George Granville, was a peer at the time of appointment. Many of the principal officers of the period, however, were well-educated younger sons drawn from the gentry classes or above. Only about one in five principal officers were likely to have been first sons, whereas one in three were likely to have been educated at an inn or a university. Of the twenty-six officers of whom we have information, moreover, five were the sons of peers, ten of baronets or knights and six of untitled gentlemen. Only five were of poorer birth — Moore senior appears to have come from a poor northern background; Fortrey was of mercantile origins; Sheer was the son of a naval captain; Craggs, the son of a barber; and Wharton, the son of a yeoman. With the exception of Craggs, all of these men held office prior to the Revolution. At this level at any rate, social mobility within the service became increasingly restricted.[1]

The background of many of the remaining Ordnance personnel — described in the 1683 instructions as being 'the inferior officers, under the chief officer of our Ordnance, who were either to attend the officers as their clerks or the Office as the deputy keeper of the Armoury, keeper of the small gun office, storekeepers, engineers, master gunner, master firemaster, proofmaster, clerk of the check, purveyor, messenger, labourers, gunners, etc'. — is obscure. Some of their names may be culled from internal Ordnance records, but, in contrast with their seniors, it is difficult to obtain information of their personal histories because they did not generally take such a prominent part in national affairs as the principal officers. Nevertheless, it is possible to paint an impressionistic portrait of the type of men holding the more junior clerical and military offices by drawing together a number of case studies.

1 This is tied up with the fact that promotion to this level from other ranks gradually became closed. (See below, p. 76). By the end of the period it was expected that a member of the board of Ordnance should be a man of some substance prior to his appointment. See *Marlborough-Godolphin Correspondence*, ed. Henry L. Snyder. 3 vols (Oxford, 1975), p. 1366, Marlborough to Godolphin, 5 Sept. 1709, for following re. Ash: 'This gentleman will have £2,000 a year, and be a credit to your board of Ordnance'.

48

It is clear from the fact that a number of Ordnance clerks are mentioned in the principal officers' wills, as well as from other internal evidence,[1] that many clerks were simply the personal servant of the principal officer. The difference in status, therefore, between the senior clerk in the department, the master-general's secretary, and the most junior position on the board, the clerkship of deliveries, was likely to be negligible. Indeed four clerks — Philip Musgrave, John Pulteney, James Craggs and Newdigate Ousley — held the two offices concurrently. Two other secretaries to the master-general — Matthew Baylie and Richard Beck — were well-endowed,[2] and a third, Richard Graham, was a principal of Clifford's Inn and a Treasury solicitor to James II. The other clerks were generally likely to have been of a much lower social standing than the principal officers, although there was some progression between the two ranks in the early part of the period as we shall see. There was also some movement between the ranks of clerk and storekeeper. Those storekeepers who were not clerks prior to their appointment, however, came from a variety of backgrounds. Some were artisans — Browne, storekeeper at Chatham in the early 1660s, possibly belonged to the family of gunfounders, and Richard Ridge, the Portsmouth storekeeper, was a cooper by trade.[3] Others were military men — John Fortescue and Robert Mynors at Upnor, and Peter Shackerley at Chester were governors of their respective garrisons; whilst Fleetwood at Portsmouth, Brockhurst at Upnor and Idell at Hull (who was also a substantial tobacco Merchant) all held Army commissions.[4] A number of storekeepers were small landowners — both Francis Povey, a clerk to the surveyor, 1670-80, and then storekeeper at Tangier, and John Watkinson, the Hull storekeeper, owned small estates. Many storekeepers, moreover, had to be sufficiently well-connected to be able to give substantial sums of money as security for their offices.[5] In this period, therefore, storekeepers of the outports were well-endowed and well-positioned members of the local community.

---

1 See below, pp. 74-5.

2 Baylie, clerk to Compton and the first commissioners, was wealthy enough to hold a bank account at Backwell's, and Richard Beck, master-general's clerk 1670-1, was able to lend over £4,000 to the king between 28 Feb. 1671 and 29 Apr. 1671 at six *per cent* interest. Glynn Mills, Backwell Ledgers I, fo. 301, K, fo. 353; WO 51/12, fo. 121, repayment 2 Jan. 1572.

3 *Pepys Diary* (ed. Matthews and Latham), IV; 260, n. 3. WO 51/7, fo. 128.

4 Charles Dalton, *English Army Lists and Commission Registers, 1661-1714,* I (1892), pp. 110, 298, 329; WO 51/15, fo. 156; WO 51/19, fo. 77; WO 51/34, fo. 46; WO 47/8, Mar. 1666; *Cal. SP Dom. 1690-1,* p. 472, Sidney to Goodricke, 6 Aug. 1691; WO 47/25, p. 290, 22 Jan. 1708; Bodl. A475, Duxbury to O.b., 28 Oct. 1685.

5 See below, p. 97.

The Ordnance gunners places too were usually filled by men from the middling ranks of society. For in the seventeenth century gunnery was esteemed as being a genteel employment, which was not suitable to be practised by the lower orders. The extant list of feed gunners for 1664, which states the gunners occupation as well as his name and dwelling place, certainly corroborates this view. Edward Arhber was listed as a mast maker, Captain John Brooke as a master attendant at Chatham, Captain Thomas Taylor and Captain Valentine Pyne as master gunners on ships, Augustine Blackwood as a boatswain, Joseph Hone as a mathematical instrument maker and Thomas Hodgkins as a master smith to the Office. A number of other men like George Wharton, Matthew Baylie and Geoffrey Fleetwood were also clerks in the department as well as being feed gunners.[1] A document on the gunners establishment drawn up for Lord Dartmouth when he was master-general in the early 1680s, makes it perfectly clear that 'servingmen, watermen, tradesmen, [and] prentices' generally discharged the duty of gunner before the reforms of 1682.[2] The engineers were, like the gunners, the bourgeoisie of seventeenth century military life. They were required to read and write, digest complex technical manuals and execute intricate plans of bastionised fortifications. A number of military officers were of foreign extraction. Sir Martin Beckman, chief engineer, 1685-1702, and comptroller of fireworks, 1688-1702, and the fireworkers Neilson and De Rüis were Swedes; Sleinsteine was formerly the Prince of Orange's firemaster, and men like Circlebach and Schlundt were clearly of foreign background.[3] In 1692-3 the House of Lords thought that the situation was so serious that they addressed the queen that Meesters should not be employed as principal storekeeper, and that, 'for the encouragement of the English, there may not be so many strangers employed in the Office of the Ordnance'.[4]

The functions of the Ordnance office-holder to a certain extent reflected their social status. The artistocratic master-generals acted as the official receiver of the Crown's pleasure on its passage from the central administration to the Ordnance board; the gentry on the board actually made the decisions as to how the department was to be run; and these decisions for the most part were carried out by the clerks, storekeepers, gunners, engineers and labourers who came from the middle and lower social orders.

1 WO 49/112, list of Tower gunners, 15 Apr. 1664.

2 D.1778/V 71. For these reforms, see below, p. 65.

3 *DNB;* WO 51/26, fo. 57, payment 10 Oct. 1682; WO 47/15, p. 64, minute 30 June 1685.

4 *LJ* XV, 235, 18 Feb. 1693; *Luttrell Diary,* P. 325, 16 Dec. 1692; *HMC* 17, 14 Rep. VI, *House of Lords,* pp. 181 ff.

The master-generals themselves were not concerned with the detailed management of Ordnance administration, but they were kept informed of the board's proceedings, either through their attendance at its meetings or the reports made to them by their chief clerks or principal officers, and they did make periodic inspections when cannon were being proved or new fortifications built.[1] Nevertheless, their precise line of duty was never as clearly defined as that of other officials. In the 1683 instructions, for instance, the department's government was committed to five principal Ordnance Officers rather than the master-general, whose specific duties were not separately outlined. Although it is clear from a reading of these instructions that the master-general had power to suspend any offending officer, and was also responsible for counter-signing warrants for supplies of stores, authorisation of contracts and payments of money. The principal officers were further enjoined to consult him over various aspects of Ordnance affairs and to present to him a regular statement of the size of the Office debt.[2]

So the master-general's function was essentially supervisory. Sir William Compton considered that his position gave him powers of 'general inspection into the affairs of the Office' and an 'interest' in business whenever the board gave him 'particular notice of such occasions', a view confirmed by the principal officers' admission in a later period that they simply looked to the master-general 'for countenance and support'.[3] It is also evident, however, that the master-general held a vast reserve of powers if he chose to exercise them. Wellington's statement that 'the whole power of the Ordnance is by his patent vested in him', the master-general,[4] applies equally to the master-general's position in the earlier period. Yet the fact that no appointment was made to the mastership, 1663-4, 1690-3, 1713-14, shows that he was not indispensable to the actual day to day ordering of Ordnance business.[5] This was the responsibility of the principal officers who constituted the working officials of the Ordnance board.

1 E.g. the following payments in the treasurer's ledgers: WO 48/12, pp. 163-4, 5 Dec. 1673; WO 48/13, p. 69, 8 Sept. 1675; WO 48/34, p. 449, 29 Apr. 1696. For evidence of their being kept informed of Office business see my thesis, pp. 116-17.

2 King's 70, fos. 6, 9-10, 12-13, 18-19, instructions 25 July 1683.

3 WO 47/5, p. 96, Compton to O.b., 2 Sept. 1663; WO 46/4, p. 57, O.b. to Romney, 12 Sept. 1699.

4 Quoted in D.M.O. Miller, *The Master-General of the Ordnance: A Short History of the Office*, p. 17.

5 During these periods the lieutenant-general became the nominal head of the Office. See WO 55/388, fo. 12, warrant to Legge, 24 Nov. 1663. Goodricke accused the principal officers of usurping this function. SP 32/4, no. 30, Goodricke's representation and O.b.'s answer, 19 Apr. 1962.

The principal officers were allocated different tasks which covered every aspect of Ordnance administration. These duties were incorporated in the instructions drawn up in 1683 for each individual Ordnance officer. The lieutenant-general held a general brief, supervising the tabling of estimates and contracts and keeping watch over the conduct of the other officers. The surveyor-general's responsibility was more specific as he was obliged to ensure that all stores were well-ordered and proved, that all bills were passed within ten days of their receipt, and that all works were accurately estimated and measured. The clerk of the Ordnance was the departmental scribe and archivist. He was to keep all records 'for the justifications and satisfaction of the Office', and to indite all 'letters, instructions, commissions, deputations, contracts or bargains'. These included debentures, bills of imprest, annual ledgers of store receipts, issues and returns, accounts of money received and paid by the Ordnance treasurer, quarter book payments and a quarterly state of the Office debt. The principal storekeeper had to take care of, and stand security for, all stores within the Tower. Strict regulations governed the receipt and issue of stores: no stores were to be received until a warrant had signified that they had been surveyed; bills of receipt were to be drawn up within ten days after delivery; and proportions of issue were to be regularly presented to the board. The storekeeper was also to keep a daily journal of all receipts, issues and returns of stores, from which day book an annual register was to be compiled for the benefit of the board and the auditors of the imprest. The issue duties of storekeeper were complemented by those of the clerk of deliveries, who was responsible for drawing up all proportions for the delivery of any stores of war. He again was to keep a strict account of his proceedings by maintaining records of all proportion warrants and delivery indents. All store deliveries and store remains were to be strictly witnessed by this official or his clerks. Finally there was the Ordnance treasurer, an office originally executed by the lieutenant-general, but one which from the death of Colonel William Legge in 1670 was performed by an accounting official who had no other departmental responsibilities.[1] This new officer was not, however, a permanent member of the Ordnance board.[2] Nevertheless, he was an extremely important official, responsible for soliciting money from the Treasury, receiving the cash that had been assigned to the department and paying out all money that had been so authorised. He was also to keep periodic duplicate accounts of the state of the Office cash. One

1   By the important order of 13 Feb. 1665. See SP 29/112, fo. 167.

2   An order of 8 Oct. 1669 stated that the treasurer was not to sit at the board (SP 29/266, fo. 104, 8 Oct. 1669) and although this order was soon countermanded (see SP 29/280, fo.234, Chicheley's warrant, 2 Dec. 1670) after Wharton's death the treasurer was not registered as having attended board meetings.

of these was to be retained by the clerk, and the other delivered, after internal examination, to the auditors of the imprest every Michaelmas.

The separate duties of each principal officer were, however, less important than the sum total of their powers, for officers exercised many rights of check on their colleagues. The surveyor and the clerk kept check books on the storekeeper and treasurer; the treasurer and the clerk of deliveries' indents served as a counter to the storekeeper's accounts; stores were not to be issued without the authorisation of at least three principal officers; the treasurer was forbidden to pay money unless directed to do so by the master-general or a quorum of the board; the board further examined the accounts of its individual members. These rights of surveillance were supplemented by the board's corporate duties. Money expended on stores was to be considered jointly, a proportion of what was needed being drawn up by the clerk of deliveries and then estimated by the clerk of the Ordnance before being submitted to the Treasury. The officers were then to negotiate with the most reliable artificers or merchants before a contract was made. Once the stores were supplied they were to be proved by the principal officers, one of whom was to be the surveyor, and received by the board, after due entry had been made by the surveyor, clerk and storekeeper. The principal officers were also involved in signing debentures for payment. These were to be passed within one month of the final delivery of stores. The principal officers were collectively liable for the issue and care of stores, as well as for their contracting and payment. Every month they were to present all proportions that had been signed by them and delivered to the storekeeper for the issuing of any stores, so that an examination could be made as to whether the original warrant had been executed. The board was further collectively responsible for the repair and sale of stores, for making allowances for wasted stores, and for the taking of remains and the security of the powder room. Building work was also to be agreed by all the principal officers. The officers were finally enjoined to see that their subordinates performed their duty by 'encouraging the faithful and punishing the negligent and unfaithful', and to do their own duties 'by the allowance, direction and signification of the masters of the Ordnance in all matters of weight, and in all courses by common advice and consent of most voices, and especially by following the literal prescripts of their warrants'.[1]

The 1683 instructions for the Ordnance board are a magnificent piece of late seventeenth century draftsmanship. They underline, how-

[1] The above account of the board's duties has been taken from the 1683 instructions. King's 70, fos. 9-16, 18-23, 49.

ever, the extent to which the individual initiative of each board member was restricted: the opportunities for anyone to have acted on his own without first consulting a colleague were limited. The board's corporate duties might have been devised to encourage vigilence among each serving member and thereby limit the opportunities for corruption, but they were not necessarily an aid to efficient administration. If an official's individual initiative was restricted, no one officer could be personally held responsible for inefficient work. An extensive system of checks and balances, however, might also have exacerbated differences among each board member. Pepys's comments on the efficacy of this system of management in the Navy Board in the 1660s might well have applied to the Ordnance board of the same period.[1]

The 1683 instructions were not confined to the master-general and Ordnance board. The duties of the Ordnance clerks, who acted under the supervision of the principal officers, were also outlined. The chief clerk to the master-general was his personal servant in matters of Ordnance business. He and his clerks were responsible for drawing up, signing and transmitting the master-general's warrants, and making out all commissions for the admission of under ministers. The chief clerk was also required at board meetings, although his presence was not recorded in the minute books, so that he could inform the master-general of all the board's transactions and make entries of all Office orders. These orders were then delivered to the clerk of the Ordnance. The other Ordnance clerks were similarly to attend and act under the direction of their respective officers.[2]

These clerks were likely to be engaged in most aspects of Ordnance business. They attended the delivery of stores to the fleet and took a ship's remains before supply was made. Once the ship was munitioned, the clerks took charge of the storeships which followed the fleet, and attended on them until the action was over, returning with the fleet to take the store remains.[3] The clerks also waited on artillery trains, ensuring that the trains were properly equipped and assisting in paying the ministers and attendants.[4] Clerks were further concerned with the delivery of saltpetre to the gunpowder makers, the proof and marking of ordnance, the recovery of arms from disbanded regiments, and the

1   See conclusion, p. 213.

2   King's 70, fos. 25, 27.

3   E.g. PRO 30 37/9, fos. 48, 54, payments to Townsend and Bennett, 11 May, 17 June 1665; WO 50/1, pp. 160, 166, payments to Whiteing and Barton for taking remains; WO 48/6, pp. 223, 225, payments to Cheltenham and Bennett; WO 48/32, list 1 May 1694, payment to Thomas Smith.

4   E.g. WO 48/7, p. 169, payment to Townsend; WO 48/25, p.303, payment to Whittaker, 22 Mar. 1687; WO 48/31, list 30 June 1693, 32nd payment to White.

surveying of fortifications and taking of garrison remains.[1] Ordnance business might, therefore, result in the clerks travelling as far afield as Flanders or the remoter regions of England.[2] A proportion of their work, however, was conducted within the Ordnance Office in the Tower. The clerks belonging to the clerk of the Ordnance were more concerned with routine book-keeping than the other clerks. They were involved with writing up states of garrison stores, making up minutes of board meetings, although they were not allowed to be present at any private debate at the board until they were called in by the officers, and in listing estimates, abstracting charges and accounting for naval gunnage.[3] By the end of the period there was some distinction between the duties of the clerks, one of whom was termed a 'receiving clerk', another a 'ledger keeper' and another, a 'minuting clerk'.[4] Extraordinary clerks undertook the more menial copying tasks.[5] Treasurer's clerks had more specialised functions. The treasurer was obliged to keep annually three ledger books of all receipts and payments, and his three clerks were each ordered to engross one of the books, 'in such order and method', as directed by the chief clerk. They were also to assist him in entering privy seals, warrants and orders, and in copying accounts and filling up receipts. A considerable amount of time was spent by the first two clerks 'soliciting for, receiving in and paying out of moneys'.[6] Other Ordnance clerks were concerned with different aspects of Office routine. Conyers, as clerk to Storekeeper Marsh, was paid for sweeping the stores and the chimneys of the officers' houses for the prevention of fire, for marking the powder in the stores and for keeping filled three water engines, and other clerks were required to receive messages from the Council at Whitehall and deliver them to the Office.[7]

1 E.g. WO 48/17, p. 50, payment to Hubbald, 14 June 1679; WO 48/9, p. 346, payments to Rothwell; WO 51/1, p.184, payments to Whittaker and Barton; WO 48/9, p. 344, payment to Jonas Moore, junior.

2 E.g. WO 50/1, p. 109, payment to Povey, 12 Aug. 1678; WO 50/1, p. 184, payment to Barton.

3 E.g. WO 48/12, p.51, 1 Aug. 1673, payment to Townsend; WO 48/49, list 14 Apr. 1711, 5th payment to Lister; WO 55/389 fo. 145, order 2 Sept. 1667; WO 55/336, fo. 1; WO 48/41, 69th payment to David Mercator, 30 June 1703.

4 Blenheim B I. 23, Eustace's list c.1709. The 'minuting clerk', the second clerk to the clerk of the Ordnance, was in existence as early as 1665. By the 1720s it had become recognised as the office of secretary to the board, although its existence was not acknowledged in the public directories until 1784. See the order of 13 Feb. 1665, above, p. 49, n. 1, and *Cal. SP Col. Am. & W. Indies 1720-1*, p.5, Popple to Bell Jones, 4 Mar. 1720. I am grateful to Mr John Sainty for this information.

5 E.g. WO 51/7, fo. 3, payments to Candland for work done by Cheltenham.

6 WO 55/468, Bertie's order, 30 June 1692; D.1778/V 71.

7 WO 48/9, p.511; WO 55/389, fo. 23, 12 June 1667.

The Ordnance clerks, therefore, to a certain extent reflected the activities of the principal officers: the clerks of the clerk of the Ordnance and the treasurer were more likely to be involved in book-keeping than those of other officers. There was not necessarily a strict dividing line between the duties of the clerks of each office, however, and all clerks could be engaged in such duties as taking store remains or making up accounts.[1]

A storekeeper's duties were clearly defined in the instructions. The deputy-keeper of the Armoury, and the keeper of small guns were to take good care of their respective arms, to receive no stores before they had been proved, marked and recorded, and to issue none without sufficient authority. Journals were to be kept of all receipts, returns and issues of stores, a yearly account being given to the board. The instructions for the storekeepers of the outports and magazines were more onerous. They were enjoined not to issue stores without a proper proportion signed by at least three principal officers, to give a report to the master-general of the condition of the stores and storehouses, and to inform the master-general before they laid out money, their expenses being registered in a monthly account. Monthly abstracts were also to be made out of the daily receipts, returns and issues, and those were to be sent to the Office every three months. The details of the receipts, returns and issues were to be set down in four separate journals, which were to be sent to the board at the end of every quarter and compared with the monthly abstracts.[2] The storekeeper's activities might also involve making arrangements for housing stores, taking remains, helping to prove ordnance, and ensuring that provisions were delivered for both garrisons, ships and artillery trains. The storekeepers might even be required to attend and make payments at the building of fortifications at their ports or garrisons.[3]

The clerks and storekeepers were by no means the only under ministers of the Ordnance Office. Messengers, miscellaneous store officers, clerks of the check, labourers, fireworkers, gunners and engineers also came under the Office's jurisdiction.

The messenger was to attend the board on office days, to summon those persons whom the board required to be present at meetings, and

1 WO 48/7, p.53, payment to Ball; WO 48/22, 15 Dec. 1683, payments to clerks for taking an Armoury account in Oct. 1682.

2 King's 70, fos. 28-30.

3 WO 48/6, pp. 357-8, payment to Robson at Chatham; WO 48/18, p. 212, payment to attorney of Perkins; WO 48/25, p. 406, payment to Peach; WO 50/1, pp. 158-9, payment to Cheltenham; WO 55/389, fos. 12-13, instructions for Povey at Portsmouth; WO 48/21, 18 July 1681, payment to Newby.

to take into custody anyone who had committed a misdemeanour until they were discharged by the board. He was responsible for carrying and delivering the board's letters, directing the artificers to make contracts with the principal officers and ensuring that the provisions were promptly brought into store. He was also to inform the board of the current market prices for stores so that it might make contracts at the most reasonable prices.[1] The messenger was further responsible for making payments to Ordnance officers which could amount to considerable sums.[2]

There were numerous minor officials who had responsibility for stores. The purveyor was to observe the orders he received from the board in the provisioning of ships, and to bring the owners of vessels to the board to contract at the most reasonable rates for the transportation of stores. He was to ensure that there was no delay in the shipping of stores. Once stores had been shipped he was not to disembark until the ship had sailed passsed Gravesend. The waggonmaster took charge of waggons for the use of the Office and the artillery trains, ensuring that they were kept in good repair and reporting any defects to the board. Proofmasters were to be skilled in the manufacture of ordnance so that they could make proof of all ordnance and mark the ordnance once it had been tested. One or more of them were to sign a report on the proofs, which was to be registered in the Office. Gentlemen of the Ordnance undertook the management of the artillery guns and carriages in the Tower, at Whitehall, and in the outports, to prevent embezzlement and to ensure that the various artillery trains were 'in constant readiness'. Furbishers and armourers were likewise responsible for keeping small arms and armour in good order, and from 1685 a yeoman was accountable to the Office for looking after the tents and toils.[3]

The clerks of the check looked after the Office labourers. They were to keep a check-roll, which was to be called four times a day, and to see that all labourers came to work early, setting down the time of their arrival and how long they continued at work. With the assistance of one of the surveyor's clerks a daily account was to be kept of all materials used and a weekly return was to be made to the Office, detailing all people employed, their rate of work and the amount of stores used. A similar function was undertaken by the garrison clerks

1 King's 70, fos. 40-1.

2 WO 48/26, 30 June 1688, payments to Anne Ball; WO 48/49, list 21 Nov. 1710, 1st-75th payments for Snapes and Harrison; WO 44/714, Snapes's petition to Dartmouth.

3 King's 70, fos. 36-7, 39-40. *See Cal. SP Dom. 1686-7,* no. 915, p. 244, warrant to Dartmouth, 21 Aug. for the appointment of gentlemen of the Ordnance, and below, pp. 105-6, for the amalgamation with the Office of Tents and Toils.

of the works, who were required 'to write all orders, letters, contracts, and to keep books of entries of the same . . . as also to make out bills of the day labourers'.[1]

There were also numerous master labourers or artificers connected with the Ordnance, who were to supply all manner of stores to the Office. These men were to perform their work substantially and at reasonable prices, and within ten days of the delivery of stores to deliver their bills in to the storekeeper so that debentures might be passed. The master artificers would also be required to provide men to act as skilled labourers on the marching trains of artillery.[2]

Finally, there were the technical and military Ordnance officers — the fireworkers, gunners and the engineers. The comptroller of fire-workers was to inspect and order all the other fireworkers and to give account of their performances to the master-general. The firemaster was to exercise those under his command with great and small mortar pieces, to keep them continually at work in the laboratory, and to train the fireworkers so that they might demonstrate their proficiency before the board. He was also to ensure that his department was well prepared for any expedition, and was to be able to estimate all the materials necessary 'upon any expedition or upon any occasion for fireworks, either of war of pleasure'.[3] The master gunner was to train the gunners in the shooting of great ordnance — once a month in the winter and twice a month every summer — and to inform the board of any qualified and capable gunner that he had instructed. He was to keep a register of all gunners, which was to be kept by the clerk of the Ordnance so that quarterly musters could be made, and another ledger of all great guns belonging to any ship, garrison or magazine, detailing their weight, lengths and dimensions.[4] The engineers were similarly organised under a chief engineer, who was to examine the qualifications and abilities of all prospective engineers. The engineers themselves, however, were likely to be far more expert in the practice of their trade, for they were required to be 'well skilled in all the parts of the mathematics . . . in all manner of foundations, in the scantlings of all timber and stone and

---

1 King's 70, fo. 38. I have only come across one muster book of the clerk of the check. This was compiled by William Wright and shows weekly musters from 7 Sept. 1712. (WO 54/680). For garrison clerks of the works, see WO 44/714, Duxbury's petition to Schomberg.

2 King's 70, fo. 42; WO 51/33, fo. 96, payment 30 Nov. 1686 to Bateman *et. al.*

3 For the duties of the comptroller see *Cal. SP Dom. 1687-8*, p.249; for the duties of the firemaster and fireworkers see King's 70, fos. 35-6. For a list of rules to be observed by the fireworkers at Greenwich see D.1778/V 71.

4 King's 70, fo. 34.

of their several natures, and to be perfect in architecture civil and military'. They were to keep drafts of all the king's forts, and to be able to draw plans and estimate the charge of all proposed fortifications. The engineers were to represent to the board the necessary materials to be used, to instruct the clerk of the check and the master workmen in their respective jobs, to supervise the building and design of fortifications, and to conduct sieging operations. They were to visit all existing fortifications as often as directed, and to report on their condition to the master-general, which report was to be presented to the king.[1]

The 1683 instructions and the other internal records give an extremely informative account of the functions of all Ordnance officials. This account, however, is necessarily unbalanced. The instructions paint an idealised picture of how Ordnance officers should perform their respective responsibilities, but they do nothing to illustrate the extent to which these rules were obeyed. How capable were the Ordnance officials of the period and how effectively did they fulfil their instructions? It is only when these questions have been answered that a meaningful assessment may be made of the responsibilities of office and the responsiveness of Ordnance office-holders towards those duties.

The department throughout the period was served by many conscientious officers. At the highest level some of the master-generals of the period were considered as able and hard-working men. Pepys, for example, thought Compton 'one of the worthiest men and best officers of state . . . in England' and Duncomb 'a very proper man for business, being very resolute, proud and industrious'. Dartmouth was even more widely respected by Pepys as a man of judgement and industry, and he declared that he had never seen 'greater prudence, justice and diligence . . . in any management' than was shown by Dartmouth in organising the destruction of the Tangier defences in 1683.[2] Pepys was not necessarily the most impartial observer, but some of these judgements were endorsed by others.[3] They also may be corroborated by an examination of internal Ordnance records. Attendance lists registered in departmental minutes, where they are available, indicate that the master-

---

1 *Ibid.* fos. 31-3.

2 *Pepys Diary* III, 286, 19 Oct. 1663; VI, 226-7, 329; *Life, Journals and Correspondence of Samuel Pepys,* ed. J. Smith, (1841), I, 395, Pepys to Houblon, 3/14 Oct. 1683.

3 E.g. Oliver Cromwell's opinion of Comptom, Burnet's of Duncomb, and those of Savile and Judge Jeffries on Dartmouth. See *Pepys Diary* III, 286, n. 1; *Bulstrode Papers,* p. 28 n.; *HMC* 20, 11 Rep. V, *Dartmouth I,* p. 93, Musgrave to Dartmouth, 24 Sept. 1683.

generals of the time, with the exception of Marlborough who was campaigning abroad for most of his period in office, attended not less than one in three and frequently more than one in three board meetings. The figures are especially impressive during part of Sir Thomas Chicheley's sole tenure of office (1670-9) as they indicate that he missed only thirty-six meetings out of the 285 from July 1673 to November 1678.[1] Dartmouth's attendances at the board were significantly less frequent than Sir Thomas Chicheley's, but it cannot be doubted he was an ardent administrator. Scattered references in the Office journals and accounts, and the vast stock of Ordnance material surviving in his personal papers, bear witness to Dartmouth's preoccupation with Ordnance affairs during the 1680s.[2] As might be expected, moreover, most of the master-generals had had extensive experience as serving officers in either the Army or the Navy prior to their Ordnance appointment.

Many of the principal officers were also well-suited to their posts — both by temperament and experience. Among the lieutenant-generals, William Legge, the father of Lord Dartmouth, had distinguished himself in the Royalist cause during the civil war and was considered a man of high integrity, who 'was a very punctual and steady observer of the orders received'. Two other lieutenant-generals were well able to direct Ordnance business — both within the House of Commons and the department. Sir Christopher Musgrave was a man of wide experience in parliamentary committees and in Ordnance procedure (he having been a master-general commissioner, 1679-82), and Sir Henry Goodricke was also active as an administrator and committee member in Parliament and the Privy Council. Sir Thomas Erle was a man of different sorts. He was not an active parliamentarian, but he, like William Legge, was an energetic and capable military officer. According to one contemporary he was of 'very good sense' and 'a hearty man for his country'. Of the surveyor-generals, Sir Jonas Moore, Sir Bernard de Gomme and Sir Henry Sheer were ingenious engineers — a necessary prerequisite for the job. William Bridges was a more obscure figure, but he too apparently was 'well-skilled' in building and architecture. The interests and background of some clerks of the Ordnance again made them particularly suited to their positions. Sir Edward Sherburne was a minor poet and classical scholar. More significant administratively was the fact that prior to his entry into office he had been brought up in the methods of his department by his father, who had been clerk of the Ordnance before the civil war. John Swaddell, who succeeded

---

1 For a discussion of these figures see my thesis, pp. 113-15, 118. They may be compared with the Privy Council attendance lists. *Ibid.* pp. 109-10.

2 *Ibid.* p. 119.

Sherburne as clerk of the Ordnance in 1689, was 'well versed in all . . . forms of ordinary domestic dispatches and in the books of entries and their indexes' from his experience in the secretaries Office under Lord Arlington. Sir Thomas Littleton, too, was well acquainted with administration, having been a commissioner of prizes before his entry into the clerkship of the Ordnance in 1690. His parliamentary expertise again was no doubt of great help to the Office during the supply debates. Of the treasurers, Sir George Wharton – a noted classicist, astrologer and mathematician – succeeded to the post in 1670, having served his apprenticeship as a clerk to the lieutenant-general in the 1660s, when the offices of lietuenant and treasurer were combined; and Charles Bertie had vast experience in money matters as secretary to Treasurer Danby in the 1670s prior to his admission as Ordnance treasurer in 1681. Many of the storekeepers of the period had practical experience of Ordnance business before their appointments. Richard Marsh had organised the Royalist supply services in Bristol during the first civil war. His son, George, was made his assistant in 1667, and succeeded as principal storekeeper when his father died. Conyers was elevated from the position of first clerk. Bridges, Gardiner and James Lowther were promoted storekeeper from the clerkship of the deliveries. Meesters, who was made storekeeper in 1691 after Gardiner's death, does not appear to have officially served the Office in another capacity, but Goodricke had recommended him for the post because he preferred 'some person of known fidelity and experience in affairs of the Ordnance' and had found him 'most diligent in that service and helpful to the board'.[1]

The figures for attendance at board meetings also reveal something about the industry of certain principal officers. Of those officers for which a reasonable record of meetings exist, only Meesters, Trumbull and George Wharton (as treasurer) were absent for significantly less than half of the meetings they could possibly have attended. A number of officers – Sir Christopher Musgrave, both Moores, William Bridges as surveyor, Richard Marsh and James Lowther as storekeeper – attended on average about three out of every four meetings. Charlton, Sherburne, Christopher Musgrave junior as clerk of the Ordnance, and Thomas Gardiner senior as storekeeper, attended even more frequently than this. The records of Sherburne and Musgrave as clerks of the Ordnance are especially remarkable, for during the period for which minute books are extant, they were never absent from the board for

1 The careers of many of the above officers may be found in *DNB* and in the draft biographies held by the History of Parliament trust (for those officers who were also MPs). For more detailed references, see my thesis, pp. 132-45. Also see below, pp. 84-5, for Moore, de Gomme, Sheer, Wharton, *et. al.*

any extended period.[1] For one or two officers information from official Ordnance minute books may be supplemented by material from private collections. It is evident from an examination of James Lowther's letters to his father, for example, that he was a thoroughly conscientious and well-organised Ordnance officer.[2]

The capabilities of the under ministers are much more difficult to assess because of the relative obscurity of many of the officials, and the consequent lack of material on which to base any qualitative judgement. One or two figures, however, do emerge from the gloom. Of the clerks, Edward Hubbald seems to have been particularly conscientious. Charles Bertie, the treasurer had a high opinion of him, and was constantly referring to his thoroughness and regard for his duty. Similarly James Lowther thought that his chief clerk, Nicholas Whittaker, was 'a most extraordinary careful and knowing man in his business'.[3] There is more evidence about some of the military officers. Sir Bernard de Gomme has already been mentioned but he was not the only engineer of ability of the period. De Rüis, the chief firemaster, was, in Prince Rupert's view at least, 'the ablest man in his profession' that he had ever seen and 'very extraordinary in all mechanics'. Sir Martin Beckman, Jacob Richards, Thomas Phillips and others were also prominent in both designing artillery weapons and planning notable fortifications. Richard Leake, too, it seems had 'a particular genius' for gunnery and engineering. The one surviving labourers' muster list, of 31 December 1712, indicates that the majority of labourers of that period were 'able and willing'. A similar list of December 1682 marks the majority of feed gunners as 'able'.[4]

For the clerks, the labourers and the military officers there are no pieces of statistical evidence, like the attendance figures for the master-general and principal officers, to ascertain their activities. Nevertheless, it does seem from an examination of miscellaneous sources that many of these officers were prepared to work long hours in difficult conditions. A number of clerks, together with Edward Sherburne and Jonas Moore senior, remained hard at work at their posts in plague-infested London during the summer of 1665. The clerks at the time of

---

1 See my thesis, p. 146.

2 In Dec. 1702 Lowther was especially proud that the books and business of his office of storekeeper had been 'regularly and duly kept up' since he entered office. This he claimed had not been so in his predecessor's time. See Cumbria RO, Carlisle, Lonsdale MS., James to Sir John Lowther, 8 Dec. 1702.

3 *Ibid.* James Lowther to Sir John Lowther, 10 Mar. 1702; WO 55/1796, Bertie to Edward Hubbald, 31 Mar. 1685, 3 May 1687, 2 Sept. 1690, 28 Aug. 1692.

4 For details of the above see my thesis, pp. 175, 177-9, 185.

the 1685 rebellions in Scotland and the West petitioned that they 'were both day and night employed in dispatching those extraordinary services which then obliged them to their utmost care and pains'. John Hooper, a clerk under Sherburne, was involved for several years in making up the receipts and returns of stores, which frequently meant his staying 'till the locking up as well as opening the Tower gates'. Other clerks were required to dine together at the time of the making up of their accounts so that no time might be lost. Thomas Townsend, another clerk to the clerk of the Ordnance, also listed several services which he had undertaken, forcing him 'to write many extraordinary hours in the night time, by which means — through the extraordinary colds by him taken — [he] hath [had] many fits of sickness, to his very great charge and expense'. A minute of 1720 provides further evidence that Ordnance clerks were expected to work long office hours — 8 a.m. to 1 p.m. and 3 p.m. to 8 p.m. — which could be extended if necessary.[1] Other Ordnance posts were as demanding. The post of storekeeper of the outports — especially at a place like Chatham — could be all consuming at a busy period of the year when ships needed re-fitting.[2] The life of an Ordnance labourer or an artificer was sometimes extremely arduous. Their normal working day started at 6 a.m. and ended at 6 p.m., with a strict time allowance for breakfast and lunch, but these limits were extended in the summer-time or when an expedition was being prepared.[3] Sometimes labourers were required to work all night, as at Chatham in 1681, when three men each had a three months stint of guarding the stores in order to prevent their embezzlement.[4] Engineers might also be involved in tiring and time-consuming work. Beckman at Hull, for instance, asked the board for money for boat-hire because he was unable to travel four miles every day to work 'in the clay up to the ankles, and stand all the day in wet . . . '; and a few months later he apologised because he could not supervise the works as well as draw up drafts and estimates of fortifications.[5]

The evidence advanced so far indicates that there were many able Ordnance officials in the late seventeenth and early eighteenth centuries, who were prepared to work long hours, sometimes in difficult condi-

1 WO 55/332, pp. 23, 28, warrants 12 Oct., 1 July 1665; WO 44/714, petitions to Dartmouth, 1685(?), 23 Feb. 1685; WO 48/7, p. 53, payment to Ball; WO 55/336, fo. 1; WO 47/33, p. 167, 19 Mar. 1720.

2 See e.g. WO 49/112, letter from Batchler, 22 July, 10 Aug. 1665.

3 WO 47/31, p. 324, order for clerk of check, 31 Oct. 1718; WO 55/389, fo. 114, instructions for Fisk; WO 47/32, p. 156, 13 Apr. 1719, p. 292, 21 July 1719; WO 44/714, petition of labourers to Dartmouth, 11 Feb. 1686.

4 WO 49/180, Cheltenham to O.b., 6, 15, Oct. 1681.

5 WO 46/1, p. 314, Beckman to O.b., 9 Nov. 1681, 29 Sept. 1682.

tions, to serve the department. This does not mean, of course, either that all the officers of the period were suited to government service or that government service was a full-time occupation in early modern Britain.

The characters of a number of Ordnance officers were unsuited to departmental work. Among the master-generals, Berkeley had little capacity for high office. Clarendon noted that Berkeley as a navy commissioner 'understood nothing that related either to the office or employment and therefore very seldom was present in the execution', while Pepys commented that Berkeley was 'brought into the Navy for want of other ways of gratification'.[1] Romney, too, was incapable of executing high office competently — at least according to Burnet who remarked that 'he was so set on pleasure that he was not able to follow business with a due application'.[2] Among the principal officers, Sir Henry Tichburne, it seems, was not a man of great resolution.[3] Few contemporaries had a high opinion of the younger Sir Jonas Moore. Aubrey compared him unfavourably with his father; Anthony Wood observed that he was 'a foolish fellow'; and Flamstead, his father's friend, remarked that no-one he knew either loved or feared him.[4] Robert Lowther was adicted to intrigue and was unable to work with his fellow board members, and he proved just as unpopular in his succeeding post as governor of Barbados as he had been at the Ordnance board. Edward Conyers seemed to be in office for what he could get out of it rather than from any notion of public service.[5]

The capacities of some under-ministers were also suspect. Among the clerks, James Godfrey absconded and 'deserted the service', George Billinghurst, Thomas Rogers and Henry Coles neglected their duties and were replaced, and Alexander Eustace apparently failed either to issue stores by proportion or to keep the clerk of deliveries journals in

1 *Own Life* II, 459; *Naval Minutes*, p. 257.

2 Burnet IV, 8.

3 See e.g. *HMC* 20, 11 Rep. V, *Dartmouth I*, p. 36, James II's observation to Dartmouth, 22 July 1679.

4 John Aubrey, *Lives of Eminent Men*, printed in *Letters Written by Eminent Persons in the Seventeenth and Eighteenth Centuries*, 2 vols. (1813), II part ii, 462; *The Life and Times of Anthony Wood . . . by Himself*, 5 vols. (Oxford, 1891-1900), III. 24, 12 July 1682; NMM, Old Royal Observatory, Flamstead/Townley letters, (transcripts of those at Royal Society). P.82. For further contemporary comments see D. 1778/V 24, Duxbury's indictment, May 1679; WO 44/714. Potenger's petition. In 1680 Moore was suspended from office. WO 47/9, fo. 89, 28 Sept. 1680; WO 49/111, minute 12 Oct. 1680.

5 See below, p. 81, and Hist. of Parl. draft biographies for Lowther, and the author's Place and Profit: An Examination of the Ordnance Office, 1660-1714', *TRHS* 5th ser. 25 (1975), 71-2, for Conyers.

due order.[1] This last charge was made by the storekeeper and may well have been unfounded, Lowther's desire to appoint his own clerk was motive enough for his fabricating the evidence against Eustace, and Eustace himself vigorously denied the accusation of incompetency levelled against him, but there is no denying the condemnatory nature of the minute of March 1720 which stated that the Office's business was much in arrears because of the neglect of the extraordinary clerks. In the future all clerks were to keep regular office hours, and they were prohibited from leaving town without the board's permission and from staying away from the department without first acquainting their chief clerks.[2] Other Ordnance officials were also inefficient or incapable. Compaints of the storekeepers being absent from their duty were made against Watkinson and Idell at Hull. Browne at Chatham, Newby at Harwich, Marbury at Landguard Fort and Jackson at Berwick failed to observe the rules for the fitting out of ships, or issued stores or took up bills without the board's permission. Some storekeepers were clearly unfit for their posts. Batchler observed that the governor of Upnor Castle, who was to have charge of the stores there, was 'an unfit person and behindhand'; reports circulated that the Harwich storekeeper drank and gamed; and a storekeeper at Carlisle suffered from blindness.[3] Labourers and artificers, too, could be negligent. Edward Blagrave was dismissed because of his practice of 'undertaking other private employment abroad to the dis-service of his majesty'; Barrett, a furbisher, had his salary stopped by the board because he had failed to take care of the arms in the Hull stores; and Powell, a labourer at Portsmouth, was displaced 'for being frequently drunk on his watch at the gunwharf at Portsmouth, abusing most people as they pass and re-pass, and in a particular manner for ill treating Captain Pattison'.[4] Occasionally a large number of labourers and artificers might forcibly absent themselves from work.[5] Engineer officers, like the civilian officials, could be incompetent, irascible and disobedient.[6] Gunners

1 WO 48/9, p. 282, payment to Townesend; WO 55/487, p. 10, warrant 3 Apr. 1702; Blenheim B I 23, Eustace's note, and petition by Lowther.

2 WO 47/33, p. 167, 19 Mar. 1720.

3 WO 46/1, p. 250, 7 Sept. 1680; WO 47/25, p. 290, 22 Jan. 1708; WO 47/6, fos. 54, 55, 120; WO 47/8, 20 Feb., 7 July 1666; WO 47/19b, 10 Feb. 1674; WO 47/25, p. 512; WO 49/112, Batchler to Wharton, 25 July 1665; WO 47/8 O.b. to Newby, 3 Mar. 1666; WO 47/28, p. 119, 6 May 1715.

4 WO 47/7, fo. 112, warrant 23 June 1665; WO 47/25, pp. 412, 428, 1, 10 Apr. 1708; WO 47/32, p. 374, 10 Nov. 1719.

5 E.g. see following minutes: WO 47/5, p. 161, 18 Dec. 1663; WO 47/30, p. 80, 26 Mar. 1717.

6 See e.g. the comments of Pepys, Duxbury and Phillips about de Gomme (Naval Minutes, p. 205; D. 1778/I i 591. 1077, letters of 17 Oct. 1680, 1684) Pepys's observation about Sir Charles and Godfrey Lloyd (Naval Minutes, p. 28)

also were sometimes remiss in their duties. Days were appointed for the feed gunners to attend the master gunner for practice, but there is evidence that many gunners neglected their duty, especially in the years before the reform of the establishment in 1682. As we have already seen, in this period the office was generally held by men who had other occupations. Many gunners, moreover, resided miles away from the Tower — the 1664 muster shows that three men lived as far distant as Plymouth, Northampton and Reading — before the order of 1682 that they should lodge constantly in the Tower and exercise as a company under the master gunner.[1]

Pluralism indeed did not die out within the department in this period. It could take the form of a single man holding more than one Ordnance post. The offices of master-general's secretary, keeper of rich weapons, gentleman of the Ordnance and feed gunner, for example, were often held in conjunction with another Ordnance post. More commonly, however, Ordnance officers would hold a position outside the department. This applied to the master-generals, principal officers and the under ministers of the period. Marlborough, for example, played little part in internal Ordnance administration because of his responsibilities as commander in chief. Other officers could not attend to their departmental duties because of their military commitments elsewhere. Meesters was an active serving officer who took charge of the bomb vessels in the attempt on St. Malo in 1694. His duties as comptroller of the Flanders artillery train also meant that he was 'not always upon the place', which the board minuted was a 'great prejudice and detriment' to his majesty's service. Erle was also an active military officer, and he rose to high rank in the Army. In July 1706, whilst Ordnance lietuenant-general, he was appointed to accompany the Earl of Rivers on an expedition to Spain. He did not return until March 1708 and in the summer and autumn of that year he commanded a further expedition to France and Ostend. The departmental responsibilities of John Hill, Erle's successor as lieutenant-general, must also have been limited because of his appointment to command the forces sent to hold Dunkirk as a security for the enactment of the Treaty of Utrecht. Another principal officer, Richard King, was established as an engineer and a colonel of foot in the Army. At a lower level storekeepers also held Army commissions. The office of storekeeper could further be combined with that of master gunner or governor of a garrison. It was not unknown, indeed, for principal

and the refusal of Romer, Blood and Phillips to serve abroad (WO 46/4, p. 15, O.b. to Romney, 9 Feb. 1697; WO 46/5, p. 87, Same to Same, 16 Apr. 1702; WO 46/6, p. 9, O.b. to Marlborough, 30 Mar. 1704).

1 For this see my thesis, pp. 182-4.

officers to be garrison governors – George Legge, Christopher Musgrave and Thomas Erle all held the office of lieutenant-general in conjunction with a garrison governorship, and Colonel James Pendlebury was a deputy governor of the Tower and master gunner. Most officers had civil responsibilities as well. Philip and Christopher Musgrave (the younger) were clerks of the Council as well as members of the Ordnance board. More than half master-generals and principal officers of the period also had parliamentary commitments – twenty-six of them were members of the House of Commons and six of the House of Lords. Their membership of Parliament, however, did not necessarily signify that they were neglecting Ordnance business. For one of their chief functions in the House of Commons debates on supply and other matters would have been to have acted as spokesmen for the board – as John Duncomb did in 1667, during the debates on the Dutch Medway raid. For many principal officers, moreover, these military and civil duties were quite apart from their local responsibilities as lord lieutenant of the county, alderman or justice of the peace.[1]

The prevalence of pluralism necessitated the appointment of deputies to execute the place of principal Ordnance officer during the period of absence. Only a few days after Sir William Trumbull had been upbraided by the board to attend every Office day 'for the better dispatch of his majesty's service at this juncture' he was seeking permission from the king for his post of clerk of the deliveries to be managed by a deputy while he was away on ambassadorial service.[2] This instance of an office being taken over by a deputy was by no means an isolated occurrence. Sir Thomas Chicheley appointed Sir James Cuffe to be his deputy to execute the mastership of the Ordnance in Ireland; successive surveyor-generals received compensation for acting as deputies to their lieutenant-generals; a Captain Charles Middleton was 'nominated and depicted' by Swaddell to his 'full right and power' of office as clerk of the Ordnance; and Meesters appointed his own clerk to be his deputy.[3] Sherburne, after he had been dismissed from office in 1688,

---

1 For the above see in general *DNB* and Hist. of Parl. draft biographies. Also *Cal. SP Dom. 1694-5*, p. 254, Trenchard to Berkeley, 6 Aug. 1694 and WO 47/18, p. 53, 7 Dec. 1695 for Meesters; and B. Withall, *A Detection of the Exhorbitant Oppressions, Public Frauds and Mismanagements . . . in his Majesty's Victualling and Ordnance Officers* (1717) (Univ. of London, Goldsmith's Library), pp. 67 ff., for King and Pendlebury. This latter source, however, is suspect, for Withall was giving vent to his feelings because of his own lack of preferment in the Ordnance service.

2 WO 47/15, p. 78, 6 July 1685; Add. MS. 52279, Trumbull's diary, 27 Aug., 17, 30 Oct. 1685.

3 *Cal. SP Dom. 1676-7*, p. 274, 11 Aug. 1676; *Ibid. 1687-8*, p. 76, 26 Sept. 1687; WO 48/29, 13 Aug. 1690, payment to Charlton; T. 1/117, fo. 72, Bridges's memorial; WO 55/395, Schomberg's warrant, n.d.; WO 55/402, p. 25, May 1691.

even argued that it was the 'indubitable right of his patent' to appoint a deputy to execute the office in his stead.[1] The practice had become so prevalent by 1690 that a warrant was issued by the king urging the principal Ordnance officers to 'personally and constantly attend the execution of their several offices and places . . . and not by deputies'. The use of deputies had not died out by the following war, however, and James Craggs could report to Erle in 1705 that the new treasurer, Harry Mordaunt, had made a Mr. Lansdell his deputy and he was to 'have the disposing of everything'.[2]

A position in the Ordnance Office in the late seventeenth and early eighteenth centuries, therefore, was not necessarily a full-time commitment. For the principal officers the burdens of office need not have been excessive. All the principal officers, except the lieutenant-general, had their own departments to run, yet their individual initiative was limited because of the extent of their collective responsibilities. The board in fact could only do business when a quorum of principal officers actually met together, and this did not occur particularly frequently. A minute of 13 May 1669 stated that the board was to sit on Thursdays and Saturdays every week, and the 1683 instructions directed that the principal officers were to meet together at 8 a.m. in the Tower at least twice a week on Tuesdays and Thursdays. In the 1690s, however, the board was meeting on all three days.[3] Only in times of emergency, as in June 1685 or October 1688, did the board meet more frequently than this. There are other indications that the tempo of work in the Ordnance Office was by no means always intense. In October 1684, for instance, Edward Hubbald could report to his chief, Charles Bertie, that there was 'little action' within his department. A few years later Edward himself received similar reports from William Hubbald. On 10 November 1692 he was informed that there had been no business in the Office that day; and some months later William could again write: 'All things in the Office goes as you could wish, no list signed, nor anything of moment since you went'.[4] These reports of leisurely activity were mirrored in the board's letters to Romney in

1 *HMC* 20, 11 Rep. V, *Dartmouth I,* p. 252, Sherburne to Dartmouth, 18 Jan. 1689.

2 WO 55/338, fo. 22, warrant 20 Mar. 1690; Erle MS 3/13, Craggs to Erle, 7 July 1705. Also see WO 54/679, p. 46, Eversfield's declaration, 10 Feb. 1713, appointing Joseph Lee his deputy.

3 WO 47/19a, 13 May 1669; King's 70, fo. 20; WO 46/4, p. 18, Griffith to Phelps, 3 May 1697. A hundred years later it was still the general practice for the board to sit twice or three times a week. Glover, p. 37. In this period meetings generally took place before noon, and sittings were usually suspended for the Christmas 'holy days'.

4 WO 55/1796, Hubbald to Bertie, 4 Oct. 1684, William to Edward Hubbald, 10 Nov. 1692, 20 Apr. 1693.

August and September 1700 and July of the following year, when the master-general was informed that there was not much business in the department. Marlborough was the recipient of similar news from Erle in July 1706.[1] During these summer months the principal officers retired from London. Charles Bertie, for example, invariably stayed at his family seat at Uffington during the summer; on 8 June 1703 James Lowther took leave of the board to go into the country for six weeks, as did his colleagues Granville, Bridges and Musgrave in August of that year; in July 1705 James Craggs could afford to write to Erle that he would 'make an indifferent correspondent for some time' as he intended to be 'as much out of town as he could' because of the heat and want of company; and in October 1712 Bridges could inform Lord Cowper that he had spent the previous five months in the country in order to recover his health.[2] Other officers, too, were granted periodic leave when business was slack.[3]

The life of an Ordnance officer, however, was not always peaceful, for at certain times he was working under extreme pressure. For some months after the Restoration the activities of the principal officers in issuing arms 'to quell the present disorders' and in receiving stores from disbanded regiments was so great that Compton had to defer a survey that was to be made of the condition of the garrisons.[4] In August 1665 Storekeeper Richard Marsh informed his subordinate at Chatham that the officers were 'all very busy' in setting out a train of artillery, and in the following March Duncomb was urging Sherburne that 'no stop in any kind' was to be made in preparing stores for ships of war.[5] Various other letters from the board reveal the intense activity of Ordnance officials when they were preparing to meet the Revolutionary invasion. Tichburne wrote to Dartmouth on 3 October 1688 that the king had commanded him to attend daily to receive his commands, and that he himself intended to call the board to meet every

---

1   WO 46/5, pp. 19, 20, 21, 42, letters 17, 30 Aug., 17 Sept. 1700, 10 July 1701; Blenheim A I 45, 12 July 1706.

2   See WO 55/1796, *passim*, letters from Bertie to Hubbald; Cumbria RO, Lonsdale MS., James Lowther to Sir John Lowther, 8 June, 24 Aug. 1703; Erle 2/12, Craggs to Erle, 31 July 1705; Herts. CRO, D/EP F.53, fo. 76, Bridges to Cowper, 31 Oct. 1712.

3   E.g. see WO 47/23, p. 327, 22 May 1706; WO 47/29, p. 207, 23 Aug. 1716, for requests made by storekeepers for extensive periods of leave. Also *Cal. SP Dom. 1667-8*, p. 93, 20 Dec. 1667; WO 47/30, p. 195, 16 July 1717; WO 47/31, p. 17, 21 Jan. 1718, for leave granted to engineers.

4   WO 55/330, p. 253, Compton's signification of 27 May 1661 on warrant of 27 Oct. 1660. For an idea of their activities see PRO 30 37/6, *passim*, various warrants.

5   PRO 30 37/16, 31 Mar. 1666.

day. Later reports to Dartmouth confirm that the principal officers at this time were both attending the board and waiting on the king at Whitehall daily, and were 'hourly busy' in loading stores for the artillery train.[1]

After the Revolution newsletters for the winter and spring of 1691, 1695 and 1702, which reported that Ordnance officials were having to work 'day and night' to prepare stores for expeditions,[2] indicate that the story was the same in the later part of the period. Internal evidence also suggests that the spring of 1694 was a particularly busy time for the department. For in March of that year the board informed Romney that even if it had been in its province to do so, it would have been impossible for the Office to supply garrison provisions because it was so concerned with setting out the Flanders train, preparing sixteen bomb vessels, and supplying the fleet. Eight years later at the same time of year, a similar report was made to him that the officers were 'very much straitened in time' as so much was required from them[3] — thereby confirming the newsletter report for that year. We also have the corroborative account of an eye witness, James Lowther, for the spring of 1702. As early as 24 February he wrote to Sir John Lowther about how busy the department was in supplying the fleet and fitting up bomb vessels and the artillery train for Holland. On 26 March he informed Sir John that departmental business had prevented him from attending the House of Commons as frequently as he would have wished, and that he was 'not . . . able to get there four or five times a week till twelve [noon], one or two a'clock'. By 7 April he was complaining that members of the House had had three or four days holiday, but during that time the board had been required to sit every day at the Tower until three. His letter to his father two days later was written in a similar vein:

> I am at the Tower every day till 2 or 3 a'clock and sometimes till the evening. There must some of us be continually present to give directions and to see everything comply'd with, with all the dispatch that is possible. We shall be forced to work on Sundays till this business is over, so that I am like to be very little at Westminster the remainder of this session. I have been all this day at the Tower from 8 a'clock in the morning, being now in the midst of the greatest business that ever we had since I have been in the Office. We have so many employ'd that I hope we shall go a great way with it in a fortnight or three weeks time.[4]

1 D.1778/I i. 1323 a, 3, 4 Oct. 1688; WO 55/335, fos. 94-5, 13 Oct. 1668.
2 *Cal. SP Dom. 1690-1*, p. 313, 17 Mar. 1691; Luttrell III, 422, 5 Jan. 1695; *Ibid.* V, 164, 21 Apr. 1702.
3 WO 46/3, p. 25, 15 Mar. 1694; WO 46/5, p. 85, 8 Apr. 1702.
4 Cumbria RO, Lonsdale MS., James to Sir John Lowther, 24 Feb., 26 Mar., 7, 9 Apr. 1702.

If Lowther's estimate of completion was correct, it would seem that the department was working at a feverish pace for well over two months in the spring of 1702. This may not have happened to such a marked degree in the years between Lowther's entry into office in 1696 and 1702, but it could not have been such an exceptional occurrence in the years of the Spanish Succession War when quite apart from the vast Flanders trains and its augmentations, the department fitted out at least fifteen bomb vessels and sixteen other artillery trains in a period of a dozen years.[1]

An Ordnance officer, therefore, would find that at certain times he was working feverishly hard and that at other periods he had little Ordnance business to occupy his time. His activities depended partly on his position in the Office. If he was an official who executed his office by patent, he could appoint a deputy and therefore take little part in the routine of Office administration. If he was especially favoured, he might hold a sinecure, like the place of assistant surveyor or the storekeepership at Windsor Castle in the post-Revolutionary period.[2] For those actually involved in running the Office, however, the time of year was an important factor in determining the extent of Office activity. The spring and autumn in all probability would be the busiest periods, when expeditions were being fitted out and were returning. At other times, however, an officer would have to work hard if an emergency artillery train had to be prepared, a general remain taken, or an account made up. Generally his activities in wartime would be greater than those in peace,[3] although extraordinary staff would be employed in those periods and this lessened the burden on any one officer. So the Ordnance Office administrators were by no means full time civil servants and their activities depended as much on external factors as their own inclination to work.

Place: Appointment, Promotion and Dismissal

As we have seen the later Stuart Ordnance Office was particularly fortunate in having a number of able and conscientious principal officers to administer its affairs, but this circumstance was as much a matter of luck as a reflection on the merits of the method of appoint-

---

1 For details of some of these expeditions see Chandler, *Art of Warfare,* p. 169.

2 The assistant surveyorship was described by Schomberg as being 'unneedful' and 'more charge than use to the king'. See WO 55/337, fo. 60, 6 Dec. 1689. For the Windsor place see T.1/20, fo. 186, O.b. report, 12 Dec. 1692.

3 Six volumes of letters between the Ordnance board and the Admiralty cover for instance, the nine war years, 1703-12. There is only one volume for the following six years, 1712-18, which were largely peaceful. See Adm. 1/3999-4005.

ment to places within the department in the late seventeenth century. For ability and suitability for the particular job was probably no more important as a factor determining entry to principal office than either purchase or patrimony and certainly less important than patronage.

Purchase, patrimony and patronage had been three common ways of securing entry to office in the 1630s.[1] By the late seventeenth century however, at least as far as the Ordnance Office was concerned, the relative importance of each of these factors had altered. Purchase was not unknown as a method of entry into the department at this time, but in contrast to the Army, where purchase was a 'universal element' in the system of appointment and promotion throughout the period and beyond,[2] purchase within the Ordnance Office appears to have declined. Nearly all examples of venality that have been uncovered, and these examples relate to all ranks of Ordnance official, occurred in Charles II's reign, although the board made proclamations against trafficking in offices as late as 1719. This suggests that the practice continued among the lesser officers (especially it seems among some military officers in the artillery trains) even though officially it was held in disfavour.[3]

Patrimony, too, was still in evidence in the department in this period, but it was not such a decisive factor in the appointments to the principal Ordnance offices. Indeed, if it is interpreted strictly to mean filial heritage, of the principal officers appointed, 1660-1714, only John Chicheley, Jonas Moore junior, Edward Sherburne and George Marsh, who all succeeded to their positions through reversions that came into effect immediately after their father's death, could have claimed to have gained their office in this way. Two of these reversions, however, were granted prior to the Restoration. George Legge's name might be included but he was not granted a reversion during his father's life and he did not immediately succeed his father as lieutenant-general. Philip Musgrave too might be added to the list. Although he did not gain the office by reversion, his father's influence as lieutenant-general in obtaining the clerkship of the deliveries for him was probably paramount. If patrimony is thought of in the wider sense of family patronage, the appointment of Philip Musgrave's brother, Christopher, as clerk of deliveries immediately after Philip's death in 1689 might be

1   See Aylmer, *King's Servants,* pp. 69-96, 274-5.

2   See I.F. Burton and A.M. Newman, 'Sir John Cope: Promotion in the Eighteenth Century Army', *EHR* 78 (1963), 655-68.

3   See my 'Place and Profit' p. 67. Also Withall, *Exhorbitant Oppressions,* p.67, for a suggestion that one Bousfield sold or exchanged his major's post in the Flanders artillery train in 1710 for a commission in the guards.

termed patrimonial – as might that of Robert Lowther, a kinsman of James Lowther, who preceeded him as storekeeper. Nevertheless, even if it is accepted that all these officers were primarily obliged for their positions to the workings of patrimony, only about one in ten principal officers were appointed in this way in this period. After the Restoration, moreover, there is no instance of a principal office being in the same family continuously for more than two generations. Among the under-ministers, whose appointments were less subject to political controls, patrimony was probably a more pervasive influence, judging by the number of instances we have of members of the same family being employed in the service. Sir George Wharton's eldest son, Sir Poly-carpus, for example, was a powder contractor to the Office; another son, was an Ordnance engineer. William Hubbald, paymaster of an Irish artillery train, was possibly the son of the Ordnance treasury clerk, Edward Hubbald. Francis Felton, junior, succeeded as storekeeper at Portsmouth after his father's demise. Sir Godfrey Lloyd followed his younger brother Charles as chief engineer. The sons of engineer Captain James Archer were Ordnance engineers, and John Romer, son of engineer Wolfgang William Romer, also entered the Ordnance service. Among the artificers son followed father as master wheelwright, master bricklayer and furbisher of small guns.[1]

Patrimony was an influence in late seventeenth century Ordnance appointments but it could not work in isolation from patronage. Of the above patrimonial appointments to principal office, only in Chris-topher Musgrave's case have we evidence of a man gaining office despite the fact that his patron had fallen into disfavour.[2] But this was an exceptional circumstance. Normally patrimony would work hand in hand with patronage as a method of entry to office, as it did with George Legge who would have depended as much on the friendship of the Duke of York as the posthumous influence of his father in gaining the reversion to the place of lieutenant-general in 1672. And for many appointments – of the forty-six master-generals and principal officers of the period for whom we have evidence of their method of entry to office, it is estimated that about half owed their position to the unaided form of patronage – a man depended solely on his patron for gaining

1 *DNB;* WO 55/1796, Rich. Wharton to Ed. Hubbald, 12 June 1686; *Cal. Treas. Books 1703,* pp. 345-6, 22 July 1703; WO 44/715, petition; *Cal. SP Dom. 1678,* p. 536, 22 Nov. 1678; WO 48/47, list 31 Dec. 1708, 16th payment to John Romer; PRO 30, 37/13, warrant 15 June 1661; WO 44/714, Fitch's petition; WO 47/5, p. 211.

2 See Schomberg's comment after the Revolution that he did not think the king would be 'well served in the Tower by Musgrave, depending wholly on Lord Dartmouth', who was believed to have remained loyal to King James. See Hist. of Parl. draft biography of Christopher Musgrave.

office. How then did the patronage network operate? Who held the right of appointment?

The principal Ordnance officers and some other office-holders (notably the master gunner and the chief engineer) were appointed by letters patent under the great seal of the Crown and were, therefore, directly in the Crown's gift. This does not of course mean that the monarch of the day personally decided who was to be recruited for the Ordnance service. The extent of the monarch's involvement depended on his or her personal initiative, and temperament. James II and William III were probably more concerned with Ordnance appointments than either Charles II or Anne. It also depended on the level of appointment to be made. If a master-general was to be appointed, the monarch would generally nominate the candidate for office. It is likely, for example, that William III exercised a personal choice in the appointments of both Schomberg, his second in command during the invasion, and his friend Sidney, later Earl of Romney, (who was passed over on Anne's succession in favour of Marlborough) to the mastership in 1689 and 1693. For the offices below that of master-general, however, the monarch would generally give formal approval to the choice of his principal advisers. By Anne's reign the lord treasurer seems to have played a role in negotations for these offices,[1] but it was not only the head of the Treasury who acted as the king's intermediary. In 1691 when the storekeeper's place was vacant, Godolphin, Sidney and Admiral Russell all wrote to the king suggesting their own nominees; some years later the Earl of Peterborough informed Secretary Vernon that his brother, Colonel Mordaunt, had gained an Ordnance place through the good offices of the Duke of Shrewsbury; and in 1701 Hedges and Vernon, the two secretaries of state, Lord Rochester, and Romney, the master-general, all interceeded with the king before James Lowther kissed hands as principal storekeeper.[2]

The patronage of the master-general could indeed be of crucial importance in the disposal of a principal Ordnance place, as Sir William Trumbull found to his cost in 1685 when he negotiated with the king to keep his position at the Tower during his period of absence abroad as

1 Both Godolphin and Oxford were consulted re. the disposal of principal Ordnance places. See Cumbria RO., Lonsdale MS., James Lowther to Sir John Lowther, 4, 25 July 1702; HMC 29, 15 Rep. IV, Portland IV, pp. 39, 28 May 1702, HMC 29, Portland V, p. 171, 2 May 1712, pp. 136-7, Rivers to Oxford, 9 Jan. 1712, p. 192, Walpole to Oxford, 23 June 1712; The Marlborough-Godolphin Correspondence, pp. 1047, 1366, Marlborough to Godolphin, 22 July, 2 Aug. 1708, 5 Sept. 1709.

2 Cal. SP Dom. 1690-1, pp. 286, 290, 295, 29 Feb. 3, 6, Mar., 1691; HMC 45, Buccleuch (Montague House) II, pt. ii, p. 626, 16 Aug. 1699; Cumbria RO, Lonsdale MS., James Lowther to Sir John Lowther, 23, 25, 28, 30 Jan. 1701.

extraordinary envoy to France. Dartmouth's influence as master-general was paramount in persuading James II not to allow Trumbull to hold his Ordnance place as a sinecure, despite promises elicited from the king by Lord Sunderland that Trumbull should keep the office.[1] Dartmouth won this struggle, but this does not necessarily mean that the master-general's influence was always decisive. In 1690, for example, Schomberg championed the cause of a Charles Middleton, who had been Swadell's deputy, for the position of clerk of the Ordnance, but Sir Thomas Littleton gained the post instead.[2] The master-general's influence over the provision of major Ordnance places was no greater than his influence with the Crown.

His right of appointment to the more minor posts was less likely to be challenged as it was authorised by his own warrant, rather than letters patent under the great seal of the Crown. This meant that the master-general was consulted over most appointments, even when he was away from the Office. The Duke of Marlborough, for example, formally directed the disposal of the most menial places, even though the board had been vested with full power during the duke's absence abroad.[3] Marlborough's position at this time may be compared with that of his predecessors in an earlier period, when the master-general's patronage powers were less formidible. In the 1660s the storekeeper's patent undoubtedly gave him authority to make appointments at the Tower, the Minories, Woolwich and Chatham. The first Restoration storekeeper, Richard Marsh, had indeed styled himself storekeeper-general and claimed that he also had rights over the places of Portsmouth storekeeper and keeper of the small guns, rights that were vigorously and successfully challenged by Sir William Compton, the master-general of the period.[4] The appointment procedure for minor offices did not necessarily mean that the master-general personally chose his subordinates. It is clear that recommendations for office were made by other persons in authority – the principal officers, for in-

1 For a relation of the incident see the entries in Trumbull's diary, (Add. MS. 52279) Aug.-Sept. 1685.

2 WO 55/338, fo. 52, Schomberg to O.b., 12 Apr. 1690.

3 See WO 46/5, pp. 111-12, 131, 4, 28 July 1702, 18 Feb. 1703; Blenheim A I 11, Craggs to Marlborough, 8 June 1703; Blenheim B 1 2, Same to Same, 21 May 1708; Erle 2/40, Marlborough to Erle, 9/20, Sept. 1711. For an indication of Marlborough's powers when abroad see *Marlborough-Godolphin Correspondence*, pp. 195, 214-5, Marlborough to the duchess, 31 May/11 June, 1/12 July 1703.

4 For details see WO 55/330, pp. 333-4; WO 55/425, no. 32; *Cal. SP Dom. 1660-1*, p. 402, Compton to Nicholas, 3 Dec. 1661; *Cal. SP Dom 1664-5*, p. 238, 4 Mar. 1665; PRO 30 37/15, Compton's warrant, 30 Apr. 1663; WO 47/5, pp. 56-7.

stance, were responsible for making nominations to vacant clerkships[1] – and that the master-general's duties in this respect were formally to recognise the appointment by counter-signing a stereotyped warrant.

The importance of patronage as a way of gaining office in the late seventeenth century is quite apparent. Other factors, however, should not be entirely excluded. A number of principal officers of the period were given Ordnance places partly as a reward for services rendered to the Crown. Of the principal officers, Sir William Compton, Lord John Berkeley, Sir Thomas Chicheley, the Duke of Schomberg, Sir Christopher Musgrave (as lieutenant-general), Sir Henry Goodricke and Sir Henry Sheer all fell into this category. Compton, Berkeley and Chicheley were all active Royalists during the Interregnum, and Chicheley also lent the king considerable sums of money at the Restoration; Schomberg and Goodricke were both prominent on King William's side in the Revolution; Musgrave played an important role in parliament against Exclusion; and Sheer was active in the campaign against Monmouth. In all these cases it is of course impossible to determine whether the service rendered was the decisive factor in entry to office. As most of these office-holders also had powerful patrons, such as the Duke of York, the Earl of Danby and Lord Dartmouth, to promote their interests, it is likely that the service that they had rendered to the Crown simply tipped the balance in their favour.

Ability, too, should not be discounted as an influence in Ordnance appointments. Indeed for the more technical posts within the department an ability to perform the office effectively was an important prerequisite for the job. It is instructive that all the surveyor-generals of the period of whom we have knowledge were competent engineers prior to their appointment. Similarly military engineers were required to have a degree of expertise before they were appointed. Engineers were largely self-taught in this period, although payments were made by the Ordnance Office to encourage practitioners to travel abroad to study the art of fortification.[2] The chief engineer, however, did examine

---

1 See WO 55/488, *passim,* letters from various officers for their clerks to be entered on the quarter books.

2 E.g. *Cal SP Dom. 1668-9,* p. 267, warrant to Ordnance commissioners, 6 Apr. 1669; *Ibid. 1675-6,* p. 509, warrant to Chicheley, 11 Jan. 1676; *Ibid. 1685,* p. 283, warrant to Dartmouth, 29 July 1685. There was no official government establishment for the training of cadet engineers until the founding of the Woolwich Academy in 1741, but as early as 1718-19 some cadets attended 'Mr Weston's mathematical school at Greenwich' and in 1720 the board raised money for a mathematics master to be employed 'for educating of youth and improving the officers of artillery and engineers in their respective duties'. It also suggested that a school of instruction should be erected at Woolwich, and a second great room was built there for this purpose. WO 47/31, p. 330, minutes 7 Nov. 1718;

prospective candidates before they were put on the Ordnance establishment. Withall, for instance, was examined 'as to his knowledge and abilities in the rules of fortification' before he was recommended by Beckman as an under-engineer.[1] For the majority of civil posts, where the only abilities required were literacy and diligence, merit was less likely to be an influential factor in appointment.

Once an appointment had been gained there were opportunities for promotion within the department, although the operation of purchase, patrimony and patronage made it inevitable that there was no systematic advancement. There was little chance of promotion, however, to the mastership or lieutenantship in this period. George Legge did indeed gain the position of master-general in 1682 after having served as lieutenant-general, and Sir Christopher Musgrave was moved from the post of master-general commissioner to that of lieutenant-general at the same time, but these appointments were unusual. It was far more likely for there to be advancements from the rank of clerk of deliveries, the officers holding this place generally being younger than the other principal officers. Christopher Musgrave (junior) became clerk of the Ordnance after having held the clerkship of deliveries, and Bridges, Gardiner and James Lowther were all promoted from that rank to the principal storekeepership. According to James Lowther many of the duties of the latter post required 'neither more knowledge nor trouble' than his former place of clerk of deliveries,[2] and this no doubt facilitated promotion from the one to the other. The fact that there was no direct interchange between the officers holding the positions of surveyor-general, clerk of the Ordnance, storekeeper and treasurer indicates that these offices were held to be equal in status if not in antiquity. By the end of the period, moreover, they were also equal in pay. Promotions from the clerical ranks to the position of principal officer were also unusual occurrences. Wharton (who was soon afterwards made departmental treasurer) and Conyers gained this reward in 1670 and 1673, but they were the last clerks to be promoted in this way. By 1714 the distinctions between the grades of clerk and principal officer were too rigid for there to be any direct progression between the two. As might be expected the practice of promoting a chief engineer to the surveyor-generalship did not die out in this period: both de Gomme and Michael Richards held the surveyorship after having been chief engineer. It was not until later in the eighteenth century, after the surveyorship had

WO 47/32, pp. 306, 340, minutes 28 July, 18 Aug. 1718; WO 47/33, pp. 269-71, minute 31 Aug. 1720; Hogg, *Royal Arsenal I*, 346-7.

1 Withall, *Exhorbitant Oppressions*, p. 5.

2 Cumbria RO, Lonsdale MS., James Lowther to Sir John Lowther, 22 Feb. 1701.

become a purely civil office, that the military and civil branches of the service were mutually exclusive.

Among the under-ministers, where office tenure was more secure, (at least by 1714), there was a more defined system of promotion. For the aspiring junior clerk, if the incumbent stayed long in Office service, there was the possibility of elevation to the position of first clerk, or that of storekeeper at one of the Ordnance depots. Blake, Rothwell, Criche, Harrison, Allen senior, Sparkes junior, Whittaker, Leece and Edward Hubbald all served as junior clerks before they were made first clerk. Edward Hubbald, Duxbury, Hooper, Povey, Fleetwood, Robson, Cheltenham, Thorpe, Charles White, Longstaffe and Griffith gained their positions as storekeepers after having been permanent or extra-ordinary clerks. It became increasingly customary in fact for the position of storekeeper to be an internal appointment. In December 1692 the Ordnance board were greatly insulted when one John Morris petitioned the king independently in order to gain the Windsor Castle storekeepership, and stressed that the position ought to go to one of the clerks. At the end of the period the board again recommended that clerks 'bred up in the Office' should succeed as storekeepers when vacancies fell.[1] For the more lowly under-ministers like the office labourers there was less chance of promotion, although Edmund Snapes was appointed the Office messenger after having been a labourer for over twenty years. Among the fireworkers, engineers and gunners, however, promotion generally came from within the ranks. Woolfson, Neilson, Pendlebury and Hara were fireworkers before they were pro-moted chief firemaster, all the first, second and third engineers had experience as practising engineers before their appointments, and the majority of master gunners had served their apprenticeships as ordinary gunners.

The extent of mobility within the Ordnance service, therefore, was not strikingly high. Only ten of the sixty-five or so appointments made to the rank of master-general and principal officer in this period were from within the department, and the majority of these promotions were from within the rank of principal officer. There are no instances, moreover, of a principal officer being promoted more than once. By 1714 the practice of promoting an ordinary clerk to a principal office had been discontinued, and it had become increasingly less likely for a military officer to be advanced to a position on the board. Nevertheless despite the fact that opportunities for lateral promotion within the Ordnance were decreasing, there is sufficient evidence to show that among the junior and military officers the opportunities for advance-

1   T.1/20, fo. 86, report 28 Dec. 1692; WO 47/27, p. 84, 26 Oct. 1714.

ment within each sub-department were improving. By the end of the period there is also evidence to suggest that at this level of government both merit and seniority were important criteria in deciding whether an officer was to be promoted, or, at least, kept on in the service following a post-war reduction in personnel. In 1717, for example, on the death of Captain Goodricke, the Chatham storekeeper, the board desired that the Office clerk who had 'the most right and merit' should be appointed to the vacancy; on the reduction of the establishment at the end of the Spanish Succession War provision was made for those who had served the Office diligently abroad; and it was similarly ordered in 1719 that preferment in the newly established royal artillery marching companies should be made to those who had 'served longest' and had the 'best pretensions'.[1] At the same time as the opportunities for advancements among the principal officers were diminishing, a career structure was gradually evolving for those in the lower ranks of Ordnance service.

The change in the nature of the tenure of patent offices in the Ordnance in this period confirms the impression gained from the survey of promotions within the department that for those at the highest level of appointment, Ordnance service was becoming less career orientated than for the clerks at the lower end of the scale. Whereas at the Restoration, in accordance with the practice earlier in the century, life tenures had been awarded to principal officers — with the exception of Francis Nicholls, whose patent had been granted during his good behaviour — thereafter all non-reversionary grants were given during pleasure. This reform coincided with the demise of the reversionary grant. A few reversionary grants were awarded in this period — to Compton for life, and to George Legge, Sir John Chicheley, Bertie and Jonas Moore junior during pleasure — but among the principal officers at least there is no instance of a reversionary grant being awarded after 1675.[2] The consequenses of these reforms are obvious. With the elimination of life tenures and reversionary grants tenure became far less secure. About half of the principal officers appointed in this period were dismissed from the service, and of the remaining twenty who died

---

[1] WO 47/28, pp. 2, 48, 53, 4 Jan. 18, 24 Feb. 1718: WO 47/32, p. 184, 28 Apr. 1719; Withall (*Exhorbitant Oppressions,* pp. 49, 56-7, 59) suggests that the system of promotion among the military branch of the establishment was grossly unfair, but his criticisms must be treated with a degree of scepticism.

[2] Although Beckman was granted one for the place of chief engineer in 1678, (*Cal. SP Dom. 1678,* p. 40, 13 Mar. 1678) and James II also promised Trumbull the reversion to Sherburne's office in Oct. 1685, (Add MS. 52279, 30 Oct. 1685) but the promise was never fulfilled. For a full discussion of these reforms in the Ordnance and other departments see J. C. Sainty, 'A Reform in the Tenure of Offices during the Reign of Charles II', *BIHR* 41 (1968), 150-71.

in office all but seven died before the Revolution. After 1688 moreover, the ratio of dismissals to deaths increased threefold. This does not necessarily signify that those officials holding life tenures would die in office. Newport was replaced as master-general in 1660 even though he had been granted a life patent in 1634, and Sherburne's life tenure of the clerkship of the Ordnance was terminated in 1688 because he was a Roman Catholic. Nor does it mean that those holding pleasure tenures would always be dismissed. Of the principal officers, Schomberg, Rivers, Hamilton, Walter, Tichburne, both Moores, De Gomme, Bridges, Conyers, Gardiner, Meesters, Fortrey, Philip Musgrave and Wharton all died in office after having been granted their patents at the king's pleasure. The granting of pleasure tenures, however, did ensure that there would be fewer complications when an officer was dismissed. In Newport's case, for instance, three separate sets of letters patent were required before Newport surrendered his life interest and Compton officially came into office. Pleasure tenures, in contrast with life tenures, also had to be renewed at the beginning of each reign if the officer was to be retained. This lessened the officer's personal stake in his office. If he was then dismissed he could not legitimately claim, as Sherburne did after his dismissal in 1688, that his proprietary rights were being invaded.

As the principal officers became less secure in their job, they also became increasingly subject to political controls. The adoption of the pleasure tenure had made it more likely that officials would be dismissed for incompetence. Initially this gave the Crown a far greater freedom of action in its choice of servant. Prior to the Revolution the monarch only rarely bowed before the prevailing political wind in his Ordnance appointments and dismissals — as in 1679, when Charles II was obliged to dismiss Sir Thomas Chicheley as master-general and appoint Sir William Hickman, a follower of Shaftesbury and a moderate Country leader, as one of his three master-general commissioners in an attempt to split the opposition and fashion an administration representing moderate elements from the Court and Country parties.[1] More usually the Crown could act independently of party considerations. An officer might be dismissed because he had lost the confidence of the king, as Sir Christopher Musgrave was in 1687 for refusing to support the repeal of the Test Act, but he would not generally be dispensed with because he had lost the confidence of Parliament. After the Revolution, however, the monarch's choice was more circumscribed.

1 A similar scheme was adopted at the Privy Council and Admiralty. See W.A. Aiken, 'The Admiralty in Conflict and Commission, 1679-84', in *Conflict in Stuart England: Essays in Honour of Wallace Notestein*, ed. W. A. Aiken and B. D. Henning (1960), pp. 205-6.

Annual sessions and the development, albeit a temporary one, of a two party system ensured that dismissals of principal officers were increasingly inspired by party political motivations. Indeed the fact that dismissals among principal Ordnance officers were twice as frequent after the Revolution as before was not only a result of the demise of life tenures but also a direct consequence of the growth of parliamentary government. The party political appointments and dismissals are most apparent in 1712 with the dismissal of the predominently Whig coterie of Marlborough, Erle, Ashe and Harry Mordaunt, and their replacement by officers with Tory sympathies and connections – Rivers, the malcontent Whig, who had formed an alliance with Harley, and who, after his death in 1712 was succeeded as master-general by the Jacobite Duke of Hamilton; Jack Hill, the brother of the queen's favourite Abigail Masham, who like Rivers had been baulked of advancement in the Regiment Crisis of 1710; Dixie Windsor, a Hanoverian Tory; and Charles Eversfield. All the former group were to resume office in 1714. Of the Tories, only Dixie Windsor retained his place on George I's accession. It should not be assumed from this, however, that principal Ordnance officers were invariably dismissed at the onset of each new ministry simply because they were not of the right political persuasion. Even at the height of the party debate in the age of Anne few of those principal officers who sat in the Commons could be definitely classified as either Whig or Tory. It would be impossible, for example, to attach a party label to a man like William Bridges, who succeeded in retaining the Ordnance surveyorship through every political crisis of the early eighteenth century. For Bridges was an inveterate placeman, that is a government supporter no matter what the political hue of the government, although like most later Stuart Ordnance officers who were also members of Parliament, he was not returned for a government borough. There was no other pure government member among the Ordnance officers of the period but there were a number like Sir Henry Goodricke, Christopher Musgrave, Charles Bertie, Thomas Littleton, John Pulteney and the young James Lowther, whose loyalties were as much directed towards the Court as either political party. This gave them a greater chance of being able to hang on to their place through successive ministerial changes than the 'party' officeholders.[1]

So the use of the pleasure patent at first increased the Crown's freedom of choice of servant, but later made it more likely that appoint-

1   The politics of a number of Ordnance officers are described in Geoffrey Holmes, *British Politics in the Age of Anne* (1967), *passim.* One important reason for the department not becoming a party-political battleground during the reign of Anne (until 1712) was the restraining influence of Marlborough. See *Godolphin-Marlborough Correspondence*, pp. 195, 214-15, Marlborough to the duchess, 31 May/11 June, 1/12 July 1703.

ments and dismissals of principal officers would be subject to parliamentary pressures. The clerks in ordinary, who were not appointed by the instrument of the Crown's patent, however, were largely immune from these pressures. Their tenure of office, therefore, was generally more secure than that of the principal officers. Normally the principal officers held the right of appointment to a clerkship when a vacancy occurred through death or resignation, but they were unable to dismiss their clerks unless it had been proved to the master-general's and board's satisfaction that they had been guilty of serious misconduct. That this convention became established in this period is clear from a number of precedents cited by Alexander Eustace, a storekeeper's clerk, in a letter to the board in 1709 defending his right to office after he had been removed by the incoming storekeeper, Robert Lowther. According to Eustace, George Billinghurst, third clerk to Sir George Marsh, and Thomas Rogers, a clerk under Samuel Fortrey, had both been dismissed for neglect of duty after due inquiry had been made. Eustace cited instances, however, where the officer's right of dismissal had not been upheld. The removal of Conyers and his grandson, Roger Fowke, from office had resulted in Conyers's re-instatement when the Ordnance commission found that there had been no valid reason for his dismissal. This case was used as a precedent when Conyers himself, after he had been promoted storekeeper, attempted to get rid of a rival clerk Abel Barton on purely personal grounds. The master-general's ruling on that occasion, 'that after any clerk was presented and endorsed by order into the quarter books of the Office . . . it was not in the power of any officer to remove him without his and the board's consent', had been adhered to in 1687 when Sherburne had endeavoured to substitute Samuel Pelling as his clerk in the place of William Phelps. Eustace also brought to his defence a further list to show 'how long clerks in ordinary have served in the office and not been removed upon the changes that have been made of the principal officers'. The list reveals that death or preferment elsewhere, rather than dismissal, were the most common reasons for new appointments to be made to clerkships. Eustace's evidence was further supported by the board's observation that since 1683 there had been only two instances of clerks having been removed by the incoming principal officer. Both Granville and Erle had dismissed their second clerks, but in neither case had any appeal been made against the decision. Erle later claimed moreover, that he would not have removed the man had he made any complaint. It is quite apparent from all this, therefore, that right was on Eustace's side. It comes as no surprise to find that his vigorous appeal, the board's friendly support, and its distrust of Robert Lowther's conduct, was sufficient to get Eustace re-instated in office.[1]

1   Although it is not quite clear whether Marlborough settled the dispute or

The documentation surrounding the Eustace affair may be supplemented by the evidence of the quarter books, in which the clerk's name was recorded after he had been appointed to office. For the lists (reproduced in the appendix) that may be drawn up from these pay books, also demonstrate that appointments and dismissals to the position of clerk in ordinary were generally made irrespective of changes among the principal officers. The major exceptions to this rule seem to have been the master-general's secretaries, and the first clerks to the lieutenant-general (before 1687) and treasurer. Nevertheless for the majority of clerks it may be said that by 1714 they had ceased to be the mere personal servants of the principal officers and had become more public officials with a moderately secure tenure of office.

The disadvantages of having clerks, and as far as it can be ascertained other under-ministers, that did not change with the incoming principal officer were far outweighed by the merits of the system. Robert Lowther might have argued that it was necessary for him to remove Eustace in favour of someone in whom he could confide in order for him to be able to execute properly his instructions for the care of the stores, but it was more than probable that if all principal officers had been generally accustomed to making new appointments as soon as they came into office the Ordnance service would have suffered. If this system had prevailed there would have been no opportunity for a defined system of promotion to have developed among the ranks of under-minister. It would then have been even more likely that experienced administrators would have been dismissed and that preferment to clerkships would have been made for reasons which may not necessarily have been conducive to the good of the department. This indeed would certainly have happened if Eustace had lost his place, for Lowther wished to appoint in his stead someone who was totally unacquainted with Ordnance business. Unless his nominee was appointed Lowther claimed that a 'multitude of inconveniences' would have followed and that his interest in the country would have been destroyed. As it was, however, a man who had many years experience in Ordnance business was kept in office. This necessity of having experienced junior officials in the department was of overwhelming importance as it was these men who kept the wheels of government turning at each change of principal officer. The advice the lord treasurer gave Mordaunt, when he was appointed treasurer for the second time in 1705, that James Leece should be continued as one of his clerks 'for his own ease and safety

whether Lowther himself acquiesced in the board's resolution. For details of this affair see Blenheim B. I 23, Eustace's list, Lowther and Eustace's letters to the board, and letters from Erle and Lowther to Marlborough of 20 May, 17 June and 16 Aug. 1709. Also Cumbria RO, Lonsdale MS., Robert to James Lowther, 4 Aug., 1, 24 Sept. 1709.

as for the good of the service in general',[1] might well have been given to any incoming member of the Ordnance board. Men such as Leece, and other clerks like John Blake, Samuel Criche, Edward Hubbald, Nicholas Whittaker and John Allen senior, who all held office for more than twenty years,[2] provided the continuity so necessary to any administrative system. These officials and others like them ensured that the political upheavals of 1660, 1689 and 1714 would not necessarily disrupt the government of the realm.[3]

The Rewards of Office

The practice of granting reversions may have died out during this period, but this did not limit the numbers who petitioned for office. Indeed as far as it can be ascertained it seems that the competition for an Ordnance place was severe throughout the period.[4] Men were quite willing to pay handsomely for the right to hold office as well as give substantial security for the privilege if the office to be administered was of great responsibility. Why this should have been so is as difficult to answer as why a particular man should have been appointed to a particular office. Even if a prospective office-holder of the seventeenth century knew in his own mind why he wished to enter the royal service, it is unlikely that he would have left the prospective seventeenth century historian with any indication of his motivation. And if he did, it is more than probable that his reason for entering public life would have been different from the next man. The historian cannot hope to disentangle the complexities of human motivation. All we can do is suggest some of the advantages of Ordnance service which might have attracted the aspiring office-holder, and weigh these against some of the costs of an Ordnance place.

The late seventeenth century Ordnance Office certainly offered an

1 See *Cal. Treas. Books 1705-6*, p. 340, Lowndes to Mordaunt, 12 July 1705. The advice, however, was ignored.

2 In some cases much more. Whittaker and Allen held office for nearer forty than thirty years. See Appendix, pp. 226-9.

3 At the Restoration, for instance, a number of the under-ministers employed before the Restoration continued in office. (For the list of officials on the quarter books for Dec. 1658 — the last complete exant quarter list before Sept. 1660 — see WO 54/19). The junior officials, moreover, were unaffected by the almost complete substitution of principal officers in 1714, although a change may be discerned throughout the establishment in 1689. (See appendix).

4 See WO 44/714, 715 for miscellaneous petitions. The increase in the Ordnance establishment during the war years may, of course, have made it less difficult for an Ordnance place to have been secured at these times — a point that is impossible to prove quantitatively.

opportunity for advancement, both within the department and in the general context of government service. As we have seen few aspiring Crown servants could hope to gain office without the help of someone within the department, or at least without the assistance of someone in a position of influence outside the service, but once an office-holder had gained the first rung on the ladder of preferment there were possibilities of promotion. There are one or two instances of administrators of relatively humble backgrounds, for example, becoming principal officers after having spent their entire careers, or at least most of their post-Restoration careers, in the Ordnance service. The rise of George Wharton, like Sir Edward Sherburne's (senior) before the civil war, may be described as that of an authentic administrative careerist. Wharton, who had gained an early opportunity to enter the Royalist Ordnance service at Oxford in the Civil War, was successively first clerk to the lieutenant-general (dealing mainly with financial business), clerk of the deliveries and departmental treasurer in the years after the Restoration. He also held the keepership of saltpetre for most of this period. In 1677 Wharton was created a baronet for services to the Royalist cause. At his death in 1681 he bequeathed £6,425 in cash and the leases of ten houses in central London, as well as his personal estate. Apart from the profits from the sale of his almanacs, this wealth must mainly have accumulated from his Ordnance career, for he seems to have sold his inherited estates in 1642 when he raised a troop of horse for the king.[1] The advancement of Wharton from the son of a Westmoreland yeoman to a wealthy baronet was not dissimilar to that of Sir Jonas Moore senior. Moore, too, came from an obscure northern background. His early administrative career, like that of many of Charles I's officials, was started in private service — as a clerk to the chancellor of Durham. During this early period of his life he was encouraged to undertake mathematical study and his proficiency in this subject seems to have been the main reason for his rise. It enabled him to enter the royal service in 1647 as mathematical tutor to the Duke of York; two years later it helped him gain the position of surveyor of the fen drainage scheme, during which project he possibly met Sir Thomas Chicheley the future master-general of the Ordnance. The experience he gained at this part of his career, as well as the contacts he made, was no doubt invaluable in his rapid post-Restoration advance in the Ordnance service from engineer at Tangier to knighted surveyor-general.

---

[1] For Wharton see *DNB; Alumni Oxonienses,* ed. Joseph Foster, IV, 1607; Prob. 11/367. fos. 232, ff. For Sherburne see Aylmer, thesis, p. 100, and *King's Servants,* pp. 79-80, 291. Bodl. Wood F 44, fos. 226 ff., letters from Sir Edward Sherburne to Wood, 1675-95, also contains interesting details of the backgrounds of Wharton and Sherburne.

The rise from obscurity of both Wharton and Moore to positions of power within the department was not typical of the period. Their periods of service may be paralleled by those of other career Ordnance officers, such as Sir Bernard de Gomme, a Dutchman who had accompanied Prince Rupert to England in the Civil War, served Charles I as engineer and quarter-master general, and in the years after the Restoration became surveyor-general via the position of chief engineer; Sir Henry Sheer, the son of a Deptford naval captain who, like Moore, attained the surveyorship after having been resident engineer at Tangier; Michael Richards, another career engineer who worked his way up the Ordnance military establishment, was promoted chief engineer by Marlborough, and then, in 1714, surveyor-general and deputy to the ageing lieutenant-general, Thomas Erle; and Edward Conyers who gained his position as storekeeper's clerk in 1660 through the good offices of General Monck, and was promoted storekeeper on the death of Sir George Marsh in 1673.[1] But the opportunities within the department for the careerists became increasingly limited as the opportunities for advancement to the board decreased. For as we have already observed, except for an engineer, who by 1714 could still hope to gain the surveyorship, it became extremely unlikely for an office-holder to be promoted from outside his own grade in the service.

The closing of the rank of principal officer to the career administrator meant that by this period a number of positions on the board were looked upon as 'middling' places, providing opportunities for further advancement outside the department rather than being ends in themselves.[2] The offices of master and lieutenant-general were not, of course, 'middling' places, as they were generally held by senior ministers. The surveyor-generalship similarly was nearly always the office of an experienced servant of the Crown — it is interesting to note, moreover, that with the exception of Sheer, all the surveyor-generals of whom we have knowledge died whilst they were in office. In contrast, the offices of clerk of the Ordnance, storekeeper, clerk of deliveries, and treasurer were usually held by younger men, especially in the later period. After the Revolution it was the tendency for men under the age of 45 to be appointed to these positions.[3] As a result, it was invariably the case that office-holders in these posts were promoted

1 For Moore, De Gomme, Sheer and Richards see *DNB;* for Conyers, Blenheim B I 23, Eustace's list.

2 See below, pp. 100-1, for James Lowther's description of the storekeeper as a 'middling place'.

3 Some were a good deal younger. The Lowthers (James and Robert) were 22 and 27 on their first call to office, Christopher Musgrave was 26, Mordaunt, *c.* 36, and Eversfield *c.* 30

to positions outside the department. Trumbull and Littleton were promoted Treasury lords, Ashe and Pulteney became Trade commissioners, Robert Lowther was assigned as governor of Barbados and James Craggs was appointed joint postmaster-general — all of them after having held one of these 'middling' Ordnance posts. At other levels promotions outside the department were not unknown. At the top of the service, Sir John Duncomb was made a Treasury lord in 1667 during his tenure as master commissioner. Marvell noted when this occurred that 'powder ne'er blew man up so soon as high'[1] and, apart from the instance of Sir John Chicheley being made an Admiralty lord after the disbandment of the second commission in 1681, it did not do so again at this level, if only because the later master-generals were eminent men who had already gained high office prior to their Ordnance appointment. Among the clerks in ordinary we know from Eustace's list that Harcourt Masters quitted the Ordnance Office for other preferment in 1687 and Richard Sturgeon was preferred into the Army in 1688. We can also surmise that Edward Hubbald was probably the same Edward Hubbald that was appointed accountant in the Navy Pay Office in 1699.[2] But as the Ordnance service for these grades of official became a career service, such interchanges again probably became less common.

From these lesser officers who could not gain further advancement within or without the department there were other rewards. All the under-ministers were privileged members of society. The board's petition of 1664 to the Privy Council showed that:

> The ministers, artificers and all other attendants (even to the meanest labourer belonging to the Office of the Ordnance) have by ancient privilege ever been exempt and free from all manner of personal offices and duties within the City of London and suburbs thereof, or other places of their abode, and from any arrest, prest or imprisonment, without leave first had from the master or in his absence from the lieutenant of the Ordnance.[3]

And it is clear that this 'ancient privilege' did indeed give those who worked for the department a certain immunity from local government service, naval and military impressment, and creditors who wished to bring about an arrest for debt, although this immunity was by no means absolute.[4]

---

1 Quoted in *Bulstrode Papers,* p. 28 n.

2 I am grateful to Mr John Sainty for this information. The fact that the Ordnance Hubbald's departure from the Office coincides with the appointment of the Hubbald at the Navy Pay Office; and that the latter appointment was made by Littleton, a former clerk of the Ordnance, makes it almost certain that they were one and the same person.

3 WO 47/6, fo.1.

4 For details see my thesis, pp. 207-9.

There were far more tangible incentives, however, for those who ventured into the service of the department, for an Ordnance officer of this period was well endowed with allowances from the Exchequer and the Ordnance treasury, as well as official private fee payments and various gratuities and perquisites such as travelling allowances, allowances for extraordinary services, tax exemption and a free house. There was in this period, however, a distinct and decisive change in the relative value of the two main sources of remuneration. As Table I indicates, between 1660 and 1714 a number of fee payments were abolished, and the salaries of all Ordnance officials were increased across the board. All the major changes in this context took place prior to the Revolution, and the most important of them stem from the period in office of the first master-general commissioners.[1]

The origin of such reforms may be traced back to the Cromwellian period, when the establishment was reduced, and increased salaries were paid to some of the principal Ordnance officers.[2] At the Restoration, the old Ordnance board with its pre-civil war fees and salaries had been reconstituted. A radical reformation of the fee system, however, was undertaken by the Ordnance commissioners who held office from October 1664 to June 1670. The previous master, Sir William Compton, had enjoyed 'the liberty of disposing of all places under his command to his advantage', as well as his patent fee and a sizeable pension, but on the appointment of the master-commissioners a fixed salary of £500 each *per annum* was awarded them in lieu of 'all advantages of perquisites whatsoever', at the commissioners' own request to the king.[3] At the appointment of the master commissioners the poundage fee of the clerk of the Ordnance was also abolished. But of far greater importance to the Office's future constitution was the order of 13 February 1665, which abolished the lieutenant's poundage fee after the death of the then incumbent, William Legge. After his decease the office of paymaster was to be executed separately by a treasurer, who was to receive a salary of £400 *per annum* in the place of all fees and gratuities. The succeeding lieutenant was to be compensated with a salary of £800 *per annum*. There was a further limitation of the poundage fee on saltpetre payments before it was abolished on the death of William Legge in 1670, and this cost the Crown £1,000 plus 10s. in every £100 on all saltpetre payments.

1   For detailed references to the following section, see my 'Place and Profit', pp. 58 *ff.*

2   See introduction, pp. 8-9.

3   This salary was increased to £1,000 p.a. to each commissioner in Dec. 1666. Some fifteen months later it was reduced to £600 p.a., the same salary as the 1679-82 commissioners.

TABLE I

Annual Allowances to Selected Ordnance Officers in 1660 and 1714 (in £.s.d.)[1]

Office - Holders	Exchequer Fees		Private Fees 2		Salaries 3		House/travelling 4 /Extraordinary Payments		Totals 5	
	1660	1714	1660	1714	1660	1714	1660	1714	1660	1714
Master-general	175-18-4 +4 servants' wages	175-18-4 +4 servants' wages	?	—	150	1,500	? for pension	£4p.day for travelling (1000 p.a. in 1705-06)	325-18-4 +4 servants' wages + fees' pension	1675-18-4 +4 servants' wages
Lieutenant-general	63-13-4	63-13-4	1,600 (?) (poundage of 6d. in £ on payments)	—	384	800	Minories house	£300 in lieu of house (from 1673) £3 p.day for travelling £1,239 in 1707-08)	c. 2,000max.	1163-13-4
Surveyor-general	54-15	54-15	?	—	174	400	Tower house	Tower house £2 per day for travelling, £300 for acting as Lt.-gen, deputy (intermittently from 1687)	228-15min.	754-15
Clerk of the Ordnance	36-10	36-10	c. 1,000 (?) (poundage, 3d. in £) +c. 1100(?) (Commission fees)	c. 300 (?) (commission fees)	215-14	400	Tower house	100 in lieu of house 1-10 per day for travelling 100 for keeping check ledger (from 1666)	1,350max.	c.936-10
Storekeeper	54-15	54-15	c. 200 + (?) (for showing stores, rent of king's wharf, patronage rights)	—	216-12	400	Tower house	Tower house 1-10 per day for travelling ('other advantages' worth 100 according to J. Lowther in 1701)	470 +	c. 550
Clerk of deliveries	18-15	18-15	—	—	155-16	300	20(?) in lieu of house (payment to Fortrey)	40 in lieu of house (in 1709)	c. 200	c.360

TABLE I

Annual Allowances to Selected Ordnance Officers in 1660 and 1714 (in £.s.d.)[1]

Office - Holders	Exchequer Fees		Private Fees 2		Salaries 3		House/travelling 4 /Extraordinary Payments		Totals 5	
	1660	1714	1660	1714	1660	1714	1660	1714	1660	1714
Treasurer	–	–	–	–		400		Tower house(?) 300 present (at least in 1705)		700
Master-general's clerk	–	–	c. 120 (?) (commission fees)	c. 300(?) (commission fees)	40 (for himself + clerks)	200 (for himself + clerks)			c. 160	c. 500
1st clerks to principal officers	–	–	Share of commission fees	Share of commission fees	80 (lt-gen) 60 (clk. Ord) 40 (s.-gen, stkpr, clk. del.)	115 (clk. Ord) 100 (remainder)	Tower house(?) 6s. 8d per day for travelling (payment to Fleetwood 1663) c. 20 for remains + other services	Tower house(?) 10s per day for travelling (By 1679 - payment to Hubbald) c. 30(?) for remains etc.	60-100 +	130-45 +
Portsmouth storekeeper (of port not garrison)	–	–	?	–	60	100 +20 for clerk		10 p.a in lieu of house (in 1707. Continued until re-building of wharf (?))	60 +	c. 110
Master gunner	36-10	36-10	c. 60 (?) (commission fees)	c. 100(?) (commission fees)	171	190	Tower house (?)	Woolwich house £1 per day for travelling, like ch. engineer(?)	c. 270(?)	c. 325(?)

1 The following figures are very much approximations. For detailed references see my article 'Place and Profit', pp. 56-62.

2 The figures given for fee payments have been culled from a variety of sources. The lieutenant-general's poundage fee for the first year after the Restoration was certainly less than £1,600, which was the approximate annual amount of poundage collected by the lieutenant-general between the Restoration and December 1665. The £1,000 given as the clerk's poundage fee is a contemporary estimate. The commission fees are included only in the principal officer's salary, but it is probable that they were also distributed in part among the respective clerks who worked under them. (Although it is probably too high. See Bodl. Wood F44, fo. 273, Sherburne to Wood, 23 Nov.

1686). An attempt has been made to ascertain the value of the commission fees for the clerk of the Ordnance (allowed £2 for the entry of each principal officer on the quarter books, £1 for an under-minister, 10s. for a gunner), the master-general's clerk (allowed £2 for each master-general's warrant for a labourer's place, £1 for a gunner's commission and 10s. for another warrant), and the master gunner (allowed 10s. for the examination, trial and certificate of a gunner. 5s. for taking his oath and 2s.6d. for his entry on the muster roll) by relating them to the size of the Ordnance establishment in 1660 and 1714. The actual commission fees do not appear to have changed throughout the period but their value increased with the expansion in the size of the establishment. The total annual average figures for the commission fees, however, are likely to have been higher than the figures given here. No allowance has been made in the commission fee totals for the fact that any commission could have been renewed more than once annually on the death or the dismissal of the incumbent. At the coming in of a new master-general or at the beginning of a new reign, moreover, a commission was automatically renewed. Nor has the fact that extraordinary personnel were awarded commissions on the establishment of artillery trains been taken into consideration. (In Sept. 1716, for instance, when a new artillery train was established, £61.10s. was paid to the clerk of the Ordnance and £42.5s. to the master's chief clerk). The figure listed for the storekeeper's fee in 1660 has been calculated from the subsequent level of compensation given to the storekeeper when the fees were dispensed with.

3 It seems that the Ordnance officers paid no tax prior to the Revolution. An Act passed after the Revolution, however, only exempted those military officers in muster by the Army's muster master-general. Ordnance officers, therefore, were obliged to pay tax, but were subsequently re-imbursed. (WO 46/3, pp. 11-13, O.b. to Sidney, 16 Nov. 1693, enclosing statement of their case, pp. 31-32, Same to Same, 6 Apr. 1694, p. 70, Same to Romney, 11 Aug. 1694; T.1/27, no.30, O.b. petition to the king; T.1/29, no. 45, Treasury report, 28 Sept. 1694, enclosing various reports). The total cost of the taxes paid by the entire Ordnance establishment for the years 1702, 1705 and 1714 was as follows: £479. 3s. 4d., £1,983. 6s. 8d., and £991. 12s. 6d. (WO 48/44, list 29 June 1706, 37th payment; WO 47/27, p. 42, minute 27 Oct. 1705, annual total calculated from half-yearly payment; WO 47/27, p. 9, minute 6 Aug. 1714). In 1706 the individual rate of tax was 11. 75 per cent. (WO 47/24, p. 269, minute 23 Jan. 1707, impresting £21 to Brockhurst and Flamstead). The principal officers were also allowed £4,125 in lieu of the master-general's salary for 2¾ years from 1690 to 1693.

4 It is impossible to determine precisely the annual monetary value of these payments. If an extraordinary payment or gratuity has not been recorded this does not necessarily mean that none were made but simply that I have not come across any reference to such an allowance. No account has been taken of either the allowances made to principal officers for remains (about £50 to each officer every three years), the small *ad hoc* payments made to the widow and dependents of those who had died or been disabled in the king's service, or the occasional pension payment, (See, e.g. WO /49/226, bills of £1,296. 14s. 9d. and £1,210. 1s. 3d. to various officers for remains in 1710 and 1713; *Cal. SP Dom. 1670*, p. 140, allowance to family of George Clarke, 30 Mar. 1670; *Cal. SP Dom. 1686-7*, no. 1751, warrant 9 May 1687, for continuation of Trumbull's pension of £200 p.a. to Edward Meredith).

5 The totals given are also approximations. No account has been taken of the value of a house or travelling cost reimbursements.

After the disbanding of the 1664-70 commission, the policy of abolishing private fees in exchange for monetary compensation was continued intermittently. The keeper of the rich weapons and the deputy keeper of the Armoury were allowed £70 *per annum* each, and the principal storekeeper and keeper of the small guns £50 *per annum* each, after various prohibitions were made against the showing of stores, although one observer commented that the keeper of the rich weapons continued to show the stores and to receive the fee. The principal storekeeper was also compensated for various other lost fees or rights. On 30 December 1670 Richard Marsh was allowed £30 *per annum* for rent lost when the old Woolwich gunwharf was sold, and a further £100 *per annum* was paid to his son, as storekeeper, in consideration of the loss of his patronage rights at Woolwich and Chatham.

These were the only private fees to have been abolished and there appears to have been no attempt in this period to do away with commission fees. Considering the weight of vested interest against fee abolishment, however, the Ordnance Office's success in instituting any reform was remarkable. For fee payments had been the traditional way of rewarding government officials and they had a vested interest in continuing such a system, as allowances paid in compensation were unlikely to match the profits of the private rewards. Fees, therefore, could only be dispensed with piece by piece after the death of an officer who had enjoyed the fruits of the system. The Treasury's shortage of money was also a principal stumbling block against an abolition of all fees. The argument Legge used in defence of the poundage he claimed on saltpetre payments, that the king should not be charged because the petremen had always been willing to pay the money, was a telling one if a lord treasurer was pressed for cash. It clearly illustrates the difficulties of a government financed reform being instituted, when the alternative was the continuation of private fees, which in the short term saved the Crown an enormous amount of expense.

Nor should the importance of these fee reforms be minimised. Had all the pre-civil war private fees been continued it would have been highly unsatisfactory for the department, as it would have meant that public welfare would have been completely sacrificed to private interest. As it was the continuance of commission fees in this period led to abuses,[1] and probably resulted in more officers being engaged than was desirable. The abolition of poundage, however, did eliminate the vested interest that the lieutenant-general had in purposely keeping expenditure

1 See below, p. 94.

at a higher level than was warranted. The abolition of the storekeeper's private patronage right as well as his rights to show stores and rent out the king's gunwharf, moreover, must also have promoted the development of a more rational system of appointment and have improved Office security and efficiency.

The establishment of realistic salaries for Ordnance officials was the only successful way of eliminating private fee taking within the department, as was quite clearly appreciated by the first commissioners. 'It is impossible', they wrote, '. . . by any rigour whatsoever to keep officers either in peace or war from irregular gain in their places . . . unless their lives be rendered easy and comfortable to them by constant pay of good salaries'. Some of the major salary increases within the Ordnance Office in this period, then, were a direct corollary to the fee reforms of the 1660s. As we have seen the order of 13 February 1665 that abolished poundage was to lead to a vast increase in the lieutenant-general's salary as well as the establishment of a well salaried independent treasurer. That same order also increased the salaries of the clerk of the Ordnance's first clerk, his minuting clerk (the second clerk) and the other first clerks from £50 to £75, £50 to £65 and £40 to £60 respectively.[1] Thereafter Ordnance salaries were increased intermittently. These increases were usually *ad hoc* awards for individuals. The most notable exception were the increases that occurred as a result of the instructions passed in 1683, when substantial increments were given to four principal officers, a number of clerks and one or two storekeepers. This was the one occasion after the 1660s that a co-ordinated attempt was made to enable Ordnance officials (in the words of James II) 'value their employment and not subject them to a necessity of base compliances with others to the king's prejudice'. By 1683 moreover, the salaries of all the principal officers and many of the under-ministers (with notable exception of the principal officers' first clerks), had reached the level at which they were to remain for the rest of the period. This meant that for most officials there was no compensation for the vast increase in Ordnance business during the post-Revolutionary wars. This point was forcibly made in 1696 when the clerks in ordinary argued in a petition to the board that their salaries, like those of their counterpart in the Navy Offices, should be substantially increased. Little was done about the proposal until 1705 when £40 *per annum* was added to the salaries of the first seven clerks. For the other clerks in ordinary, however, there was no such recompense.

---

1 It appears from the quarter books that the salary of the surveyor-general's second clerk was also increased to £60. The £80 salaries of the lieutenant-general's two clerks were unaffected by this order.

It is difficult to determine whether the increase in salaries for Ordnance officers compensated for their loss of fees, simply because it is almost impossible to establish the size of those fees that were superseded by increased salaries. As Table I shows, however, the value of an official's total allowance in 1714 might well have been less than his predecessor's total income from all sources (including fees) in 1660, even though it was likely that the salary due to his rank had doubled or more than doubled in that time. In the case of the lieutenant-general, for example, the new allowance did not match the annual poundage that we know Legge levied. Nevertheless in a period of general price stability, Ordnance salaries were sufficiently high to enable the office-holders to enjoy a comfortable standard of living. Nor were such salaries exceptional among government servants. By the end of the period printed lists show that in many departments high salaries had been instituted for officials. To take just random examples from among the top tier of officials, by 1708 the commissioners of Customs were receiving £1,000 *per annum* each, the commissioners for the Salt Duty £500 *per annum* each and those for Wine Licences £200 *per annum* each, the treasurer of the Navy £2,000 *per annum,* the members of the Navy Board £500 *per annum* each and the commissioners for Victualling and Transports £400 *per annum* each. Clerks in such offices could expect at least £40 *per annum* and lowly figures such as watchmen and labourers £20 *per annum* These salaries compare favourably with those of other members of the community. By the eighteenth century it has been estimated that the average annual income for the largest land-owners were no more than £5,000 for a peer, £1,200 for a baronet and £400 for a member of the gentry. At the other end of the scale, Gregory King guessed that in the 1690s the yearly income for the family of a labourer or outservant would be about £15, whilst a cottager's family might have to subsist on £6 *per annum.* King also estimated that the average family income of a merchant would be no more than £400, a lawyer £140 and a clergyman £60 *per annum.* It would thus appear from their salaries alone that government officials of this period – by the standards of the day – were generally well remunerated, and that the highest officials were among the most well-paid men in the country.

The limited nature of the evidence also makes it impossible to measure precisely whether the institution of realistic salaries was successful in limiting corruption within the department, for the official who indulged in such practices would have rarely left an account of his proceedings. Nevertheless it is apparent that some officials benefited from the unofficial rewards of office – venality, unauthorised fee taking and the embezzlement of stores and money – as well as the official fee and salary payments.

We have seen in connection with the placing of officials that purchase of office undoubtedly occurred in the early part of the period. The buying and selling of most public offices had been made illegal by a law of 1552, but in the late seventeenth century office was still looked upon as a part of a man's freehold to be bartered on the open market — although the extinction of the life tenure grant made this view even less legitimate. From the evidence that we have of the actual amounts received and paid for office within the department, it would seem that in the early part of the period a poorer Ordnance place (that of a clerk, labourer or gunner) was worth about three times, and a more lucrative office well over three times, its own annual value.

There were many other unofficial rewards which could be gained by an Ordnance officer. There are instances of travelling claims being disallowed, for example, which suggests that some officers were making excessive gains. The two orders of 1683 and 1719 prohibiting the unauthorised sub-letting of official lodgings shows that this practice was not stamped out in this period. Unwarranted fees were sometimes claimed. In the early 1660s Matthew Baylie, the master-general's chief clerk, was charging some gunners five times the annual rate for their warrants; under the Duke of Schomberg several clerks enriched themselves by collecting fees from fraudulent warrants; and it seems that this activity of undue fee-taking had not ceased by the early eighteenth century.[1] Other clerks profited by taking presents (from officers within the department or from merchants and artificers outside) to ensure that payments were made, and by collecting unofficial poundage money. Tradesmen may also have made such payments to Ordnance officers in order to gain contracts. Pepys when he was at the Navy Board was certainly handsomely rewarded for his services by William Warren, the timber merchant, and William Legge does not seem to have been averse to profiteering in this way through the manipulation of the Tangier contracts. Ordnance officials could also make profits by pilfering Ordnance stores, although the evidence suggests that acts of embezzlement were more likely to be committed by the establishment of garrisons and private persons than by Ordnance officers.[2]

Evidence also exists that petty thievery of money, as well as peculation of stores, occurred among minor office-holders. Senior artillery officers, especially, were able to cheat the Office by keeping false musters and purloining the wages of those that had · died on their

1   At least according to Withall, *Exhorbitant Oppressions*, pp. 31, 54.

2   For further details of the unofficial rewards of office, see my 'Place and Profit', pp. 67 *ff*. Also Withall, *Exhorbitant Oppressions*, pp. 19, 34, 40, 46-7, 50, 54.

establishment.¹ Those more important officials directly responsible for Ordnance finances, however, had far greater opportunities to misappropriate government money. This was a result of the confused nature of public and personal credit in the Ordnance Office at this time. Ordnance treasurers had direct control over the disposal of the public funds in their possession, and these were often administered through the private bank account of the official concerned.² Successive treasurers, therefore, could well have used to their own advantage the large cash balances that were sometimes in their hands. This had occurred at the end of the sixteenth century before interest was charged on such 'loans' in 1608.³ Although it is difficult to ascertain whether such practices had official sanction (and therefore, to determine whether the private use of arrearages was 'corrupt' in seventeenth century terms),⁴ there is little doubt that the lack of central control over the departmental accounts enabled treasurers of spending departments to use their cash balances in the interval between receiving and paying out public money. Parliamentary powers in this respect were negligible. Although attempts were made by Commons committees to examine the public accounts in the 1690s and early 1700s, they were largely defeated by the complexity of the accounts. Such committees simply became instruments of party vendettas.⁵ By the early eighteenth century departmental accounts were regularly presented for perusal by members of the Commons,⁶ but such accounts could not have been

1 See WO 46/3, pp. 115-18, report 27 Apr. 1695.

2 See Glynn Mills, Backwell Ledgers, O, fos. 204, 209; P, fo. 209; Q, fo. 109; R. fo.41; S, fo. 195, for Ordnance transactions conducted by George Wharton as first clerk to the treasurer. Lansdell, as deputy treasurer, also opened an account in his name at the Bank of England for Ordnance business, as did the following treasurer, Plumptree. See P.G.M. Dickson, *The Financial Revolution in England: A Study in the Development of Public Credit, 1688-1756* (1967) p. 389. The custody of the Ordnance cash was not officially transferred to the Bank until after Pitt the younger's death. J.E.D. Binney, *British Public Finance and Administration, 1774-79,* (Oxford, 1958), p. 161.

3 Ashley, *'Tudor Office of Ordnance',* p. 125. The balances shown to be held by the treasurers at the end of each Ordnance declared account were quite large under Wharton, 1670-81, (largest £272,364.10s.1½d. at the end of the 1678-9 account). They were reduced to a few thousand pounds in the 1680s but increased again in the following war year. See AO 1/1846, rolls 71 ff. However, it is impossible to determine from these accounts the proportion of cash in hand.

4 Wentworth, as receiver of the northern recusant revenues prior to the civil war, certainly believed that his use of cash balances was a perfectly permissible perquisite of his office. See Aylmer, *King's Servants,* p. 167.

5 Roseveare, *Treasury 1660-1870,* pp. 56 ff. For the requisitioning of Ordnance accounts by these committees see WO 55/395, extract from minutes of public account commissioners, 24 Apr. 1691; WO 55/339, p. 99, warrant, 20 July 1691; *HMC* 17, 13 Rep. V, *House of Lords,* p. 400; WO 55/342, p. 193; WO 55/404, p. 90, commissioners of accounts to O.b., 4 Mar. 1714.

6 For the Ordnance see, e.g., *CJ* XIV, p. 429, 21 Nov. 1704.

subject to searching examination. The ancient Exchequer accounting procedures also did not inspire confidence, as accounts were often not declared for many years,[1] although in the early 1700s the Commons again attempted to bring pressure to bear by asking the auditors to give certificates of the accounts they had passed.[2] The accounting system of the day, therefore, undoubtedly facilitated the private use of government money. There is little hard evidence that Ordnance treasurers misapplied the balances in their hands, but at the death or removal of a treasurer there was certainly a reluctance by the heirs of the deceased or the outgoing official to hand over the cash balances to their successors.[3]

Many Ordnance officials in this period, then, profited from the best of both worlds: the tradition of private fee payments, handed down from medieval bureaucracy; and a newer salaried system, struggling for recognition against the old. The richest officials were those who commanded a large salary and could still exact substantial private rewards: the master who had extensive powers of patronage; the master's secretary, the clerk of the Ordnance, and the master gunner who could still officially exact commission fees; the storekeeper who could show his stores and had small reservoirs of patronage in the early years after the Restoration; and the lieutenant before 1670, and the treasurer after that date, who could manipulate their control of Ordnance finances. The most lucrative of these offices probably had an annual total value (from all sources) of thousands rather than hundreds of pounds.

1   For the dates of declaration of Ordnance accounts see AO 1/1846, rolls 71 ff. *Cal. Treas. Books 1667-8*, p. 127, minute 26 Nov. 1667; *Ibid. 1669-72*, pp. 356, 409, 467-8, 587, 689, 908, 955, orders and letters 1 Feb., 19 Apr., 7, 29 June, 14 Nov. 1670, 15 July, 6 Nov. 1671; WO 55/392, pp. 42-3, 69, 73, orders and warrants, 19 Nov. 1673, 28 Feb. 1678, 8 Mar. 1679; WO 55/1795, petition of Wharton, letter of J. Ernle; T. 1/82, no. 57, Lowndes to Auditors, 7 Nov. 1702; T. 1/86, no. 43, Bridges to Godolphin, 16 June 1703; WO 47/23, p. 275, 20 Apr. 1706; WO 47/24, p. 454, 20 May 1707; WO 47/25, p.8, 8 July 1704, p. 74, 28 Aug. 1707; *Cal. Treas. Books 1709*, p. 98, warrant 9 Mar. 1709, p. 47, minute 1 Sept. 1710; T. 1/133, fo. 321, O.b. to treasurer, 31 May 1711.

2   E.g. *CJ* XVI, 149, 10 Mar. 1709, p. 155, 14 Mar. 1709, p. 329, 21 Feb. 1710; *CJ* XVII, 101, 21 Feb. 1712.

3   See *Cal. Treas. Books 1681-5*, pp. 378-9, warrant 25 Jan. 1682; WO 55/395, Bertie's representation, 25 Jan. 1683; T. 1/63, fo. 43, 23 Aug. 1699; *Ibid. 1710*, p. 6, minute 10 Feb. 1710, p. 171, Lowndes to Mordaunt and Bertie, 14 Feb. 1710; *Ibid. 1711*, p. 411. Harley to Bertie's executors & Churchill, 18 Aug. 1711; T. 1/137, no. 15, Charles Bertie (younger's) letter, 6 Sept. 1711; WO 47/27. p. 119; WO 47/28, pp. 7, 22, 26, 55, 82, 91, 119, 154; WO 47/31, p. 245, minutes re. Eversfield's balance, 21 Dec. 1714 − 28 Aug. 1718. For the dates of payment of the balance of Bertie's and Eversfield's 1698-9, 1704-5 and 1711-12 accounts, see *Cal. Treas. Books 1695-1702*, pt. I, p.d lxxvii; *ibid. 1712*, pt. I, p.ccvi.

Against these rewards of office, however, must be balanced the financial costs of a place in the Ordnance: the pledging of personal fortune for those holding the most responsible positions; the miscellaneous expenses of office for many other officers; and the irregular payment of allowances, fees and quarter salaries for all office-holders irrespective of their place in the department.

The principal Ordnance officers were required to give substantial security for their offices. Richard Marsh, as principal storekeeper, for example, was ordered to enter into security with sufficient sureties for £4,000; William Merchant, as an out storekeeper, was ordered to make a bond for £1,000, with two sureties standing £500 each; and it is clear that similar sums were required from other storekeepers[1] The security a treasurer had to give was even more demanding. Wharton had to have sureties for £30,000, 'for . . . answering what shall appear to be due upon the balance of his accounts'.[2] Bertie was ordered to give security on his own bond for only £10,000, but in 1699 the board thought it necessary that two sureties were bound with Mordaunt, the succeeding treasurer, for £10,000, as over £113,000 in money and tallies was to be paid over to him.[3] When he was again made treasurer in 1705, Mordaunt entered into a bond with four merchants, who were bound jointly as sureties for £10,000. One of these, John Lansdell, was to be his deputy, even though it was strictly against the department's rules for one officer to stand security for another.[4] The majority of Ordnance officers who held responsible offices must not only have been sufficiently well endowed or well connected to afford the costs of entering into a bond for large amounts of money as security, but must also have had the wherewithal to advance money for the service.[5] The close inter-communion between public and private credit might have resulted in undue private gain, but it also meant the pledging of personal fortunes in times of stringent credit to ensure the completion of the king's service.[6]

1 PRO 30 37/17, warrant 17 Oct. 1668; WO 55/340, fo. 143, 1 Mar. 1694; WO 46/2, p. 14, minute 13 Nov. 1683, p. 185, Watkinson to O.b., 10 Nov. 1683. The security requirement even extended to Office labourers. See WO 47/19b, minute 14 May 1675.

2 WO 47/9, fo. 49, Guy to Ordnance commissioners, 29 July 1680.

3 WO 46/4, p. 49, O.b. to Romney, 23 June 1699, pp. 49-50, Same to Same, 6 July 1699, p. 58, Romney to O.b., 25 July 1699; T. 1/65, fos. 9-11, 15, 21, 23.

4 WO 47/22, p. 254, 10 July 1705; WO 47/13, fo. 28, 13 Feb. 1683.

5 *Cal. SP Dom. 1690-1*, p. 290, Godolphin to the king, 3 Mar. 1691. Also see WO 51/8, fo. 131, payment to Nicholls, 25 Nov. 1667; WO 51/9, fo. 24, payment to Moore, 16 Dec. 1667; WO 51/12, fo. 121, payment to Beaumont, executor of Beck, 2 Jan. 1672.

6 Roseveare, *Treasury 1660-1870*, p. 53; John Childs, *The Army of Charles II* (1976), pp. 53-4.

Patent expenses, which by 1701 were as high as £60 for the office of storekeeper,[1] were a further outgoing for those holding high office on their first obtaining a place and, if they were still in office, at the beginning of each new reign when their patents (if they were held at the Crown's pleasure) would be re-newed. For other officers lower down the departmental hierarchy — especially the storekeepers of the outports — many miscellaneous expenses could be incurred. Towards the end of his long tenure of office at Hull, storekeeper Watkinson complained that he was owed several hundred pounds for his salary and for the disbursements he had made to keep the stores from 'utter ruin', and desired that these sums might be paid him in order that he could leave the town without being indebted to anyone. Another Hull store-keeper, William Idell, found that he was 'a great deal . . . out of purse' because his bills had not been passed by the board.[2] The cost of being an engineer or a gunner could be as considerable. Sir Godfrey Lloyd, the chief engineer, spent £600 of his own money in the king's service, and his brother, Sir Charles Lloyd, who died in office soon after the Restoration, had been obliged to borrow money to pay off his debts.[3] Other more humble feed gunners petitioned that they were unable to manage because out of the half years salary that had been listed to them, £3 was to be sent out for their clothes, 30s. each for their warrants and 20s. each for their badges.[4]

As may be gathered from some of the above petitions there was never a certainty of compensation for Ordnance personnel. The payment of patent fees was invariably in arrears.[5] Quarter salaries were also paid irregularly. Advances were sometimes made,[6] but it was much more usual for quarter payments to be made in arrears, the length of time before payment depending on the Treasury's financial state. Government officials in this period had to become accustomed to savage retrenchments, and this could result in a suspension of their salary payment.[7] Yet even when there was no official retrenchment

1 Cumbria RO, Lonsdale MS., James Lowther to Sir John Lowther, 22 Feb. 1701.

2 WO 46/2, pp. 208-9, Watkinson to Dartmouth, 20 Apr. 1684, pp. 209-10, declaration of Watkinson to Dartmouth; WO 55/1796, Duxbury to Hubbald, 31 Mar. 1686, Idell to Hubbald, 16 Jan. 1692.

3 Cal. SP Dom. 1670, p. 621; Ibid. 1661-2, p. 223, petitions of Blanch, and Honoria.

4 WO 44/715, petition of feed gunners to Goodricke.

5 Cal. Treas. Books 1667-8, pp. 545, 547, 555, 557; T. 1/16, fo. 63, Howard's certificate, 23 Nov. 1691; T. 1/80, fo. 109, Howard's certificate, 27 Jan. 1689; Sloane 836, fos. 85-6.

6 WO 55/1796, 21 Sept. 1686; WO 47/31, p. 307, 21 Oct. 1718.

7 See e.g. the order in Cal. Treas. Books 1676-9, pp. 116-18, 25 Jan. 1676.

there was no guarantee that salaries would be paid in time. This uncertainty is reflected in a note written from Robert Mynors, storekeeper at Upnor Castle in June 1692. 'Pray two words the next when you think we shall have any salary', he wrote, 'for at this time I have more than ordinary occasion for money'.[1]

The Ordnance often owed money to principal officers at the time of their death or dismissal from office. Ten years after William Billers had been dismissed from office as clerk of deliveries, he was still claiming the £264. 14s. 10d. owed him for his salary and travelling expenses prior to his dismissal in June 1660. Edward Conyers petitioned for a similar sum after his dismissal. Nearly £750 remained unpaid of Sir Edward Sherburne's patent fee at the time of his dismissal in 1688, and this sum was quite apart from the £943. 9s. 8d. that was due to his father as clerk of the Ordnance on his death in 1641. The Duke of Schomberg was owed £4,000 on his death for two quarter payments as master-general, for his allowance of £10 per day as master of the Irish artillery train, and for money lent the Office to buy arms. The executors of William Meesters maintained that he was owed over £7,000 by the Office at the time of his death, and although some of the claims for disbursements made by the king's verbal order were challenged by the board, it had no objection to the claims totalling over £1,500 for his unpaid allowances.[2] Storekeepers also petitioned for unpaid allowances. Francis Povey begged Dartmouth that his disbursements, stopped because he provided stores at the insistence of the governor but without the board's order, should be allowed him, because the greatest part of his small estate depended on the payment; and John Duxbury at Hull claimed that for about eight years he had not received an allowance for his work as clerk of the works there.[3] Ordnance military personnel suffered from similar debts. De Gomme's pension of £300 *per annum* was unpaid, 1663-6, despite it having been ordered that payments should continue during the stop of pensions; at the time of the death of Captain James Archer, an Ordnance engineer, it was certified that £350 was owed his widow because of the arrears due to her husband and her two sons; the widow of Captain Thomas Phillips petitioned for the £811 unpaid to her husband during his life-time; and Withall claimed that he was owed over £3,000 by the department, nearly £1,400 of which was arrears of full and half pay, travelling charges and other

1   WO 55/1795, Mynors to Hubbald, 4 June 1692.
2   *Cal. SP Dom. 1670*, pp. 664-5; WO 44/714, 16 Feb. 1689; See below, p. 100 n. 4; *Cal. SP Dom. 1661-2*, p. 229; Notts. CRO., DDS 49/46, certificate 30 Dec. 1690; WO 46/4, pp. 50 ff., report of the board and account; WO 46/5, pp. 30 ff., O.b. to Romney, 4 Mar. 1701 and account.
3   D.1778/V 32, n.d.; WO 44/714, petition to Schomberg.

disbursements.[1] In June 1682 there were arrears due to gunners on the quarter books of the Office amounting to £573. 10s. 8d., and several other gunners remained unpaid by the Office for their work in demolishing Tangier, years after the operation had been completed.[2]

A place in the Ordnance Office, therefore, was not necessarily commensurate with wealth. Some officers did indeed succeed in making a great deal of money from their place in the Ordnance Office. The names of William Legge, Sir Bernard de Gomme and Michael Richards, who all left sizeable bequests in their wills as well as large personal estates, may be cited with that of Sir George Wharton as examples of officers who made small fortunes in the king's Ordnance service.[3] But there were also other officers who did not gain great wealth from their Ordnance careers. Both Sir Edward Sherburne and Sir Henry Sheer, for example, after they had been dismissed at the time of the Revolution, found it difficult to subsist on what they had gained from office. Sherburne, who had spent half a life time as clerk of the Ordnance, was reduced 'to the lowest of extremities and a deplorable poverty' towards the end of his life and depended on charitable handouts from the Treasury, whilst Sheer could only boast of a 'poor fortune' when he made his will in 1709.[4]

An Ordnance place at best provided a chance for the career administrator to better himself and to make a small fortune. But there was no guarantee of wealth from an Ordnance career, nor a certainty of preferment or a surety of income. Nor was the encumbent ensured of permanent tenure devoid from the responsibilities of his office. Indeed for the vast majority of principal officers of the period who came from the gentry classes, an Ordnance place might well not have lived up to their initial expectations. Many such officers might have agreed with James Lowther that 'for a man that had a good clear estate and a handsome parcel of money in his pocket', there was 'not so much to be got

---

1 SP 44/18, p.115; Cal. SP Dom., 1665-6, p. 421, May? 1666; Ibid. 1667-8, p. 141, 1667?; Ibid. 1680-1, p. 136, warrant 17 Jan. 1681; WO 46/3, p. 38; Withall, Exhorbitant Oppressions, pp. 28 ff., (Withall's figure was probably a gross exaggeration).

2 D. 1778/V 79; WO 44/714, petition of 16 gunners and endorsement by Leake, 19 Dec. 1689, petitions of Hunter and Jackett, gunners at Tangier.

3 Legge left £4,000 (in 1670) and estate and lease of Alice Holt Forest, de Gomme, c.£3,750 in bequests (in 1685) and various manors in Kent, and Richards, c.£8,200 (in 1722) and estates. Prob. 11/335, fo. 178; Prob. 11/381, fos. 199 ff., Prob. 11/584, fos. 270-1. For Wharton, above, p. 84. Although all these men were career officers, it is impossible to determine how much of their wealth was made in the king's service.

4 See Sloane 836, fos. 85-6; Sloan 1048; Sloane 4067 fo. 148; T.1/80, fo. 108; Prob. 11/515, fo. 57. Again it is not possible to gauge the wealth of either man at the time of his dismissal.

by a middling place as people imagine considering the confinement withal'.[1]

Conclusion

On one occasion Pepys spoke to Christopher Wren 'of the corruption of the court and how unfit it is for ingenious men, and himself particularly, to live in it where a man cannot get suitability without breach of his honour', and on another occasion he noted that:

> an ignorant pretender to an office has but, by his interest, to get himself put into one, how unfitsoever he knows himself and indisposed for the labour necessary to render him otherwise. For, from all my observation and more particularly in the Navy, no degree of inexperience or unusefulness by age or otherways, provided he can but keep himself from making enemies by being troublesome in his office, can suffice to turn a man out on't, without some provision made for rendering such his removal easy to him by pension or other equivalent, if not advantage, *verbi gratia*.[2]

Some Ordnance personnel undoubtedly lived up to Pepys's condemnation of office-holders. A number of Ordnance officers such as the Duke of Marlborough, Thomas Erle, and Sir William Trumbull, attended board meetings infrequently and could have taken little part in the actual running of affairs. Some, such as John Swaddell and Harry Mordaunt, appointed deputies to do their work in the Office. Some, like Richard Marsh, were too old to perform their functions efficiently.[3] Others, like Jonas Moore junior and Robert Lowther, were unsuited temperamentally to working as a member of the board. The characters of a number of Ordnance officers were also unsuited to government service.

Nevertheless, there were some hardworking and ingenious men who held places in the Ordnance Office in this period. Duncomb and Dartmouth were rigorous heads of the department; Goodricke, Sherburne and Christopher Musgrave junior were efficient and painstaking administrators; and Jonas Moore senior, Edward Sherburne, George Wharton and Samual Fortrey were enlightened office-holders, who also made a significant contribution to the advancement of science and the arts. Little is known of the officials in subordinate positions, but there were

---

1 Quoted in Holmes, p. 127.

2 *Pepys Diary*, **VIII**, 108, 27 Sept. 1668; *Naval Minutes*, p. 256.

3 George Marsh was appointed as assistant to his father because of the 'great age' of Richard Marsh (WO 55/425, p. 106, warrant 19 Mar. 1667). Sherburne's efficiency as an administrator may also have been impaired because of his age. For some fifteen years before his dismissal at the age of 70, the observation was made that he was 'unable through his age and infirmities' to attend the train of artillery. See *Letters . . . to Sir Joseph Williamson . . .* ed. Christie, Camden Society new series VIII (1874), I, 45, Swaddell to Williamson, 16 June 1673.

some loyal servants among them who held office for long periods of time and who must have gained an enormous amount of expertise in the running of Office affairs.

Indeed the period witnessed notable developments in the professional standing of some Ordnance officers. The senior ranks of the service may have been staffed for the most part by dispensable gentlemen amateurs, but their clerks had ceased to be mere personal servants and had become permanent salaried public servants. The opportunities of promotion to the rank of principal officer had declined for such men but their chances of advancing within their own grade had increased, especially if they were able and conscientious officers. The beginnings of a distinction between civil and military personnel was a part of this process of professionalisation. In the late seventeenth century there was little distinction between the civil and military Ordnance officer, but as the department expanded it grew more specialised, and by the early eighteenth century distinct civil and military branches of the service were recognised.[1]

The growth of the idea of a public service, in which profit was not the sole criterion of place, may thus be discerned in the Ordnance Office in this period. Richmond's observation when he was master-general in 1785, that the officers of the board were executing a 'public trust' without 'prejudice or inclination one way or other',[2] might equally have been said by his predecessor in the early eighteenth century. Allied to this was the emergence of a tradition of service among successive generations of the same family. The Legges, the Musgraves and the Moores were the counterpart in the government service of the military families of Restoration England.[3] As one historian has rightly pointed out, 'merit as the basis of appointment and promotion, permanent tenure and complete aloofness from all political bias and subservience did not begin in 1853, and may be applied to some parts of the administration in the first generation of the eighteenth century'.[4]

1 The two branches were certainly in existence after the French Wars. (See King's 70, fos. 64-5, warrant reorganising the civil establishment, 1 July 1718). The last time that both civil and military establishments were listed together on the same quarter book appears to have been for the quarter ending 31 March 1719 (WO 54/77). This does not of course mean that the two branches were mutually exclusive. See Withall, *Exhorbitant Oppressions*, pp. 19, 58.

2 See WO 46/19, p.30, Richmond to Laver, 3 June 1785.

3 Such as the Cravens, the de Veres, the Russells and the Sidneys. Childs, p. 36.

4 E. Hughes, *Studies in Administration and Finance, 1558-1825* (Manchester, 1934), p. 267.

3

ORDNANCE STORES

Types

The Ordnance Office was responsible for supplying the armed forces with a vast range of military equipment. Ordnance stores included brass and iron guns of a wide variety of different types, and a corresponding profusion of different shots and carriages for the guns; a host of different kinds of firearms and hand weapons; gunners' and musketeers' accessories; gunpowder and primitive explosives; and innumerable miscellaneous habiliments of war.

There was a proliferation of different types of weapon in this period. Mortars — usually of brass with short barrels, thick walls and wide bores, throwing the missile in a high trajectory — were commonly used.[1] Heavy artillery guns and ships' pieces ranged in size from the cannon to the diminutive falconet.[2] In between these extremes there were demi-cannon, culverin, demi-culverin, saker, minion, and falcon, each of a different size and range, and each carrying a different weight shot.[3] Within this broad classification of guns there were sometimes several varieties of one particular type, but by the end of the period many of the varieties had disappeared and heavy ordnance was classified by the weight of the shot discharged.[4] It was impossible, however, for there to be complete standardisation within the different categories of cannon — despite the lists of regulation sizes for ordnance published by the department[5]— for the process of casting involved the making of a clay mould, which had to be broken every time a gun was made to retrieve the cast gun, so that no two pieces of heavy ordnance could be made

---

1 *The Armouries of the Tower of London*, Vol. I: *Ordnance*, ed. H.L. Blackmore, (HMSO 1976), contains an excellent catalogue and glossary relating to cannon, mortars, carriages and gunners' accessories.

2 *Ibid.* p. 16; W.Y. Carman, *A History of Firearms to 1914* (1955), pp. 55-8.

3 Cf. the cannon and the falconet's estimated weight, calibre, shot and point-blank range (*c.* 7000 to 300 lbs; 8 to 2 ins; 50 to 2 lbs; and 350 to 200 yards). Few contemporary writers, however, agree on the size and range of types of ordnance. See *The Naval Tracts of Sir William Monson*, ed. M. Oppenheim, vol. III, Navy Records Soc. 45 (1914), pp. 36-42; C.J. Ffoulkes, *The Gunfounders of England* (Cambridge, 1937), pp. 92, 103; O.F.G. Hogg, *Artillery; Its Origin, Heyday and Decline* (1970), pp. 266-72; D.E. Lewis, 'The Use of Ordnance in Early Modern Warfare', (unpublished Manchester M.A. thesis, 1971), p. 52; Chandler, pp. 177 ff.; *The Armouries of the Tower of London,* 1,391.

4 Hogg, *Artillery*, pp. 57-8. The 1665 remain is one of the earliest inventories to describe cannon by weight of shot, as well as by name. *The Armouries of the Tower of London*, I, 306.

5 See e.g. the list drawn up by the surveyor-general in 1725. *Ibid.* pp. 399-400.

exactly alike. Consequently, it was not unusual to find that there were several hundredweights difference in the weights of guns cast in any one batch.[1]

Cannon could also be distinguished by the type of metal used in their manufacture. The great majority of guns made for the Ordnance Office in this period were iron cast. A number of guns, however, were made from bronze, an alloy of copper, tin, and other elements,[2] and these were referred to as 'brass' ordnance. Brass cannon did not rust and were not as susceptible to fracture as iron. Because of the strength of the metal, guns of a similar calibre could be made much smaller in bronze than iron and were consequently lighter.[3] The lighter and more durable brass ordnance was, therefore, favoured for use in the field, whilst iron ordnance was preferred for the larger pieces mounted in garrisons and on board ship, although this distinction was by no means always adhered to.[4]

The number of different kinds of firearm in use in this period for which the Ordnance was responsible, was as great as the many types of cannon. The matchlock musket, fired by a separate charge of match, was still being used, but the snaphance musket, operated by a piece of flint in the cock striking a serrated steel hammer and giving a charge to the priming powder, was becoming increasingly popular. In addition to these firearms, musketoons, blunderbusses, pistols, dragons, carbines, fusils, and numerous other weapons which are almost impossible today to identify, were also issued.[5]

Miscellaneous accessories, which were all provided by the Ordnance Office, accompanied these weapons. Gunners required ladles for deter-

---

1 A.R. Hall, *Ballistics in the Seventeenth Century* (Cambridge, 1952), p. 12. It was not until the end of the eighteenth century that the Ordnance Office insisted that guns should be bored from the solid state rather than cast. (See H.C. Tomlinson, 'Wealden Gunfounding: An Analysis of its Demise in the Eighteenth Century', *EcHR* 2nd Ser. 29 (1976), p. 388). This process may well have resulted in a more uniform weight of gun.

2 For a chemical analysis of bronze cannon, see, *The Armouries of the Tower of London*, I, 406-9.

3 A.P. McGowan, 'The Royal Navy under the First Duke of Buckingham, Lord High Admiral, 1618-28' (unpublished London Ph.D. thesis, 1967), p. 259; Lewis, p. 24.

4 *Ibid.; Cal. SP Col. Am. & W. Indies 1693-6*, p. 123, O.b. to Lords of Trade, 1 July 1693; 'none but iron guns are allowed for any garrisons at home or abroad'. *Cal. SP. Dom. 1670*, p. 556, warrant Nov. 1670 for recasting brass guns from garrisons for first rate frigates.

5 Ffoulkes, *Arms and Armament*, pp. 52 ff.; H.L. Blackmore, *British Military Firearms, 1650-1850* (1961), pp. 32, 38; J.F. Hayward, *The Art of the Gunmaker* (1962), pp. 263-70; Carman, pp. 126-7.

mining the correct amount of charge, rammers for securing the charge, linstocks for holding the match, pick or priming wire for clearing the vent of a gun, sponges for cleaning out the bore of the gun and searchers for discovering defects in the bore. Other accoutrements were hand-spikes, wedges, tackles, gyns, levers, gundrugs, slings and sheers for moving, mounting and dismounting guns from gun carriages.[1] The musketeers were also furnished by the Ordnance Office with numerous miscellanies: bandoliers for holding charges, though cartridges carried in a cartouch box were increasingly being used; powder horns; supplies of match (smouldering cotton cord carried in a metal tube), or flints for flintlocks which had to be replaced every twenty rounds; and ram-rods (scouring sticks) for ramming the charge. Bayonets were also an attachment the musketeer might carry, especially after 1678, when, instead of the medieval pike, the bayonet was issued as a standard piece of military equipment to the grenadier companies that were added to the British regiments in that year. At first the bayonet was plugged in to the muzzle of the musket, thereby preventing the gun from being fired, and only later fixed externally by the means of a ring or socket.[2]

It was also the responsibility of the Ordnance Office to ensure that the ammunition for these guns and firearms was supplied. Gunpowder, shot of different kinds (round, barred, double-headed, musket), primi-tive shells, carcasses, grenades, fireworks and bombs were some of the explosives in use in this period.[3]

Guns and explosives were not the only kinds of store that came under the jurisdiction of the Ordnance Office. The Armoury was joined to the Ordnance Office in 1671, after the death of the master of the Armouries, William Legge, and from this date the Ordnance was responsible for the store and distribution of armour.[4] It is likely, how-ever, that armour was used mainly for ceremonial occasions at this time, judging by the Armoury issue book which records only eighty-eight issues from 7 December 1682 to 20 October 1714.[5] A similar amalga-mation of the Tents and Toils with the Ordnance Office occurred in

---

1 Ffoulkes, *Arms and Armament*, p. 100, fig. 111, for the diagram of parts of a gun carriage and some gunner's accessories; Hogg, *Artillery*, pp. 235-8.

2 Ffoulkes, *Arms and Armament*, pp. 53-4, 69 ff.; Blackmore, pp. 31-2; Childs, pp. 61-2.

3 Carman, pp. 161 ff., Ffoulkes, *Arms and Armament*, p. 65.

4 *Cal. SP Dom. 1667-8*, p. 291, 16 Mar. 1668; PC 6/18, pp. 134-5, order 8 Oct. 1669; SP 29/266, fo. 163, 8 Oct. 1669. For the declared account of the old Armoury Office, 1 Oct. 1660– 31 Oct. 1670, see AO 1/2300, roll 10.

5 WO 55/1656. For the types of store under the surveillance of the keeper of the Armoury, 2 Nov. 1682 – 30 June 1686, see AO 1/2301, rolls 11, 13, 14, 15.

October 1685, which resulted in the Ordnance having the direct supervision of the storage and issue of tents, waggons and other accompanying utensils.[1] Beds, bedding and flags for garrisons, and uniforms for
the Ordnance establishment were some of the other non-military stores
provided by the Office.[2]

This brief survey of the stores for which the Office was accountable
cannot possibly indicate the many types of Ordnance stores in use in
this period. A greater insight into the mass of different Ordnance
equipment may be gained from a study of one of the Ordnance store
registers. A huge ledger of the receipts, returns and issues of Ordnance
stores from 21 June 1675 to 2 September 1679, has recently been
analysed by an historian, who has identified about 500 classes of items
in the ledger, each of which may be subdivided into many different
types of store. Twenty-five different types of brass and iron cannon,
for example, were listed. Each class, moreover, contained a number of
guns of different lengths, so that in all there were 160 varieties of
name, material and size of gun. Ammunition varied from massive
eighteen inch projectiles to shells for three pounder guns. Other projectiles included double-headed shot, cross-barred shot, chain shot,
langer shot, fire shot and round shot, all in a number of different
calibres. Among the artillery stores were halberds, bills and five different lengths of pike for use in the Army and Navy. Finally, at the end of
the volume came lists of armour and a huge alphabetical list of the
general habiliments of war from adzes to yarn.[3]

Contracting and Manufacture

Although the Ordnance Office was accountable for this vast range of
military equipment, the department itself did not directly manufacture
the goods that it was responsible for supplying. At this time the
principal officers of the Ordnance simply bargained 'with the ablest and
fittest artificers or merchants and such as will be ready and willing to

---

1 *Cal. SP Dom. 1685*, p. 340, warrant to Dartmouth, 4 Oct. 1685. Prior to this
date the Tents and Toils Office was under the command of the Lord Chamberlain
of the Household. It appears, however, that even before 1685 the Office had
some responsibility for the issue of their stores. For issues of waggons by the
Ordnance prior to 1685 see *Cal. SP Dom. 1661-2*, p. 436, warrant to Legge, 13
July 1662. For tents see *Cal. SP Dom. 1661-2*, p. 536, Williamson's memo. Oct.
1662.

2 For issues of beds and bedding for garrisons see WO 47/19a, p. 70, 11 Nov.
1668, p. 101, 5 Dec. 1668. For flags WO 47/5, p. 81, 23 July 1661; WO 47/24,
p. 338, 4 Mar. 1707, p. 469, 17 May 1707, p. 503, 19 June 1707. For uniforms
WO 47/31, p. 302, 17 Oct. 1718.

3 See W. Reid, 'Balkes, Balls and Bandoliers: A Stores Ledger in the Tower of
London', *Journal of the Society of Archivists, 2* (1960-4), pp. 403-10.

serve . . . in every kind the best stuff and the best cheap'[1] and contracted with them for the stores. The state did not directly intervene in the provision of cannon, gunpowder and handguns, for example, until the building of Woolwich foundry for brass ordnance in 1716, the assumption of control by the government in 1759 of the Faversham gunpowder works, which became the Royal Gunpowder Factory, and the creation of a government handgun establishment in Birmingham in 1804.[2] Until the eighteenth century the members of the Ordnance board were simply middlemen, untimately accountable for the goods being produced but having no immediate concern in their manufacture, although Ordnance engineers occasionally produced designs for stores and sometimes even supervised casting operations.[3]

The Ordnance officers, then, were not generally involved in the process of manufacture of the stores they supplied. Nevertheless, it is necessary to examine briefly the internal organisation of one or two of the key Ordnance industries (in particular gunfounding, small arms manufacture and gunpowder making), in order to appreciate some of the difficulties with which the department had to contend in maintaining ordnance supplies.

The internal organisation of the cannon foundries was under the control of the gunfounders who leased the land, provided the ore and fuel for the working founder, and generally organised production. For most of the seventeenth century, the monopoly of providing iron guns and shot[4] for the Ordnance Office was in the hands of the Browne family, who owned furnaces at Buckland in Surrey, and at Spelmonden and Horsemonden in Kent. In the early years after the Restoration the family was by far the biggest ordnance suppliers to the government. From July 1664 to May 1678, bills were made out to George and John Browne worth c. £136,693 for about 3,871 tons of iron guns, which sums were greatly in excess of those of any other iron ordnance contractor. It should not be surmised, however, that the Brownes executed all the contracts for which this money was paid. Indeed we know that the Browne family had business connections with such ironmasters as

1 King's 70, fo. 21, 1683 instructions.

2 See Ffoulkes, *Gunfounders*, pp. 61-3; Hogg, *Royal Arsenal*, pp. 250-1, A. Percival, *The Faversham Gunpowder Industry*, Faversham Society Papers no. 4 (1967), p. 7; Hogg, *Artillery*, p. 133; Glover, p. 61.

3 Particularly the firemasters, it seems. See WO 55/475, Dartmouth to Tichburne, 1 Mar. 1688; WO 47/12, fos. 9, 19, minutes 7, 21 Oct. 1682; WO 48/22, payment to De Rüis, 30 June 1684. The master gunner was also sometimes involved. See *The Armouries of the Tower of London*, I, 94 re. 1687 bronze mortar.

4 For bronze cannon (many of which were made at Moorfields prior to the opening of the Woolwich foundry in 1716) see *ibid*. pp. 15-16.

the Courthorpes, William Dyke and Thomas Foley. Arrangements like these facilitated sub-contracting between the various Wealden gunfounders.[1]

Such co-operation was necessitated because of the huge contracts made by the Brownes with the Ordnance Office. The largest single contract made by the Brownes in the early 1660s was for 1,500 iron guns,[2] and this order could not possibly have been executed by only one contractor because the unit of production of any one furnace was small. Less than seven tons of ordnance could generally be produced in any one found-day (which lasted a week), and there were only about thirty found-days in any one year, so that one furnace was usually capable of smelting no more than 200 tons of metal *per annum*.[3] In such circumstances co-operation between gunfounders was inevitable. Even then there was no guarantee that ordnance would be quickly delivered from the foundries. A letter from George Browne to the Ordnance board in September 1664, reveals some of the difficulties of gunfounding, which made delays unavoidable. He had received a note from his brother that the Ordnance Office required that forty-one cannon of seven, 200 demi-cannon, fifty demi-culver cuts, and 100 saker cuts be delivered within three months. Browne pointed out that the cannon of seven could only be made of brass, because if they were of iron the metal would have to be kept so long in the mould that the piece would be liable to fracture. If the weather was suitable for the transportation of the brass, however, he promised to undertake to cast one cannon of seven weekly, this being as much metal as the furnace could contain at any one time. Browne also considered that it would be 'very uncertain' to cast the demi-cannon of iron, but he did not doubt he would be able to deliver fifty such guns at or before the following midsummer. The delivery of the remainder of the order, however, could not be guaranteed before the midsummer of 1666, because the only available furnace could not cast more than fifty guns at one blowing. Provisions for other furnaces could not be made before the following summer, which meant that the rest of the order would not be ready until the spring of 1666.[4] Over seventy years later it was

1   For the above see 'Wealden Gunfounding. . .', pp. 384-6.

2   D.C. Coleman, 'The Economy of Kent under the later Stuarts' (unpublished London Ph. D. thesis, 1951), pp. 182-3.

3   Hall, p. 14. This is, of course, an average estimate rather than a general norm. For the capacity of any one furnace depended on its size and the duration of the annual blasts (which, in turn, depended on the water supply). Output, therefore, fluctuated violently from year to year. See Tomlinson 'Wealden Gunfounding' p. 399, appendix table IV, for the output at Heathfield furnace, 1725-39.

4   Kent CRO, transcripts 1295/69, Browne to ?, 21 Sept. 1664.

still not possible for a batch of guns to be delivered in less than a year.[1]

The difficulties of production of iron cannon were compounded by the difficulties of carriage in the Wealden area. A sufficient quantity of rain was necessary to enable the blow furnaces to function effectively, but such rain made transportation almost impossible. Water carriage was available for the transportation of ordnance in the latter stage of its journey to Woolwich for proof, but in the immediate vicinity of the furnace, gunfounders were dependent on land carriage. Such roads that were available for the use of the gunfounders in the Weald were little better than clay tracks, which were difficult to negotiate in the summer months and impassible in winter.[2]

Firearms were more easily supplied than heavy iron ordnance. There were few problems of transportation as firearms were lighter and easier to handle than cannon. Moreover, contracts were usually made with London gunmakers who worked in the Minories and East Smithfield in the vicinity of the Tower, and so firearms only needed to be carried a few miles at most to the Tower proofyard. It was also less likely that contracts for small arms would be subject to delays because of problems of manufacture.[3] The trade of gunmaking, unlike gunfounding, was not so directly dependent on the weather, and could be practised all the year round. Consequently orders could be fulfilled relatively quickly and regularly. In times of emergency in wartime, for instance, gunmakers were able to supply the Office with 2,000 firearms a month.[4]

Firearms do not seem to have been made in the Tower in this period, although they were in the sixteenth century.[5] A number of gunsmiths worked in the Small Gun Office under the furbisher and his assistant, but they were generally preoccupied with the repair rather than the manufacture of firearms. The furbishers officially attached to the Ordnance Office were capable gunsmiths in their own right, responsible

---

1   See, e.g. Fuller to Remnant, 19 Sept. 1735, in Herbert Blackman, 'Gunfounding at Heathfield in the Eighteenth Century', *Sussex Archaeological Collections* 67 (1926), pp. 39.

2   Straker, pp. 183 ff. For a discussion of water transport in the Wealden area see Coleman, 'Economy of Kent', pp. 289-96.

3   Although the making of a handgun was a complex operation involving the assembly of a number of separate items of manufacture – including barrels, locks, flints, and stocks, ramrods and bayonets – which were each made by different skilled artisans working in distinct trades, and then assembled by the gunmaker. See Glover, pp. 47 ff.

4   Blackmore, pp. 23, 39-40. WO 55/344, p. 128, letter 7 Feb. 1706.

5   Ashley, 'Tudor Office of Ordnance', p. 57.

for the viewing of arms, the producing of pattern muskets and the supervising of other gunsmiths in the fixing of weapons.[1] Contracts for the manufacture of firearms, however, were made by the Ordnance board with external gunmakers, who were not necessarily officials of the Office, although the master gunmaker, like the master founder, presumably had a significant share of the contracts.

The Company of London Gunmakers, of which the Ordnance master gunmaker was usually a member, played an important part in the negotiating for contracts from its gaining independence from the tutelage of the Armourers and Blacksmith's Company in the 1630s. The strength of the Company was such by 1657, that an agreement was made between the gunmakers and Ordnance officers that all arms contracts should be assigned to the Company, which would undertake distribution to the various gunmakers, rather than contracts being assigned directly to individual contractors.[2] By the early years of the eighteenth century there were open contracts with the Company of London Gunmakers to provide arms according to their own pattern and prices.[3]

In the later period, however, the London gunmakers were not able to monopolise the contracts. The first orders for snaphance muskets were made with the Birmingham gunmakers in 1689, and from 1692 more regular contracts were made with them for the delivery of 200 muskets a month. A further attempt was made to reduce the control of the London gunmakers and build up a store of parts, by the placing of separate orders for barrels and locks with the Birmingham gunsmiths. These were then proved and stored in the Tower and distributed to the London gunmakers to make into firearms.[4] The London gunmakers represented to the board the hardships that this system caused among their members, but it was continued with, as the board considered that previously the service had been interrupted by the London gunmakers not being furnished with sufficient supplies of barrels and locks.[5] The London gunmakers were further displeased when the pressure of war necessitated large orders to be made with gunmakers in Holland. When a contract which had been made with a gunsmith at Rotterdam, for instance, was not liable to be fulfilled in time, the board considered that it would give the home gunsmiths 'a handle to renew their clamour

[1] WO 47/24, p. 66, order 12 Sept. 1706; Blackmore, p. 41; Walter M. Stern, 'Gunmaking in Seventeenth Century London', *Journal of the Arms and Armour Society* 1 no. 5 (March 1954), 68-9.
[2] *Ibid.;* Blackmore, pp. 23-4; Stern, p. 66.
[3] WO 47/29, p. 232, 19 Aug. 1718, p. 284, 7 Oct. 1718.
[4] Blackmore, pp. 37, 39.
[5] WO 47/32, p. 39, 31 Jan. 1719, report on petition of London gunmakers.

in Parliament, under pretence they could have made them in less time'.[1]

The manufacture of gunpowder, like that of firearms, involved the putting together of a number of different constituent parts. Unlike firearms, however, the ingredients which made up gunpowder — 75 *per cent* saltpetre, 15 *per cent* charcoal and 10 *per cent* sulphur (brimstone) — were not found in the immediate vicintiy of the Tower. There were no great problems about obtaining the lesser ingredients. Charcoal was made simply by charring coppice wood in open pits and could, therefore, be obtained locally. Sulphur on the other hand had to be imported from Sicily and Italy. But the Ordnance was not solely dependent on it being supplied by merchants, and it could be brought to England in naval vessels as ballast if merchants were unwilling to supply it at a reasonable rate.[2] Saltpetre, however, was required in much greater quantities than sulphur and was not so accessible. The finer quality saltpetre could only be obtained from India and Persia, and the Office was dependent on it being imported by the East India Company.

Nevertheless it was possible to manufacture saltpetre artifically. The process, involving the mixing of earth and animal excrement with lime and ashes and the watering of the compound with urine, had been introduced into England in the Elizabethan period and was continued throughout the first part of the seventeenth century.[3] In 1666 an attempt was made to revive this method of manufacture.[4]

Such a method of procurement of saltpetre was very unsatisfactory. The quality of the petre was poor; the yield was inadequate; and the disturbance caused to the countryside was liable to bring into question the royal prerogative that had sanctioned the activity, as had occurred in the early Stuart periods.[5] It was also argued that commissions for making saltpetre encouraged illicit powdermaking, which increased the likelihood of 'plots and conspiracies'.[6] The economic factor was as

1 Blackmore, pp. 37-8; PRO, MS. Cal. SP Dom. Anne, p. 276, order in council, 7 Feb. 1706; Blenheim A II 25, O.b. to Marlborough, 8 Aug. 1707.

2 PC 2/73, p. 309, report from Ordnance officers and order, 12 Dec. 1689.

3 E.W. Boville, 'Queen Elizabeth's Gunpowder', *Mariner's Mirror* 33 (1947), p. 183; *VCH Surrey, ii* 307-8.

4 PC 6/18, p. 96, 25 Apr. 1666; *Cal. SP Dom. 1665-6*, p. 539, proclamation 16 July 1666; *Evelyn Diary*, ed. E.S. de Beer, 6 vols. (Oxford, 1955), III, 442, 2 July, p. 443, 3 July, p. 445, 14 July 1666; PRO 30 37/9, pp. 106-9, various contracts. July 1666; WO 55/1785, indenture with George Perdue, 5 July 1666; SP 29/189, p. 71, Legge to Arlington, 23 Jan. 1667.

5 See *VCH Surrey*, II 308-9.

6 D.1778/V 33.

important an argument against the production of English saltpetre. The cost of gunpowder made from the eighty-one tons of English petre produced, 1666-7, was £4 14s. 7d. per barrel. This compared with the gunpowder made from the 1,568 tons of imported East India Company saltpetre, 1664-7, which varied in price from £3 6s. 3d. per barrel in 1664 to £4 9s. 4d. per barrel in 1667.[1] As a result the commissions for the making of English saltpetre were terminated, and the petremen were allowed to keep the £200 which had been imprested to them.[2]

The post-Restoration experiment in the home manufacture of saltpetre had only been attempted as a last resort because of a lack of a sufficient alternative source of supply. In the contract with the king's powdermaker immediately after the Restoration, it was agreed he should procure his own saltpetre and keep a stock of seventy tons constantly in store to enable him to fulfill his obligations,[3] but there was no guarantee that he could then obtain a sufficient supply.[4] After the demise of the gunpowder monopoly and the onset of war, the Ordnance Office itself obtained supplies of petre by making contracts directly with the East India Company and individual merchants,[5] the saltpetre then being given out to the gunpowdermakers. This may have ensured a more rational distribution of saltpetre, but it did not alter the fact that the Ordnance Office was still directly dependent on the uncertainty of imported supplies. In wartime this meant at best paying an inflated price for the commodity, and at worst no supplies at all. An alternative system was needed for the procurement of saltpetre, which would reduce the dependence on the vagaries of importation but would not mean being dependent on the unsatisfactory method of home manufacture.

A solution was found when it was decided that there should be a store of saltpetre, to be supplied by the terms of a long standing agreement with the East India Company. Proposals were made to this effect in the years immediately after the conclusion of the Second Dutch War,[6] and an attempt was made to implement some of these propositions. On 12 August 1670 a warrant was made out to Chicheley to

1   WO 55/392, p. 3.

2   *Cal. SP Dom. 1670*, p. 377, warrant to Treasury commissioners, 16 Aug. 1670; WO 55/392, pp. 7-8, warrant 15 Aug. 1670.

3   T.51/1, p. 67, contract 3 Aug. 1660.

4   WO 55/388, p. 87, warrant, 26 May, 1664 to provide petre to assignees of O'Neal.

5   See WO 55/388, pp. 146-8, 20 June 1664; WO 47/8, 8 Mar. 1666; PRO 30 37/9, p. 113, agreement with George Smith, 19 Nov. 1666.

6   See e.g. the draft proposals in D.1778/V 33 (William Legge's ?); D.1778/V 20, Chicheley's representation, 26 July 1670.

augment the supply to 1,000 tons of saltpetre, and in the following October a contract for 500 tons was made with the East India Company.[1]

The agreements with the East India Company, however, by no means provided the ideal solution. A series of memorials by Edward Hubbald, the storekeeper of saltpetre, reveal the difficulties raised by their contracts.[2] The Company could charge whatever price it liked for the commodity, as it claimed the monopoly of the trade with India. No other merchant could import without the king's special licence, and Hubbald argued that as a result the king was cheated and the powder-makers deprived of their former trade in saltpetre. He compared the current price of saltpetre imported by the Company with that brought from India by the Dutch, and reckoned the Dutch saltpetre was cheaper by at least 8s. per cwt. and of far better quality than the Company's petre. He claimed that the real problem was that since 1664 contracts with the East India Company had been made by the directions of the lord treasurer, on a different fund from that allocated to the Ordnance Office, without any examination being made by the Ordnance officers into the quality of the saltpetre. Hubbald made a number of proposals in an attempt to remedy the situation: the money needed for salt-petre payments should be included in the ordinary estimate of the Ordnance Office, and extraordinary charges awarded to the Company for interest should be abated; assays of the quality of the saltpetre should continually be made by Ordnance officers to avoid dead stocks of saltpetre being foisted upon the king; the saltpetre should be brought in as refined petre, as unrefined was subject to evaporation; and a rate of refraction should be agreed by direct negotiations between the powdermaker and the merchants. Such proposals, Hubbald thought, would ensure that the king knew 'what he hath for his money and what petre he hath really in his stores', remove 'frequent doubts and hazardous uncertainties which arise about settling the refraction of petre that is bought rough', free the Ordnance Office of the 'labyrinth' of working out amounts to be allowed for refraction, and prevent 'foul and rubbish petre' being sold to the king.

Not all Hubbald's conditions were met in subsequent contracts made with the East India Company for saltpetre. Responsibility for the signing of such contracts continued to be shared by the Ordnance and the Treasury,[3] and payments continued to be made out of the customs

1 *Cal. SP Dom. 1670*, p. 374; WO 55/392, pp. 6, 11-12, 12 Aug., 18 Oct. 1670.
2 D.1778/V 20, 1371.
3 *Cal. Treas. Books 1693-6*, p. 1402, minutes 10 Sept. 1695, p. 1427, 24 Jan. 1696; *Ibid. 1696-7*, p. 63, 16 Oct. 1696; T.1/63, fo. 286, O.b. to Treasury

arising from the goods of the East India Company rather than from the Ordnance estimate.[1] It does seem that the powdermakers had some say as to the refraction of the saltpetre, but all too often there were disputes as to the proposed refraction which had to be resolved at the Treasury.[2] Long term contracts with the East India Company, then, did not solve all the problems attached to the supply of saltpetre but they were a substantial improvement on artificial methods of manufacture. Moreover, clauses written into charters which incorporated successive East India Companies, ensured substantial concessions for the Crown, both as to the price and the quantity of saltpetre to be imported.[3]

The monopoly of making and repairing the king's gunpowder from 1660-4 was in the hands of one Daniel O'Neal, a groom of the king's bedchamber, who held the office of sole gunpowdermaker to the king. [4] O'Neal, however, did not personally execute the monopoly as he appointed James Lloyd and Thomas Carter his deputies, and it was they who actually fulfilled the contract.[5]   After the termination of the monopoly on the death of O'Neal in 1664,[6] the making of gunpowder was to be maintained by 'our commissioners of the office of master of the Ordnance for our best advantage', and in November 1664 the commissioners were ordered to contract for such quantities of gunpowder and saltpetre as they should judge necessary.[7] By the end of the year contracts had been made with seven gunpowdermakers to supply 1,580 barrels of gunpowder a month. By April 1665 the total monthly supply by the same powdermakers was 2,620 barrels, and two months later it had been increased to 2,780 barrels from nine con-

---

lords, 3 Oct. 1699, fo. 288, Same to Same, 14 Oct. 1699.

1   WO 55/340, fos. 8-9, O.b. to Goodricke, 27 Aug. 1692.

2   WO 46/3, p. 127, O.b. to Romney, 31 Aug. 1695; *Cal. Treas. Books 1693-6,* p. 1402, 10 Sept. 1695, p. 1427, 24 Jan. 1696, p. 1428, 27 Jan. 1696; T. 1/98, fo. 153, O.b. to Treasury, 7 May 1706; WO 47/25, p. 44, 7 Aug., p. 57, 14 Aug., p. 84, 4 Sept., p. 92, 11 Sept., p. 112, 23 Sept. 1707.

3   A peacetime and a wartime rate were fixed. See *Cal. SP Dom. 1691-92,* p. 387, warrant 28 July 1692; PC 2/74, p. 257, 16 Oct. 1693; *HMC* 17, *H.L.N.S.* I, 370, debate 16 Mar. 1694; *Cal. Treas. Books 1697-8,* pp. 71-2, 12 Apr. 1699, p. 101, 12 July 1698; *Ibid. 1700-1,* p. 44, 11 Feb. 1701; *Cal. Treas. Papers 1708-14,* p. 451, 31 Dec. 1712.

4   *Cal. SP Dom. 1660-1,* p. 369, warrant Nov.? 1660. For proposals re. his contract see 1.51/1, pp. 66-70, 3, 18 Aug. 1660; *Cal. SP Dom. 1663-4,* pp. 456, 547, 28 Jan., 7 Apr. 1664.

5   WO 55/386, p. 113, 11 Dec. 1660. Randyll, Samyne and Dewy were also working for O'Neal at this time. *VCH Surrey,* II 324. From October 1660 to December 1663 the required monthly proportions, worth £1,800, were delivered into the stores by Lloyd and Carter. See WO 51/3, *passim.*

6   *Cal. SP Dom. 1664-5,* p. 77, 17 Nov, p. 87, 23 Nov. 1664.

7   WO 47/6, fo. 79, 16 Nov. 1664; SP 44/16, p. 262, warrant 4 Nov. 1664.

tractors.[1] By June 1667 contracts had been made with sixteen gun-powdermakers,[2] but three years later the demand had slackened so markedly that only two powdermakers, Richardson and Buckler, were maintained as contractors.[3] In 1675 the gunpowder monopoly was re-introduced and awarded to William and Thomas Buckler.[4] The Bucklers' patent did not last long, however, for in July 1682 a contract was made with Peter Rich to supply 1,000 barrels of gunpowder from the king's saltpetre at 16s. per barrel, 6s, of which was to be allowed by way of discount towards satisfying the debts owed by William Buckler.[5] From this time onwards the board continued the policy of the late 1660s by contracting with a number of gunpowdermakers.[6]

With the ending of the powder monopoly, the board was able to deal with those powdermakers who failed to comply with their contracts or who made inferior gunpowder.[7] Nevertheless in 1706-7 it was unable to resist the demands of a combination of gunpowdermakers, who, 'knowing the necessities of the Office', successfully brought pressure on the board to increase the price of gunpowder by 4s. beyond its market price of 16s. per barrel.[8]

Gunpowder production suffered from some of the disadvantages of cannon manufacture. Both industries required quantities of imported

1   PC 6/18, p. 81, 18 Jan. 1665; WO 55/1756. The biggest suppliers at this time were Josias Dewy with 900 barrels per month, James Lloyd with 700 barrels, John Samyne with 300 barrels, a Mr Randyll with 240 barrels and Thomas Carter with 200 barrels per month.

2   WO 55/389, fo. 38, order to several powdermakers to continue contracts, 17 June 1667.

3   *Cal. SP Dom 1670*, p. 428, warrant 9 Sept. 1670; WO 55/392, pp. 9-10, warrant of same date specifying powdermakers. The signing of the contract was delayed because Moore objected to the terms. see WO 55/1756 for an interesting interdepartmental wrangle over this contract.

4   See *Cal. Treas. Books 1672-5*, p. 818, Sept. 1675; WO 55/393, fo. 16, 4 Oct. 1675, for patents to William and Thomas Buckler.

5   For a draft contract see WO 55/1756. For negotiations with Rich re. the price of powder see D. 1778/V 33. Rich stated that the cost of new powder would be 54s. per barrel, so the price of 16s. in the contract presumably allowed a consider-able abatement for the saltpetre delivered.

6   See minute WO 47/14, p. 64, 10 Nov. 1684. In 1687 there were eight gun-powdermakers operating eleven mills with a total yearly output of 34,706 barrels. The major owners were Sir Polycarpus Wharton with mills at Chilworth, Clapton and Susam (with a total capacity of 18,134 barrels p.a.) and Sir Peter Rich with mills at Wandsworth and Molsey producing 7,488 barrels p.a. WO 49/220.

7   E.g. PC 2/78, p. 62, order on petition of Gruber; WO 47/23, p. 341, 29 May 1706, stopping of contract with Madam Rich.

8   T.1/99, fos. 50/2, 11 July 1706; Blenheim A I 46, O.b. to Marlborough, 25 June 1706; WO 46/6, p. 65, O.b. to Marlborough, 4 Dec. 1707; WO 47/25, p. 245, 23 Dec. 1707.

raw material; both were dependent on huge supplies of charcoal; both were dependent on water power, production being halted by frost or drought. The transportation of gunpowder for proof at the Tower, and later at Greenwich magazine,[1] was also as problematical as the carriage of cannon. The commodity was lighter and easier to handle than ordnance but it was far more volatile. In 1666 a committee was appointed to consider a suitable place for storing gunpowder and an alternative route for the carriage of gunpowder to the Tower, because of the great danger to which the City was exposed by the passage then used. It proposed that the landing and proving of gunpowder should take place by the Tower wall near the wharf and the waterside, and that a passage should be made from the wharf into Cold Harbour, thereby reducing the expenditure of carriage and decreasing the time taken to supply the fleet from twenty to four or five days.[2] These proposals, some of which seem to have been acted upon,[3] might have made more secure the internal storage arrangements of the Tower, but they did little to relieve the anxiety of the citizens of London and its environs about the carriage of gunpowder, which continued to be transported by road.[4] By March 1707 this nuisance had reached such heights that a bill was introduced to prevent the carrying of large quantities of gunpowder within the vicinity of London Bridge. The bill was dropped with Parliament's prorogation, but the powdermakers subsequently promised not to ship off any powder within half a mile of the bridge, or to carry more than twenty barrels in a covered waggon within the City.[5]

Despite the hazards accompanying the carriage of gunpowder, it could be transported far more quickly than cannon. This was not only because of the difference in the weight of the two commodities, but also as a result of the places of manufacture. Gunpowder was made on the fringes of the Wealden ironfounding area and so did not have to be carried such long distances. Transportation was made easier, moreover, as most of the powderworks were situated on accessible routes.

There was an important powder mill at Waltham Abbey to the north

1 For the proof of gunpowder see WO 47/24, p. 494, 14 June 1707; WO 47/29, p. 207, 23 Aug. 1716.
2 *Cal. SP Dom 1665-6*, p. 288, 6 Mar. 1666; SP 29/450, no. 5a; WO 47/8, warrants and reports, Mar. 1666.
3 See SP 44/23, pp. 440-1, warrant 24 Apr. 1667.
4 See e.g. WO 55/344, pp. 176 ff.
5 WO 47/24, p. 361, 13 Mar. 1707; *HMC* 17, *H.L.N.S.* VII, 89, 3 Apr., p. 96, 21 Apr. 1707.

of London. This had been originally adapted from the corn mills of the sixteenth century monastery, but by 1735 the works comprised of twenty-two buildings in addition to a saltpetre refinery, a charging house, a composition house, a corn and glazing engine and several drying stores. In a survey of gunpowder mills, carried out in 1687 by Sheer and Gardiner, the powderworks at Waltham Abbey were the seventh largest in the kingdom, capable of producing 2,016 barrels of gunpowder a year. The largest gunpowderworks, however, was south of the river Thames. Surrey men had usually been appointed as the monarch's gunpowdermaker, so that until the civil war the only authorised gunpowder mills in the country were in Surrey, and even after that date Surrey never lost its pre-eminence as the gunpowder county. The largest mills in the country were at Chilworth near Guildford. In 1677 Sir Jonas Moore surveyed the mills and reported that 1,000 barrels could be made there monthly. He added that the mills were convenient for the delivery of gunpowder at London or Portsmouth, 'and may be constantly employed as well in dry years as in the greatest frosts'. In 1687 they were capable of producing 12,960 barrels a year, more than three times the capacity of any other works in England. At the beginning of the 1689-97 war, Sir Polycarpus Wharton, who leased the mills for the Crown, added several new works, which increased the output capacity to 300 barrels a week throughout the year. He claimed this output was more than all the other powderworks in the kingdom. Other mills mentioned in the 1687 survey were situated at Wandsworth (4,032 barrels *per annum*), Molsey (3,456 barrels *per annum*), Clapton (3,446 barrels *per annum*), Hounslow (2,880 barrels *per annum*), Faversham (2,304 barrels *per annum*), Susam (1,728 barrels *per annum*), Walthamstow (1,152 barrels *per annum*), Temple Mills (432 barrels *per annum*), and Crawford (288 barrels *per annum*).[1]

The gunfounders, small arms manufacturers and gunpowdermakers have been highlighted as some of the main ordnance contractors, but they were by no means the only artificers to have dealings with the Ordnance Office. Contracts were also made with numerous manufacturers — ironmongers, armourers, wheelwrights, cutlers, brasiers and a host of others — who supplied the Office with the many varieties of Ordnance store. The Ordnance Office was a huge employer, from whose tentacles extended a spider web of contractors and subcontractors, who in the main depended on the Office for their prosperity. It was, therefore, the department's responsibility to keep its

---

1   Hogg, *Artillery*, pp. 132-3; T.1/13, fo. 79, report 2 Feb. 1691; WO 49/220, 1687 survey; *V.C.H. Surrey*, II, 306; WO 46/5, pp. 155 ff.

118

credit buoyant with this army of skilled craftsman; to co-ordinate their activities; and thereby to maintain its supplies of Ordnance stores. How successful the department was in achieving this end will be the subject of the following two chapters. But first it is necessary to examine the storage facilities available to the Office once the contracts had been implemented.

Storage

Ordnance storehouses were scattered throughout the kingdom. The major central depository was at the Tower, which continued to be the premier Ordnance stronghold for most stores. Other store depots, however, were established in this period and these replaced the Tower as the key magazine for some stores: notably Woolwich, for iron ordnance and saltpetre, and Upnor Castle and Greenwich, for gunpowder. Woolwich with Chatham, Sheerness, Portsmouth and Plymouth were the major ports for naval ordnance, although supplies were also to be found at Harwich, Hull, Kinsale, Dover, Berwick, Tynemouth and Leith in the 1702-13 war.[1] In addition, every garrison had its own supply of Ordnance stores.

The main Ordnance storehouses at the Tower were situated within its inner walls to the north, south and east of the central White Tower, which was itself used as an Ordnance store.[2] There was considerable re-development, however, of the central site at the Tower in this period. In the 1660s the existing storehouses were insufficient to deal with the mass of ordnance that had been reclaimed from the localities, and a number of new storehouses were erected.[3] By the early 1670s, however, the pressure on space within the Tower had slackened so marked-ly — as a result of the building of new storehouses and the rearrange-ment of the storehouse facilities in the mid 1660s, necessitated by the redirecting of the gunpowder route — that the Office was able to dispense with an appendage store. In 1673 the Ordnance Office sold storehouses and workshops situated to the North of the Tower in the Minories, which had originally been bought by the Crown in the 1560s as a store for heavy weapons to relieve the central Tower stores. The

1 Adm. 1/3999, 29 Apr. 1704; Adm. 1/4002, 23 Sept. 1707; Adm. 1/4003, 28 May, 15 Dec. 1709; Adm. 3/18, 14 Apr. 1703; PC 2/82, p. 51, 15 Apr. 1708. For further details of Ordnance ports see my 'The Ordnance Office and the Navy', *EHR* 90 (1975), pp. 35-6.
2 For a description of the history of the Ordnance buildings at the Tower see Ffoulkes, *Inventory and Survey*, I, 18-35.
3 E.g. the new storehouse within the Wardrobe garden. PRO 30 37/14, 27 Jan. 1663; WO 47/5, p. 5; PRO 30 37/9, fo. 21, warrant 24 Nov. 1663.

Office reported that there was greater room for Ordnance stores within the Tower than at any time previously, because of the new buildings and the removal of naval stores to Woolwich, and that the Minories stores could be conveniently lodged with the other artillery stores in the upper storehouses of the Tower fitted out for that purpose[1]

The largest and grandest of the Tower storehouses were erected in the late 1680s immediately to the north of the White Tower. In January 1687 the Ordnance officers had represented to Dartmouth 'the crazy condition of the old storehouse and how little safety his majesty's stores were there lodged', and Dartmouth had ordered a draft and estimate to be made for the building of a new storehouse. After a year's deliberation the plans were approved and in March 1688 Dartmouth ordered that the new building should be started. The grand storehouse was completed early in the 1690s. The two storied building was 345 feet long and 60 feet wide, crowned by a martial tympanum and cupola. The central room on the ground floor of the storehouse was fitted up as an armoury for small guns, around which were a series of racks, each capable of holding over a thousand small arms. The armoury was entered at the west end by a magnificent baroque screen. On the top floor of the building were stored tents and miscellaneous military stores.[2]

The Tower remained pre-eminent as a store for general Ordnance equipment, although not for heavy artillery, throughout the period.[3] It did, however, decline in importance as a gunpowder magazine. In November 1678, for instance, Sir Thomas Chicheley was ordered to move gunpowder from the Tower to other magazines because of the great quantities which were stored there, and on 9 July 1691 the board received a warrant from the Privy Council to consider an alternative place for a gunpowder store, 2,000 barrels having fallen through one of the floors of the White Tower that very morning.[4] One reason

---

1 Ashley, 'Tudor Office of Ordnance', pp. 91-2. For details of the sale see Hogg, *Royal Arsenal*, I, 67; *Cal. Treas. Books 1672-5*, pp. 452-3, report from Latimer, 30 Dec. 1673.

2 WO 55/335, fo. 475, Dartmouth to O.b., 1 Mar. 1688; *Wren Society.*, XVIII, 187, plate V; WO 47/18, p. 173, agreement with Hayward, 11 Jan. 1696; PRO, Works 31/106, 115, Tower plans; Ffoulkes, *Inventory and Survey*, I, 23; *Armouries of the Tower of London*, I, 17. The original intention that the grand storehouse should be a complete Army store was not realised. Nevertheless the storehouse served as a central ordnance depository and trophy room until it was destroyed by fire in 1841. The tympanum alone escaped and may still be seen at the Tower.

3 See below, p. 124.

4 *Cal. SP Dom. 1678*, p. 535, 22 Nov. 1678; PC 2/74, p. 106; WO 55/339. p. 87.

for this dispersal of gunpowder from the Tower to remoter magazines was the extreme hazard of having large stores of highly volatile material within such a short distance of the City.[1]

Most of the other major gunpowder magazines in the kingdom were, like the White Tower, makeshift stores. The gunpowder stored at Windsor Castle in the late 1660s and 1670s was lodged in the Great (Devil's) and Little Towers, which were especially repaired for the purpose in 1668-9.[2] A little prior to that, the garrison at Upnor Castle had been disbanded and its rooms converted to receive large quantities of gunpowder, but it was hardly sufficient as a magazine, for in July 1714 the chief engineer could report to the board that it was simply covered by a lead roof which exposed it 'to a single bomb'.[3] Gravesend Blockhouse, like Upnor Castle, was also converted into a gunpowder magazine.[4] Across the river at Tilbury Fort, however, two new powder magazines were built in 1716-17 with a huge domed storage chamber, each capable of holding nearly 3,000 barrels of gunpowder.[5]

A new magazine was also constructed at Greenwich in the 1690s. Prior to this, however, a number of important government establishments had been located at Greenwich. An armoury was situated there until the civil war; the Royal Observatory, which was built at the instigation of Sir Jonas Moore to Wren's design in 1675 and was directly under Ordnance Office control, was sited within Greenwich Park; and Greenwich was also the home of the Ordnance fireworks laboratory from 1683 to January 1696.[6] There had been no major Ordnance store at Greenwich, however, although a house had been built in Greenwich Park in 1669 to accommodate ordnance for the use of practitioner gunners, and in the early 1690s the grounds of the royal palace had been used to lodge the gunpowder taken from on board the fleet at

---

1 Although the Tower was never actually damaged by fire in the period, the great fire of 1666 and another fire of 1680 stopped within yards of its walls. See PC 6/18, p. 103, order 6 Sept. 1666; *Cal. SP Dom. 1680*, pp. 80-2, 28 May 1680.

2 WO 47/19a, pp. 98, 113, 137, 141-2, 160, 232, 276. Also see report of Jonas Moore (senior?), D.1778/V 71, 19 Apr. (no year).

3 *Cal. SPDom. 1666-7*, p. 247, warrant 8 Nov. p. 287, warrant 24 Nov. 1666; *Ibid. 1667-8*, p. 417, warrant to Legge, May? 1668; Stowe 477, fo. 21, report of Richards, 18 July 1714.

4 PRO, MPHH 45, plan by John Romer, 1 June 1715.

5 King's Top. Coll. XIII, 57 d, e, plans and section of the magazine, 1716, 1717; WO 47/29, pp. 109, 121, 131-2, 201; WO 47/30, p. 150, orders re. surveying of magazine, contracts etc. 11, 25 May, 6 June, 14 Aug. 1716, 4 June 1717.

6 See Hogg, *Royal Arsenal*, I, 103-4; SP 44/44, fo. 15, 22 June 1675; WO 47/13, p. 101, 24 May 1683; WO 47/18, p. 153, 7 Jan. 1696.

their return.[1] The immediate reason for the building of the Greenwich magazine was the preparation of the palace for the reception of the Queen in the summer of 1694. The principal Ordnance officers, however, were allowed to retain the use of the royal residence as a gunpowder store until February 1696, by which date it had been handed over to the Navy for use as a seaman's hospital.[2] By this time preparations had been made for the building of the new magazine.[3]

Upstream from Greenwich was the arsenal at Woolwich. There had been an Ordnance store at Woolwich since early in the sixteenth century, but there was a great expansion in the size of the arsenal in this period. In the early 1660s Woolwich was certainly only a minor store. There was no resident storekeeper, and the buildings consisted simply of a wooden wharf with a ninety yard river frontage and a depth of about eighty yards, upon which were a number of storehouses, some of which were in a state of ill repair. In 1664 a more substantial naval carriage shed of brick with a tiled roof was constructed there. The Anglo-Dutch war, 1665-7, increased the importance of Woolwich as an Ordnance base, and by October 1668 its storehouse capacity was sufficiently large to receive the guns, carriages and stores, which had been removed from Deptford.[4] Woolwich gunwharf, however, was not an ideal site, as the available storage space was limited to about half an acre, and it was subject to flooding by the spring tides. It also appears that the wharf actually belonged to the Navy Board, who had a small ropeyard enclosure at its north-west corner. The wharf by the early 1670s was in any case in a bad state of repair, as a naval official could report in February 1671, that although repaired only three years previously, it was so much ruined by the weight of heavy guns being laid upon it, that men were 'forced to go up to their ankles in mire'. The depth of water at the foot of the wharf had apparently been raised by three feet because of its use by the Ordnance Office. Such a

1 WO 47/19a, p. 311, 10 May, p. 437, 23 July 1669; *Cal. Treas. Books 1689-92*, p. 1279, warrant to Wren, 26 Aug. 1691; WO 46/3, p. 52, Romney to O.b., 19 June 1694, p. 64, O.b. to Romney, 26 June 1694.

2 See WO 46/3, pp. 52, 64, Romney to O.b., 19, 26 June 1694; WO 47/18, p. 11, 26 Nov. 1695, p. 267, 4 Feb. 1696.

3 An estimate for over £6,000 was presented to the Treasury in Oct. 1694, but the magazine had not been completed by June 1696. For details of the progress and siting of the building see T.1/29, fo. 214, 6 Oct. 1694; WO 46/3, p. 63, O.b. to Romney, 30 May 1695; WO 46/4, p. 2, Same to Same, 21 Jan. 1696; WO 47/18, p. 33, payment 3 Dec. 1695; Hogg, *Royal Arsenal* I, 107.

4 *Ibid.* pp. 161, 167-8; WO 47/5, pp. 46, 48, 163, repair of wharf and house on wharf, 14, 16 Apr., 22 Dec. 1663; WO 48/8, pp. 98, 99, payments to Norfolk and Scott; WO 47/6, p. 16, order for contract, 22 July 1664; WO 47/19a, p. 19, minute 10 Oct. 1668.

situation was hardly satisfactory, and arrangements were made by the Ordnance for the purchase of Sir William Prichard's mansion house and land at Tower Place, the old Ordnance storehouses and wharf being given to him in part exchange for the property.[1]

The new Woolwich arsenal had a number of advantages over the old site: it had already been made defensible by the establishment of a battery of sixty guns by Prince Rupert in June 1667; the existing buildings and wharf, which had been built by Prichard, could be immediately utilised; and above all there was sufficient land for future expansion. Even before the acquisition of Tower Place in April 1671 there had been a spate of building activity there, and this was to continue throughout the period.[2] Woolwich was clearly destined to be an important Ordnance site, and in 1682 the old Tudor mansion was divided in order to provide accommodation for the resident storekeeper, the lieutenant-general and the master gunner, the last two officers having been deprived of their official residences with the sale of the Minories and the old artillery ground. Manufacture of ordnance commenced at Woolwich in the mid 1690s with the establishment of the laboratory there after its removal from Greenwich, and in the following year an elaborate new carriage yard was built within the line of Prince Rupert's battery.[3]

A copy of a plan of Woolwich arsenal drawn by Albert Borgard in 1701 does exist,[4] revealing the expansion that had taken place there since the Ordnance Office acquired the site in the 1670s. The drawing shows the laboratory, outside of which are stacked thousands of shells, gun and mortar stands, the old and new carriage yards, the powder house, a line of three cranes on the waterfront, the shot yard, the old mansion house, several storehouses and the proof yard to the south of the main buildings. Even more dramatic, however, were the developments that took place immediately after 1714: the building of the brass foundry and a series of carriage sheds and artificers houses, and

---

1 Hogg, *Royal Arsenal* I, 156-7, 185 ff.; SP 29/296, fo. 149, Bodham to Navy commissioners, 23 Feb. 1671, fo. 150, sketch of wharf; *Cal. SP Dom. 1671*, p. 211, Apr. 1671.

2 See Hogg, *Royal Arsenal* I, 177, 196 ff.; WO 48/11, pp. 38-9, payment to Pyne, 16 Sept. 1671, p. 49, payment to Clare, 23 Dec. 1671; WO 47/12, p. 40, 14 Nov. 1682; WO 47/13, p. 92, 12 May 1683.

3 Hogg, *Royal Arsenal*, I, 206, 227. For details also see D.1778/V 41, estimate by De Gomme, 17 Mar. 1682; WO 49/182, pp. 18 ff., 224. The carriage shed estimate (£2,961 12s.) was presented to the Treasury in Oct. 1694, (T. 1/29, fo. 216) and the building was almost complete in Jan. 1696. WO 47/18, p. 217, minute to Hayward.

4 PRO, MP I 296, copy by J. Bellamy, Nov. 1869.

the complete remodelling of the great Tudor mansion. Such buildings are fine examples of bold baroque architecture and John Vanbrugh may have been concerned in their design.[1] By the end of the period, then, Woolwich was clearly recognised as being of pre-eminent importance in Ordnance administration.[2]

The Tower and Woolwich storehouses and the powder magazines described were the major central Ordnance supply depots. The other storehouses at the ports and garrisons, however, were often inadequate. At Chatham in the mid 1660s an Ordnance officer could complain that there was no fit place in which to lodge powder securely, although by the end of the period a plan of the Ordnance wharf shows a number of imposing storehouses, including one which had been built in 1717 in the grand manner of those at Woolwich.[3] The storehouses at Harwich were insufficient to hold the stores necessary for the fleet, whilst those at Sheerness were plainly inadequate.[4] At Portsmouth, before the new wharf was built 1705-10, the arrangement of the existing naval storehouses was quite unsatisfactory, for they were rented and situated in several places about the town at a great distance from each other, most of them being inconveniently placed for shipping off and taking in the Ordnance stores and incapable of holding the stores necessary for supplying the ships.[5] At Plymouth the situation was similar. The main naval storehouses were sited at Cockside in Sutton Pool and were some distance from the new naval dock at Hamouze, although they were 'situated the most commodiously' of any storehouses in Plymouth. The buildings were rented at a rate of £60 *per annum* and by 1715 they were in a state of ill repair, 'the owner having been so negligent of their repairs knowing his lease was near expired'. The storehouses enclosed three sides of a square of about 100 feet and were capable of receiving stores from over thirty ships, but they could not accommodate cannon and gunpowder. Nor was there a suitable place for trimming gun-

---

1 Hogg, *Royal Arsenal*, I, 245 ff.; WO 47/29, pp. 138, 139, 140, 192, 201, 202, 264; WO 47/30, pp. 1, 191, 284; WO 47/31, p. 98; King's Top. Coll, XVII, 25, d, e, g, plans and elevations, 1715, 1717; K. Downes, *English Baroque Architecture* (1966), pp. 112-13; L. Whistler *The Imagination of Vanbrugh and his Fellow Artists* (1954), pp. 216 ff. I have found no documentary evidence connecting Vanbrugh with the design.

2 E.g. see WO 47/33, p. 240, minute 14 June 1720; D. Defoe, *A Tour Through the Whole Island of Great Britain*, ed. G.D.H.Cole, 2 vols. (1927), I, 98.

3 WO 49/112, Batchler to Marsh, 5 July 1665; PRO, MPH 247, Lemprière's plan of yard and wharf, 1719; King's Top. Coll. XVI, 42 e – g, storehouse plans.

4 Adm. 1/4003, 27 May 1708; Adm. 1/4001, 28 Nov. 1706(?).

5 See D.1778/V 55, report of Conyers and Fortrey; WO 46/5, Bridges's report, 17 Jan. 1703; WO 48/46, list 14 Aug., 15th payment, rents of Portsmouth storehouses.

powder that had been put on shore whilst a ship refitted, because Cockside was too near the rest of the town. In December 1716 the Plymouth naval storehouses were insufficient to house ship's carriages, and it was ordered that they should be left on board ship until the new storehouses were built the following year.[1]

The garrison storehouses at Plymouth, within the Royal Citadel, were more substantial.[2] Many of the other garrison stores, however, were not so well built. In the 1680s the storehouses at Hull, for instance, as important a garrison for the north as Plymouth was for the south-west, were in complete disarray.[3]

It would be an impossible task to give a survey of the amounts of all stores kept in the Ordnance storehouses in this period, because of the many different types and categories of stores which were detailed by the Ordnance officers in their remains. The numbers of brass and iron cannon and matchlock and snaphance muskets, and the amount of gunpowder and saltpetre in the major Ordnance stores, however, have been calculated from a sample of Ordnance remains and reports on the state of Ordnance stores. Such a survey necessarily has its limitations. There are not enough extant remains after the 1670s to give a fair picture of the state of the various Ordnance strongholds in the later period, and by selecting certain types of Ordnance stores there is no indication given of the total volume of stores in any one depot. There is moreover no indication given of the vast range of different types of cannon and muskets. Table II, however, does serve as a general guide to the relative importance of the major storehouses in the kingdom in relation to some of the main Ordnance stores.

A number of conclusions may be drawn from this survey of guns, gunpowder, saltpetre and muskets. The chief general Ordnance arsenals for these commodities were the Tower and Woolwich. The Tower remained the chief depot for small arms, and probably numerous miscellaneous stores, and with Chatham, the main arsenal for brass ordnance, although it declined in importance as a depot for iron guns and as a gunpowder magazine and saltpetre store.[4] In its place, Wool-

---

1 *Ibid.;* King's 45, fos. 41 ff., Lilly's report and plans, 1715; New Bodleian Library, Gough Maps 5, fos. 15b, 16b, further plans of the storehouses by Lilly, 1715; WO 47/29, p. 305, 14 Dec. 1716.

2 See King's 45, fo. 36, for plans and sections of the principal buildings in Plymouth Citadel, by Lilly, 1716.

3 See WO 46/2, pp.178, 190, 278, Watkinson's letters, 9 Oct. 1683, 12 Jan., 6 Oct. 1684.

4 The decline of the Tower in this period as a main artillery store may be traced in the remains printed in *The Armouries of the Tower of London,* I, 306-84.

TABLE II

A State of the Remains of Brass and Iron Cannon, Gunpowder, Saltpetre and Muskets at the Major Ordnance Stores[1]

Brass and Iron Ordnance*

	Chatham		Portsmouth		Tower		Woolwich	
	Brass	Iron	Brass	Iron	Brass	Iron	Brass	Iron
19 Oct. 1660	468	865	168	718	240	2,609		
31 Dec. 1662	463	1,040	193	645	536	2,804		
31 Dec. 1663	442	895	317	811	367	2,797		
18 Mar. 1669	429	1,320	116	1,275	205	1,504	131	1,946
31 Jan. 1671	425	1,239	146	1,107	193	1,610	112	2,181
11 Dec. 1672	394	1,327	57	470	288	904	66	1,224
1 Jan. 1676	470	1,659	42	1,538	301	721	22	1,792
31 Nov. 1679	350	1,323	106	1,154	301	551	90	2,090
c. 1691	343	1,189	123	1,470	226	152	166	3,558

* I.e. the number of all types of brass and iron cannon (including mounted, unmounted, train, naval or garrison guns), except mortars.

Gunpowder*

	Berwick	Greenwich	Hull	Plymouth	Portsmouth	Sheerness	Tilbury & Gravesend	Tower	Upnor	Windsor
19 Oct. 1660					1,076½			4,096		
31 Dec. 1662					905			4,061		
31 Dec. 1663					1,144			3,863		
17 June 1667			300	700	1,800			9,677		2,000
31 July 1668			780	800	2,519			7,663	3,100	1,300
18 Mar. 1669	64		915	283	2,620	27	23	6,767	1,300	1,326
31 Jan. 1671	104		900	437	2,223	20	100	4,948		1,250
11 Dec. 1672	250		375	735	2,608	270	73	4,876	3,900	283
1 Jan. 1676			494	521	3,695	136		3,981	5,127	24
31 Nov. 1679	572		412	2,377	1,684½	46	57	3,198	4,521	2
1 Jan. 1685	459		551	1,289	677	392		3,191	811	10
c. 1691	863		504	1,111	3,287	597	696	3,692	5,207	11
1 Sept. 1695	447	1310	228	2,082	2,591	632	2,521	970	84	13
10 Jan. 1702		4793		1,178	3,696	471	699	667	4,104	

* To the nearest barrel. Including stored, repaired and unserviceable gunpowder in both garrison and navy stores.

Saltpetre*

	Tower/Minories†	Woolwich
18 Mar. 1669	480	
8 Mar. 1670		385
31 Jan. 1671	1,033	
23 Aug. 1672	53	322
3 Sept. 1673	12 cwt.	67
30 July 1678		480
28 June 1683	207	844
16 June 1685	582	1,109
30 June 1688	171	387
5 July 1689	75	144
28 May 1691	5	277
13 Mar. 1695	3	74

* To the nearest ton (except where stated). Including refined and rough saltpetre.

† On the sale of the Mansion House and other storehouses to Sir William Prichard in 1673, the saltpetre was removed from the Minories to Woolwich. See D. 1778/V 1393, entries 3 Sept. 1673.

Muskets*

	Hull		Plymouth		Portsmouth		Tower		Windsor	
	Matchlock	Snaphance	Matchlock	Snaphance	Matchlock	Snaphance	Matchlock	Snaphance	Matchlock	Snaphance
17 June 1667	1492	100	50		2216	381	12,687	2,415	756	35
31 Dec. 1671							8,678	7,337		
7 Mar. 1678	1,277		1,006		6,170		17,835		2,544	
31 Nov. 1679							5,842	1,844		
21 Nov. 1687							6,111	6,945		
25 Feb. 1689							1,947	1,540		
27 Nov. 1705							1,676	9,726		

* N.B. The totals include both serviceable and unserviceable muskets.

[1] The following remains have been sampled: WO 55/1694, 19 Oct. 1660, 31 Dec. 1662; WO 55/388, 31 Dec. 1663; WO 49/110, 17 June 1667, 7 Mar. 1678; WO 49/112, 31 July 1668; Harl. 4247-9, 18 Mar. 1669, 31 Jan. 1671, 11 Dec. 1672; D.1778/V 1393, saltpetre remains, 8 Mar. 1670, 23 Aug. 1672, 3 Sept. 1673; WO 55/1714, 31 Nov. 1679; D.1778/V 1395, 28 June 1683; D.1778/V 55, 1 Jan. 1685; WO 55/1708, 1 Jan. 1676; WO 55/1757, saltpetre remains, 5 July 1689-13 Mar. 1695; D.1778/V 71, 16 June 1685, 30 June 1688; D.1778/V 39, 21 Nov. 1687, 25 Feb. 1689; WO 55/1757, saltpetre remains, 5 July 1689-13 Mar. 1695; SP 8/10, no. 131, c.1691; WO 46/3, p. 131, 1 Sept. 1695; WO 46/5, p. 69, 10 Jan. 1702; SP 41/34, 27 Nov. 1705.

wich was established as the main arsenal for iron ordnance and the central store for saltpetre, though not for gunpowder. Chatham and Portsmouth were the largest naval outports for both types of cannon, and Portsmouth, Plymouth and Hull held the largest stocks of gunpowder for the Navy. There was a significant increase in the capacity of the powder depositories at both Portsmouth and Plymouth. Windsor Castle, on the other hand, declined in importance as a gunpowder store. The evidence presented in the Table, however, confirms the establishment of Upnor Castle and Greenwich as important magazines.

4

THE ORGANISATION OF ARTILLERY TRAINS AND SUPPLY

The last chapter gave some indication of the endless variety of Ordnance stores, as well as an insight into the problems associated with their manufacture and an assessment of the capacities of the major Ordnance strong-holds. Such a structural analysis, however, needs to be complemented by a dynamic survey of the department in action. How were artillery trains organised? What was the state of Ordnance reserves? How successful was the department in mobilising the vast resources at its command? These will be the themes of the following pages.

Artillery Trains[1]

When an artillery train was required to accompany the troops on any expedition it was the responsibility of the Ordnance Office to equip the train with guns, stores and artillery officers. For most of the period there was no permanent establishment of artillery officers, who were simply drafted into Ordnance service for a limited period and were discharged once their services were no longer required.[2] An observation of the clerk of the Ordnance in December 1691, 'that it has not been the practice of former times . . . . to have officers etc. established and in pay unless the train were in some few days ready to march',[3] reveals the impermanent nature of artillery service at this time. An important development in the staffing of artillery trains occurred after the peace of Ryswick, with the first permanent English establishment of artillery officers in a regimental form.[4] Early in 1699 the regiment was disbanded. A new establishment of engineers, gentlemen of the Ordnance, bombardiers and gunners, formed in 1697, was continued, however, and additional allowances of £1,400 *per annum* were given to the old

---

1 For a general discussion also see Chandler, pp. 167 ff.

2 E.g. see WO 47/15, p. 106, 25 July 1685; *Cal. SPDom. 1691-92*, p. 488, warrant to Goodricke, 25 Oct. 1692.

3 WO 55/339, p. 127, 22 Dec. 1691.

4 See WO 46/4, pp. 23 ff., letter 25 Nov. 1697, for initial proposals. Four companies were eventually established at a cost of £4,482 10s. p.a., *Cal. SPDom. 1698*, p. 263, warrant to Romney, 21 May 1698; Ducan, I, 61-2; F.D. Cleaveland, *Notes on the Early History of the Royal Regiment of Artillery*, ed. Lieut.-Col. W. Lambert Yonge (Woolwich, 1892 (?)), p. 142. For the names of those in the companies see WO 48/37, pp. 66-70, quarter book, July 1698.

regimental officers who were not re-called.[1]   The disbanding Act of 1699, which stated that all regiments and companies, except 7,000 men, should be dissolved, was thereby circumvented.[2]   The experiment of regimenting artillery officers was not to be repeated until 1716, when two companies of artillery were formed.   This was done in an attempt to remedy the deficiency in trained men on the military establishment, in the light of the failure to organise artillery trains to combat the 1715 rebellion.   Prior to this a large sum had been advanced on the military establishment in half pay, to a largely non-effective body of men, who had to be supplemented by inexperienced artillery officers when emergencies arose.[3]

The size of an artillery train was dependent on the type of expedition on which it was to be engaged.   Until the onset of the wars against France, there was little continental campaigning, and the size of artillery trains was comparatively small.[4]   One of the largest trains to be assembled before the Revolution, was that organised in October/November 1688 against the invasion of William.   A warrant for a train of twenty-six pieces to attend the king's forces of 15,000 foot and 5,000 horse was made out on 8 November, although a preparatory warrant had been issued several days before on 15 October.   By mid-November, the certain weekly charge for the artillery train amounted to £2,280. 2s. 10d.[5]   After the Revolution, vast artillery trains were assembled much more frequently.   In 1689 a huge train was sent over to Ireland under the Duke of Schomberg.[6]   The Flanders trains were even larger. On 27 February 1692 warrants ordered the lieutenant of the Ordnance to prepare 'a train of brass ordnance with all fitting equipage' to be immediately transported into Flanders, and the following day another warrant was issued for a train of seventy-six pieces to be established. The estimate for the first train came to £70,804. 11s. 9d., whilst that designed to be shipped with the summer fleet was calculated to cost £119,333. 2s. 4d. An indication of the number of officers required

---

1   *Ibid.* p. 147; SP 44/167, pp. 416 ff. warrants to Romney, 14 Feb. 1699; *Cal. SP. Dom. 1699-1700,* p. 36, warrant to Romney, 30 Jan. 1699. The new establishment cost £2,573 p.a.

2   *Ibid.* pp. 227-8, Pulteney to Galway, 4 Apr. 1699; WO 46/4, p. 43, letter 10 Jan. 1699.

3   Cleaveland, pp. 185, 189, warrants 10 Jan., 26 May 1716; O.F.G. Hogg, *English Artillery, 1326-1716* (1963), pp. 266 ff.

4   *Ibid.* pp. 235, 241; Cleaveland, pp. 98, 108; NMM Dartmouth MS. 1, abstract 13 Feb. 1678; *Cal. SP. Dom. 1685,* p. 219. 21 June 1685; *Ibid. 1686-7,* p. 131, 12 May 1686; *Ibid. 1687-8,* p. 4, 5 June 1687.

5   Cleaveland, p. 109; WO 55/395, warrant to Ranelagh, 13 Nov. 1688.

6   Add. MS. 5795, fos. 20-9

to man these trains is provided by the computation of the allowances for the artillery officers which came to £220. 7s. 2d. and £99. 13s. 6d. per day respectively.[1] The artillery trains in the War of Spanish Succession in the early eighteenth century, however, were not as large as those formed in the previous war.[2]

The actual estimate of stores and artillery officers for these trains, was considered by the principal Ordnance officers in conjunction with the commander of the expedition. The Ordnance officers were allowed some initiative in altering small matters in the agreed estimate, although they were expected to adhere to the main parts of the established proportion once it was fixed and signed by the king.[3] The Ordnance officers, however, were not usually in a position to evaluate the cost of an estimate for stores submitted by a commander abroad, as they often did not know the number of troops to be employed or the nature of their service.[4] In such circumstances the board complied with the submitted estimates, despite the fact that it invariably considered them wildly extravagant.[5]

Once the estimate had been decided upon it was the task of the Ordnance Office to man and equip the artillery trains. Such trains might consist of hundreds of men responsible for maintaining, transporting and using the artillery: comptrollers; rank and file conductors; engineers and battery masters; gunners and matrosses; craftsmen; commissaries of stores; waggon masters and commissaries of horses; and chaplains, surgeons and clerical officers. Each type of officer was given instructions as to the way in which they were to conduct themselves on the train. The comptroller was to see that the train marched to its required destination, and all officers performed their duty, and to keep the board informed of all proceedings. The commissaries were to indent for the stores they received from the Ordnance storekeeper and to record all receipts and deliveries made, which books were to be returned into the Office when the train was disbanded. No issues were to be made without warrant from the commander of the forces,

---

1 *Ibid.* pp. 36, 41; Cleaveland, p. 119; Hogg, *English Artillery,* p. 250; Add. MS. 5795, fos. 34-46.

2 See e.g. the cost of the Holland trains in Feb. 1702 and in 1705. SP 32/13, fo. 87; Stowe 470.

3 WO 55/339, pp. 224-5, O.b. to Duke of Leinster, 7 Apr. 1692.

4 See e.g. complaints by the board, WO 46/6, p. 128, 20 Jan. 1711; WO 55/344, p. 69, O.b. to Harley, 9 Aug. 1705; SP 41/34, O.b. to Dartmouth, 31 July 1712.

5 See e.g. Erle 2/40, Erle to Marlborough, 11 June 1706; Blenheim CI 30, O.b. to Marlborough, 14 Jan. 1708.

except for those stores for guns, which were to be supplied on the comptrollers' instruction. Issues of money by the paymaster were also only to be made by order of the comptroller or commissary, and all books of account and receipt of payment were to be kept, states of cash being weekly exhibited to the comptroller, and a monthly return being made to the board in order to renew money supplies. The waggonmaster was to see that each waggon, under the charge of a conductor, carried the same load, and that artificers repaired all waggons or took up others at reasonable rates. The commissary of draught horses was similarly to have oversight of all horses and drivers, who were to be immediately supervised by a number of assistants. The gentlemen of the Ordnance were responsible for an allotted number of guns and gunners, and were to give notice to the comptroller of the munitions spent. The Ordnance quartermaster was to attend the commander or Army quartermaster-general regarding the route the train was to march, and to take up convenient quarters for the officers of the train. The ordinary conductors of ammunition were to ensure that stores were properly kept and not embezzled, and to issue no stores without authority. Before they were discharged at the end of the service, they were to take receipts of all deliveries to the commissary of ammunition.[1]

In addition to getting together large numbers of men of different skills, the Office had to collect the multifarious pieces of *impedimenta* which formed the equipment of the train. Key garrisons held a number of resident pieces of equipment which were mobilised when required.[2] The state of the marching trains was described by Chamberlayne in his *Present state of England* in 1682:

> The train of artillery within the Tower is very considerable and worthy of particular observation, consisting of fifty pieces of brass ordnance mounted on travelling carriages with all its furniture necessary and fit for marching, besides several mortar pieces, some whereof an extraordinary bigness . . . . There are other trains of artillery in his majesty's magazine abroad, as at Portsmouth, a very considerable one, at Plymouth, Windsor etc.[3]

A few years later a survey of artillery trains in England showed that there were eighty-nine pieces of brass ordnance on travelling carriages at the Tower, and seventy-two waggons for the artillery train there. There

1 WO 55/1728, June 1685; T. 1/94, fo. 133, 1 May 1705; T. 1/98, fo. 310, 1 June 1706.

2 E.g. WO 55/339, pp. 178-9, O.b. to Nottingham, 29 Apr. 1692; WO 47/30, p. 30, 15 Feb. 1717.

3 Chamberlayne, *The Present State of England* (11th edn. 1682), part II, pp. 217-18.

were twenty brass artillery pieces and eleven waggons at Whitehall and St. James's Park, and thirty-seven pieces and twenty waggons at Portsmouth. Plymouth, Hull, and West Chester had twelve artillery pieces, and Yarmouth and Berwick ten each, and there were a small number of waggons at Hull and Berwick.[1] After the Union an artillery train was established at Edinburgh Castle. By the early eighteenth century permanent artillery trains were also established abroad.[2]

As well as finding the basic pieces of equipment, the Office had to calculate the number of carts, horses, and drivers required to transport them. Military manuals such as Markham's *Five Decades of War* set out tables to show how many horses were needed to carry a given weight of gun or size of waggon. Thirty horses were required to draw the largest field pieces, a team of eight or twelve horses was expected to draw a medium sized field piece, and five or six animals, a cart laden with four barrels of gunpowder.[3] Draught animals were sometimes impressed if they were required at short notice, but it was more usual for a contract to be made with an undertaker to supply and maintain a certain number of horses and carters, if they were required for a foreign campaign.[4]

Some indication of the many different types of stores and the number of skilled men required on an artillery train, may be provided by a recitation of the orders the board demanded to be observed during the march of the artillery train in June 1685.[5] The march was to take place in three divisions. In the vanguard came the captain of pioneers and his men followed by the chief officers of the train. The gunners and gentlemen of the Ordnance were to march alongside their allotted guns, which were to be placed in order of size, the greatest pieces coming first. Before the pieces of ordnance were carts with working materials, and after them waggons with budge barrels, cartouches, shot and spare equipment. Next came the waggons of the principal officers, the powder and match carts, and the tent waggons in the care of the tent master and his servants. Carts of spare material and waggons for artificers completed the first division. Ammunition for foot and

---

1   D. 1778/V 71, survey by De Gomme, n.d. (*c.* 1685).

2   Add. MS. 5795, fo. 170, queen's warrant, 16 Dec. 1708; WO 55/488, p. 63, master-general's warrant, 16 July 1709; Duncan, I, 70.

3   See table given in Hogg, *Artillery: Its Origin, Heyday and Decline*, p. 57, for horses required for 1684 train. Also Roy, p. 290.

4   WO 47/15, p. 40, minute 19 June 1685; WO 55/399, pp. 17, 50, 71, 79, 151; WO 55/400, p. 73. Sloane 443, fos. 22-3, contract Nov. 1694.

5   WO 55/1728.

horse, and bridge boats, were appointed to the second division, and the standing magazine and a reseve train for the third division.

TABLE III

The State of Ordnance Reserves (in store), 1669-1704

	Brass Cannon (Nos.)	Iron Cannon (Nos.)	Gunpowder (Barrels)	Salt- petre (Tons)	Muskets
18 Mar. 1669 (Harl. 4247)	956	6,796	13,440	480	
31 Jan. 1671 (Harl. 4249)	990	7,022	10,974	1,032	
31 Dec. 1671 (WO 55/1704)	1,042	6,859	13,355	1,152	
11 Dec. 1672 (Harl. 4248)	912	5,227	15,323½		
Mar. 1676 (D.1778/V 20)			14,135	3,540	
Mar. 1683 *(Ibid.)*			13,869	2,107	
1 Aug. 1686 (D.1778/V 1395)				1,373	
30 June 1688 *(Ibid.)*				557	
26 July 1690 (WO 55/1757)				912	
1691 (SP 8/10, no.131)	992	8,513	18,883		
12 May 1692 (WO 55/1757)				101	
13 July 1693 (WO 55/1757)				77	
13 Mar. 1695 *(Ibid.)*				84	
Early Nov. 1701 (WO 49/119)			14,180	1,007	38,399
Nov. 1704 *(Ibid.)*			19,179	177	15,562

The State of Ordnance Reserves

The Ordnance Office was not only concerned with the organisation of artillery trains, but also was involved with the supply of munitions to the Navy, to the Army at home and abroad, and to plantations overseas. How did the Office cope with these extraordinary demands?

It is possible to gain some idea of the overall capacity of the Office in certain types of stores, by an examination of extant remains. From Table III it may be gathered that the Office was generally tolerably well provided for in cannon, gunpowder and saltpetre, although there was a shortage of the latter commodity in both post-Revolutionary wars. Table IV, which indicates the value of Ordnance reserves in store at various dates, also suggests that the total state of Ordnance stores was quite healthy. Indeed the valuations in Table IV show that the wealth of Ordnance store reserves gradually increased in the late 1680s and early 1690s (apart from the two remains of 1688 and 1690). This is not surprising considering the persistent increase in the size of both the Army and the Navy in those years.[1]

TABLE IV
The Total Value of Ordnance Reserves (in store),
1679-93

8 Sept. 1679 (D.1778/V 1373)	£333,237. 19s. 10½d. (excluding ordnance)
1 Jan. 1682 *(Ibid.)*	£318,360. 17s. 2½d. (excluding ordnance)
30 Sept. 1684 (D.1774/V 1375b)	£790,720. 6s. 6d.
1 Jan. 1686 (WO 55/1729)	£778,622. 12s. 5¾d.
30 Jan. 1687 (D.1778/V 1376)	£839,256. 11s. 10¾d.
Jan. 1688 (Harl. 7459, fo.27)	£721,373. 18s. 8¾d.
Jan. 1690 (Harl. 7461, fo. 30)	£735,477. 14s. 5d.
Jan. 1693 (WO 55/1734)	£940,358. 15s. 8d.

Such remains, however, are misleading. They give no indication of the yearly demand for stores,[2] and therefore can shed no light on whether there was a sufficiency of stores for all requirements. For a more realistic picture of the state of Ordnance reserves, it is necessary to turn away from lists of store remains towards evidence presented by the Ordnance officers and others regarding supply.

From this evidence a different picture emerges: one of insufficiency rather than plenty. Clarendon declaimed his surprise at the beginning of the fifth session of the second Parliament held at Oxford in October 1665, that:

> a triumphant nation that had made itself terrible to Christendom . . . should at the time of his majesty's happy return, as if on the sudden all their arms had been turned into plough shares and their swords into pruning hooks, not have in all the magazines . . . arms enough to be put into the hands of 5,000 men, nor provisions enough to send out ten new ships to sea. His majesty . . . made it his first care, without the least noise and with all imaginable shifts, to provide for the full supply of these important magazines and stores, which have ever since replenished as they ought.[3]

Very little evidence survives from the 1660s to test Clarendon's observation, but it appears that the state of war stores at the Restoration was

1 See conclusion, pp. 208-9.
2 General remains were usually only taken at the time of a storekeeper's replacement. See *The Armouries of the Tower of London*, I, 251-2, re. Tower remains.
3 Cobbett, IV, 319.

quite chaotic, judging by a Privy Council order of 11 September 1663 to account for 'our store and provisions of war . . . that so it may appear to us what quantities of each are in our stores and what further is yet wanting for the full completing those magazines royal'. In the following year, the Office still needed several species of cannon to complete the wartime gun establishment for the fleet.[1] It also appears that in certain periods of the second Dutch war, reserves of gunpowder and saltpetre were extremely low.[2] This is hardly surprising considering the vast quantities of saltpetre and gunpowder expended in that war, compared with the expense in peacetime. 46,051 barrels of gunpowder were made from 1,994 tons of saltpetre during the three year war with the Dutch, at a cost of over £170,000. The fleet alone was furnished with 16,000 barrels in 1666, although half was returned. This may be compared with the peace-time expenditure of gunpowder issued for all services from the Tower in the 1660s: 2,602 barrels in 1662; 3,527 in 1663; and 1,604 from December 1668 to December 1669.[3]

The story of shortages of essential supplies was often repeated in the following years. In September 1673, at the height of the third Dutch war, the board reported that there were many stores required before the fleet could be re-fitted for another season's campaigning.[4] It also appears there was an insufficiency of stocks for a complete gunning of the Navy in the 1680s. In January 1684, forty twelve pounders and fifteen sakers and saker cuts were wanting to complete the naval ordnance proportion. Nor did the situation improve, for in mid-December 1686 the board estimated it would take two years before the Office would be in a position to completely fit out the fleet to put to sea.[5] This estimate proved only too accurate. In March 1688, 1,026 carriages and fifty-three twelve pounders were still wanting for the Navy, although there were nearly 1,900 other guns spare; and as late as 30 June 1688, nearly £30,000 worth of carriages and other stores were necessary to fulfill the complete naval proportion. These reserves, moreover, proved insufficient for supplying the fleet in the 1688 campaign against William of Orange.[6] The supply of small arms was also very much exhausted at this time because of the issues to the land

1 ·WO 47/5, pp. 142-4, 244.

2 WO 47/7, fo. 33, minute 28 Mar. 1665, fo. 78, 4 June 1665.

3 WO 55/392, pp. 3 ff.; D.1778/V 64, note in Dartmouth's hand, 19 Apr. 1681; WO 49/112.

4 Add. MS. 28082, fo. 51, O.b. petition 22 Sept. 1673.

5 PL 2879; D.1778/V 47, abstract 12 Dec. 1686.

6 WO 55/1762; D.1778/V 55; *HMC* 20, 11 Rep. V, *Dartmouth I*, p. 211, Musgrave to Dartmouth, 22 Nov. 1688.

forces. A year later Schomberg could still report that there was a great want of small arms.[1]

A varied picture of the state of stores was presented by Ordnance officers in August 1689. 740 cannon were wanting for the supply of the English fleet, plus the proportions for ten new first and second rates. The 600 spare guns in store, moreover, were not of the correct size to answer the demands of the new ships. There was a sufficient supply of shot and shells for the whole Navy, however, and all the garrisons were reported as being well furnished with cannon. Contracts had been made for the supply of 7,727 barrels of gunpowder, 8,000 small arms and 1,500 tents, to supplement the stock of 5,500 barrels of naval powder, 5,500 small arms and 500 tents in store, but the board surmised that any order that had been contracted was likely to be 'very uncertain' unless 'seasonable supplies of money' could be granted.[2] Other reports from Ordnance officers in August 1689 implied that the stock of arms for the land forces was extremely low, and that without considerable sums of money they could not be replenished in less than twelve months. The want of small arms continued throughout the early 1690s, despite contracts with gunmakers for a supply of 3,000 arms per month.[3] Indeed the unexpected demand for all types of store was such that the board could report in March 1692 that existing stocks would soon be exhausted, despite the fact that the reserves were 'never so full' as at the beginning of that year. The gunpowder stores, especially, were likely to be quickly spent because of the demand for that commodity.[4] By March 1694 the gunpowder stocks had been replenished,[5] but the reserves of saltpetre were slender. (See Table III). The board, therefore, advised Romney against obstructing the bill for the free importation of saltpetre, which measure was subsequently passed.[6]

---

1 WO 55/335, fos. 94-5, O.b. to Dartmouth, 13 Oct. 1688; D.1778/I i, 1643, Gardiner to Dartmouth, 6 Dec. 1688; WO 55/336, fo. 136, 26 June 1689.

2 SP 8/5, no. 76, report 2 Aug. 1689. Also see *ibid.* no. 76i, Goodricke's report, giving a slightly different picture.

3 *Cal. SP. Col. Am. & W. Indies 1689-92,* p. 134, commissioners to the king, 24 Aug. 1689, pp. 136-7, Same to lords of Trade, 31 Aug. 1689; *Cal. SP. Dom. 1688-9,* p. 238, Shrewsbury to Trelawny, 31 Aug. 1689; Browning, *Danby* II, 179, Carmarthen to the king, 9 July 1690; WO 55/339, p. 32, O.b. to the king, 19 Mar. 1691; *Cal. SP. Dom. 1691-2,* p. 225, Nottingham to Treasury commissioners, 9 Apr. 1692.

4 WO 55/339, pp. 138-9, 2 Mar. 1692. 64,304 barrels of gunpowder were spent in the four years from Jan. 1690 to Jan. 1694. WO 46/3, p. 27, computation dated 26 March 1694.

5 Nearly 30,000 barrels being in reserve and over 26,000 barrels on board the fleet. WO 46/3, p. 30.

6 *Ibid.* p. 29, 28 Mar. 1694; *HMC* 17, HLNS I, 370-2.

The pressure on Ordnance stores was as great at the start of the following war. At the beginning of 1702, the Office found that it would be impossible to find gunpowder for the King of Sweden or to answer the demands of the Duke of Ormonde for gunpowder for a sea train. Over 22,000 barrels of gunpowder remained to be found to supply the fleet with forty rounds, and there were only about 16,475 barrels available in naval Ordnance stores.[1] On 31 March 1702 the principal officers informed Romney that the demand of the master of the Ordnance in Ireland for 1,258 barrels of gunpowder, 6,917 barrels of shot, and 850,000 flints would 'put the Office upon the utmost difficulties' and 'very much exhaust our stores'. They proposed deferring supply because of the pressing needs of the fleet and the descent trains for all types of stores. By the end of May there were only 3,000 barrels of gunpowder in store, even though the powdermakers in England had been employed to capacity in supplying 400 barrels a week, and 4,000 barrels had been contracted for in Holland.[2] The Duke of Ormonde's demand for stores had been so great that in November 1702 little was left, 'except powder and some small emptions', to answer the Earl of Peterborough's request for over £30,000 worth of stores.[3] In 1703, judging from the lack of complaints, the Office was able to cope with the demand for stores, although it became impossible in that and subsequent years to comply with naval demands according to the new gun establishment devised in 1703.[4] The only spare naval guns the Office possessed at this time were being saved for new ships, which presumably were being gunned according to the new establishment.[5]

In 1704, 1705 and 1706 the board renewed their pleas to the secretaries of state about the extraordinary claims on Ordnance stores. In July 1704, the board acquainted Hedges that because of the recent issues to Portugal, they had only 3,059 serviceable muskets in store, out of which the new levies were supposed to be supplied with 2,556. It reckoned the Office would have difficulty in immediately supplying 3,000 arms overseas, although it was expected that such a quantity would be available in a month's time. The arms, however, were ordered to be sent abroad, despite Ordnance protestations that if this happened

1 WO 46/5, p. 50, O.b. to Romney, 3 Jan. 1702, p. 67, Same to Same, 14 Feb. 1702, p. 68, calculation 10 Jan. 1702.

2 *Ibid.* p. 83, p. 99, O.b. to Romney, 21 May 1702.

3 WO 55/342, p. 297, O.b. to Nottingham, 7 Nov. 1702.

4 WO 55/343, p. 136; Adm. 1/3999, O.b. to Admiralty, 5 June, 20 July 1703, 13, 31 Jan. 1704; Adm. 1/4002, O.b. to Admiralty, 3 July 1707, 15 Apr. 1708; Adm. 1/4003, O.b. to Admiralty, 2 June 1708.

5 WO 47/25, p. 11, 8 July 1707.

there would be no arms left for the new levies or for extraordinary occasions.[1] In September the Office was partly able to comply with a demand from the Prince of Hesse in Gilbraltar, although only ship carriages were in store for the cannon and there was an insufficient number of gunners or engineers to be sent over. Two months later the board observed that if 3,000 muskets were then issued there would be only about 2,000 left in store for land service.[2] A review of the position of the Office at the beginning of 1705, for the first time suggested that there might be a serious dislocation in the provision of ordnance. The saltpetre reserves which had stood at 800 tons at the beginning of the war had been reduced to 170 tons, and there were only about 6,000 small arms in stock, whereas previously there had been 60,000. 'We are like to be in a little time', Marlborough was informed, 'without stores, money and credit'.[3] A great demand for officers and stores for Gibraltar amounting to over £164,000 produced this reaction from the board in a letter to Secretary Sunderland in February 1705:

> your grace very well knows by the extraordinary issues during this war for which no money has been given by Parliament or otherwise to resupply, the magazines are at this time very indifferently furnished with those three considerable species of stores, [gunpowder, small arms and cannon shot] notwithstanding by your Grace's directions the beginning of this winter we have made large contracts hoping to prevent any disappointment for want of the same.[4]

Further letters from the board to the secretary of state in June, August and December of 1705 confirmed that the stocks of small arms were low,[5] and early in the following year the board was empowered to contract for arms abroad as the home gunmakers supply of 2,000 arms a month was insufficient to meet the extraordinary demands.[6] At the beginning of 1706 there was also a shortage of saltpetre, but the situation was saved with the arrival of 1,500 tons on board the East India ships.[7] The stores were so poorly stocked, however, that the Office was unable to meet the demand for an additional supply of mortars, shells, handgrenades and other arms for the Navy. It was ordered that these stores were to be furnished only to such ships and in such proportions

---

1 SP 41/34, no. 4, 8 July 1704; O.b. to Hedges, 10 July 1704.

2 PRO, MS Cal. SP Anne, p. 150; Same to Same, 23 Sept. 1704; SP 41/34, no. 9, O.b. to Hedges, 11 Nov. 1704.

3 WO 46/6, p. 21, O.b. to Marlborough, 9 Jan. 1705.

4 Blenheim CI 30, 10 Feb. 1705.

5 SP 41/34, no. 27, 28 June, no. 30, 3 Aug, 6, 8, 29 Dec. 1705.

6 PC 2/80, pp. 90-1, order 7 Feb. 1706; WO 55/344, p. 128, warrant 7 Feb. 1706.

7 WO 46/6, p. 41, O.b. to Marlborough, 8 Jan. 1706.

as the lord high admiral judged necessary, until the magazines were able to cope adequately with the increase.[1]

Some idea of the amounts expended of the two principal stores which seem to have been in shortest supply in these years, may be gained from an examination of the accounts of the state of small arms, salt-petre and gunpowder, 1702-4, submitted to Parliament in conjunction with the 1705 estimates. These figures, which are reproduced in Table V, show the heavy outlay in these stores at the beginning of the Spanish Succession War.

Such general lists again give no indication of local shortages of Ordnance stores. It was of little use for the immediate dispatch of a ship or for the munitioning of a troop of garrison soldiers if the general state of stores was satisfactory, but the stores at a number of outports and garrisons were totally inadequate. Throughout the period there are indications that the stores at some garrisons and ports were not as well supplied as they might have been.

The outlying garrisons were likely to be poorly supplied, especially it seems in the 1660s, when there were frequent complaints about the inadequate state of garrison stores from the governors of such places as Pendennis Castle and the Isles of Wight, Scilly and Guernsey.[2] Nor was it only the outlying garrisons that were likely to be badly equipped. The governor of Tilbury for example, requested in January 1665 that a supply of carriages and gunpowder might be sent to the garrison, 'it being destitute of all manner of store'. The garrison had formerly been assigned a constant yearly allowance by Sir William Compton, and the board reported in favour of its continuance.[3] The order of June 1670, which instructed the master of the Ordnance to supply forty rounds of gunpowder, shot, and proportionable stores to any garrison when necessary, provided an account of the stores expend-ed had been received from the garrison commander,[4] may have contri-buted to the decline in the number of petitions from governors about the lack of supply. Although after this date the outlying garrisons were still liable to be neglected.[5]

---

1   WO 55/344, p. 124; Corbett 14, fo. 165.
2   E.g. see WO 47/5, p. 64, Arundell's petition; WO 47/5, p. 66, Sir Willaim Godolphin's petition, Nov. 1664, p. 183, petition of deputy-governor of Isle of Wight, 1664; WO 47/6, fo. 111, Hatton's petition; WO 47/19b, p. 436, O.b. to PC, 23 July 1669.
3   WO 47/6, fo. 109, report 3 Jan. 1665; PC 6/18, p. 62, petition 26 Feb. 1664; WO 55/388, fo. 69, O.b. to PC, 20 May 1664; WO 47/5, pp. 229-30.
4   SP 44/35a, fo. 14, warrant 18 June 1670.
5   E.g. see SP 44/111, St. John to O.b., 20 July 1711, enclosing letter of 9 July,

TABLE V
The State of Small Arms. Saltpetre and Gunpowder
1702-4

Small Arms (Nos. of)

State of Small Arms	Issues	Receipts & Returns	Arms Expended for Which No Return Made
1 Jan. 1702 47,625	36,642½	19,586½	
1 Jan. 1703 30,569	26,274	24,778	70,721 (Value £78,179.8s.)
1 Jan. 1704 26,274	7,804½	3,704½	
30 June 1704 24,973			

Saltpetre (To Nearest Ton)

State of Saltpetre	Saltpetre Received	Saltpetre Issued to Powdermakers
Beg. Nov. 1701 1,007		
1702	400	1,056
1703	443	379
30 June 1704 177		238

Gunpowder (In Barrels).

State of Gunpowder	Gunpowder Received	Gunpowder Expended
Beg. Nov. 1701 14,180		
1702	15,513	13,949
1703	17,637	15,331
30 June 1704 19,179	5,747	4,618

Note:

    These figures have been adapted from those in CJ XIV, 416-17, 13 Nov. 1704. Copies of these accounts may be found in WO 49/19 and T.1/92, fos. 193 ff.

There were fewer complaints in the 1660s of the ports being inadequately furnished with ordnance.[1] It should not be supposed, however, that lack of evidence means there was no shortage of war

re. Scilly Isles; WO 49/120, the Earl of Leven's, demand for the Scottish garrisons.
1 Although see WO 49/112, Batchler to Marsh(?), 5 July 1665, re. Chatham.

stores at the ports in this period. In the War of Spanish Succession, 1702-13, for which there is a complete set of correspondence between the Ordnance board and the Admiralty, there were constant complaints from the Navy that Portsmouth, Harwich, and Plymouth, in particular, were inadequately supplied with Ordnance stores.[1] One of the main reasons for this must have been their comparatively isolated position from the central Ordnance bases around the Thames and Medway.

The quality of ordnance did not always make up for the insufficiency in quantity. At intervals the Office was authorised to dispose of a number of unserviceable stores which were 'utterly decayed and useless and do so much fill up and encumber the stores, particularly those within his majesty's magazine in the Tower of London, that there is not conveniency for receiving and lodging such good and serviceable provisions. . .'[2] Despite these injunctions there is evidence that some Ordnance stores were plainly inadequate. The bedding in the barracks quickly became worn.[3] Reports were not infrequently made that carriages were unserviceable, or that cannon were rusty or over-mettled.[4] Above all, complaints were lodged with the board about the defectiveness of small arms. The quality of the arms in the 1689 Irish expedition under Schomberg seem to have been especially poor, and various representations were made at other times about the inferiority of weapons.[5]

The Efficiency of Supply[6]

A review has been made of the organisation of artillery trains and

1 Adm. 1/3999, O.b. to Admiralty, 19 Apr., 21 June, 6, 20 July 1703, 31 Jan., 10 Mar. 1704; Adm. 1/4000, O.b. to Admiralty, 13 June, 15 July, 12 Sept., 21 Nov. 1704, 20 Jan. 1705; Adm. 1/4001, O.b. to Admiralty, 29 Jan. 1706; Adm. 1/4002, O.b. to Admiralty, 21 Oct., 25 Nov. 1706; Adm. 1/4004, O.b. to Admiralty, 22 June, 29 Aug. 1710, 15 Mar. 1711.

2 WO 55/330, pp. 309-10, warrant 6 July 1661; PC 6/18, p. 116, warrant 27 Nov. 1667, pp. 151-2, 23 Feb. 1676.

3 WO 47/9, p. 134, minute 12 Apr. 1681; WO 47/12, p. 23, minute 28 Oct. 1682; WO 47/25, p. 10, minute 8 July 1707; WO 47/29, p. 250, minute 12 Oct. 1716.

4 PL 2862, p. 120, Pepys to Dartmouth, n.d. (c. Oct. 1688); WO 55/335, fo. 99, Dartmouth to O.b., 13 Oct. 1688; WO 55/1792, fo. 28, Bowles to O.b., 10 Jan. 1690; WO 46/1, fo. 153, account of carriages at Hull, 30 Mar. 1680; WO 47/7, p. 47, Pepys to Sherburne, 13 Apr. 1665; Adm. 3/9, 8 Feb. 1694; Adm. 1/4002, O.b. to Admiralty, 3 Feb. 1708; Adm. 1/4004, 21 Mar. 1712.

5 Cal. SP. Dom. 1689-90, p. 36, Schomberg to the king, 22 Mar. 1689; WO 55/337, fo. 55, Schomberg to O.b., 16 Nov, fo. 79, Same to Same, 27 Dec. 1689, fo. 90, PC to O.b., 31 Jan. 1690; SP 8/6, no. 66 n.d. c. 1690; WO 55/343, p. 173, Nottingham to O.b., 10 Sept, 1703; Cal. SP. Dom. 1703-4, p. 162, Same to Same, 19 Oct. 1703; WO 47/29, p. 160, 10 July 1716; WO 47/32, p. 130, 27 Mar. 1719.

6 A part of the following section has been published in my, 'The Ordnance

the state and quality of Ordnance stores in this period, but it is also important to examine the efficiency of this organisation, and the effectiveness of the supply of stores to the forces, and to try and explain why deficiencies occurred and to what extent the Office was responsible for these deficiencies.

Some military and naval historians have castigated the Office for its indifferent supply of munitions throughout its existence. Ehrman observed that 'from the sixteenth to the nineteenth century the Ordnance enjoyed an unbroken reputation for procrastination and corruption'. Oppenheim's verdict was even less charitable. His researches into the administration of the Navy led him to the conclusion that by 1638, 'the Ordnance Office had already obtained that evil pre-eminence in sloth and incapacity it has never since lost'. More recently Marcus wrote that the mismanagement of the Ordnance Office was primarily responsible for the poor provision of munitions to the fleet in 1688.[1] How accurate are these observations?

Not all contemporaries echoed these historians' damning judgements. In the summer of 1666, for example, the leader of the fleet was clearly pleased with the supply of naval ordnance. On 23 August of that year Coventry was informed: 'The commissioners of the Ordnance have expressed great care. We have no reason to complain of them. They have supplied us well in everything except junk, which, it seems, was not to be gotten'. These and other compliments contrast strongly with the failure of the victuallers in the same campaign.[2] In May 1673 Prince Rupert was again warmly appreciative of the punctual performance of the Office in supplying the fleet and ammunition ships.[3] The principal Ordnance officers alluded to these commendations in 1674, when they attempted to rebut the charges which were made against them of having failed to supply the fleet adequately in the campaign the previous summer. The board vigorously defended itself by giving a detailed account not only of the amount of ordnance that had been delivered to the fleet during the 1673 campaign, but also the

Office and the Navy, 1660-1714', *EHR* 90 (1975), pp. 19-39.

1 J. Ehrman, *The Navy in the War of William III* (Cambridge, 1953), p. 176; M. Oppenheim, 'The Royal Navy under Charles I, part III: The Administration', *EHR* 9 (1894), p. 482; G. J. Marcus, *A Naval History of England*, I: *The Formative Centuries* (1961), p. 190; Chandler (p. 156) presents a more balanced conclusion.

2 *Rupert and Monck Letter Book 1666*, ed. J. R. Powell and E. K. Timings, Navy Records Soc. 122 (1969), pp. 133, 138, 139. See also N.A.M. Roger, 'The Ordnance Board in 1666'. *Mariner's Mirror* 62 (1976), 91-4.

3 *Cal. SP. Dom. 1673*, p. 280, Hamilton to Arlington, 21 May. p. 301, Same to Same, 27 May.

quantity of the supplies that had remained over after the engagements had taken place. Indeed, contrary to the allegations that had been made, the board asserted that the issuing of such great quantities of stores for land and sea forces was a notable achievement. As the principal officers observed:

> at the last going out in July [1673] they [had] provided, besides the supply of gunners' stores for the whole Navy with all its tenders, all fitting stores and equipage for the land forces, and train of artillery then designed. That is to say, all manner of arms offensive and defensive, ammunition of all sorts, horses, tents for 10,000 men, habiliments of war of all kinds, and other utensils and instruments, as well for entrenchments as surprises, in case a descent had been made either upon the coast of Holland or elsewhere. All which to the value of £40,000 and upward have been supplied by them, sent out extraordinarily and upon the credit of the Office the last summer without one penny advanced for the same.

Evidence from such a polemical work must inevitably be treated with a degree of circumspection, but the favourable opinion of Prince Rupert about the supplying of the fleet before the first engagement in May 1673, suggests that the Office was not dilatory in its efforts to munition the fleet in this campaign. The board's observation that 'if success had been answerable to . . . supplies, this apology had not been needed', certainly rings true.[1]

The number of complaints about the inefficiency of naval ordnance supply made by naval administrators and sea captains alike, however, vastly outweigh the favourable reports and it is folly to ignore them. Pepys's Admiralty letter books for the 1670s and 1680s, the Admiralty minute books from 1689, and scattered miscellaneous correspondence, all point to delays in the provision of gunpowder, guns, and petty emptions to naval ships.[2] The extent of the delay varied from a few weeks, if the captain was fortunate, to a number of weeks or even longer.[3] Very often ships waited only for guns and were in all other respects ready to sail.[4] If a ship was ordered to carry guns to a station abroad and they were not ready, she was hindered from taking in her other provisions. The consequences of the failure of the Ordnance Office to supply stores on time, were more serious in the case of the squadron which was unable to chase after Dunkirk privateers, because

---

1 For the Board's rebuttal see *A Just Vindication of the Principal Officers of his Majesty's Ordnance* . . . (1674). Both tracts are to be found in the Goldsmith Library Collection, London University (nos. 2061, 2103).

2 See my, 'Ordnance Office and the Navy', p. 19, n. 3, and the references there cited.

3 *Ibid.*, p. 20, n. 1 and references there cited.

4 *Ibid.*, p. 20, n. 2 and references there cited.

of the alleged mismanagement of the Ordnance in the fitting out of the ships.[1] But the most notorious example of departmental inefficiency in the supply of naval ordnance during the whole period was the ill-organisation of the Office during the latter months of 1688, when the fleet was assembling to meet William's invasion.[2]

The dispatch of the artillery train in 1688 was more efficiently handled than the supply of naval stores. The warrant for the marching of the train was not delivered until 8 November, but a preparatory warrant had been issued several days before this on 15 October.[3] Yet by the date the first warrant was signed, preparations had already been made for the assembly of the train,[4] and it would seem that by the end of October the train was in a condition to march — although it was not finally dispatched until November, by which time the train had been radically altered in design from that originally intended.[5]

There is very little further evidence about whether the preparation of other artillery trains and land expeditions was efficiently managed by the Ordnance Office. According to the account of the Ordnance officers themselves, the stores for the 1673 expedition, for instance, were adequately dealt with, although the artillery officers on that particular expedition were criticised for being negligent.[6] In 1694 the stores for the artillery train were shipped away in good time.[7] In the War of Spanish Succession, judging by the reports from the Office

---

1 Adm. 3/2, 10 Dec. 1689; Adm. 3/18, 1 June 1703.

2 As early as 11 Sept. Pepys informed the Ordnance Office of the complaints that had been made by naval commanders concerning the tardiness of the Ordnance officers in supplying naval stores. Such complaints were constantly re-iterated in the following weeks. (For details see my, 'Ordnance Office and the Navy', p. 20). It may well be that some of the criticisms from naval personnel were politically inspired by officers who were sympathetic to William's cause, but the very number of complaints to Pepys from disillusioned captains, the re-iteration of such criticisms by Lord Dartmouth, and above all, the evidence about the state of the department from the Ordnance officers themselves, would seem to suggest that there was something seriously amiss with Ordnance naval administration at this time.

3 Above, p. 131.

4 See WO 55/335, fos. 98-9, for Dartmouth's instructions re. train, 11 Oct. 1688; D.1778/I i 1392, Sheer to Dartmouth, 12 Oct. 1688; WO 55/335, fos. 94-5. 13 Oct. 1688; D.1778/I i 1504, Philip Musgrave to Dartmouth, ? Oct. 1688.

5 D.1778/I i 1449, Tichburne to Dartmouth, 20 Oct. 1688; D.1778/I i 1572, P. Musgrave to Dartmouth, 22 Nov. 1688.

6 Above, p. 144-5; Cal. SP. Dom. 1673, p. 448, Schomberg (to Arlington?), 21 July 1673.

7 WO 46/3, p. 62.

to the secretary of state,[1] there was no serious dislocation in the preparation of artillery trains and land expeditions abroad. The most serious failure of the Office in the preparation of land expeditions during the whole period, seems to have been in 1667 at the time of the Medway incident,[2] and in 1689, when Schomberg commanded the Army for the reduction of Ireland. In 1667 there was very little time to assemble an artillery train, but there was no such excuse in 1689. Schomberg arrived in Chester on 20 July of that year to embark for Ireland, to find there was a complete lack of artillery, baggage and provisions in the magazines. He was compelled, therefore, to stay in Chester for twenty-two days arranging stores, and he did not set sail until 12 August. Even then he had only 10,000 men and part of his artillery ready to sail.[3]

It is not enough, however, for the historian to relate stories of failure. His more important task is to ask why such failures happened. The failure of the Office to answer consistently all demands for stores in wartime, the poor quality of some of those stores, and above all the inadequacy of aspects of their supply must be explained. Some of these mistakes may be put down to personal negligence. On other occasions it was the unweildiness of the administrative machine that could be faulted. But at many other times the resources of the state were such, that it lay quite outside the power of the administrator to control events.

The Ordnance Office was only a cog in a very large administrative machine. As has been discussed in an earlier chapter, before supplies could be made, a warrant had to be gained from an appropriate authority: the Privy Council, the Admiralty, or one of the secretaries of state. In addition, the Ordnance was dependent on the co-operation of other departments and personnel over whom it had no direct control. Garrison commanders at home and abroad and Army commanders in the field had to inform the Office of their wants; naval personnel had to work

---

1 SP 41/34, *passim.*

2 See *CJ* IX, 11-14, Albermarle's report; *Pepys Diary,* 17 June, 23, 25 Oct. 1667.

3 *Dalrymple,* II, 130-1. The extent of the Office's responsibility for this debacle is debatable. Goodricke, the lieutenant-general, certainly denied that there was any delay in the supply of artillery horses, although the department may be held responsible for the appointment of inferior artillery officers and the provision of poor quality arms. The real author of the intrigue seems to have been one Shales a commissary of the train and a suspect Jacobite, who was believed to have deliberately sabotaged supply efforts. See Cobbett, V, 453 ff.; *Dalrymple,* II, 167-8, Schomberg to the king, 9 Aug. 1689, p. 168, Same to Same, 27 Aug. 1689, p. 171, Same to Same, 6 Oct. 1689.

with the Office in refitting a ship; Transport commissioners had to ensure a sufficiency of vessels to carry ordnance overseas; the Admiralty had to safeguard Ordnance convoys; above all Parliament had to vote, and the Treasury to supply, or promise to supply, a sufficiently attractive fund to maintain the Office's credit. In order to mount an expedition successfully the secretaries of state were responsible for co-ordinating these agencies, and it needed only one to fail to hold up the entire operation. It is hardly surprising that in such an interdependent system the chain of command snapped whever sufficient pressure was exerted upon it. Very often it was the central links in this chain which broke first.

Delays in the munitioning of ships and in the provision of ordnance for expeditions were sometimes caused by the failure of the secretaries to inform the board of the king's intentions. On 9 January 1692, for example, the principal officers wrote to Secretary Nottingham for information about the nature of the artillery to be prepared for that year's service. The earlier that this was known, the better the management of the king's affairs. Notwithstanding this plea, the 'king's pleasure' regarding the Flanders train for that year was not signified until 4 February. Later in the year the board was kept in ignorance of the expected time and place of its embarkation, and its destination.[1] At times it was the short notice given which made it very difficult for the board to comply with the demand, and on other occasions the secretaries completely ignored the board's request for directions.[2] The lack of clarity in the orders to the board could be just as tiresome. In March 1692 Secretary Nottingham was informed that the Office was at a loss to know where to send stores for the Irish train. Directions were at first given to send them to Waterford; then on further advice from Whitehall, Cork was decided upon; finally the Irish lords justices had instructed the board that Kinsale was the most suitable place.[3] At other times the estimate was insufficiently detailed for the board to act upon it, or the amount of stores originally intended to be sent was altered midway through the preparations for supply.[4]

1 WO 55/340, fo. 30, 9 Jan., fo. 42, 4 Feb. 1693; WO 55/339, p. 165, O.b. to Nottingham, 9 Apr., p. 167, Same to Same, 15 Apr. 1692.

2 WO 46/6, p. 34, O.b. to Marlborough, 10 Apr. 1705; Blenheim C I 20, O.b. to Sunderland, 10 Dec. 1708; SP 41/34, O.b. to Dartmouth, 16 Oct. 1711, 29 Feb. 1712, 11 Apr., 16 June 1713.

3 WO 55/339, p. 156, 18 Mar. 1692.

4 Add. MS. 29588, fo. 421, O.b. to Nottingham, 18 Mar. 1703; SP 41/34, no. 6, O.b. to Hedges, 15 July 1704, no. 18, Same to Same, 22 Mar. 1705; SP 44/105, Hedges to O.b., 12 June 1706.

It was not only the secretaries, however, who were liable to give inadequate directions to the board. The Admiralty officers were also responsible for imprecise messages and incorrect orders. In the summer of 1703, for instance, the board asked the Admiralty why directions had been given that the *Assurance* was to be gunned like the *Content,* and the *Moderate* like the *Dreadnought,* when it resulted in ten more guns being assigned to each than they had gun-ports for. The letter was endorsed, 'to be told 'twas meant guns of the same nature as those in the *Content* and *Dreadnought'*. Less than a year later, however, the Admiralty had indeed mistaken the number of gun-ports on a ship.[1] At other times the Admiralty failed to specify the nature, length, and position of guns to be altered,[2] or gave an incorrect order, or changed the order about the gunning of a ship.[3] The Admiralty was also responsible for delays in the issuing of orders. Despite the Ordnance board's protestation that the king's warrant to the Office directed through the Admiralty should keep pace with those to naval officials, and Pepys's assurance that warrants for gunning a ship were usually dispatched on the same day as warrants for fitting a ship, delays did occur through the Admiralty's failure to send out orders on time.[4] The Admiralty's negligence in giving a sufficient warning to the Office that a new ship was being built was also likely to cause a protracted delay, as the provision of suitable heavy ordnance for a whole ship took some time to assemble.[5]

Delayed orders were not necessarily caused by the negligence of any one party. Sometimes delays were unavoidable because of the length of the winding tunnel of communication between the central executive authorities and the dependent administrative departments. This was especially the case in the gunning of a ship. Before a ship could be supplied the king's warrant had to be obtained through the Admiralty, passed on to the Ordnance board in the Tower, who in turn referred it to their own storekeepers in the ports. Although in an emergency the direct authority of a naval officer would suffice.[6] Frequently, therefore,

1 Adm. 1/3999, 27 July 1703, O.b. to Adm., 18 Apr. 1704.

2 Adm. 1/4003, O.b. to Adm., 30 Sept., 14 Oct. 1708; Adm. 1/4004, Same to Same, 19 Sept. 1710.

3 Adm. 1/3999, Same to Same, 7 Dec. 1703; Adm. 3/1, p. 126. Adm. 3/17, minute 12 Dec. 1702.

4 See *Cat. Pepys* III, ed. J.R. Tanner, Navy Records Soc. 36 (1909). pp. 250-1, and PL 2862, p. 21, for the board's protestation and for Pepys's assurance. For examples of Admiralty delay, see Adm. 1/3999, O.b. to Admiralty, 17 Mar., 5 Apr. 1704; Adm. 1/4001, Same to Same, 21 Mar. 1706.

5 Adm. 1/4001, O.b. to Admiralty, 21 Aug. 1706.

6 Above, p. 32.

an Ordnance storekeeper justified his inaction through his lack of orders from his own superiors,[1] and even in wartime the power of flag officers to give orders for the munitioning of ships was sometimes questioned by the Ordnance storekeeper.[2] On such occasions the only remedy was for the naval officer to inform the Admiralty board, the Admiralty would then contact the Ordnance board in the Tower, and that board would finally inform the Ordnance storekeeper of the captain's wants.[3]

Supplies for garrisons were less likely to be delayed, for, as we have seen, the master-general himself had the executive authority to supply fortifications when necessary. In an emergency Ordnance storekeepers could also issue stores when they were demanded by garrison governors, as long as they indented for them.[4] However, it is clear from an account of the attempts of Lieutenant-Governor Hales to strengthen the Tower batteries overlooking the City in November 1688, on the authority of the king's verbal order rather than the king or Council's written warrant, that governors did not possess automatic powers to requisition stores.[5] If regimental arms were needed similar formalities were observed. The commander of a regiment could not order the Ordnance storekeeper to deliver arms, as the storekeeper could only act on the board's authority. Such procedures inevitably caused frustration and delay.[6]

As important a reason for inefficient supply as the intractable and inflexible chain of command between the central executive and the departments, was the interdependence of the departments themselves. It simply needed obstruction from one of them for the whole operation of supply to be placed in jeopardy.

One of the chief problems was the repeated failure of the Transport commissioners. The Ordnance board sometimes assumed direct respon-

---

1 *Cat. Pepys* II, 225 *Cat. Pepys* III, 20; WO 55/338, fos. 36, 38; WO 55/1792. fo. 38; Adm. 3/3, p. 251.

2 WO 55/1792, fo. 10; WO 46/3., p. 124; Adm. 1/4000, O.b. to Adm., 13 May 1704.

3 The time taken for some orders to be transferred to the Ordnance store-keeper was quite remarkable. See e.g. my, 'Ordnance Office and the Navy', p. 23, re. the gunning of the *Namure*.

4 WO 55/1795, Dartmouth's order, 16 Dec. 1682; *Cal. SP Dom. 1685*, p. 206, no. 919, warrant to Dartmouth, 17 July 1685.

5 Although in this case Shales succeeded in getting the master gunner to mount a mortar on the Tower (the proportion having been signed by Hales himself and two Ordnance officials), despite the demands of Philip Musgrave, the clerk of the deliveries, that the formal departmental procedures should be observed. See D. 1778/I i 1572, P. Musgrave to Dartmouth, 22 Nov, 1688.

6 See e.g. *HMC* 43, 15 Rep. VII, 118-19, Portmore to Somerset, 9 Feb. 1704.

sibility for contracting vessels for the transportation of stores abroad,[1] but more usually it relied for its shipping on the Navy Board and, after its formation in March 1690, the Transport Board. The early history of this latter body, in particular, was one of confusion. The poor financial provision for the Board was among the worst of its problems. There was no separate parliamentary grant for the Transport Office — money for the department being provided by the Army and Navy funds — no treasurer and no regular course of payment. The commission, moreover, was not directly responsible to any person or body, as its orders emanated directly from the Treasury, Admiralty and secretaries of state. Partly as a result of this haphazard organisation, the first Transport commission appears to have been a thoroughly inefficient body.[2] The Ordnance board certainly had cause to make more than one complaint in the early 1690s about the poor standards in the provision of transports maintained by the Transport commissioners.[3]

In the following war, however, the Transport service appears to have worked more smoothly. By that time the old commission had been disbanded, a treasurer had been appointed, and financial instructions had instituted a regular course of payment.[4] This seems to have had a marked effect on the Transport Board's credit and its administrative efficiency, at least as far as the Ordnance was concerned. For the Ordnance board made no adverse criticism of the transport commissioners in its letters to the secretaries of state during the Spanish Succession War.[5]

If the story of the provision of transports is one of steady improvement, the same cannot be said of the provision of convoys, on which both the Ordnance and Transport Offices depended for its shipping to be safeguarded. Ordnance shipping was hindered throughout the period through the inability of the Admiralty to provide suitable escorts. Delays of some weeks were frequent, whilst those of months were not

---

1 See PC 6/18, p. 131, letter to Ordnance commissioners, 26 Mar. 1669; *CJ* X, 436, account 10 Oct. 1691; *Cal. SP Dom. 1703-4*, p. 15, Nottingham to O.b., 15 June 1703; SP 44/108, fo. 231, Sunderland to O.b., 17 May 1710.

2 For the history of the Transport Board, 1702-14, see Watson, pp. 260 ff.

3 E.g. WO 55/339, p. 23, 7 Mar. 1691, p. 47, 2 Apr. 1691; *Cal. SP Dom. 1691-2*, pp. 176-7, O.b. to Goodricke, 10 Mar. 1692; WO 55/339, pp. 165, 167, 214, 220, O.b. to Nottingham, 9, 15 Apr., 30 June, 16 July 1692; WO 55/340, fos. 27-8, report 17 Nov. 1692, fo. 71, O.b. to Nottingham, 2 May 1693.

4 Watson, pp. 260-1, 286, 288, 291-2.

5 Indeed, on one of the few occasions the board mentioned the Transport commissioners in the extant correspondence, they appeared in a very different light from the earlier commissioners. See SP 41/43, nos. 22i, 23, 9, 14 Apr. 1705.

uncommon.[1] To lessen such delays during the 1702-13 War, the Office suggested that information about convoys should be sent to the Ordnance by the Admiralty prior to the vessel's loading.[2]

The Admiralty, however, was not always culpable. The master of the vessel to be conveyed had every incentive to delay, for the longer he waited the higher his demurrage would be. In certain cases, the Ordnance clearly suspected that the vessel owners had neglected their opportunity of returning with a convoy.[3] The lack of convoys may also be partly imputed to the negligence of naval officers. On application for convoy, the Admiralty, instead of appointing a specific ship, sometimes asked the master of the Ordnance hoy to apply directly to flag officers for escort.[4] Captains, however, were inclined to disregard the request, either through sheer obstinacy or because they lacked specific Admiralty orders.[5]

Of more consequence was the commander's want of care whilst actually convoying, for the charge of the loss of the vessel was likely to fall on the Crown rather than the vessel's owner. In the Dutch Wars, the king encouraged commanders to take enemy privateers instead of merchantmen, by giving them the entire benefit of their capture, and this had a decidedly ill effect on their care of convoys.[6] Delays in the sailing of vessels could be as disastrous, for they caused a heavy charge on the Office for demurrage,[7] and they also meant that vital services could not be performed on time. Stores could not be sent to the fleet or the garrisons, new iron ordnance was held up at the south coast outports to the foundries, and works on new wharves and fortifications came to a standstill through lack of stone.[8] Those vessels that attempted a voyage without support ran the risk of being ransacked by the privateers who haunted the coast.[9]

The Admiralty was ultimately responsible for the provision of

1   See my, 'Ordnance Office and the Navy', p. 30, n. 7, and references there cited.
2   Adm. 1/4000, O.b. to Adm., 21 Nov. 1706; Adm. 1/4001, Same to Same, 11 Aug. 1705.
3   Adm. 1/4002, O.b. to Adm., 27 Oct. 1707, 20 Apr. 1708; Adm. 1/4004, O.b. to Adm., 10 July 1711.
4   Adm. 3/7, 14 May 1692; Adm. 3/17, 7 Dec. 1702; Adm. 3/19, 18 May 1704.
5   Adm. 1/3999, O.b. to Adm., 27 Apr. 1703; Adm. 1/4000, Same to Same, 13 Sept. 1704; Adm. 1/4004, Same to Same, 28 Oct. 1710; Adm. 3/19, minute 3 Nov. 1703.
6   *Cat. Pepys* IV, 10, 14.
7   In the early 1680s John Holmes demanded 50s. a day. WO 44/714.
8   See my, 'Ordnance Office and the Navy', p. 30, n. 9, and references there cited.
9   Adm. 1/3999, 23 Sept., 20 Oct. 1703.

Ordnance convoys, and that Office must bear the largest portion of the blame for the failures in the escort of Ordnance shipping. The Admiralty may also be blamed for disrupting supply by authorising the impressment of Ordnance personnel, notwithstanding the official protections that had been granted to the men concerned.[1] In their defence the Admiralty protested against the large numbers of good seamen protected by the Ordnance and other offices, and claimed that the pressing of all men was directed by order of council, which order could only be retracted by the Privy Council.[2]

Captains also caused difficulties by their provocative behaviour. It was the captiains' responsibility to order their master gunners to contact an Ordnance official in order to receive orders for stores to be sent on board ship, but it frequently happened that the guns and stores were ready some time before they were collected from the Ordnance Office.[3] It may well not have been the captains' fault that their gunners were not sent more expeditiously to receive the guns, for very often the Navy Board had failed to make ready their ships to receive them on board,[4] but captains were certainly responsible for other misdemeanours which impeded the steady dispatch of ships' stores.[5] A further cause of friction was the unwarranted requests made by some captains that their ships' munitions should be changed, or other groundless complaints of lack of stores.[6] The board claimed that if such extraordinary requests for ordnance had been acceded to, there would have been 'no method or certainty in fitting out her majesty's Navy.'[7]

1 WO 55/339, p. 189; WO 47/8, Duke of York's warrant, 2 July 1666; WO 55/340, p. 72; Adm. 1/3999, O.b. to Adm., 6 Nov. 1703; Adm. 1/4004, Same to Same, 12 July 1710; Adm. 3/1, minute 25 June 1689.

2 Adm. 3/3, p. 272, 5 Aug. 1690; HMC 17 HLNS VII, 524; Cal. SP Dom. 1697, p. 165; WO 55/339, p. 189. See Tomlinson, 'Ordnance Office and the Navy, p. 29, n.7, re. lists of protections granted by the Ordnance Office.

3 NMM Dartmouth MS. XV, p. 66, Dartmouth to Pepys, 22 Oct. 1688; Adm. 1/3999, O.b. to Admiralty, 8, 29, Jan. 1704; Adm. 1/4000, Same to Same, 16 May, 21 July 1704; Adm. 1/4001, Same to Same, 10 Apr. 1705; Adm. 1/4002, Same to Same, 29 May 1707.

4 Cal. SP Dom. 1667-8, p. 403, O.b. to Navy commissioners, 21 May 1688; SP 46/137, part IV, no. 328, p. 641, Same to Same, 16 Mar. 1672; Adm. 1/3999, O.b. to Admiralty, 15 Apr. 1704; Adm. 1/4001, Same to Same, 28 Nov. 1705; Adm. 1/4003, Same to Same, 13 Mar. 1709.

5 Such as dragooning Ordnance hoys when a ship was re-fitting. See Adm. 1/4001, O.b. to Admiralty, 12 Jan. 1706; Adm. 1/4003, O.b. to Admiralty, 24 Dec. 1709, 17 Jan. 1710, 25 Apr. 1714; Adm. 3/4, 29 Nov. 1690. Also see Tomlinson, 'Ordnance Office and the Navy', p. 24, for a further instance of friction.

6 Adm. 1/4001, 3 July 1705; Adm. 1/4002, O.b. to Admiralty, 12, 16 Apr. 1707; Adm. 1/4004, Same to Same, 21 Mar., 25 Apr. 1712.

7 Adm. 1/4002, O.b. to Admiralty, 1 Feb. 1707. When such demands were

The neglect of stores by gunners was a further source of complaint[1]. Various regulations were made in an attempt to limit the extravagant use of naval ordnance. Dartmouth moved Pepys to approach the king on the subject, and in February 1686 James ordered the principal naval officers to make good out of the responsible gunner's pay, the value of stores damaged by neglect[2]. James as Duke of York and head of the Admiralty, also elaborated several rules for regulating salutes at sea and for preventing the unnecessary waste of gunners' stores, which rules were modified in 1688[3]. Judging by the complaints of the Ordnance Office these rules were not entirely successful[4], although the Office did attempt to check the disorder by demanding that the captain pay for excessive salutes, or by delaying the authorisation of a captain's certicate until he gave account of his stores[5].

The failure of naval officers to give account for stores at home, was matched by their irresponsibility in not sending remains of stores whilst at sea, which inevitably caused delay and frustration before a ship was re-stocked[6]. An Ordnance storekeeper at Barbados observed that the moment the captain crossed the line he became 'as absolute as the French King', refusing to obey orders, firing gunpowder aimlessly, and replenishing his stocks by drawing expensive bills of exchange on the Ordnance Office[7]. It was this habit of captains drawing large sums of money on the Office for stores bought abroad at several times the normal cost without giving account for them, that was one of the greatest causes of complaint in correspondence between the Ordnance Board and the Admiralty[8]. Indeed, Pepys himself admitted that the practice was: 'an evil that of all others we also do not only most labour under, but find the most difficult to remedy in reference to the stores that come within the direction of the officers of the Navy'[9].

made, the Office naturally suspected embezzlement. Adm. 1/4001, O.b. to Admiralty, 11, 14 June 1705, 16 Mar. 1706, 1 Feb. 1707.

1 Adm. 1/4001, O.b. to Admiralty, 21 Feb., 16 Mar. 1706, 1 Feb. 1707; Adm. 1/4001, Same to Same, 1 May 1705; Adm. 1/4002, Same to Same, 17 July 1707; Adm. 1/4004, Same to Same, 29 Aug. 1710.

2 PL 2858, p. 567; WO 55/334, fos. 32-3.

3 *James, Duke of York, Memoirs of the English Affairs, chiefly Naval from the year 1660 to 1673* (1729), pp. 80-5. Harl. 1898, fos. 119-24.

4 Adm. 3/15, minute 22 Feb. 1700; Adm. 3/16, minutes, 15, 22 May 1700.

5 WO 47/8, p. 333; WO 47/25, pp. 326, 443.

6 Adm. 1/4001, O.b. to Admiralty, 4 Nov. 1706.

7 Adm. 1/4004, Lowther to O.b., n.d.

8 See my, 'Ordnance Office and the Navy', p. 29, n. 5, and references there cited.

9 P.L. 2859, pp. 333-4, Pepys to O.b., 1 Nov. 1686.

It was not only the naval captains who were guilty of maltreating Ordnance personnel. Garrison governors were also sometimes responsible for these abuses.[1] Governors at the outports, moreover, were often as lax as naval captains in informing the Ordnance board of their wants. This was especially the case with governors of overseas garrisons. The Ordnance Office furnished large quantities of stores to overseas plantations, and although their dispatch was under the immediate jurisdiction of the Privy Council, and later the Board of Trade, the co-operation of that Council, and the plantation governors whom it controlled, was required before an effective supply could be made. The instructions drafted by the Council enjoined that a yearly account of the expenditure of ordnance should be returned by the plantation governors,[2] but it is clear that this instruction was not strictly heeded, despite repeated warnings from the lords of Trade that they should certify to the Office the amount of stores expended.[3] As a result the Ordnance Office was unable to determine whether the demand for stores was a justifiable one or not.[4]

Nor was the misuse of stores a prerogative of naval personnel. Bedding and barrack furniture in general suffered badly from maltreatment by garrison soldiers, despite an order of 1685 that the garrison commander was to take a particular indent of barrack stores from the captain of every troop, who was to give satisfaction for any embezzlements or breakages.[5] The regulation had little effect, judging by representation made to Marlborough in December 1716 about 'the ill state and condition of barracks in general in England from the embezzlements and disorders of the soldiery', and a further set of barrack rules were submitted for approval.[6] Other types of stores were also liable to be pilfered by gunners and other soldiers.[7] When regiments

---

1 See D.1778/I i 1669, Ridge to Dartmouth, 12 Dec. 1688; NMM Dartmouth MS. XV, p. 164, Dartmouth to Ridge, 12 Dec. 1688, Dartmouth to Scott, same date; SP 44/106, fos. 348-9, O.b. to Sunderland, 24 June 1708.

2 E.g. see *Cal. SP Col. Am. & W. Indies 1669-74*, p. 569, instructions for Earl of Carlisle at Jamaica, 23 Mar. 1674.

3 E.g. see *Cal. SP Col. Am. & W. Indies 1681-5*, p. 555, Musgrave to Blathwayt, 30 Nov. 1683; *Cal. SP Col. Am. & W. Indies 1689-92*, pp. 136-7, O.b. to lords of Trade and Plantations, 31 Aug. 1689; *Acts of PC Col. 1680-1720*, pp. 482-3, 11 Jan. 1705.

4 E.g. *Cal. SP Col. Am. & W. Indies 1693-6*, p. 123, O.b. to Lords of Trade, 1 July 1693.

5 *Cal. SP Dom. 1685*, pp. 340-1, warrant 4 Oct. 1685.

6 WO 47/29, p. 297, minute 11 Dec. 1716. For the state of barracks in Plymouth at this time see King's 45, fos. 32, 48, Lilly's reports.

7 E.g. WO 47/6, fo. 110; WO 47/19a, pp. 250-2; WO 49/111, articles against

were disbanded, it was quite likely that their arms would be lost, as they were often simply left in the alehouse or place where they were quartered.[1] A similar wastage of stores occurred when excessive amounts of gunpowder were discharged in salute.[2] In an attempt to remedy the situation, detailed orders were made out to every garrison commander. No commander was to waste gunpowder 'otherwise than in fight with an enemy'; in answer to a ship's salute, no more than five lesser cannon were to be fired; salutes were only to be made to persons of the rank of admiral, general or ambassador; and no salute was to be made upon 'any festival or entertainment'. Further rules governed the surveying, accounting, and issue of stores.[3] The constant re-iteration of such instructions suggest that they were as much honoured in the breach as in the observance.

The failures of the central administration and obstruction from other offices and officers goes some way to explain the difficulties the Ordnance Office laboured under with regard to Ordnance stores and supply. The situation at the dockyards and garrisons, however, was also a key factor in the despatch of such stores. At the ports the Ordnance clerks did the detailed work of taking the remains of gunners stores on a ship, but they were dependent on the ordinary seamen to do the manual work.[4] The actual carrying of guns from the wharf to the ship was under the charge of naval masters of attendance and boat-swains, who were paid a gratuity by the Ordnance board for their co-operation.[5] The Ordnance Office, therefore, was dependent on naval provision of freight vessels and larger sea transports for the removal of guns.[6] This situation was hardly satisfactory, for neither masters of attendance nor naval vessels were to be relied on to perform Ordnance Office tasks.[7] The Navy continually complained to the

---

one Thomas Paris; NMM Dartmouth MS. XVI, pp. 187-8, Dartmouth to Ridge, 21 Dec. 1688.

1 See e.g. WO 55/336, fo. 56, Schomberg's Warrant Mar. 1689.

2 See e.g. WO 46/2, p. 107, O.b. to Duxbury, 8 Apr. 1684; WO 47/16, fo. 36, 3 Nov. 1685; WO 55/345, p. 311, O.b. to Granville, 1 Nov. 1711.

3 WO 47/5, pp. 92-6; PC 6/18, pp. 44-6, 69, 137-8, 193-5; SP 42/1, no. 8, 13 Mar. 1690; D. 1778/I i 294; D.1778/V 42.

4 Adm. 1/4002, O.b. to Admiralty, 20 Nov. 1707.

5 WO 47/9, fos. 135, 141; WO 51/7, fo. 182, 14 Mar. 1667; WO 51/8, fos. 101-2, 31 Aug. 1667.

6 See my, 'Ordnance Office and the Navy', p. 33, n. 4, and references there cited.

7 See e.g. Cal. SP Dom. 1663-4, p. 249, Sherburne and Nicholls to Mennes; WO 47/5, p. 85, Aug. 1663, WO 55/342, pp. 76-80; PL 2858, p. 90; Adm. 1/3999, O.b. to Admiralty, 26 June 1703.

Ordnance about the lack of hoys for transporting guns,[1] but the Office simply did not have many of their own vessels, and had to rely extensively on the co-operation of others for the service to be performed. The root of the problem was that there was never an established agreement between the Ordnance and the naval commissioners as to who was responsible for taking the guns on and off the ships, and although the Ordnance board attempted to lay down a set convention regarding the procedures to be adopted,[2] this convention was by no means recognised by the Navy. Throughout the period, therefore, there were altercations, especially at Portsmouth it seems, regarding the extent of the naval officers' responsibility for the carriage of Ordnance stores.[3]

The lack of adequate Ordnance hoys was matched by a shortage of suitable labour at some ports and garrisons.[4] Speedy despatch was also incommoded because of inferior storage facilities at some of the major ports and garrisons. The storehouses at Sheerness, Harwich and Hull were totally inadequate to meet the demand, whilst the naval stores at Plymouth and Portsmouth, for most of the period, were situated some distance from the naval dockyards.[5] Henry Hooke, the Ordnance storekeeper at Plymouth, observed that the remoteness of the sites of some of the naval storehouses meant that business could not be dispatched 'as soon as if they were nearer', although he claimed that he 'never knew any ship hindered from going to sea by reason of any delay by us'.[6] Storage space at overseas garrisons was even more meagre.[7] Yet it was precisely these places that needed good storage facilities, because arms were likely to decay much more quickly abroad.[8]

At most dockyards and garrisons other essential requirements were in short supply. In 1681 the Hull storekeeper could report: 'the inconveniences are so bad for delivering and receiving of stores, that

1 WO 55/1792, p. 52; Adm. 3/3, minute 15 July 1690; Adm. 3/7, 16 Aug. 1692, 12, 26 June 1693; Adm. 3/10, 6 Aug., 3 Sept. 1694.

2 See SP 29/235, no. 40, O.b's report, 22 Feb. 1668.

3 E.g. WO 46/3, pp. 71-2, O.b. to Romney, 22 Aug. 1694; WO 46/5, p. 34, Same to Same, 25 Mar. 1701; WO 55/342, pp. 76-80, Sept. 1701; SP 29/221, fos. 145-6, Middleton to Navy Board.

4 E.g. WO 49/112, Batchler to Wharton, 5 July 1665; Bodleian, Rawl. A.475, Duxbury to O.b., 20 Oct. 1685.

5 Above, p. 123.

6 Adm. 1/4000, 12 May 1704, enclosed in a letter to Admiralty of 16 May.

7 E.g. see HMC 20, 11 Rep. V, Dartmouth I, Povey to George Legge, 23 Sept. 1680; WO 55/1786, pp. 143 ff., Povey's Tangier reports; Cal. SP Col. Am. & W. Indies 1702-3, pp. 854-5, O.b. to Council of Trade.

8 See WO 55/344, pp. 155-6, O.b. to Hedges, 1 July 1706.

men toil like beasts, and waggons and carts go axletree deep, which advances the rates and number of workmen.' A few years later we find his successor moving cannon from their emplacements by rolling them down the bank because of the lack of a crane.[1] At Harwich the Ordnance officer depended on the use of the Navy's crane for taking in and putting out a ship's guns.[2] The lack of suitable strong wharves was a great problem in all the sea ports. Many of the wharves belonged to the Navy, which service strongly objected to their use by the Ordnance Office, for the wooden wharves, as well as the cranes, were likely to be severely damaged by guns and gun carriages, thereby interrupting naval business.[3] Yet if, through lack of space, heavy ordnance was kept on board ship when it refitted, the ships themselves were endangered.[4]

The problems posed by the lack of suitable Ordnance wharves at Portsmouth and Plymouth, for example, seemed especially severe. As early as 1663 a gun wharf had been projected at Portsmouth,[5] but it probably remained unbuilt, for in 1668 the Ordnance officers could write to the Navy commissioners that they had no place to put the guns at Portsmouth other than on ground which inconvenienced the Navy.[6] *Ad hoc* purchases of quays and further building in the 1680s[7] did not alleviate the problem. In November 1699, the board admitted to Romney that the Navy at Portsmouth were 'greatly incommoded in the despatch of their own affairs by interfering of ours', and in September 1701 the Admiralty was informed by the board that 'nothing would be of greater service than the building of a wharf to receive the said guns'. By this time the naval business at Portsmouth had reached such proportions that it had become absolutely imperative to build a new gun wharf, with magazines and storehouses, for sixty or eighty ships.[8] Various suggestions were made for a new wharf in the 1690s and early

---

1 WO 46/1, fo. 320, Watkinson to O.b., 13 Dec. 1681; WO 46/2, p. 219, Duxbury to O.b., 19 May 1684.

2 Adm. 3/17, minutes 3, 21 July 1702.

3 See my, 'Ordnance Office and the Navy', p. 35, n. 2, and references there cited.

4 SP 29/221, fos. 145-6, Middleton to Navy commissioners, Oct. 1667; Adm. 1/3999, O.b. to Admiralty, 13 May 1699.

5 *Cal. SP Dom. 1663-4*, pp. 348, 589; WO 47/5, p. 135; PC 6/18, pp. 65-6, estimate 6 May 1664.

6 *Cal. SP. Dom. 1667-8*, p. 266, 3 Mar. 1668. Also see Add. MS. 38849, fo. 74. observation of Sir John Kempthorne. 28 Aug. 1672

7 WO 47/19b, 18 Jan. 1676; WO 47/9, fo. 109, 29 Nov. 1680; WO 47/16, fo. 70, 5 Dec. 1685; T. 1/28, fo. 291, O.b. to Romney, 7 July 1694.

8 WO 46/4, p. 60, O.b. to Romney, 25 Nov. 1699; WO 55/342, p. 81, Same to Same. 25 Sept. 1701; WO 46/6, p. 78, O.b. to Marlborough, 23 Mar. 1704.

1700s,[1] but it was not until July/August 1705 that the surveyor-general marked out the ground for its construction. The masons did not proceed to work on the wharf until early the following year, and it was not fit to lay guns on until December 1709.[2] The building of this gun wharf was a great step forward in advancing naval business at Portsmouth. It was built of stone instead of wood, it gave the Office adequate storage room all on one site, plus houses for most of its officers, and it meant that Ordnance officials were not so dependent on the tide before a ship could be dispatched.[3] Plymouth's old gun wharf adjacent to Mount Wise was again not large enough to cope adequately with the gunning of large numbers of ships.[4] An even greater problem after the Revolution, however, was the remoteness of the site of the wharf from the Plymouth fortifications and, more importantly, from the new dockyard. But it was not until the end of the period that plans were implemented for erecting a more conveniently sited wharf to the north of the naval yard at Hamouze.[5]

It may well be argued that the Ordnance Office should have improved their services at ports and garrisons. Why could it not have provided larger wharves and stronger storehouses to save stores from being damaged? Indeed, why did it not always ensure a constant supply of stores to cover all contingencies and meet all the needs of the Army and Navy? It is not difficult to find an answer to these questions, for the Office simply did not have the resources to answer all the demands made upon them. It was the inadequate credit facilities of the Office that was the most important single reason for failures in supply, and this subject is given separate consideration in chapter 5.

---

1 Adm. 3/7, 19 Sept. 1692; Adm. 3/8, 13 July 1693; Adm. 3/15, 19 Jan. 1700; Adm. 3/16, 11 Dec. 1700; SP 32/11, p. 329; SP 44/100, pp. 343-4; WO 46/3, estimate Nov. 1694; WO 46/5, pp. 151-2; WO 49/119, Bridges's report, 17 Jan. 1702; *Cal. SP. Dom. 1700-2*, p. 20; *Cal. Treas. Books, 1704-5*, p. 29.

2 WO 47/22, p. 223; WO 47/23, p. 101; Adm. 3/24, minute 21 Dec. 1709. Also see Adm. 1/4003, O.b. to Admiralty, 9 Mar. 1710.

3 For plans of the wharf and its buildings see PRO, MPHH 29, 516; King's Top. Coll. XIV, 42 t, u, w, x, y. For some of the problems relating to the building of the wharf see WO 46/6, p. 70; WO 47/24, pp. 150, 302, 359, 363, 396; WO 47/25, pp. 39, 187, 234, 310, 321, 324, 400, 444, 470.

4 In 1715 Col. Lilly observed that at least 300 ft. of land was required to be taken up to the north of the wharf in order for it to be adequate to serve the new yard at Hamouze. King's 45, fo. 43.

5 See WO 47/18, p. 302, minute 22 Nov. 1717; WO 47/31, p. 8, 14 Jan. 1718; WO 47/31, p. 350, minute 21 Nov. 1718; WO 47/32, p. 123, 24 Mar. 1719, p. 425, 30 Dec. 1719; WO 47/33, pp. 3-4, 2, 17 Jan. 1720. For plans of the new wharf see King's Top. Coll. XI, 89; Bodl., Gough Maps, 5 fos. 10b, 17a, 18, 18b, 19, 20, 20b, 21b, 25; PRO, MPH 216.

Other factors which delayed Ordnance supply were quite outside the power of any department or individual to control. In the days of sail, there was no certainty that stores would be delivered to outlying regions, or even to a ship at sea, on time, because of the likelihood of bad weather.[1] Indeed, contrary winds at the outports sometimes made it impossible for any services to be performed. At Plymouth, when strong south and south-west winds blew, no vessel was able to pass through the Sound to supply any ships at all.[2] Dependence on the tides also often meant that ships could only be refitted at the most inconvenient times.[3]

Bad weather might also affect the time taken for orders to reach the appropriate department. It sometimes took several weeks for requests for supply to be sent from the outlying garrisons to the appropriate authority, and it would take even longer for similar demands from the colonies.[4] By the time the demand was complied with and the stores received, the emergency for which they were needed might well have passed.[5] Internal communication within England was slow and its costs prohibitive. In May 1691, for instance, the board informed Nottingham of the difficulties of sending 1,000 arms and 2,000 barrels of gunpowder with flints and lead to Berwick, because of the length of the journey, and the necessity to press at least thirty teams of horses for every ten or fifteen miles at a cost of £450.[6]

The physical situation of the departments within London must also have meant a delay in the dispatch of orders. From Whitehall, where the offices of the secretary of state and the Admiralty were situated, to the Navy Office in Crutched Friars Lane in the City, was a distance of well over two miles, and it was even further from there to the Ordnance Office in the Tower and the Victualling board on Tower Hill.

The lack of technological advance did not only mean poor communications, but also directly affected the manufacture and quality of Ordnance stores. It took many months before cannon could be made and several weeks before a contract for small arms could be ful-

1 See e.g. WO 47/5, p. 157, minute 14 Dec. 1663; SP 29/106, fo. 101.

2 King's 45, fo. 43, Lilly's report, *c.* 1714.

3 E.g. WO 50/1, p. 159, payment for candles burnt when ships re-fitting.

4 See e.g. *Cal. SP. Col. Am. & W. Indies 1701,* nos. 666, 683, 770; SP 44/111, St. John to O.b., 20 July, enclosing letter from lieut.-governor of Scilly of 9 July.

5 *Ibid; The Correspondence of Henry Hyde, 2nd Earl of Clarendon, and Lawrence Hyde, 1st Earl of Rochester,* ed. Samuel Weller Singer, 2 vols. (1828), II, Chatham to Rochester, 30 May 1686; SP 34/1, no. 45, O.b. to Prince George, 6 June 1702.

6 WO 55/339, p. 73, 19 May 1691.

filled.[1] Once these stores were made and once they had been proved there was no guarantee that they would be serviceable, but often this was no fault of the Office. The keeping of stores adequately aired and free from damp was a constant problem for which there was little remedy.[2] The ravages of rats and other vermin were a further source of mischief that was difficult to control.[3]

Another problem was the lack of standardisation of many types of stores. Great efforts were made during this period to obtain a gun establishment that might be 'standing, certain and indifferent from all ships both built and to be built',[4] but it was impossible for complete standardisation to be achieved, because, as we have seen, the gun-founders were unable to cast cannon of exactly the same weight. This usually resulted in cannon being too heavy for a ship.[5] The gauges used to measure the size of cannon, moreover, were crude and inexact instruments, as is shown by the board's order of February 1715, requiring one Mr John Rowley to provide a set of brass gauges and a stop rule, so that 'the calibres of great ordnance' might 'be more exactly ascertained than hitherto'.[6] Nor was complete standardisation achieved with other stores. This was not necessarily caused by the inadequacies of the manufacturing process. The profusion in the different types of firearms in this period must have been partly the result of the seizing and subsequent reissue of arms from rebel forces.[7] The Office's policy of making only one issue of arms to regiments, after which issue they were required to buy their own weapons, also resulted in the use of different sorts of firearms and other stores.[8] There was an attempt,

1 See e.g. WO 46/5, p. 126, O.b. to Marlborough, 8 Feb. 1703; SP 41/34, O.b. to Dartmouth (1st Earl of), 17 May 1711. Also, above, pp. 108-9.

2 See e.g. WO 47/19a, p. 64, 10 Nov. 1668, p. 195, 25 Feb. 1669; WO 47/9, p. 77, 7 Sept. 1680; WO 47/14, p. 36, 30 Sept. 1684.

3 WO 47/19a, p. 208, minute of letter, 4 Mar. 1669; WO 47/13, fo. 177, 15 Sept. 1683; WO 47/16, fos. 51, 57, 17, 24, Nov. 1685; WO 47/23, p. 240, minute of letter, 4 Apr. 1706; WO 47/25, p. 521.

4 *Cat. Pepys.* IV, 418. For the various gun establishments see Admiralty Library Corbett XIV, fos. 133 ff.

5 WO 47/25, p. 303; Adm. 1/4002, O.b. to Admiralty, 3 Feb. 1708, Adm. 3/9, minute 8 Feb. 1694.

6 WO 47/28, p. 29.

7 E.g. *Cal. SP. Dom. 1684-5,* pp. 26-8, 20 May 1684, warrants to various governors, pp. 83-4, warrant to Dartmouth, June 1684; WO 55/1760, account of arms seized.

8 See WO 55/334, fo. 58, the king's warrant, 4 Aug. 1686; WO 55/345, pp. 156-7, O.b. to ?, 17 Oct. 1710, p. 175, report of O.b; WO 55/344, pp. 148-9, O.b. to ?, 17 June 1706; SP 41/34, O.b. to ?, 21 Mar. 1702, 17 Oct. 1710. For the department's inconsistency re. issue of arms to regiments, see Chandler, p. 173.

however, to standardise the pattern of these arms, for an Ordnance minute of 28 July 1722 required that all colonels were to have arms made according to an approved pattern, and those arms were to be viewed by Ordnance officers. A similar order, issued a few years previously, attempted to standardise the pattern of gunpowder barrels.[1]

Conclusion: The Extent of the Office's Responsibility

An attempt has been made to show the magnitude of the problems of ordnance supply in this period, and some reasons have been advanced for such failures that occurred. Is it possible to determine the extent of the responsibility of the Ordnance Office for these failures, now that some appreciation has been made of the other factors involved in ordnance supply?

The Ordnance Office may certainly be criticised, with some justification, for the lack of stores and inferior quality of those stores on certain occasions. At other times, expeditions were badly supplied: notably the supply to the Navy in 1688 and the organisation of the Irish expedition in 1689. Ordnance officers, however, were certainly not solely responsible for such inefficiences that occurred. The secretaries and Admiralty officials were often dilatory in directing orders to the board; the Transport commissioners were sometimes thoroughly negligent, especially in the years immediately after the Revolution; the Admiralty failed to provide sufficient convoys and impressed Ordnance personnel; captains and governors caused difficulties by their provocative behaviour; and they and others wasted Ordnance stores and failed to keep the board informed of their needs.

Ultimately, however, it is impossible to differentiate between the culpability of the Ordnance Office and the other departments. It is simply necessary to take one example to show the difficulty of weighing the responsibility of each department for each offence. The fitting out of bomb vessels for service in 1694 has been chosen, as a detailed account of the affair has survived among the records of the Office. There was no clear culprit who had direct responsibility for the delay of over three months in the fitting out of these vessels, although Romney boasted that his Office was not to blame. 'Let', he wrote, 'the lords of the Admiralty in whose province it is to provide them men, provisions, and give the sailing orders, answer for it. If I am rightly informed the neglect has lain there'.[2] To whom does one apportion responsibility for

---

1 Blackmore, p. 44; WO 47/31, pp. 105-6, 22 Apr. 1718.

2 There seems to be some substance for this claim. For a detailed account see WO 46/3, pp. 55-62, 9 Feb. – 5 June 1694, and Tomlinson. 'Ordnance

the delay of the bomb fleet in 1694: to the Ordnance Office, whose founders failed in some of their contracts; to the Navy Board officials for not commandeering the bomb vessels; to the owners who refused to part with their vessels; to the Admiralty who failed to provide convoys; or to the captains of those ships who did not join the fleet as soon as they might have done? If it is invidious to accuse one party of being primarily responsible for neglect in this incident, how much more so to estimate the overall culpability for failure in supply over the whole period? There were so many variables in ordnance supply, that even if a judgement was made about the degree of responsibility of any one department in any one incident, it would be quite another thing to imply that that department was generally responsible for inefficiencies in supply, for in another incident, circumstances, and, therefore, the degree of responsibility, might well have changed. What can be said with more certainty is that the root causes of inefficiency lay quite outside the power of any one department to control.

One of the major causes of inefficiency was the antiquated administrative system of the day. A successful expedition depended on the co-operation of so many different departments, each of which had a different sphere of influence, and each of which was dependent on commands from different parts of the central administration. As Sir Thomas Clarges forcefully observed in a debate on the state of the nation in 1689 after the failure of the Irish expedition:

> We shall hardly have success in Ireland unless the king employ some actual executive power in that affair, and in some emergency put the absolute executive power in some persons, that if they want a rope here or there they need not go to seek it in several Offices but may have power to use the Treasury to issue out money as occasion requires.[1]

This comment may well be applied to the whole of this period. There was little absolute control from one central agency which could command total respect from all the departments involved in supply. The fewer the departments involved in the supply operation, the less the likelihood of conflict between them. It is perhaps significant that there were fewer complaints about the inefficiency of the Ordnance Office in the dispatch of artillery trains than their supply of naval stores. In many ways the spheres of action of the Ordnance Office and the Navy were far too close, and this inevitably led to conflict over the exact duties of each body. Who was to provide shipping when naval and

Office and the Navy', pp. 27-8.
1 Cobbett V, 454.

Ordnance goods were sent abroad? Who was responsible for the repair and victualling of the Ordnance Office yacht? How much was each office to pay for bomb ships fitted out by both? Which stores were to be provided by the Navy and which by the Ordnance Office? These questions were debated by both departments throughout the period, but answers to them were very rarely found.[1] The inter-relationship between the Ordnance Office and the Navy was so close, that sometimes even the secretary of state did not know which department was responsible for what service. On one occasion, the secretary had to be informed by the board that the sailing of bomb vessels was under the direction of the Admiralty, and the Ordnance Office was simply responsible for supplying the vessels with munitions, bombardiers and carpenters. On another occasion, the board felt it was necessary to remind secretary St. John that it was not within the Ordnance's province to furnish provisions for an expedition abroad, and this perhaps suggests that secretaries had hitherto been unsure of the exact distinction between the Victualling and Ordnance Offices. [2]

This inadequate definition of the jurisdiction of the Ordnance and naval Offices, must inevitably have exacerbated an innate rivalry that already existed between them. Both Offices were anxious to be recognised in what they considered to be the correct mode of address, and during the course of the period there was a great altercation as to the form the actual warrants would take in correspondence between them.[3] Petty jealousies also existed between members of different departments. Pepys's comment when he learned that Ordnance officers were partly to be blamed for the Medway incident, was that he was glad at their fate.[4] A Navy Board officer at Chatham observed, that Ordnance officers believed naval officers were 'equally at command with their own servants', whilst the Ordnance board warned their master-general that 'the Navy . . . expected more subservience than is proper to be allowed'.[5] The Ordnance Office so feared for its independence when the Admiralty requested a copy of the establishment of naval Ordnance stores, because of complaints that some stores were wanting, that the matter was brought before the lords justices, who

[1] See my, 'Ordnance Office and the Navy', p. 26, notes 2-5, and references there cited.

[2] Blenheim C I 20, O.b. to Sunderland, 11 Mar. 1709; SP 44/109, St. John to O.b., 16 Feb. 1711.

[3] See my, 'Ordnance Office and the Navy', pp. 26-7, based on Admiralty Library, Corbett XIV, fos. 129-30; PL 2867, pp. 224-5.

[4] *Pepys Diary* VII, 161, 26 Oct. 1667.

[5] SP 29/234, fo. 346, Gregory to Navy commissioners, 17 Feb. 1668; WO 46/3, pp. 71-2, 22 Aug. 1694.

ordered that they should be sent a copy of the establishment in order to dispose of it as they thought fit. The Ordnance officers explained the situation in a letter to Romney:

> It seeming to us as if thereby their lordships [of the Admiralty] did expect a further compliance from the Ordnance than is, as we conceive, consistent with the dignity of a separate Office which has hitherto performed their business without reproach. Nor can we well imagine for what reason the Admiralty should insist so much upon this occasion . . . unless it were by this means to draw the Ordnance Office more under subordination than it hitherto has been . . . Because we have often heard it said, even by some of the lords of the Admiralty, that it would be better for the king's service if our board were absolutely under their control, as is the Navy Board, we are the more cautious of advising your lordship to anything that might fortify their pretensions to that purpose.[1]

Yet in many ways those Admiralty lords were right when they considered that the Ordnance Office should be directly under their jurisdiction. If the Admiralty lords had had coercive powers over the Ordnance officers for naval supply, many of the conflicts of jurisdiction would have been ironed out, and many of the rivalries which existed between the naval and Ordnance departments would have disappeared. Above all, one of the chief causes of inefficiency, the undue strain to which an overburdened supply department was subject in wartime, would have been eliminated, for the failure of the Ordnance Office to mobilise after a long period of peace must in good measure be put down to its great commitments on many different fronts. In 1688 both Pepys and Dartmouth advanced the proposition that one of the chief reasons for failure in supply of ordnance, was the extraordinary demands made on the Office by both the Navy and the Army.[2] If this observation was true in 1688, it was even more accurate in the following wars, when many artillery trains were organised, and huge supplies were made to the Navy, to the forces abroad, to various garrisons throughout the world, and even to foreign princes.[3] In such circumstances it was miraculous that the Office coped so well. After 1689, although there are isolated complaints of lack of naval ordance, there is little evidence of there being a serious dislocation in the organisation of expeditions abroad. Indeed, there is much more evidence about the Office being

---

[1] *Ibid.*, p. 129, 30 Sept. 1695; *Cal. SP Dom. 1695*, pp. 74, 75, lords justice's minutes, 2, 3 Oct. 1695.

[2] PL 2861, pp. 380-1, Pepys to Aylmer; NMM, Dartmouth MS. XV, p. 26, Dartmouth to Pepys, 8 Oct. 1688.

[3] The Office was obliged to furnish the king of Portugal with 3, 413 barrels of gunpowder p.a. (WO 46/6, p. 85, memo 28 Feb. 1708), although by 1710 the board was behind on its commitments. *Cal. Treas. Books 1710*, p. 434, report 1 Sept. 1710.

able to ship stores abroad within a matter of weeks of receiving the order from the secretary of state.[1]

There is, therefore, no simple answer as to why delays occurred in the provision of ordnance and who was responsible for them. A host of reasons may be pointed to as possible causes of inefficiency: the ineptitude of individuals; the failure of convoy; the pressing of Ordnance personnel; the embezzlement of stores; the lack of facilities; poor munitions and the technical deficiencies of ordnance; the unwieldy administrative machine; the lack of credit. Some of these, no doubt, could have been avoided. A possible remedy in the supply of naval ordnance, as has been postulated, might have been the establishment of a separate naval Ordnance Office directly under Admiralty jurisdiction.[2]   As it was, the old Ordnance administrative machine remained essentially unaltered throughout the eighteenth and greater part of the nineteenth centuries, inevitably making the same kind of mistakes as in this period.[3] Such mistakes were inevitable, however, not necessarily because of the arrangement of the organs of government, but because the good quality of administrative officials could not be reasonably ensured, the technical resources of the state could not surmount the problems of communication and difficulties relating to the manufacture of ordnance, and — as we shall see in the following chapter — a comparatively smooth money flow could not be guaranteed. It is not until comparatively modern times that more favourable conditions have prevailed.

---

1   WO 46/5, p. 71, O.b. to Romney, 28 Feb. 1702;   SP 41/34, O.b. to Hedges, 10 Apr. 1705, 13 Aug. 1706, Same to Dartmouth, 31 July 1712.

2   Although there is no reason to suppose that in the late sixteenth century, when there was a master of the Ordnance of the king's ships, or in the mid 1650s, when the Admiralty commissioners were entrusted with the direct management of the Ordnance Office and its stores, the fleet was any more effectively supplied than in the late seventeenth century.   See Oppenheim, *History of Royal Navy,* pp. 158-9; Hammond, pp. 271-85.

3   For the activities in the Office in the later period see C. R. Middleton, 'The Administration of Newcastle and Pitt: the departments of state and the conduct of the war, 1754-60, with particular reference to the campaigns in North America' (unpublished Exeter Ph. D. thesis, 1968), pp. 268 ff.; Mackesy, *passim;* Olson, pp. 94 ff.

5

THE MANAGEMENT OF ORDNANCE FINANCES

The most important task for any department of state is to manage its finances effectively. The Ordnance Office was no exception to this rule, for without an adequate supply of money it could not perform its functions adequately. This chapter will examine how estimates were made for Ordnance expenditure; the amounts expended by the Office; the extent of its debt and the effect of that debt on Ordnance credit facilities.

Estimates

There was a great change in the nature of parliamentary supply for the forces in this period. In the years before the Revolution there was no detailed parliamentary supervision over the way the peace-time supply it granted was to be spent. In 1660 an annual subsidy with an estimated yield of £1,200,000 was awarded for the entire reign of Charles II, which grant was expected to cover both civil and peace-time military expenditure. The same life revenues were renewed on the accession of James II. The general nature of these supplies meant that they could be distributed to the various departments in such proportions as was thought expedient, although in war-time the Bills granting additional aids were usually accompanied by strong appropriation clauses. After the 1688 Revolution the annual granting of supply for military purposes strengthened parliamentary control over the executive. The appropriation clauses in money Bills were more rigidly enforced, and departmental estimates of expenditure, on which the parliamentary votes were based, were generally laid before the Commons every year.[1]

The increased financial control of the Commons makes it possible from the 1690s to determine the annual estimated expenditure of the Ordnance Office, but before this time there is little evidence on the nature of Ordnance estimates. In the early period a simple estimate for peace-time Office activities, called the ordinary, was used for internal purposes. £12,000 was estimated as the ordinary Office allowance in the early 1660s: £3,500 for the supply of all stores except gunpowder

---

1 For a general discussion of these questions see P. Einzig, *The Control of the Purse: Progress and Decline of Parliament's Financial Control* (1959) *passim;* C. D. Chandaman's, *The English Public Revenue, 1660-88* (Oxford 1975), chapter VI, provides a detailed account of the parliamentary grants to Charles II in 1660 and to James II in 1685.

for ships for the ordinary guard; £4,000 for travelling charges, carriage of stores and repairs; and £4,500 for salaries and allowances. This ordinary estimate, as the board pointed out, scarcely exceeded the £10,000 per annum allowance of November 1626 'in times of much less action'.[1] Later in the 1660s the Office estimate for all services was calculated at £30,000, and then £40,000 at the time of the proposed retrenchment of governmental expenditure. By 10 May 1675 the ordinary Office estimate had increased to £72,701. 9s. 4d. £8,871. 9s. 4d. for salaries; £44,680 for sea service; and £19,150 for land services. But this sum was reduced to £40,000 out of a total of £1,175,315. 1s. 6d. in the retrenchment scheme of 1676.[2] It was not until the further retrenchment of 1679 that there are other extant calculations of the ordinary Ordnance expenditure. One proposal drafted by George Legge intended to reduce the ordinary to £44,589. 13s. 1d., a sum which was considered too excessive by the Treasury commissioners; the other ordinary allowance totalled £37,526. 8s., which, including an allowance for extraordinaries, resulted in an Office charge of £60,000 per annum out of an estimated total of £1,161,975. 15s. 10d. for all government expenditure.[3] Later in the mid 1680s, the board considered that the ordinary Office estimate, exclusive of the saltpetre charge, could not be defrayed for less than £1,000 per week. A further £30,000 per annum at least was estimated as necessary for extraordinary occasions.[4]

It should be emphasised that these estimates were in no way comparable to the later parliamentary estimates. They were simply devised by the Office, in response to a directive from the king or Privy Council, in accordance with a general scheme of retrenchment or in order to give the Treasury some indication of ordinary Ordnance expenditure. They were not submitted for parliamentary approval, although there are instances in the 1670s of Ordnance estimates for extraordinary expenses being debated in the Commons and meeting with a particularly frosty reception.[5]

After the Revolution estimates were regularly submitted to Parliament by the Ordnance Office. The earliest, however, were 'very few

---

1 WO 49/112, paper presented to Sir Philip Warwick, n.d. but early 1660s.
2 See D. 1778/V 79, for the 1675 estimate, and below, pp. 175, 178, for the retrenchment schemes.
3 See D. 1778/V 1371, Legge to the king (n.d.); *Cal. Treas. Books 1679-80*, p. 223, 20 Oct. 1679 Harl; 4251, fos. 1 ff.; *Cal. Treas. Books 1681-5*, p. 1653,
4 D.1778/V 94, n.d. but after Sept. 1684.
5 See below, pp. 187-8, for estimates presented to the Commons 1678.

and imperfect', and it was not until January 1691 that regular estimates were brought into the Commons.[1]   The first Ordnance estimate
was in fact submitted in October 1690 for the following year. It divided
into sea service and land service sections, each estimate being further
sub-divided into distinct articles. The sea service estimate, for example,
detailed the following charges: £138,164. 17s. for re-supplying the
previous summer's fleet with half a proportion of gunners' stores;
£20,500 for two storeships to attend the fleet; £7,500 for freight and
other incidental charges; £9,000 for carriages and other stores for the
ships then building; a further £15,000 for ordnance and carriages
that were likely to be lost or broken in an engagement; and £70,000
for 20,000 barrels of gunpowder to replenish the naval stores. The
individual value of gunners' stores for a ship of each rate was also
listed. The Ordnance land service estimate for that year was similarly
itemised: £46,574. 9s. and £16,240 for arms and ammunition for the
Army; £12,000 for new tents; £15,612. 13s. 4d. for the garrisons;
£59,000 for a spare artillery train; and £9,000 for cleaning and repairing stores.[2]   The succeeding estimates were generally itemised in
this manner.[3]

The year 1690, however, was one of the few years when separate
Ordnance sea and land service estimates were presented to the
Commons.[4]   It appears that the estimates for the years 1694-6 were
deliberately included in the general naval and land estimates in order
to prevent the 'canvassing' of particular articles in Parliament, which
the board considered 'might occasion great delays in granting their
majesty's necessary supplies for prosecuting the war'.[5]   It is probable
that this happened again with the 1700 Ordnance estimates, about
which there is no separate record in the Commons Journals.

Although the Ordnance board was responsible for drawing up the
estimates after the Commons had addressed the Crown and this address
had been communicated to the board via the secretary of state,[6]   they

---

1   *HMC* 17, *HLNS* VII, 173, report of parliamentary account commissioners,
24 Jan. 1708; *Ibid.* 17, *HLNS* I, 16, report of same, 5 Dec. 1693.

2   *CJ* X, 436-7.

3   Except in the years 1690, 1693, 1705-6 and 1708 when separate sea service
estimates were presented to the Commons. For details see *CJ* X, 436-7, 713;
CJ XIV; 401, *CJ* XV. 20, 407.

4   Littleton, the clerk of the Ordnance, presented the Ordnance estimates for
1692-3, Bridges, the surveyor-general, for the years 1705, 1707, 1708 and 1711,
and Windsor, the storekeeper, for 1714.

5   WO 46/3, p. 80, 19 Nov. 1694; WO 47/18, p. 19, minute 30 Nov. 1695.

6   See e.g. SP 44/109, St. John to O.b., 3 Dec. 1710; SP 44/111, Same to

were submitted to the Treasury lords for their perusal before they
were submitted to Parliament.[1] Copies of Ordnance estimates exist
among the Treasury papers, and while some of these agree with the
final estimate, a number of them do not.[2] In these cases the estimate
had probably been altered by order of the Treasury. There is no direct
evidence to support this conclusion in these instances, but in a number
of other cases it it clear that the Treasury had the final word as to
whether a particular article should be included in an Ordnance estimate
before its submission to Parliament.[3]

There was a fundamental difference in the treatment of sea and land
service estimates once they had been presented to the Commons. An
anonymous contemporary outlined the distinction between the methods
used in granting supply:

> It is very well known that in the committee of supply the method of
> giving money for the use of the Navy is different from the manner
> of providing for the land service. In the latter case exact estimates
> of the whole expense are given in to the Parliament. According to
> those estimates the respective sums are granted, and persuant to
> them, establishments are made regulating the whole expense of the
> Army and subject to no alteration or enlargement. But the annual
> provision of the Navy is made by granting a general sum, not adjusted
> or limited by any particular estimate, but by computation.[4]

This observation can be shown to be sound in relation to Ordnance
estimates. The few detailed sea service estimates submitted by the
Office were ignored by the parliamentary committee of supply. All
figures of naval expenditure were simply translated into the cost of a
seaman's maintenance per month, under wages, wear and tear, victualling and ordnance. The monthly figure for one seaman, kept separately
under these different heads, were then multiplied by the thirteen lunar
months of the year to establish the yearly totals, which sum was then
multiplied by the estimated number of seamen in the Navy to find part
of the annual naval charge.[5]

Marlborough, 12 Dec. 1711, Same to Rivers, 13 Mar. 1712.

1 See WO 47/22, p.399, 11 Oct. 1705; WO 47/25, p. 162, minute 30 Oct.
1707; WO 55/404, p. 58, Lowndes to O.b., 26 Feb. 1713.

2 E.g. T.1/97, no. 1; T.1/100, no. 36b, land service estimate; T.1/103, no.
39; T.1/112, no. 1; T.1/119, no. 37.

3 See *Cal. Treas. Books, 1703*, p. 298, Lowndes to O.b., 9 June 1703; *Ibid.
1712*, p. 7, 31 Jan. 1712; *Ibid. 1714*, p. 25, 12 Mar. 1714; T.1/173, no. 52,
O.b. to Treasury, 13 Mar. 1713; WO 55/404, Harley to O.b., 2 May 1713.

4 *Lord Somers Tracts* XIII (2nd edn. 1815), p. 308. 'A Letter to a Friend
Concerning the Public Debts, Particularly that of the Navy.

5 Ehrman, p. 158. A fixed ordinary estimate and other extraordinary grants

This rude method of calculating the naval estimate did not work to the benefit of the Ordnance, for the Office had no direct control of the amount of money that it would be allocated for sea service. For the years 1689 and 1690 a lump sum of money was appropriated by Parliament to the Admiralty for the use of the Navy and Ordnance. There was no specification in the £4 per man per month allowance of the amount to be used on Ordnance services, and the Office had no say in its distribution which was completely in Admiralty hands.[1] For the following three years 5s. per man per month was allotted to the Ordnance out of the naval estimate. This sum was hardly commensurate with the Office's needs, as Goodricke argued in the Commons, and for the years 1694-7 the Office was apportioned 7s. per man per month.[2] Extraordinary grants were also made to the Navy for building ships and bomb vessels and docks at Portsmouth and Plymouth, but there was no parallel grant to expedite Ordnance costs in these ventures, despite estimates having been put forward by the Office.[3] In 1694, for instance, the king directed the Admiralty to leave out of their estimates the Ordnance charge of fitting out fourteen bomb vessels, and Parliament struck out two more articles for furnishing bomb vessels and for transporting stores to the Mediterranean, besides 1s. out of the 8s. per man per month estimate.[4] The Ordnance naval proportion, moreover, was reduced to 2s. 6d. per man per month in the peace years immediately after the ending of the war. The Office considered that this allowance was totally inadequate compared with that in the previous peace, when the Office was smaller, there was no fleet at sea and extraordinary services were provided by the Treasury.[5] It was augmented to 5s. for the year 1701, but reduced to 4s. for the following year and kept at that figure for the remaining years of the war.[6] The Ordnance sea service proportion in these years was usually not determined by Parliament, which body simply granted a lump sum for maintaining 40,000 seamen for thirteen months at £4 per man per month (including ordnance),[7]

were also added to the total. For naval supply 1688-97 see *HMC* 17, *HLNS* VII, 173-8.

1 *Ibid.* p. 173; WO 55/339, O.b. to the king, 23 Apr. 1691 p. 97, Same to Same, 29 July 1691.

2 *Luttrell Diary*, pp. 18-19, 14 Nov. 1691; *HMC* 17, *HLNS* VII, 174 ff.

3 *Ibid.; Luttrell Diary*, p. 279, 1 Dec. 1692; T.1/30, no. 53, O.b. to Treasury, 24 Nov. 1694.

4 WO 46/3, pp. 101-2, Romney to O.b., 3 Dec. 1694.

5 Admiralty Library Corbett XI, fo. 102; WO 46/5, pp. 4-5, Ob. to Romney, 23 Apr. 1700.

6 WO 49/119; WO 46/5, p. 43; WO 46/5 O.b. to Marlborough, 19 Dec. 1702; WO 55/344, p. 254.

7 See *CJ* XIV, 11, 31 Oct. 1702, 238, 25 Nov. 1703, 403, 7 Nov. 1704; *CJ*

but by the lord treasurer, who had been empowered by Parliament to apportion the sea service money as he thought fit.[1] A proposal to increase the allowance to 6s. was rejected,[2] but further additional grants were made by the Commons for extraordinary supplies and for building Portsmouth gun wharf.[3]

The supervision of Ordnance land service estimates by the Commons was in marked contrast to its attitude over sea service supplies. A far greater time was taken over scrutinising these estimates in a select committee or Committee of the Whole House, consequently the Ordnance land service supply vote was invariably made a number of days after the sea service vote. It is also clear from the *Commons Journals* and the few extant debates that even after the Revolution, Parliament still looked upon the provision of supplies for land services with suspicion. This usually resulted in the reduction of the submitted Ordnance land service estimate (SeeTable VI, p. 173).

The Ordnance Office estimates in the later part of the period, therefore, were no guide to the eventual parliamentary supply. Its few sea service estimates seem to have been very largely ignored, provision being made for naval ordnance out of a lump sum, crudely calculated by a method that had been in use well before the Revolution.[4] This was in contrast to Ordnance land estimates after the Revolution, which were more numerous and more carefully considered by Parliament, and were generally reduced by the rigorous Commons supply committees. It could be argued that such estimates were being unduly inflated to allow for the expected reduction and to gain an increased parliamentary supply. This criticism, however, is more valid after the ending of the Spanish War. During the war years, the board's letters show it endeavoured to limit its estimates by not inserting many items of anticipated extraordinary expenditure, and by making calculations of necessary expenditures as low as possible.[5] After the war, however,

---

XV, 27, 15 Nov. 1705, 209, 9 Dec. 1706, 419, 18 Nov. 1707; *CJ* XVI, 23-4, 27 Nov. 1708, 220, 21 Nov. 1709, 416, 4 Dec. 1710; *CJ* XVIII, 8, 13, Dec. 1711, 157, 27 Mar. 1712 (allowing 4s. for Ordnance), 351, 14 May 1713, 513, 18 Mar. 1714.

1   WO 46/5, p. 138, Same to Same, 25 June 1703.

2   Largely because of Admiralty opposition. See WO 46/6, p. 23, Same to Same, 29 Jan. 1705.

3   *Ibid.; CJ* XIV, 408. 9 Nov. 1704; *CJ* XV, 30, 20 Nov. 1705. 228, 9 Jan. 1707, 485, 23 Dec. 1707; Chandler XIII, 117-22.

4   See e.g. PL 2266, no. 155, resolution on naval expenditure, 12 Feb. 1678.

5   See e.g. WO 46/6, p. 21, O.b. to Marlborough, 9 Jan. 1705, p. 50, Same to Same, 16 Nov. 1706.

TABLE VI

Ordnance Land Service Estimates and Supplies, 1692-1714

DATE	ESTIMATE	AMOUNT VOTED	AMOUNT BY WHICH ESTIMATE REDUCED
Feb. 1692	£254,608. 16s. 3d.	£210,773. 4s. 5d.	£43,834. 11s. 10d.
" 1693	£320,075. 10s. 11d.	"	£109,302. 6s. 6d.
" 1694-6	?	"(in 1694)	?
" 1697	£354,184. 7s. 6¼d.	?	?
" 1698	£99,570. 12s. 6d.	£60,000	£39,570. 12s. 6d.
" 1699	£87,585.	£50,000	£37,585
" 1700	?	£25,000	?
" 1701	£30,273. 3s. 9d(?)	£25,000	£5,273. 3s. 9d.
" 1702	£104,478. 16s. 9d.	£70,973. 13s. 9d.	£33,505. 3s. 9d.
" 1703	£104,478. 16s. 9d(?)	"	" (?)
" 1704	£176,169. 13s. 6d.	£118,362. 13s. 6d.	£57,807
" 1705	£161,184. 7s. 1½d.	£120,000	£41,184. 7s. 1½d.
" 1706	£172,980. 18s. ½d.	"	£52,980. 18s. ½d.
" 1707	£169,757. 1s. 3d.	"	£49,757. 1s. 3d.
" 1708	£157,173. 3s. 9d.	"	£37,173. 3s. 9d.
" 1709	£200,488. 0s. ½d.	£180,000	£20,488. 0s. ½d.
" 1710	£153,368. 3s. 6d.	£130,000	£23,368. 3s. 6d.
" 1711	£144,675. 0s. 10d.	"	£14,675. 0s. 10d.
" 1712	£130,091. 19s. 7½d.	£116,411. 17s. 1d.	£13,580. 2s. 6½d.
" 1713	£71,244. 10s. 6d.	£66,698. 3s. 6d.	£ 4,546. 7s. 1d.
" 1714	£55,281. 16s.	£55,281. 16s.	-

The figures have been calculated from those given in *CJ* X-XVII, except those listed for the estimates for the years 1697, 1701 and 1703, which figures have been taken from WO 49/117, p. 210; *Cal. SP Dom. 1700-2*, p. 312; and WO 46/6, pp. 20-1. These latter estimates, therefore, have been questioned as there is no specific evidence that they were presented to parliament. No land service estimates appear to have been submitted for the years 1694-6 and 1700, and a lump sum was awarded for general land services for the years 1695-7, rather than a specific annual supply. (*CJ* XI, 182-7, 363, 576).

the increase in the Ordnance estimate from £55,281. 16s. to £170,991. 10s. 2½d. for the peace years 1714-15 seems excessive. In these years the Office also again indulged in the practice of submitting an un-differentiated estimate, which practice seems to have been a return to a dubious procedure. Moreover, the vigilance of the Commons' supply committees relaxed after the 1702-13 war, and whole Ordnance estimates were accepted without detailed examination.[1]

Just as the figures on Ordnance estimates are no guide to the amount granted by Parliament, the parliamentary Ordnance vote gives no firm indication of actual Ordnance receipts, still less than the total Ordnance expenditure. The Commons' resolutions ordaining supply specifically mentioned that 'a sum not exceeding' the vote was to be passed, and all too often the Office did not receive the anticipated sum, despite constant complaint to the Treasury lords who administered the funds.[2] For an idea of the money received and spent by the depart-ment, it is necessary to turn away from parliamentary evidence of estimates and supply to the internal departmental records of the Ordnance Office.

Expenditure

When investigating Ordnance expenditure for the late seventeenth and early eighteenth centuries, the historian is not beset to such an extent with those problems that confront the researcher investigating the financial history of the Office in an earlier period.[3]

Nevertheless, some of these problems still remain to confound the historian of the Ordnance Office after the Restoration. This is especially so during William Legge's lieutenantship, when there were only two Ordnance accounts declared: 24 June 1660 - 24 June 1662 and 24 June 1662 - 13 October 1670. So it is impossible from these de-clared accounts to gain any definite indication of the yearly Office expenditure in the 1660s. Nor do the treasurer's ledgers help, for they are incomplete and do not indicate the total payments made over any given period. The Exchequer issues give some indication of the annual sums given to the Ordnance[4] but they do not reveal the

---

1 See *The Case of Great Britain in Relation to His Majesty's Office of Ordnance, represented by Benjamin Withall, Engineer*, London Univ., Goldsmiths Library. Broadsides III, (1713-20), no. 270; and Withall, *Exhorbitant Oppressions*, pp. 83-4.

2 See below, pp. 179-205.

3 For a discussion of these problems see Aylmer, thesis, pp. 28 ff.

4 The Exchequer issues are given in Chandaman, pp. 350-1, 354. These figures

gross Office receipts during the 1660s, as a proportion of an Ordnance treasurer's credit was gained from sale of stores and other assignments known as his voluntary charge, which sums did not go through the Exchequer. Nor do they give any more than a rough guidance to Ordnance expenditure in this period.

More revealing are abstracts of receipts and payments. Although no regular series survives, the following figures taken from an account of William Legge's do show the vast increase in Ordnance expenditure during the Second Dutch War.[1]

	Receipts	Payments
Restoration - 18 Feb. 1663	£102,051.9s.2d.	£97,594.0s.1¼d.
6 Aug. 1664 - 1 Sept. 1666	£242,946.19s.8d.	£243,483.17s.3½d.
Sept. 1666 - 29 Sept. 1667	£208,217.8s.3½d.	£211,988.2s.8½d.

These figures may be compared with the £521,145, later calculated by the board as the total three year expense of the Office in the war, and the £495,083. 13s. 9½d. accounted by the Brooke House commissioners as given to the Ordnance to finance the Second Dutch War, nearly £55,000 of which was applied to uses other than the war.[2] The annual Ordnance charge from 1668 to 1670 was reduced significantly,[3] but not as dramatically as the authors of the retrenchment scheme, implemented after the ending of the war, had hoped for.[4]

After the appointment of an independent Ordance treasurer in 1670, there is no immediate improvement in the Office's accounts, which makes it as difficult to discern Ordnance receipts and expenditures on a yearly basis as in the 1660s. Wharton's treasury ledgers

differ substantially from Shaw's (cf. *Cal. Treas. Books 1660-7*, vol.I, xxxii-xxxiii; *Ibid. 1667-8*, vol. II, xv; *Ibid. 1669-72*, vol. III, part i, xiv) which seem far too low. The 1662-70 declared account reveals that £934,382+ was issued to the Ordnance from the Exchequer, which is more in keeping with Chandaman's record of issues.

1   D.1778/V 71. For a monthly account of all money paid and imprested by Legge, 1 Sept. 1664 – last Feb. 1668, see WO 49/215.

2   Add. MS. 28082, fo.53, O.b. to Danby(?), 8 Oct. 1673; *Cal. Treas. Books 1667-78*, vol. II, 1iv-1xi; Egerton 2543, fos. 217-19, report 28 Jan. 1670; *HMC 8 Rep.* (1881), part I, Appendix (H. of L. MSS.), pp. 128-33, report 25 Oct. 1669 and appendages.

3   The figures are as follows: £100,937.14s.2½d. for 1668; £46,222.19s.11¼d. for 1669; £66,497. 9s. 10½d. for 1670. WO 49/217.

4   They at first planned to reduce Ordnance expenditure to £30,000 p.a. (SP 29/233, fo. 249, warrant Jan. 1668) out of a total expenditure of £996,475. 15s.10d. *Cal. Treas. Books 1667-8*, pp. 1651-2. Later the Ordnance estimate was increased to £40,000 p.a. out of a total expenditure of £1,006,370. SP 44/30, fos. 40-1, 49; SP 29/236, no. 193, order 18 Mar. 1668; WO 55/388, pp. 196 ff., warrant 16 Mar. 1668; *Cal. Treas. Books 1681-5*, p. 1649.

for the early 1670s, for instance, show no improvement on those drawn up by his predecessor and give no indication of total yearly payments. His first two declared accounts, moreover, were not based on a regular yearly period.[1] After the early years of Wharton's treasurership, however, there is less need to refer to sources other than the declared accounts and ledger books for an annual account of Ordnance expenditure, because of a change in accounting methods. This change in Ordnance book-keeping was in direct response to an initiative from Treasurer Latimer (Danby), who on 23 January 1674 made this declaration to the master-general of the Ordnance:

> Whereas several inconveniences have heretofore happened for want of a due and exact method in the accounts . . . It is hereby ordered that on the last day of June in every year, the officers of the Ordnance . . . shall deliver into the auditors of his majesty's imprests . . . one fair book containing all the debentures and quarter books of the said Office which have been signed and listed within the precedent year for payment.

Two such ledger books were, in fact, to be made and kept by the clerk of the Ordnance and treasurer, wherein the debentures and quarter books were to be 'entered in such course and method as they were listed', the balance on every list being subscribed to by the Ordnance board. Within three months from 30 June the treasurer was to deliver to the auditor one of the books to be checked against debenture and quarter payment receipts, the board giving the auditor at the same time an account of all money delivered to it in order to facilitate the checking process.[2] This declaration did not solve all the accounting problems and shortly afterwards Latimer announced proposals to regularise the accounting of Exchequer imprests in the Offices of the Navy, Ordnance, Works and Wardrobe.[3] It did, however, have an immediate effect on the form of Ordnance accounts, and from 30 June 1673 there is a regular series of Ordnance declared accounts and treasury ledgers which now form the basic source for estimates of Ordnance expenditure (See Table VII, p. 177).

1 WO 48/9-11. The declared accounts cover the period 25 Nov. 1670 – 31 May 1672 and 31 May 1672 – 30 June 1673.

2 T.27/5, fos. 249-51; WO 55/392, p. 45; *Cal. Treas. Books 1672-5*, p. 465. Some reform in Ordnance accounting may have been the result of an appeal by Clifford in June 1673, to 'reduce the account and manner of proceedings in our Office to the method they had been formerly in', (Add. MS. 28082, fo.53, O.b. to Danby(?), 8 Oct. 1673) but it is clear from its reading that this directive did not demand any radical transformation.

3 See *Cal. Treas. Books 1672-5*, p. 478, order 16 Feb. 1674. The order made each departmental treasurer (rather than the auditor of the Exchequer) account-

TABLE VII

Ordnance Office Expenditure, 1660-1714

24 June 1660-24 June 1662	£ 31,061. 17s. 3d.	30 June 1692-30 June 1693	£ 258,394. 9s. 5¾d.
24 June 1662-13 Oct. 1670	£1,017,502. 13s. 9¾d.	" 1693- " 1694	£ 159,905. 10s. 9½d.
25 Nov. 1670-31 May 1672	£ 209,701. 10s. 11¼d.	" 1694- " 1695	£ 282,108. 14s. 9½d.
31 May 1672-30 June 1673	£ 220,467. 9s. 8¼d.	" 1695- " 1696	£ 113,217. 17s. 11¾d.
30 June 1673 " 1674	£ 120,477. 10s. 8¼d.	" 1696- " 1697	£ 283,854. 19s. 3¾d.
" 1674- " 1675	£ 113,825. 5s. 10¾d.	" 1697- " 1698	£ 402,987. 2s. 6¾d.
" 1675- " 1676	£ 32,163. 3s. 7d.	" 1698- " 1699	£ 646,418. 8s. 4d.
" 1676- " 1677	£ 74,519. 17s. 4½d.	" 1699- " 1700	£ 91,670. 10s. 7¼d.
" 1677- " 1678	£ 101,963. 8s. 7¼d.	" 1700- " 1701	£ 79,314. 5s. 2½d.
" 1678- " 1679	£ 112,372. 7s. 6¼d.	" 1701- " 1702	£ 143,884. 17s. 5½d.
" 1679- " 1680	£ 152,739. 1s. 8½d.	" 1702- " 1703	£ 162,323. 6s. 4¾d.
" 1680-12 Aug. 1681	£ 126,076. 14s. 6d.	" 1703- " 1704	£ 135,991. 5s. 7¾d.
12 Aug. 1681-30 June 1682	£ 23,728. 9s. 8d.	" 1704- " 1705	£ 166,626. 19s. 4d.
30 June 1682- " 1683	£ 73,861. 4s. 8¼d.	" 1705- " 1706	£ 223,916. 4s. 4¾d.
" 1683- " 1684	£ 79,179. 9s. 1¾d.	" 1706- " 1707	£ 144,097. 8s. 3¼d.
" 1684- " 1685	£ 53,892. 4s. 7½d.	" 1707- " 1708	£ 235,484. 16s. 11d.
" 1685- " 1686	£ 76,086. 18s. 10¾d.	" 1708- " 1709	£ 169,622. 16s. 4¾d.
" 1686- " 1687	£ 94,332. 8s. 11½d.	" 1709- " 1710	£ 148,712. 8s. 11¼d.
" 1687- " 1688	£ 100,913. 15s. 5¼d.	" 1710- " 1711	£ 273,147. 13s. 11¼d.
" 1688- " 1689	£ 92,448. 0s. 4d.	" 1711- " 1712	£ 520,410. 14s. 2¾d.
" 1689- " 1690	£ 223,010. 19s. 7¼d.	" 1712- " 1713	£ 150,234. 14s. 8¼d.
" 1690- " 1691	£ 328,049. 0s. 3d.	" 1713- " 1714	£ 184,845. 3s. 2d.
" 1691- " 1692	£ 191,304. 4s. 5¾d.		

Note:
The figures have been collated from the final totals given in the Ordnance ledger books (WO 48/12-52), with the exception of those for the years 1660-73, which have been taken from the Ordnance declared accounts (as listed by W.A. Shaw in *Cal. Treas. Books 1667-8,* xxvii-xxviii; *ibid. 1669-72,* pt. I xix). The totals include listed debenture and quarter book payments and Exchequer fees, but not imprest money advanced by the Ordnance treasurer, which sum was carried over from account to account. The figures for 1698-9, 1704-5 and 1711-12 were inflated by the following balances handed over to the succeeding treasurers £113,086. 17s. 7¼d., £20,700; £137,485. 14s. 4¾d. The 1711-12 figure also includes imprests cleared by debentures subscribed into the South Sea Company, worth £15,691. 6s. 3¼d.

For an indication of the annual expense of the Office for the early 1670s, it is again necessary to turn to miscellaneous abstract accounts. These show an increase in Ordnance expenditure over the previous three years: £121,270. 14s. 8½d. for 1671 and £175,377. 4s. 9½d. for 1672.[1] A substantial proportion of the increase in 1672 was caused by the Third Dutch War. Over £220,000 was spent by the Office in the first thirteen months of the War (31 May 1672 - 30 June 1673), although in its latter stages Ordnance expenditure decreased. The Treaty of Westminster of February 1674, however, did not result in an appreciable drop in the expense of the Office, and it was not until the Ordnance financial year 1675-6 that Office expenditure was severely curtailed. The major part of this curtailment must have been made in the latter part of that year, for it was not until 25 January 1676 that the king's order in council was made for a general retrenchment in expenditure from 1st of that month until 31 March 1677, 'by reason of the great anticipations upon his revenue and for preservation of the due payment thereof'.[2] As far as the Ordnance Office was concerned, however, the retrenchment was not a long term success, and for the four years from 30 June 1676 Ordnance expenditure inexorably increased. The greater part of this increase was due to extraordinary charges. Between 15 February 1677 and 14 February 1678 the board estimated that £58,563. 9s. and £37,630. 9s. 4d. had been spent on extraordinary sea and land services.[3] In the following months these charges increased substantially with the onset of preparations for English participation in the European war against France.[4] For the accounting year 1679-80, moreover, the Office was still attempting to pay off the debt left by these preparations, although in the following two years there was a substantial reduction in expenditure. Thereafter, from 30 June 1682 for the following four years, Ordnance expenditure more or less stabilised, although it increased again under James II.

Ordnance expenditure in the 1690s was on a greatly increased

able from the first for the money assigned on imprest payments, but it did not remedy the problem of imprest payments being carried over as 'supers' on Ordnance declared accounts.

1 WO 49/216, 217. Cf. above, p. 175, n.3. The Office calculated that their total expenditure for the four years 1668-71 equalled £334,928, an average of £83,732 p.a. Add. MS. 28082, fo.53, O.b. to Danby(?), 8 Oct. 1673.

2 *Cal. Treas. Books 1676-9*, pp. 116-18, 25 Jan. 1676. For a copy of Danby's preliminary calculations for the retrenchment see Browning, *Danby*, III, 22-3.

3 D.1778/V 26, estimate 13 June 1678.

4 On 3 June 1678 the board calculated land service charges for the anticipated French war at £112,178.5s.8¼d. and sea service charges at £149,000. *Ibid.*

scale compared with the preceeding years. Surprisingly, it came to a head in the financial years 1697-8 and 1698-9 after the war had ended, when the Ordnance stores were re-stocked and the arrears were paid to the officers amd ministers of the Flanders artillery train.[1] In the following two years expenditure was severely pruned, but it again increased on the outbreak of war, although the growth was not as dramatic as in 1689. Ordnance expenditure was not as great in the first years of the War of Spanish Succession as in the previous war, but it increased again in its latter years because of the expense involved in re-supplying the arsenals and paying off the artillery trains.[2] The Ordnance disbursements during this war were in excess of those during the 1689-97 conflict, but the total cost of the Spanish Succession War for the Ordnance Office was probably less than the previous war. A contemporary estimate reckoned that the Office expended £2,666,178. 8s. 1¾d. from June 1702 to 30 June 1713 for land and sea services, which compared with £2,992,569. 19s. 7¼d. accounted as paid and transferred by Charles Bertie as Ordnance treasurer for the same services between 5 November 1688 and 30 June 1699.[3] The latter figure is probably a fairly accurate representation of the total cost of the war, but for a valid comparison with the earlier figure, it is necessary to deduct the sums expended by the Office, 1697-9, during which period the country was at peace, although the expenses of the war were still being paid for.

Debt and Credit

Expenditure figures reveal what was paid out by the Office, but they neither indicate its total financial commitments nor the extent to which these commitments were fulfilled. In a word, they do nothing to illuminate the Office's credit in this period. How quickly and efficiently were Ordnance creditors paid? What was the size of its debts? To what extent did these debts jeopardise the performance of its services? These questions are of vital importance when considering Ordnance finances.

One of the most pressing of the financial problems at the Restoration was the necessity of making provision for the Army and the Navy, the maintenance of which involved a monthly charge of about

---

1 For details see *Cal. Treas. Books 1695-1702*, pp.dlxxv-dlxxvii.

2 See *Cal. Treas. Books 1711*, pt. I, ccliii-cclvii; *ibid. 1712*, pt. I, cciii-ccvi, for details.

3 *Lord Somers Tracts* XIII, 362. Also see WO 55/346, pp. 85-6, for a more detailed account of the 1702-13 war. Cf. the figures for the earlier war given in *CJ* XIII, 397, 11 Mar. 1700; Add. MS.31243, fos. 33-4.

£100,000.[1] In addition, there was a huge outstanding backlog of debt due to both services, which came to well over £1,000,000.[2] By November 1660 the committee appointed to examine the public debt estimated that £678,000 would be needed to clear the current naval debt, including £200,000 for the provision of victuals, ordnance and other stores for the fleet, but apparently largely excluding a further sum of £248,049. 8s. due for current naval wages. Another £422,819 was required to disband the Army and such of the twenty-five ships that had not been discharged. Of the total sum, which amounted to £1,300,819. 8s., £670,868 was immediately needed to pay off the naval officers and disband the Army.[3] Paying off the Army had been completed by about February 1661, but the operation accounted for a large amount of the total disbandment supply, so that by July of that year when the whole of that supply had been exhausted, arrears of £150,000 were still owing to ships in the king's service. No further provision was made to pay off these ships, or the £287,000 standing naval debt, or the £200,000 required to replenish the naval stores. The total deficiency of the parliamentary provision for the forces appears to have been £637,000, which sum is in accordance with contemporary estimates of the total obligation outstanding after the disbandment.[4]

The position of the Ordnance Office in the Restoration financial settlement is largely a matter of conjecture, for no separate Ordnance account appears to have survived. The debt of the Ordnance Office at the Restoration, however, must have been a very small percentage of the debt outstanding to the whole of the forces, because of the great difference between the total expenditures of the Ordnance Office and those of the Army and Navy in the preceding years.[5] The debt of the Ordnance at the Restoration might have been only a small amount compared with the debts outstanding to the Army and Navy, but the Office's credit at the time was clearly no better than that of the other services. The request of the old Ordnance board to the Admiralty commissioners for £5,000 to buoy up the credit of the Office, which they pleaded, 'has been frustrated by so many disappointments,

---

1 The figure has been taken from Chandaman, p. 196. Cf. W.A. Shaw's figures of £55,000 a month for the Army and £6,000 a day for the Navy in his introduction to *Cal. Treas. Books 1660-7*, p. vii.

2 At midsummer 1660. Chandaman, p. 197. Cf. the position in April 1659 Ashley, 'Financial and Commercial Policy' p. 178.

3 *CJ* VIII, 182, 12 Nov. 1660.

4 Chandaman, pp. 197 ff.

5 Ashley, 'Financial and Commercial Policy', pp. 87-8.

insomuch that we cannot supply *The Bear* and other ships, repair arms, or carry on any other services wherein there will be a necessity of using credit"[1] was a significant comment on the state of Ordnance finances on the eve of the Restoration. Nor did the situation improve dramatically when Charles was restored, for a substantial proportion of the £637,000 outstanding after the disbandment was due to the Ordnance for stores, and it is clear that these took some time to replenish.[2] In September 1662, however, an order for a warrant for the payment of £180,000 by monthly instalments of £10,000 was made out to the Ordnance treasurer. £86,106. 1s. 2½d. of this sum was earmarked for the payment of arrears, part of which must have been sustained in the pre-Restoration period.[3]

There is little indication of the ability of the Office to meet current debts in the early years after the Restoration, although towards the end of 1664 a number of creditors were clamouring for payment after having provided the Ordnance with stores.[4] It may have been this steady build up of debts owed by the Office to tradesmen for goods supplied to refurbish the magazines, that prompted the master commissioners to instigate procedural regulations for the paying of Ordnance creditors. These were issued on 13 February 1665 in conjunction with the other orders for the abolition of poundage and the amalgamation of the Ordnance with the Armoury.[5] Every artificer who provided stores for the Office was to deliver his bill to the storekeeper within ten days of the last delivery of the stores. The surveyor was to allow the bill within a further ten days, and the debenture was to pass within one month of the delivery of the goods into the stores by the clerk of the Ordnance. Any merchant failing to deliver his bills according to the time-table was to be excluded from further contracts. Further provisions were made for the regular payment of the debentures. Every payment was to be made 'in course', (i.e. in strict order) 'to prevent the unnecessary soliciting for money and the undue preference in payments'. No money was to be paid without the signature of the master of the

---

1 *Cal. SP Dom. 1659-60*, p. 418, no. 95, 18 Apr. 1660.

2 See e.g. *ibid. 1663-4*, p. 634, warrant to treasurer, 6 July 1664.

3 *Ibid. 1661-2*, p. 481, 6 Sept., p. 565, docket 21 Nov. 1662. The sum could not have solely referred to post 1660 arrears, as only a little over £30,000 had been expended by the Ordnance in the two years 24 June 1660 − same 1662 (See Table VII).

4 See e.g. WO 47/6, fo. 59, minute 2 Nov. 1664, fo.101, 29 Nov. 1664.

5 SP 29/112, fos. 166-8; WO 55/331. Part of the financial provision was written into the minutes on 18 Feb. WO 47/6, fo.134. For the other order see above p. 87.

Ordnance or three members of the board. This setting down of a firm, regular and unalterable procedure for the repayment of Ordnance creditors, which could be subject to public examination, could have had no other effect than strengthening the credit of the Office. If the system was strictly adhered to, a trader could now hope that there would be no favouritism in repayments and that ultimately his debts would be reimbursed.

The establishment of a regular procedure for the repayment of Ordnance creditors did not, of course, provide the Office with the wherewithal to furnish these creditors. It simply meant a fairer distribution of resources once money had been issued to the department. It is clear, however, that at certain critical periods during the Second Anglo-Dutch War the Office was desparately short of ready money to perform essential services. On 12 August 1665, for example, an advance of £6,000 to be repaid on the Royal Aid for Essex, was assigned to the Ordnance:

> the necessities of which Office are at this present very great, and as they have no means to find credit for the supply of the stores there, which are now so very much exhausted by the first and second setting forth of his majesty's Navy, it is endeavoured to borrow money upon that security as remote as possibly can be procured, to the end that what is nighest may be paid in ready money or give artificers encouragement the more willingly to expect it.[1]

A few weeks later money was still in short supply, for the board informed Treasurer Southampton of the necessity of provision being made to the Ordnance so that the orders for resupplying the fleet and stocking up the stores could be obeyed. Southampton gave further orders to Auditor Long that the remainder of the Royal Aid on several counties should be totally assigned to the Office from Lady Day 1665, and that tallies should be struck on any of these counties for any quarter, in order to provide the Ordnance board with such sums as it required to meet the most pressing services. The lord treasurer added that the warrant was simply to give the auditor-general directions as to how to comply with the Office's demands, in order to prevent mistakes in its Exchequer account, the state of which was not entirely clear.[2]

This warrant is instructive in that it highlights one of the defects in the system of management of the Crown revenues at this time. All

---

1 T.51/13, fos. 13-14 (at back of vol.), order for imprest to Long, 12 Aug. 1665.
2 *Ibid.* fo. 33, Southampton's warrant to Long, 7 Sept. 1665.

too often these revenues were diverted at source and transferred directly by the revenue farmer to the department, rather than being controlled by the lord treasurer through the instrument of the Exchequer. This diversion undermined the Exchequer's credit and made it particularly difficult for the treasurer to keep abreast of the assignments made to each department. The departmental treasurers, on the other hand, could not be certain when and on which county the money would be assigned.[1] Partly to alleviate this problem, as well as that of the acute credit shortage, new appropriation and borrowing clauses were added to the Additional Aid of October 1665, some of which had already been foreshadowed in the Ordnance Office by the orders of the previous February. The £1,250,000 tax was to be paid directly into the Exchequer without diversion and appropriated solely for the expenses of war. The receipts and issues of the money were to be recorded in two registers open to the public, to be kept in the Exchequer. A third public register was to record the lists of issues of the funds made in course according to the treasurer's instructions. Finally, three new instruments of credit were created: for repaying individuals for loans advanced (at a guaranteed parliamentary interest of six *per cent*); for tradesmen and contractors for goods and services supplied for the war; and for impresting funds to departmental treasurers. These were to be negotiable and payable in course, each order bearing the lord treasurer's and chancellor's signature and the same number as the register entry. The system was designed to attract members of the general public to lend money and services on the security of the supply, by guaranteeing them a regulated course of repayment, thereby reducing the rate of interest on government loans by cutting out the profits of the banking middlemen.[2]

At a departmental level the new system certainly had some short term success in creating credit. Attempts were soon made by departmental treasurers, with Treasury backing, to realise the value of orders drawn in their favour before they matured, by offering them to bankers or in exchange for departmental purchases. From about 1666 these

---

1 For the problems this caused the Ordnance Office, see D.1778/I i 155, 158, 174, 183, Wharton to Legge, 21 July, 3 Aug., 31 Oct., 30 Dec. 1665.

2 This order system was incorporated into the remaining parliamentary grants for the war and later extended to branches of the ordinary revenue. Despite the disaster of the stop of the Exchequer in 1672 (largely created by the unrestricted operation of the fiduciary order) the system was reapplied to most of the parliamentary supplies of the Restoration period, although it was not again extended to the ordinary revenue. For a full discussion see Chandaman, pp. 295 ff.; Roseveare, *Treasury, 1660-1870*, pp. 23-5; W.A. Shaw, 'The Beginnings of the National Debt', from *Owen College Historical Essays* (1903), pp. 414, 418-20.

orders were issued directly to departments as a form of paper currency, specifically for this purpose. As far as the Ordnance Office was concerned, there is evidence to suggest that its credit held up reasonably well during the later stages of the Second Dutch War. On 17 February 1667 Pepys confided to his diary that he was informed by one Captain Cocke, treasurer of the Sick and Wounded Commission, that the Ordnance Office had £300,000 worth of good tallies in their hands, 'got by their over-estimating their charge in getting it reckoned as a fifth part of the expense of the Navy', whilst the Navy itself was in dire need of disposable credit.[1] Shortly afterwards he made further comparisons about the poor state of naval finances compared with those of the Ordnance Office.[2] By April 1667 the Navy was compelled to borrow £40,000 on the Additional Aid from the Ordnance commissioners.[3] On 24 April Pepys visited Sir John Duncomb to help arrange the loan:

> Thence by coach to Sir John Duncomb's lodging in the Pell Mell, in order to the money spoken of in the morning, and there awhile sat and discoursed . . . He told me what reformation they had made in the Office of the Ordnance . . . He tells me they have not paid any increase of price for anything during this war, but in most have paid less, and at this day have greater stores than they know where to lay, if there should be peace, and than ever was any time this war. That they pay every man in course and have notice of the disposal of every farthing. Every man that they owe money to has his share of every sum they receive. Never borrowed all this war but £30,000 by the king's express command, but do usually stay till their assignments become payable in their own course, which is the whole mystery. That they have had assignments for a fifth part of whatever was assigned to the Navy.[4]

Duncomb's figure of £30,000 under-estimated the total money borrowed by the Office during the course of the war.[5] Nevertheless, it is clear that towards the end of the war the Ordnance repayment regulations were taking effect and providing the Office with a substantial store of good credit, even though Ordnance expenditure overran receipts by

1 *Pepys Diary* VI, 174, 17 Feb. 1667. Cf. Heneage Finch's observation to his brother that the Ordnance had £350,000 assigned to it on an old fund, without touching the £1,800,000 given the previous session. *HMC* 71, *Finch* I, 456, 22 Feb./4 Mar. 1667.

2 *Further Corr. of S. Pepys* I, 163. By this time Pepys estimated naval expenditure exceeded 'stock' by *c.* £1,277,161. *Ibid.* pp. 121, 125.

3 *Cal. SP Dom. 1667*, p.40, warrant 19 Apr. 1667.

4 *Pepys Diary* VI, 266-7, 24 Apr. 1667.

5 Legge himself attested to £34,000 being taken up at interest, in April, June and July 1665, as well as several smaller sums at a later date. D.1778/V 27, answer by the lieutenant of the Ordnance, n.d.

more than £26,000 for the whole war. This picture presents a sharp contrast with Coventry's mismanagement of naval finances.[1]

The mass of realisable funds of the Ordnance, however, do not seem to have lasted long after the end of the war. Indeed, only two days after the Treaty of Breda was concluded Sir Charles Littleton was warned to be frugal in the dispensing of funds on the works at Harwich, 'both in regard of the lowness of the Office cash and that the peace being now concluded there may not be that pressing necessity as formerly'.[2] In October 1668 the board pleaded to the Treasury commissioners for renewed supplies in order to keep the Office's credit afloat.[3] Shortly afterwards the listing of debentures was restricted to those persons specifically named on a £10,000 grant, not more than £2,000 of which was to be paid for the salaries and allowances of the Ordnance officers themselves.[4]

It is not until 1673 that there is further evidence of the financial capabilities of the Ordnance. In the summer of that year the Office was able to supply the land and sea forces with extraordinary stores, at an estimated cost of over £40,000 entirely on its own credit without one penny being advanced for the enterprise.[5] That operation, however, completely exhausted the department's financial and material resources. (See Table VIII, p. 186, for the size of the Office debt at this time).[6] The crux of the problem was that for the most part money was owing to those artificers who were to be contracted with for the following year's stores, which would not be supplied without ready money being advanced.[7] By December 1674 money had been assigned to the Office, but it was made on such remote funds that the Ordnance

1   Above, p. 175, for costs of the war. Re. charges levelled against Coventry see *Pepys Diary* VI, 268, 24 Apr. 1667, and Roseveare, *Treasury, 1660-1870*, pp. 52-3.

2   WO 55/389, fo.98, minute 25 July 1667.

3   WO 47/19a, pp. 14-15, 6 Oct. 1668.

4   *Ibid*. p. 30, 11 Oct. 1668.

5   See SP 30/case f, *A Just Vindication*. . . . The supplies for the fleet cost £33,390, a further £17,000 was required in ready money for the land forces and another £9,000 for munitions for Ireland. Add. MS. 28082, fo. 53.

6   In addition the department estimated that a further £149,768.7s.8d. was required for services the following year. Add. MS.28082, fo. 49, estimate 22 Sept. 1673.

7   *Ibid*. fo. 51, O.b. petition (referred to the lord treasurer on 29 Sept. 1673. *Cal. SP Dom. 1673*, p. 561). Also see Add. MS. 28082, fo. 53, for a further petition of 8 Oct. 1673.

TABLE VIII

Ordnance Office Debt and Credit, 1673-1713

REFERENCE	DATE	TOTAL DEBT [1]	CREDIT IN HAND [2] (if known)	EFFECTIVE DEBT
Cal. SP Dom. 1673, p.561	1 Sept. 1673	£238,893. 17s. 0½d.		
Cal. Treas. Books 1681-5, p.1660	31 Mar. 1679	£293,050	£ 50,833	£242,217
D.1778/V 64	25 Jan. 1687	£128,822. 7s. 4¾d.		
CJ X, 434	30 June 1690	£168,915. 3s. 6¾d.	£ 67,653. 10s. 4d.	£101,261. 13s. 2¾d.
T.1/30, fo. 32	30 Sept. 1694	£286,170. 8s. 9d.		
CJ XI, 360	" 1695	£208,990. 5s. 6¾d.		
CJ XII, 7	" 1697	£204,157. 6s. 4d.	£178,104. 14s. 10½d.	£ 36,052. 11s. 5½d.
T.1/65, fo. 59	30 Nov. 1699	£142,122. 5s. 3½d.	£ 90,522. 18s. 4½d.	£ 51,599. 7s. 9d.
T.1/69, fo. 240	30 June 1700	£ 72,615. 0s. 8¼d.	£ 46,765. 13s. 4d.	£ 25,749. 7s. 4¼d.
CJ XIII, 389	March 1701	£ 64,530. 9s. 11¾d.	£ 69,706. 8s. 7½d.	-
T.1/78, fo. 250	March 1702	£ 75,220	£ 72,890. 6s. 6d.	£ 2,329. 13s. 6d.
CJ XIV, 17	30 Sept. 1702	£166,293. 9s. ¼d.		
CJ XIV, 238	" 1703	£153,324. 19s. 4¼d.		
T.1/91, fo. 491	" 1704	£188,392. 16s. 1¼d.		
WO 49/120	" 1705	£237,379. 13s. 2½d.		
T.1/99, fo. 397	" 1706	£231,703. 15s. 1d.	£ 78,000	£153,703. 15s. 1d.
T.1/103, fo. 132	" 1707	£207,247. 8s. 2¾d.		
CJ XVI, 36-7	" 1708	£230,875. 11s. 6½d.	£ 89,760. 0s. 10¾d.	£141,115. 10s. 7¾d.
CJ XVI, 392-3	" 1709	£250,497. 7s. 6¾d.	£ 84,272. 7s. 11d. [3]	£166,224. 19s. 7¼d.
CJ XVI, 428	" 1710	£322,710. 11s. 10¾d.	£168,385. 16s. 2½d. [4]	£154,324. 15s. 8¼d.
CJ XVII, 12	30 Nov. 1711	£104,582. 13s. 11¾d.	£103,339. 5s. 5½d. [5]	£ 1,243. 8s. 6¼d.
T.1/159, fo. 204	31 Mar. 1713	£ 71,292. 10s. 10¼d.	£ 93,518. 6s. 8½d. [6]	

1. The post 1690 figures are exclusive of debts contracted prior to 1 Jan. 1689. (I.e. debts of £99,722. 19s. 8½d. and £64,176. 19s. 9¼d. contracted under Charles II and James II).

2. The credit figures do not, of course, necessarily denote realisable funds.

3. Excluding tallies that had been ear-marked for the building of fortifications.

4. *Ibid.* 5. *Ibid.* 6. *Ibid.*

treasurer was directed to borrow at a rate of ten per cent interest for immediate services.[1]

Ordnance credit, then, appears to have been reasonably buoyant during the first two campaigning seasons of the Third Dutch War. Had the war continued for a further year, however, its officers may well have found difficulty in maintaining its credit. As it was, the great debts of the Office continued to weigh heavily on their shoulders. These debts could not be met out of current assignments and could only be satisfied by such expedients as sale of stores. If the Ordnance creditors accepted payments in kind in lieu of monetary payments, however, it was likely that they would sustain considerable losses by virtue of the fluctuation of the market prices of stores and the length of time before great quantities of stores could be sold.[2]

The backlog of debt was increased with the mobilisation of 1678. Ninety ships of war and a military force of nearly 30,000 men were raised within a matter of forty days, but the Commons failed to provide an adequate supply for their maintenance or demobilisation.[3] There was especially vehement opposition to the provision of money for the land forces, 'as a matter of great danger to the laws and liberties of this kingdom'. This antipathy was extended to the land services of the Ordnance Office. On 14 February 1678 Sir Thomas Chicheley, as master of the Ordnance, presented three estimates to the Commons of £150,000, £28,000 and £55,800 for repairing fortifications, furnishing arms for the army, and providing an artillery train of twenty three pounders for Flanders. But these estimates met with a cold reception.[4] Many members of the Commons must have agreed with the arguments that Mr Powle used in answer to Chicheley in the grand committee on supply on 18 February. 'If there be ninety ships at sea', he was reported as saying, 'there is no danger of the French

1 WO 55/392, p. 44, order 8 Dec. 1673; *Cal. Treas. Books 1672-5,* p.432, same.

2 See e.g. *Cal. SP Dom. 1675-6,* p. 13, warrant to Chicheley, 8 Mar. 1675; WO 48/15, p. 25.

3 Cobbett IV, 995, the king's speeches to Commons, 18 June 1678; A. Grey, *Debates of the House of Commons from the year 1667 to the year 1694,* 10 vols. (1769), V, 148; Chandaman, pp. 241-2. In February 1678 the monthly charge for the fleet and Army was estimated at £157, 971.3s.4d. *Grey's Debates,* N.148. In June 1678, after £200,000 had been provided by Parliament for the Navy and Ordnance. Williamson calculated that £176,243.8s.6d. remained to be found for these two departments. *Cal. SP Dom. 1678,* pp. 212, 229.

4 See *HMC 36. Ormonde n.s.* IV, 403, Southwell to Ormond, 16 Feb. 1678. I have traced two of these estimates: for the fortifications and the Flanders train. Rawl. A 176, fo.6, estimate 14 Feb. 1678; D. 1778/V 26, 13 Feb. 1678.

landing and so no need of a train of artillery nor erecting forts'.[1] The result was that the advances made to the Ordnance Office were insufficient to cover its current liabilities. By 3 June 1678 the money that had been received by the Ordnance treasurer on account of the projected intervention in the European war fell short by more than £75,000 of the cost of the contracted land and sea stores.[2]

The sum outstanding on account of the projected war had increased to over £177,000 by 31 March 1679, which was exclusive of debts of over £30,000 for the thirty ships and an old Ordnance debt of nearly £116,000.[3] This figure may be compared with the unassigned debt of the Navy which stood at only £566,985, a little over twice that of the Ordnance, despite the vast disparity in the size of the naval and Ordnance services. Meanwhile, the Army debt had been totally assigned to funds.[4] There therefore seems to have been some justification for the Ordnance board claim that the department had not received a fair share of the money allotted by Parliament for the war.[5]

The attempted mobilisation against the French, therefore, was a costly enterprise which had not been supported by a sufficiency of parliamentary supplies. For the Ordnance, as for other departments, it meant a vast increase in the size of its floating debt.[6] It was not only war supplies, however, that were not forthcoming at this time. The payment of the ordinary Ordnance allowance was also being neglected.[7]

---

1 Grey's *Debates*, V. 170, 18 Feb. 1678.

2 D. 1778/V 78, estimates dated 3, 5 June 1678. For the stores contracted for the war see WO 50/1, *passim*. For petitions for the payment of the debt see PC 2/68, pp. 117, 167, 176, 198, 249, 13 June – 26 Nov. 1679.

3 D. 1778/V 79, abstract 31 Mar. 1679. See Table VIII for the size of the debt (except the Ordnance charge for the thirty ships, which was apparently included on the naval debt) and for the credit in hand.

4 For these figures see *Cal. Treas. Books 1681-5*, pp. 1660-1, list of his majesty's debts, 31 Mar. 1679 (from Add. MS. 17019, fo. 25). The total unassigned debts of all the departments came to £1,229,437.

5 D. 1778/V 27, petition, n.d.; Grey's *Debates*, VII, 264; *HMC* 36, *Ormonde n.s.* IV, 512-13, Southwell to Ormonde, 13 May 1679. The war debt had been reduced by *c.* £6,000 by early in 1680, and arrangements were later made to pay off £50,000 of the debt on the strength of the hearth money, at an interest of six per cent from Michaelmas 1679. The remainder, consisting of orders below £10, was reimbursed out of the ordinary Exchequer receipts to the Ordnance. (See T.52/7, pp. 230-3, order 23 Feb. 1680; *Cal. Treas. Books 1679-80*, p. 750, warrant 26 Nov. 1680.

6 Chandaman (p. 244) has estimated that Danby's floating debt in March 1679 equalled about £2,400,000, *c.* ¾ million more than the 1673 debt.

7 D. 1778/V 27, 71.

As a result the Office debt, exclusive of the French War debt, inexorably increased.[1]

The slow settlement of the French War debt and the gradual accumulation of debts for ordinary services inevitably had a hard effect on the mass of Ordnance creditors. In July 1680 they petitioned the Privy Council that the money due to them, exclusive of the war account which had been recently settled, should be paid in such a manner as the Navy debts 'to commiserate the deplorable condition of them and their families who have been wholly brought up and employed in the service of the said Office'.[2] In this situation it was essential that the credit of the Office was upheld. Money had to be raised not only to pay past debts of the Ordnance artificers, but also to furnish them with sufficient amounts to encourage them to undertake further services, especially repairing the garrisons which were in an appalling condition.[3] Various proposals were put forward to meet these immediate needs, and on 7 April 1681 the Treasury commissioners proposed that nearly £30,000 should be raised by selling gunpowder, the old artillery ground, and Irish stores, and by claiming an Irish debt that had been outstanding for over twenty years.[4]

Such expedients were only short-term remedies to make up for the deficiencies on the ordinary account, and did little to lessen the total Office debt, which towards the end of Charles II's reign was approaching £100,000. The total burden had:

> not only hindered the said officers from carrying on according to their duties and intentions the several services required of them, but . . . much exhausted his majesty's stores and greatly impoverished the merchants, artificers and creditors by them employed in their estates and trades, and reduced diverse others relating to the said Office to very great extremity and hardships.[5]

Nevertheless, the Ordnance artificers were induced to supply over £40,000 worth of stores at the time of the Western and Scottish rebellions. By December 1686 all but £1,375.18s.11¼d. had been paid of

---

1 From 30 June 1678 to 26 January 1682 it had increased by £62,769.18s. 3¼d. D. 1778/V 27, computed from various abstracts.

2 PC 2/69, p. 23, 14 July 1680. Also see D. 1778/V 41, artificers' petition.

3 One of the most obvious consequences of the failure to pay the ordinary was the decay of Ordnance fortifications. See D.1778/V 27, petition, n.d. c. May 1679.

4 D.1778/V 71, estimate; WO 46/1, fo. 213, Guy to O.b., 7 Apr. 1681. Also see D. 1778/V 27; D.1778/I i 639, for O.b. reports, 2, 22, Apr. 1681.

5 D.1778/V 94, O.b. to Treasury, n.d. but post Sept. 1684.

this sum,[1] but the overall indebtedness of the Office continued to rise. The increase in the Ordnance debt during the reign of James II was later calculated at more than £60,000.[2] In addition, there was the outstanding £100,000 Ordnance debt from Charles II's reign, only £1,140 of which had been repaid between January 1687 and January 1689.[3] The growth of the Ordnance debt in the later 1680s may be traced in the following series of figures detailing the size of the arrears of Ordnance ordinary and extraordinary payments for land and sea services:[4]

17 March 1687	£16,051.13s.2d.
12 October 1687	£22,551.13s.2½d.
30 June 1688	£27,551.13s.2d.
29 September 1688	£58,855.2s.2¾d.
January 1689	£64,537.14s.6¾d.

It may be seen that these arrears multiplied rapidly as a result of the mobilisation in the latter half of 1688.

These arrears had a direct effect on the performance of the Ordnance in 1688. In early October the board petitioned the Treasury to consider the pressing debts of the artificers, upon whose performance the king's service very much depended.[5] The Treasury, however, could not respond with sufficient supplies to maintain the Office's credit, and despite Dartmouth's injunction that debenture payments should be made in an orderly fashion so that there was always some cash 'to answer any emergent occasion',[6] business virtually came to a stand because of a lack of money. By the end of the month Dartmouth was receiving information from various officers on the effect of the Ordnance's poor credit.[7] The Treasury made occasional further grants, but they were irregular and small in amount and did little to encourage Ordnance tradesmen to perform further services, so that by 28 November Philip Musgrave lamented that it was no longer worth attending board

1 D. 1778/V 78, account to December 1686.

2 *CJ* XII, 55, 17 Jan. 1698. £64,176.19s.9¼d. was given as the debt on 1 Jan. 1689 (d.1778/V 79).

3 *Ibid.* account 1 Jan. 1689. Cf. account 25 Jan. 1687 (D.1778/V 64).

4 Abstracted from D.1778/V 88, 64, 27. Also see D.1778/V 64, 71, 79 for accounts of quarterly debts.

5 D.1778/V 71, n.d. but arrears calculated to 30 Sept. 1688.

6 WO 55/335, fo. 98, Dartmouth to O.b., 11 Oct. 1688.

7 See e.g. D.1778/I i 1498, P. Musgrave to Dartmouth, 30 Oct. 1688; D.1778/I i 1499, T. Gardner to Same, same date.

meetings.[1]   Some days later the board members considered that be-cause of the great Ordnance debts, the impoverishment of their best creditors, and the exhaustion of their stores, they were unable to supply the least part of the land forces or the smallest squadron or ship of the fleet.[2]

The Office's credit never again plunged to quite such depths.   In the early period of the 1689-97 war, however, it was dangerously extended by the weight of its debt, which totalled more than £100,000 on 30 June 1690 (See Table VIII). [3]

There is little extant evidence of the effects of this debt on Ord-nance services in the early months of 1689.[4] By the end of the year, however, Ordnance credit had been fully stretched so that at least one commentator feared that it might not be possible to send out the fleet the following year.[5] Ordnance artificers had petitioned the Office for money to support their credit, and Goodricke, the lieutenant-general, was acting as spokesman for the Ordnance in the Commons in order to gain an extraordinary supply to encourage the making of further con-tracts. In a further debate the following March, Goodricke claimed that £300,000 would be needed to 'put the Ordnance into its ancient course'.[6]   Master-general Schomberg, moreover, repeatedly observed from Ireland that the bills he drew on the Office were not being honoured by the board through their want of money.[7] The artificers in their turn demanded that provision should be made to settle the £170,000 due to them for recent stores, on a realisable fund so that they could gain credit to perform further services.[8] In fact, the Ordnance only maintained its credit with the major contractors by having their debts

---

1   *Ibid.* 1572. Also see *HMC* 20, 11 Rep. *Dartmouth I*, p. 211, P. Musgrave to Dartmouth, 22 Nov. 1688.

2   *Ibid.* p. 222, O.b. to Dartmouth, 1 Dec. 1688.

3   Listed debts, Dec. quarter 1688 — Sept. quarter 1690, came to the astonishing sum of £180,966.15s.1¾d. D.1778/V, 79; *CJ* X, 434-5.

4   Although see Schomberg's complaint to the King. *Cal. SP. Dom. 1689-90*, p. 36, 22 Mar. 1689.

5   *Dalrymple Memoirs* II. 202-3.

6   Cobbett V, 435 ff.; Grey's *Debates* IX, 425 ff., debate 16 Nov. 1689; Cobbett V, 564-5, 31 Mar. 1690.

7   *Cal. SP Dom. 1689-90*, p. 498, Schomberg to the king, 7 Mar. 1690; WO 55/338, fos. 51, 52, Same to board, 5, 19, Apr. 1690.

8   The £170,000 was exclusive of 'a great debt formerly owing to them', by the Ordnance Office. PC 2/73, p. 421, 10 Apr. 1690; *Cal. Treas. Books 1689-92*, p. 583.

counted as Exchequer loans, which were settled on a specific fund with a six *per cent* interest rate[1]. At the beginning of the 1691 campaigning season, the Ordnance Office was able to make contracts for stores worth £38,153.9s.10d. for the Irish artillery train, even though only £2,000 had been received in cash for them[2].

Some Ordnance contractors, however, were unable to withstand the shock of continued failure of payment in ready money. The gunmakers were particularly vulnerable as they were excluded from the ordinary course of Ordnance payments,[3] but there were other Ordnance contractors, who also felt the pinch of poor credit[4]. During the preparations for the 1692 campaign the Office's affairs were especially hampered by the money shortage, which coincided with the extraordinary demands for a third artillery train for that summer's service. The only ready cash had been strictly appropriated by Parliament for the uses of sea service, yet money was desperately needed for the land service, 'which the Parliament had not usually so much regarded to in their appropriations as they have to the Navy, which they look upon as their more immediate care'. The whole charge of setting out the two trains that had already been prepared came to £300,000, which was about one third more than the parliamentary allowance calculated for one train. The raising of a third train would cost a further £61,674.5s. All these overheads had to be borne on the credit of the department which was already more than £200,000 in debt.[5] Other aspects of Ordnance administration were as affected by the money shortage in the first part of 1692: the gunmakers' debt prevented them fulfilling their contracts at a time when the small arms store was denuded by recent issues,[6] and the £80,000 arrears of the Office ordinary resulted in a total neglect of coastal fortifications.[7]

The failure of monetary provision for the artillery train sent out in 1692 was matched by the extraordinary charges of 1693, which sums were not included in the annual Ordnance estimates.[8] That year the

1   See e.g. *ibid.* pp. 527-8, 534, 668-9, warrants 6, 12 Mar., 26 May 1690.

2   WO 55/339, p. 19, O.b. to the king, 18 Feb. 1691.

3   T.1/15, no.42, petition Oct. 1691. It is clear that the gunmakers received no immediate relief. *Cal. SP Dom. 1691-2*, p. 225, Nottingham to Treasury, 9 Apr. 1692; T.1/22, fo.79, petition 17 May 1693.

4   *Luttrell Diary*, 131, petition 15 Jan. 1692.

5   WO 55/339, pp. 138-9, O.b. to Nottingham, 2 Mar. 1692. Also see *ibid.* pp. 218-19, O.b. to William III, 11 July 1692, re. Ordnance trains.

6   *Cal. SP Dom. 1691-2*, p. 225, Nottingham to Treasury, 9 Apr. 1692.

7   WO 55/339, pp. 177-9, O.b. to Nottingham, 29 Apr. 1692.

8   WO 55/340, fo. 48, O.b. to the king, 23 Feb. 1693.

artificers had agreed to supply stores solely on the credit of the promise of funds, yet by April the sums that had been advanced on the land service estimate were so small that it was impossible for the Office to make any regular quarterly payments or give sufficient imprests for carrying on the service. This was despite the fact that prices were at least two or three shillings in the pound lower than they had been in the late 1680s. Ordnance sea services were in little better condition, for although nearly £60,000 had been received in tallies on that head, they were based on such a remote fund that no-one would pay the artificers ready money for them.[1] By August 1693 tallies worth £50,000 had also been advanced on the customs for land service, but the artificers had refused to take them without being given a third of their debts in ready money. Some days prior to this the land service charge had been eased by the order to disband the French descent train,[2] yet paying off the train itself became a burden on the Office.[3]

The dawn of Christmas 1693 brought little relief to the hard-pressed Ordnance finances. About that time the board members informed the master-general that they were anxious to comply with the artificers' expectations of being supplied with such money that could be spared, and therefore they hoped to be able to pay off some of the arrears from the previous midsummer quarter. Yet despite the board's good intentions it was difficult to find the resources to pay the artificers. There was no ready money in the Ordnance treasury and such funds as were being advanced consisted of long-dated tallies on the Million Act and the joint stocks. The only funds in the Office's possession on which ready money could be raised were the Contribution Act tallies, which the board advised should be kept for an emergency.[4] The Ordnance artificers could not have been well satisfied that Christmas, for less than two months later they were refusing to proceed in fitting out an artillery train for the 1694 campaign, because they had received such remote funds. Altogether nearly £40,000 was needed to pay the officers' and contractors' arrears and meet the immediate needs of the Flanders train,[5] quite apart from the arrears of the artillery officers employed in reducing Ireland.[6]

1   T.1/21, fo. 290, O.b. to Treasury lords, 28 Apr. 1693.

2   WO 46/3, pp. 2-3, O.b. to Sidney [Romney], 9 Aug. 1693; *Cal. Treas. Books 1693-6*, p. 292, Guy to O.b., 24 July 1693.

3   WO 55/340, fo.90, O.b. petition to the king, 22 Aug. 1693.

4   WO 46/3, p. 19, n.d. but after 12 Dec. 1693.

5   T.1/26, fos. 163-4, O.b. to Treasury, 20 Feb. 1694; T.1/27, fos. 89 ff., O.b. to Treasury lords, 22 Mar. 1694; WO 55/340, fos. 144-5, O.b. to the king, same date.

6   WO 46/3, p. 26, O.b. to Sidney, 27 Mar. 1694.

A cogent memorial presented by the board to Romney on 21 April 1694, explains the dilemmas faced by the Ordnance officers of this period.[1] The board felt the need to explain why the Office had contracted such a great debt and why its credit was so low. The sea service debt, amounting to £155,783.9s.5½d., was attributed to the fact that since the Revolution, Parliament had never allowed the department more than 8s. out of the £4.5s. per man per month given for the naval service. This sum had recently been reduced to 5s., compared with the Ordnance estimates of 14s. per man per month. Every year the Admiralty had fitted out a great number of hired ships not included in their estimates, and had built many new ships upon the Navy ordinary, without any allowance having been awarded to the Ordnance for their guns. Specific examples were given of the lack of consideration of Ordnance naval expenditure: no parliamentary allowance had been made towards the charge of gunning ten of the thirty ships built under Charles II; in 1692 the Admiralty had omitted the Ordnance charge of the eight fourth rates and four bomb vessels given in their estimate for building ships, and there was a further likelihood that no allowance would be made for other bomb vessels that needed to be fitted out; the Treasury lords had discontinued the payment of the ordinary of £1,000 per week and £2,000 per quarter for thirty-seven months, and had not made a particular appointment for saltpetre as formerly, which had to be paid out of the Office's parliamentary appropriations. Similar reasons were advanced for the size of the Ordnance land service debt of £224,436.19s.4d. The board had unwillingly submitted to Lord Ranelagh's random estimate of £210,000 for the land services, as for the past few years the cost under that head had amounted to near double that sum, besides many extraordinary services. The charge for 1694 in particular had increased because of the Flanders train, the arming of all the new levies and the vast proportion of stores ordered for Guernsey. In spite of these charges, the land service money and the ordinary, which affected both land and sea services, were much in arrears. The previous year's payments from the Treasury, moreover, (except the ready money for the Flanders train) had all been made in tallies on the three-quarter customs, a fund so bad that they were only accepted for money at a thirty *per cent* discount. The board asked Romney to prevail upon the king to give directions to the Treasury lords for a definite settlement, without which the board feared for future supply.

The memorial, like so many other Ordnance memorials, had little

---

1   The following has been taken from WO 46/3, pp. 35-7.

effect. By June 1694 the Ordnance artificers were clamouring for the two *per cent* extraordinary payment, promised by the Treasury twelve months previously upon the £50,000 worth of tallies struck on the three-quarter custom[1]. A fund of £500 per week had by this time been settled on the gunmakers, but the course of payments had been interrupted so that they had only received £16,000 of the £30,000 promised[2]. The board, itself, as in 1688, admitted that business was entirely at a stand. Payments to the artificers were seven quarters in arrears. £107,000 on the land service estimates of former years was still outstanding, and only £59,500 had been received out of the £210,000 due for 1694, all of which money had been swallowed up in supplying the Flanders train and making provision for a new expedition and artillery train[3].

Ordnance applications to the Treasury for money continued throughout that year. By early autumn the land service arrears for that year amounted to more than £77,000 and the sea service arrears to more than £50,000[4]. The total Ordnance debt (Table VIII) was continually being increased by extraordinary services. At home the artificers were demanding that the £20,000 they had received as ready money upon the previous years Aid should be made good, 'or at least transferred upon some fund that shall be money worth'. A further £7,000 was needed to honour bills of exchange for the train abroad and avoid the collapse of the Office's foreign credit[5]. During this period the board was simply being supported 'with nothing but small weekly distribution from hand to mouth for particular services', which did nothing to maintain its general credit[6], especially when many of the distributions were made on remote funds[7]. Nor was it possible for the money allotted for the sea services to be used for land services because of the strict parliamentary appropriation[8]. By November 1694 Treasury arrears amounted to nearly £133,999.3s.1d., and bad tallies in the board's possession to £140,165.13s.4d. The board commented that 'such an arrear as this' was 'enough to sink any Office', and pointed out to Romney that with-

---

1   T. 1/28, fos. 53 ff., O.b. to Treasury, 5 June 1694, enclosing artificers' petition.

2   *Ibid.* fo. 202, report of O.b., 27 June 1694, fo.266, same, 7 July 1694.

3   *Ibid.* fo. 130, Same to Same, 12 June 1694.

4   T.1/29, fo.118, O.b. to Treasury, 18 Sept. 1694.

5   *Ibid.* T.1/29, no. 39, Same to Same, 25 Sept. 1694.

6   *Ibid.* fo.210, Same to Same, 9 Oct. 1694.

7   *Ibid.* fo. 239, Same to Same, 16 Oct. 1694; T.1/30, fo. 30, Same to Same, 23 Oct. 1694; T.1/32, fo. 82, enclosed with O.b. letter of 25 Jan. 1695; T.1/31, fo. 209, n.d.; T.1/30, fo. 74, Same to Same, 30 Oct. 1694, fo. 30, Same to Same, 23 Oct. 1694; WO 46/3, fo. 78, O.b. to Romney (?), Nov. 1694.

8   T.1/30, fo. 74, O.b. to Treasury, 30 Oct. 1694.

out a sufficiency of supply the Ordnance service would inevitably suffer.[1]

The summer and early winter of 1694 marked the nadir for Ordnance credit in the War of English Succession, but the situation improved slightly the following year. Bank of England subscriptions were allocated to the Ordnance for immediate services, and in March 1695 the Treasury made a disposition of £44,408.7s. for land services, and agreed to nearly £41,000 of this sum being listed to pay off some of the artificers' past arrears.[2] These handouts, however, by no means solved the problem of the arrears or bad tallies. In early June 1695 the total arrears for land and sea services for that year equalled £196,948 9s.10¼d., whilst the total land service arrears for the years 1692 to 1694 stood at £133,999.3s.1d.[3] In addition, tallies worth over £90,000 needed to be exchanged for better funds, and a further 2 per cent paid on the three-quarter customs tallies. If this were not achieved, the board feared that the artificers would combine against giving any further credit.[4] Nevertheless, the total Ordnance war debt was reduced by over £78,000 from 30 September 1694 to Michaelmas 1695.[5]

Although the Office had some success in reducing the Ordnance debt in 1695, credit was to remain scarce until the end of the war. Early in 1696 Bertie was able to dispose of tallies on the Coal Act at low discount rates, but in late March 1696, because of the re-coinage, he was unable to get money even on the best funds.[6] The Treasury promised the Office £30,000 forthwith for the Flanders train out of the best funds. Yet two months later, at the end of May 1696, this money had been diverted and the Ordnance Treasurer could not raise any money at under 18 per cent discount on the tallies in his hands.[7] The high discount rates for Ordnance tallies, which continued throughout the rest of the war period,[8] meant that it was difficult to obtain ready money

---

1 WO 46/3, pp. 76-8, 13 Nov. 1694.

2 *Cal. Treas. Books 1696-7*, pp. 444-5, 31 Dec. 1694; *Ibid. 1693-6*, p.944, Lowndes to Ordnance treasurer, 8 Mar. 1695; T.1/32, no. 53, O.b. to Treasury, 18 Mar. 1695.

3 T.1/33, fo. 130, 4 June 1695. There were no sea service arrears for the same period. WO 46/3, p. 81.

4 T.1/33, fo. 128, O.b. to Treasury; 1 June 1695, fo. 173, Same to Same, 13 June, fo. 217, Same to Same, 27 June.

5 Cf. T.1/30, fo. 32, with *CJ* XI, 360, 13 Dec. 1695.

6 WO 47/17, minutes 14, 25 Jan., 18 Feb., 28 Mar., 4 Apr. 1696; *Cal. Treas. Books 1693-6*, p.1444, minute 27 Mar. 1696.

7 *Ibid.; Cal. Treas. Books 1696-7*, p. 17, minute 25 May 1696.

8 Discount rates of over twenty *per cent* + interest were not unusual. *Cal.*

for immediate needs, even though total Ordnance expenditure had decreased in the year 1695-6 (See Table VI).

In the spring and early summer of 1697 the situation was very reminiscent of that three years earlier. Huge sums were needed for Ordnance services that year: £80,000 for Flanders, £30,000 of which had to be sent over immediately, plus a further £16,000 due on foreign bills and £60,000 for the bomb vessels.[1] Ordnance credit was at a low point. The poorer ordnance artificers and the whole trade of gunmakers had been ruined by tally payment which involved so great a discount, and those that were able to withstand such rates charged extravagant prices for new supplies for the exhausted magazines. Even payments that had been made with bad tallies were six months in arrears, which contrasted unfavourably with advances made to naval tradesmen who had been paid up to June 1696, and were soon expecting to receive bills and good tallies for the March quarter of 1697.[2] Yet the Ordnance artificers were so desperate that they were prepared to take salt tallies that could only be sold at twenty-five *per cent* discount, as long as they received a third part payment in Exchequer bills, which would enable them to buy bank bills if the tallies were subscribed into the Bank of England. It seems, however, that this idea was scotched as no money could be raised to buy the bank bills to subscribe with the other tallies.[3] The Treasury lords simply directed the Office to issue tallies to its creditors at a discount of fifteen *per cent* in accordance with the discharging of the victuallers debt.[4] Despite these issues, the post 1688 Ordnance debt still stood at over £200,000 in December 1697.[5]

There was a notable reduction in the number of begging letters from

---

Treas. Books. 1696-7, p. 63, 16 Oct. 1696, pp. 306-7, 9 Nov. 1696, p. 324, 1 Dec. 1696, p. 359, 2, 3, Mar. 1697, pp. 415-16, 2 Mar. 1697; T.1/43, , fo. 276, 3 Mar. 1697, fo. 361, 15 Mar. 1697.

1 *Ibid.;* T.1/44, fo. 75, O.b. to Treasury, 30 Mar. 1697, fos. 228-9, Same to Same, 30 Apr. 1697.

2 *Ibid.*

3 T.1/45, fo. 33, Same to Same, 6 May 1697, fo. 177, petition of artificers, 22 May 1697; *Cal. Treas. Books 1697,* p. 19, minute 11 May 1697, p. 23, 14 May 1697.

4 *Ibid.* pp. 191-2, Lowndes to Romney, 1 June 1697; *Cal. SP Dom. 1697,* pp. 171-2, minutes of lords justices, 27 May 1697.

5 Table VIII. To set against this debt the Ordnance treasurer had tallies in his hands worth over £178,000, but they were valueless for immediate services as they could not be discounted. *CJ* XII, 7, 14 Dec. 1697. Cf. other departmental debts: £1,392,742 for the Navy, £340, 708 for transports for reducing Ireland and £125,785 for other transport services, £49,929 for quartering and clothing the Army, 1677-9, and £1,254,000 for the Army 1 Apr. 1692 – 30 Sept. 1697. Chandler III, 79, 13 Feb. 1698.

the Ordnance board to the Treasury in the peace years 1697-1702, compared with the preceding and succeeding periods, and this suggests an improvement in the Office's financial position. Some debts from the war period were still unpaid, as evidenced by petitions from artillery train officers[1] and artificers, the latter group of whom in December 1698 had received no consideration since the previous March.[2] Moreover, unpaid arrears for sea and land services on submitted estimates, which amounted at the end of 1698 to £171,100.2s.5¾d. for the previous two years,[3] caused some delay in the repayment of unfunded debts.[4] These arrears, however, were not as consequential as in the previous war, for the vast post-war reduction in the Ordnance's expenditure meant that some current advances could be used to gradually cut down the size of the total Office debt. By the end of November 1699, the board did not doubt that it would be able to discharge the difference of some £60,000 between the size of the post 1688 Ordnance debt and the money and tallies then available for payment in the Ordnance treasurer's hands.[5] Current advances, however, were unable to meet extraordinary expenditures for building wharves and fortifications, because of the size of the Ordnance parliamentary allowance. By July 1700 the board claimed that the peace-time Ordnance sea service allowance was hardly sufficient to meet current needs, although the total Ordnance debt had been reduced by nearly £70,000 since the previous November.[6] The board may well have exaggerated the insufficiency of the sea service allowance to meet current needs in order to counter naval suggestions of the disproportionate size of the Ordnance allowance, but it is clear that the board's fears about the effect of the sea service arrears on the efficiency of Ordnance administration were genuine. This is confirmed by a number of letters from the board to Romney throughout the summer of 1700, complaining about Treasury

---

1 E.g. *Cal. Treas. Books 1697-8*, p. 75, minute 5 Apr. 1698; *CJ* XII, 583, 11 Mar. 1698; WO 55/341, pp. 120-1, petition and report of O.b., 20 July 1699.

2 See T.1/58, fo. 53 ff., O.b. to Treasury, 13 Dec. 1698, enclosing artificers' petition. Payment was eventually made. See T.1/54, fos. 237 ff., Treasury endorsement (9 Nov. 1699) to O.b. letter and artificers' petition dated 10 Oct. 1699.

3 WO 46/4, p. 39, estimate 14 Nov. 1698. The total arrears, 1692-8, was computed at £303,852.6s.6¾d. at this time.

4 See e.g. T.1/52, fo. 52, O.b. to Treasury, 1 Apr. 1698; T.1/53, fo. 1, Same to Same, 10 May 1698.

5 T.1/65, fos. 57 ff., O.b. to Treasury, 12 Dec. 1699.

6 WO 46/5, pp. 4-5, O.b. to Romney, 23 Apr. 1700; *Cal. SPDom. 1700-2*, p. 20, Same to Same, Same date; T.1/69, fo. 238, O.b. to Treasury, 15 July 1700.

negligence in the distribution of sea service money, compared with the full distribution of £25,000 for land services.[1]

The Office had succeeded in maintaining its credit, despite the arrears, and keeping down the size of the Ordnance debt[2] for most of the interregnum period between the two wars. The onset of war, however, meant a vast increase in Ordnance expenditure and a resultant surge in the size of its debt, especially as little consideration was taken of its extraordinary expenses and the ordinary payments to the Office were frequently in arrears.

One constant theme of complaint of the Ordnance board during the War of Spanish Succession was the expense of extraordinary services above the allowed estimate. During 1701 alone the supply of stores for the plantations cost the Office £18,407.8s.10¼d.[3] Issues of such magnitude continued to be made by the Office to the plantations for stores and men for which no provision had been made by parliament. These issues should have been reimbursed by a four and a half *per cent* duty paid by the plantations, but all too often the duty remained unpaid.[4] Other services were affected by the lack of monetary provision. In February 1702 the board argued that because Parliament had 'chalked out the way for disposing of the money' to the department that year, specific provision should be made to cover the cost of freight charges and other incidental services, as well as Ormonde's huge demands for a descent train and sea expedition, for which there was less than half the necessary stores in stock.[5] In the following months the board had to find stores and men for Shovell's expedition, and provide a train for Newfoundland and a further expedition for Portugal, having had little money for these services from Parliament.[6] The answering of these

1 WO 46/5, pp. 14-15, 16, 19, 21, O.b. to Romney, 24 July, 1, 17 Aug., 17 Sept. 1700.

2 *CJ* XIII, pp. 388-9, 8 Mar. 1701; Add. MS. 31243, fo. 32.

3 *Cal SP Dom. 1700-2*, p. 487, O.b. to Romney, 10 Jan. 1702; WO 46/5, pp. 89-90, Same to Same, 29 Apr. 1702.

4 See WO 47/22, p. 279, minute 3 Aug. 1705; SP 41/34, no. 29, O.b. to Hedges, 3 Aug. 1705, Same to Same, 25 June 1706; T.1/101, fo. 311, O.b. to Treasury, 31 Mar. 1707; *Cal. SP Col. Am. & W. Indies 1708-9*, no. 746; WO 46/6, p. 109, O.b. to Marlborough, 17 Dec. 1709; T.1/154, fo. 142, 18 Nov. 1712; T.1/158, fo. 118, O.b. to Treasury, 27 Jan. 1713; *Cal. SP Col. Am. & W. Indies 1712-14*, no. 679, Bolingbroke to Council of Trade, 20 May 1714.

5 WO 46/5, p. 67, O.b. to Romney, 14 Feb. 1702, pp. 71-2, Same to Same, 28 Feb. 1702, p. 81, estimate 28 Mar. 1702

6 *See ibid.* pp. 119-20, O.b. to Marlborough, 19 Dec. 1702, pp. 137-8, Same to Same, 25 June 1703, for details of expeditions. *CJ* XIV, 232, for list of extraordinary services to 25 Nov. 1703.

extraordinary charges put the Office under the greatest difficulty of forwarding the ordinary services, such as the Holland train, for which money had been supplied. Later in the war further issues were made by the Office to strengthen Gibraltar, re-supply Lord Galway in Portugal, furnish private expeditions and provide an additional allowance of stores to the fleet.[1] The board also had to honour bills of exchange drawn without their knowledge by sea captains and Army commanders abroad.[2] The cost of these services made a significant impression on the total Ordnance debt.[3]

The lack of payment of the agreed parliamentary estimate was of even greater consequence. At the end of 1704, for instance, the total arrears were stated as £156,114.1s.9d. and in September 1705 the board was still receiving the arrears from their proportion for land and sea services for 1702 and 1703.[4] Arrears of this stature continued to be a burden on Ordnance finances throughout the rest of the period.[5] Whereas in the early years of the war these arrears had particularly hit the sea service estimates, in the middle and later war period land service estimates were also affected.[6]

In these circumstances it is scarcely surprising to find that the total Ordnance debt increased. indeed, in February 1702 the board forecast that it would be impossible to meet the huge charge for fitting out bomb vessels and other services out of the supplies then being advanced,

1 Blenheim C I 30, O.b. to Sunderland, 10 Feb. 1705; WO 47/22, pp. 183-4, minute 7 June 1705; SP 41/34, nos. 19, 20, 30, O.b. to Hedges, 23 Mar.1705, 2 Apr. 1705, Same to Harley, 3 Aug. 1705, Same to Dartmouth, 17, 24 Feb. 1711; T.1/94, fo. 52, O.b. to Godolphin, 12 Apr. 1705; T.1/112, fo. 203, O.b. to Treasury, 24 Feb. 1709; WO 46/6, p. 43, O.b. to Marlborough, 19 Feb. 1706, p. 50, Same to Same, 16 Nov. 1706.

2 *Cal. Treas. Books 1706-7*, p. 443, Taylour to O.b., 23 Sept. 1707, pp. 481-2, Lowndes to Same: WO 47/25, p. 247, minute 23 Dec. 1707; T.1/107, fo. 139, O.b. to Godolphin, 9 June 1708; T.1/137, fo. 156, 25 Sept. 1711.

3 WO 46/5, p. 150, abstract of extraordinary services, 31 Mar. 1702 – 30 Sept. 1703. Cf. the services for the first five months of 1709. WO 55/345, p. 49, O.b. to Sunderland, 8 June 1709; T.1/114, fo. 176, O.b. to Treasury, 4 June 1709.

4 WO 49/119; *Cal. Treas. Books 1705-6*, p. 29, order 12 Sept. 1705.

5 See WO 46/6, pp. 41, 49, 50, O.b. to Marlborough, 8 Jan., 19 July, 16 Nov. 1706; T.1/102, fo. 112, state 26 May 1707; T.1/102, no. 69, O.b. to Treasury, 13 July 1707, no. 118, O.b. to Same, 4 Sept. 1707; WO 49/120, computations 30 Nov. 1708, 4 July 1710; T.1/122, fo. 87, O.b. letter 20 June 1710; T.1/133, fo. 248, O.b. to Treasury, 15 May 1711; T.1/137, fo. 156, O.b. letter, 25 Sept. 1711; T.1/151, fo. 31, O.b. to treasurer, 15 Aug. 1712; T.1/165, fo. 129, endorsed 29 Oct. 1713; T.1/175, fo. 143, O.b. to treasurer, 11 May 1714; WO 55/346, pp. 79-80, arrears 1702-13.

6 WO 49/120, estimate 14 Aug. 1710; WO 55/346, pp. 79-80.

without running into a very great debt, which had hitherto been prevented. It doubted the wisdom of running the Office into such a debt
because of the strictness of parliamentary appropriation.[1] The gloomy
forebodings of the board were ultimately justified by a disastrous
decline of Ordnance credit in the later part of the war, but in the earlier
years the Office debt was kept in manageable proportions and its credit
maintained (Table VIII).

There is little indication in the early war years, therefore, of a decline
of Ordnance credit. As late as the summer of 1705, for instance, the
Ordnance treasurer was able to dispose of over £20,000 worth of tallies
at par to the Bank of England.[2] But less than a year later the first signs
of the impending crisis may be discerned. In mid August 1706 the state
of the Ordnance's credit was reasonably healthy on paper: £17,148.
18s.9d. in cash, £61,592.8s.6½d. in tallies on low wines, and one tally
on the two-thirds subsidy worth £1,257.11s.5½d.[3] Yet the high proportion of Ordnance funds held in tallies on low wines had for some
time been a dead weight on the office because of the difficulty caused
by their disposal. Many of these tallies were for such large sums with
such a remote course of payment that brokers were unwilling to advance
money on them.[4] The tallies carried an interest rate of six *per cent,*
yet by August 1706 the Bank of England had refused to discount any
of them, the East India Company were unwilling to accept them as
payment for saltpetre, and only a small proportion of the total Ordnance holding had been sold. Moreover, the artificers were more than a
year in arrears, and the Office was being pressed for supplies of ready
money by artillery officers abroad. More immediately, £165,068.
12s.10d. had to be found for pressing services.[5] There was no immediate danger, however, of the debt over-burdening the Office, for the board
did report to Marlborough in November that it had been able to comply
with all the demands that had been made on the Office.[6]

Yet the pressures on the department were growing, and in the
following war years it was increasingly difficult for the board to main-

1   WO 46/5, pp. 55-6, 67, 5, 14 Feb. 1702.

2   *Cal. Treas. Books 1705-6,* p. 349, warrant 18 July 1705, p. 423, Lowndes to
O.b., 29 Sept. 1705, WO 47/22, pp. 326, 334, minutes 30 Aug., 7 Sept. 1705.

3   T.1/99, fo. 198, O.b. to Godolphin, 13 Aug. 1706.

4   See *Cal. Treas. Books 1706-7,* pp. 456-7, Godolphin's warrant, 8 Oct. 1707.

5   T.1/99, fo. 198, O.b. to Godolphin, 13 Aug. 1706, and calculation to 31 Dec.
1706.

6   WO 46/6, O.b. to Marlborough, 16 Nov. 1706. For the size of the debt see
Table VIII.

tain its good reputation. In the summer of 1707 the East India Company had still not received their dues for saltpetre and were refusing to deliver any saltpetre to the gunpowdermakers until this debt had been repaid.[1] At this period the pleas of the board to the Treasury are very reminiscent of the earlier pleas during the 1689-97 war. The one and a half years arrears due to the artificers were valued at £221,000, and there was a further £4,803 a month due for the artillery trains and shipping abroad. There was only £549.9s.6d. in ready money to meet these needs, and £166,238.17s.4d. remained unpaid out of the parliamentary estimates for 1706 and 1707, besides the arrears of former years. The Ordnance credit was sinking lower even than the Navy, Victualling and Transport Offices, where the artificers were allowed interest on their bills six months after they were due.[2] The board feared that unless interest was also allowed on Ordnance artificers' bills, the artificers would be compelled to advance their prices, for they were unable to sell their debentures at any reasonable rate to gain money to perform their contracts.[3]

In many cases cash was needed rather than further advances in tallies. In April 1708, for instance, the £30,000 in tallies on the land tax advanced by the lord treasurer for works at Chatham and Portsmouth provided no real solution to the board's difficulties, as ready money was required for the artificers at the signing of their contracts. Further problems were caused by the Treasury stipulation that the tallies should only be disposed of at par, which meant that the Office was unable to give them as payment to the artificers in case they should part with them at a discount.[4] Such tally advances made by the Treasury at this time, then, were virtually useless as instruments of credit, because of the strict Treasury provisions regarding their dispersal.[5] At the end of

---

1 WO 47/24, p. 442, minute 13 May 1707, p. 500, minute 19 June 1707; WO 47/25, p. 18, minute 19 July 1707; T.1/102, no. 53, O.b. to Treasury, 19 June 1707.

2 *Ibid.* no. 69, O.b. to Treasury, 13 July 1707. The East India Company's demands for interest, however, were eventually recognised (See *Cal. Treas. Books 1706-7*, pp. 359-60, Taylour to O.b., 17 July 1707), although the Treasury countered by demanding that the Company should be strictly charged interest when it fell behind on customs payments. *Ibid.* p. 381, Lowndes to customs commissioners, 30 July 1707.

3 WO 47/25, p. 241, minute 20 Dec. 1707, p. 289, minute 22 Jan. 1708; WO 46/6, p. 69, O.b. to Marlborough, 20 Dec. 1707, p. 81, Same to Same, 22 Jan. 1708. On the other hand, the navy bills (on which interest was allowed) held up well until the general decline of credit in 1708. See J.G. Sperling, 'Godolphin and the Organisation of Public Credit, 1702-10', (unpublished Cambridge Ph. D. thesis 1955), p. 110.

4 See WO 46/6, p. 92, O.b. to Marlborough, 7 May 1708.

5 See T. 1/107, no. 39, O.b. to Godolphin, 9 June 1708.

the year the board had calculated that £92,415.3s.7½d. was needed to carry on the services of the Office. This sum represents an increase of nearly £25,000 on the calculation made at the beginning of the year, an indication of the failure of the Treasury to respond to Ordnance needs in this period.[1]

The paltry sums that the Treasury did advance did little to alleviate the crisis. The artificers were more than two years in arrears and were obliged to exchange their debentures at a rate of twenty-five *per cent* discount. Extraordinary services had reached an unprecedented level. The Bank of England had refused to discount any of the Ordnance tallies 'being at a great[er] distance than they take', and private dealers would not purchase any without a substantial allowance.[2] The tallies in hand, therefore, could hardly be claimed as realisable funds to set against the ever rising Ordnance debt.[3]

The Office's financial situation in 1710 was as severe as at any time since the beginning of the war. Ordnance credit was declining rapidly; the artificers were almost two years in arrears and their debentures were being sold at up to thirty *per cent* discount;[4] and there was an inexorable increase in the absolute size of the Ordnance debt (Table VIII), mainly because of the failure of payments to the artificers. As has been seen, many of the funds set down to balance the debts were hardly realisable assets,[5] but there was a sufficiency of good funds to carry on the service. On 20 June 1710, for instance, the board reported that the £25,000 worth of Exchequer bills in its hands would suffice for providing for the artillery trains in Holland, Catalonia, Port Mahon and Gibraltar, and carrying on the Portsmouth wharf and other fortifications.[6] Small advances could also be raised on other tallies, and loans could always be made at interest,[7] but such sums would hardly answer the £120,000 or so that the Office considered vital for continuing the service in the last quarter of 1710.[8]

---

1 Cf. T/110, no. 54, 20 Dec. 1708, and T.1/105, no. 26, O.b. to Treasury, 28 Jan. 1708.

2 WO 46/6, p. 103, O.b. to Marlborough, 30 Apr. 1709; T.1/114, no. 26, Lansdell to Lowndes, 19 May 1709, no. 45. Although the situation was eased somewhat with the disposal in July of the land tax tallies. *Cal. Treas. Books 1709*, p. 26, 29 July, p. 288, Taylour to O.b., 29 July 1709.

3 *CJ* XVI, 220, 392-3; WO 49/120; Table VIII re. increase in debt, 1707-10.

4 T.1/120, no. 6, O.b. to Marlborough, 14 Jan. 1710.

5 Above, p. 201; *Cal. Treas. books 1710*, pp. 95, 108, 420.

6 T.1/122, no. 25, O.b. to Treasury, 20 June 1710.

7 See e.g. *Cal. Treas. Books 1710*, pp. 56, 90, 19 Sept., 6 Oct. 1710.

8 T.1/123, no. 58, calculation 26 Aug. 1710; T.1/157, fo. 72.

The full Ordnance demands continued to remain unsatisfied during the first months of 1711.[1] Of the money that had been supplied, by far the largest part had been spent on the current needs of the artillery trains and establishments abroad, and only a small proportion had been given for the Ordnance artificers.[2] Nevertheless there was a serious attempt made to raise the Office's credit by settling with the artificers for their past arrears, thereby shortening the department's course of payments.[3]

Over the course of 1711, therefore, there was a significant improvement in the size of the Ordnance debt, which by the end of the year effectively stood at little over £1,000 (Table VIII). The reason for this dramatic change was the funding of the £154,324.15s.8¾d. Ordnance debt at Michaelmas 1710, plus further debts that had accrued since then to 25 December 1710, into the stock of the South Sea Company, at a guaranteed six *per cent* rate of interest for those debentures that carried interest and three *per cent* for those that did not. The dividends that accrued on the stock were to be applied by the Ordnance treasurer 'for the use of the public', as directed by the Treasury.[4] This operation did not include the old debts of the Office contracted under Charles II, although a naval debt of equal standing was provided for by the funding Act.[5]

The weight of some of the old Ordnance debts may have been lifted from the shoulders of the board, but vast sums were still needed for current services in the latter stages of the war. The Treasury enjoined the board to lessen the charge of the Office, yet no economy could reduce the great expense of the Flanders and Spanish artillery trains which amounted to over £53,000 *per annum*.[6] Moreover, in January 1712 there were three years arrears due to the artillery officers in

---

1 *Cal. Treas. Papers 1711*, p. 2, minute 5 Jan. 1711; T.1/157, no. 29c, account, n.d; T.1/133, no. 21, 12 Apr. 1711.

2 *Ibid*.

3 *Cal. Treas. Books 1711*, pp. 47, 49, 52, 110, minutes 11, 14, 19 Apr., 23 Nov. 1711, pp. 410-11, Harley to O.b., 18 Aug. 1711; T.1/133, fo. 100, O.b. to Treasury, 13 Apr., fo. 129, Same to Same, 24 Apr. 1711.

4 The Ordnance was not the only department whose debts were funded this way. For details of the funding operation see 9 Anne c.15; *Cal. Treas. Books 1711*, pp. 1-1i, 321-3, 355-6, 441, 569-70, warrants 22 June, 6 July, 7 Sept., 30 Nov. 1711; *Ibid. 1712*, p. 88, minute 3 Dec., pp. 184-5, instrument 11 Mar. 1712; *Ibid. 1713*, p. 47, n., pp. 148-50, 11 Mar. 1713; *Ibid. 1714*, pp. 87-8, Oxford to Harley, 12 Jan. 1714; Dickson, p. 68, table 5.

5 See BL 516 M18, No. 57, *The Case of the Creditors Of the Office of Ordnance* (c.1711).

6 T.1/151, fo. 35, O.b. to Treasury, 15 Aug. 1712.

Flanders and Spain, amounting to £15,779.13s.3½d.[1] In these circum-stances the board inevitably still made large demands on the Treasury. On 4 April 1712, for instance, the board estimated that £43,171.13s.1d. was absolutely necessary for carrying on the services, £30,000 of which was for the payment of two quarters arrears to the artificers.[2] By September the board reckoned that nearly £150,000 was needed for land and sea services for the following quarter, against which there was less than £50,000 in tallies and money in the Ordnance treasurer's possession.[3] Had the Treasury given the Office permission to dispose of its tallies, the board observed that business would have been at a stand, as exchange bills were daily being drawn upon the department for the money given by Parliament in the two previous years.[4] So the Office ended the war as it had begun it by demanding money from a reluctant Treasury.[5]

Conclusion

What conclusions may be reached about the management of Ord-nance finances in this period?

The Office undoubtedly suffered from poor financial provision. The Commons were suspicious of Ordnance land services and this resulted in a reduction of its estimates in an attempt to force economies. There was little consideration of the extraordinary expenses of the Office, and because of the strictness of parliamentary appropriation after the Revolution it was impossible to divert the funds supplied for other uses.[6] Even the authorised parliamentary supply rarely reached the anticipated amount. A high proportion of funds provided by the Treasury, moreover, were remote tally assignments. Invariably it was the poorer sort of tradesmen who suffered from these assignments, as they were often forced to sell their tallies at a great discount so that

1 T.1/144, fo. 19, O.b. to Treasury, 29 Jan. 1712; *Cal. Treas. Books 1712*, p.7, minute 31 Jan. 1712, p. 10, minute, 8 Feb. 1712, directing £8,659.10s. to be issued.

2 T.1/146, fo. 26, O.b. to Treasury, 4 Apr. 1712; T.1/152, fo. 17, O.b. to Treasury, 17 Sept. 1712.

3 T.1/152, fo. 17, O.b. to Treasury, 17 Sept. 1712. The dividend on the South Sea stock that was also held by the Ordnance treasurer would have done little to make up the deficit. *Cal. Treas. Books 1712*, p. 88, minute 3 Dec. 1712; *Ibid. 1713*, p. 148, 11 Mar. 1713; T.1/159, fo. 114, account 9 Mar. 1713.

4 *Ibid*. fo. 167, O.b. to Treasury, 24 Mar. 1713.

5 Although the total Ordnance debt had been significantly reduced by the end of the war. See Table VIII, figures for 31 Mar. 1713.

6 See e.g. *Cal. Treas. Books 1693-6*, pp. 153-4; WO 46/5, p. 9, O.b. to Romney, 11 May 1700.

they could gain money to fulfil their contracts. This not only worked to the disadvantage of the tradesmen but also restricted the government's borrowing powers.[1] Ordnance artificers were also disadvantaged by there generally being no interest allowed on their debentures, which resulted in their depreciation at a quicker rate than those of other Offices.

The failure of both Parliament and Treasury to make adequate allowance for the Ordnance Office inevitably affected the efficiency of its services. It was especially important that there should be a regular ordinary allowance. As the board pointed out:

> For want of it no service of how mean importance soever can be furnished without an estimate and money first had, much less the continual support and repleneshing of the growing decays and defects of the magazine, to which end it was principally intended and for which, according to the fundamental uses, it ought wholly and inviolably to be employed.[2]

Nevertheless, the ordinary allowance was rarely paid in full. From the September quarter of 1661 to the June quarter of 1671, only in one year (1663-64) did payments on the ordinary exceed £12,000. In some years payments were considerably below £12,000, and in 1670 they were as low as £6,830.6s.3d.[3] Nor was this unusual: in the 1680s the board repeatedly complained to the Treasury that their ordinary allowance remained unpaid.[4] As a result some of the most vital Ordnance services, such as the maintenance of garrison fortifications, were neglected. It was not only the ordinary services, however, that were affected by lack of money. The building of the new wharf and storehouses at Portsmouth was constantly postponed because of an insufficiency of funds, although in the long term the Office would have saved on freight charges, as well as rent on many storehouses and the storekeeper's house.[5] Similarly, the Office did not have the money always to ensure compliance with a new gun establishment,[6] and other

---

1 See *Cal. SP Dom. 1690-1*, p. 241, Godolphin to the king, 2 Feb. 1691.

2 WO 49/112, paper presented to Sir Philip Warwick, n.d. but early 1660s.

3 *Cal. Treas. Books 1667-8*, p. xxvii. The year has been calculated from 30 June. The average yearly ordinary payments for these ten years fell far short of the average for the period 1627-34. See Aylmer, thesis, p. 35.

4 Above pp. 188, 190.

5 SP 32/11, fo. 329; WO 46/5, pp. 4-5; *Cal. SP Dom. 1700-2*, p. 20; WO 49/119, Bridges's report, 17 Jan. 1703.

6 See e.g. WO 46/5, p. 126, O.b. to Marlborough, 8 Feb. 1703; WO 55/344, p. 254.

Admiralty demands for additional stores to be turned down because of lack of funds.[1] It was impossible for the Office to comply with these and other extraordinary naval demands for mortars and bomb vessels,[2] for which no parliamentary provision had been made.

Nevertheless, although some Office services were retarded by lack of funds to meet all its needs, there is little evidence for a general dislocation of Ordnance services through failure of supply, apart from 1688. Office credit reached low points in 1673, 1679-80, 1690, 1694, and towards the end of the Spanish Succession War, yet the board, through the well-ordering of its finances and its uncanny ability to live from hand to mouth, always managed to survive the crisis. Artillery officers had to be paid reasonably promptly with hard cash, but Ordnance tradesmen could generally be persuaded to perform their functions on a minimum of supply and promises of better payments in the future. This was mainly because of the absolute integrity of the Ordnance course of payments. The regularisation of Ordnance payments dated from the first commissioners' period of office in the 1660s. By the 1690s this system had become so perfectly ordered that it has been praised by an historian investigating the general financial scene at that time.[3] Considering the vast expenditures incurred by the Office, its ability generally to maintain its credit, despite incomplete financial provision, was no mean achievement.

1   E.g. WO 46/6, p. 25; Corbett XIV, 157; WO 55/344, p. 120.
2   See *Cal. SP.Dom. 1698*, p. 152, Vernon to Admiralty lords, 18 Mar; WO 46/3, pp. 101-2, 136-7, 139-40; WO 46/4, pp. 6, 31; WO 46/5, pp. 2, 155; WO 55/340, fo. 48; T.1/24, fo. 254; Adm. 1/4005, 10 July 1712.
3   See Dickson, pp. 397-8.

CONCLUSION

Important as the Ordnance Office was in matters of war and defence, England's survival did not wholly depend on its labours, for the Office's activities were only one part of the total war effort. Indeed, the maturing of Ordnance administration and the increase of its activities was largely in response to demands from the Army and Navy. It is to these services that we must turn for a full appreciation of the significance of developments within the Ordnance Office in this period.

The growth of the Ordnance Office in the late seventeenth century was matched by a phenomenal expansion in the size of the Army and Navy. Under Charles II a standing army was for the first time permanently established in England in a time of peace. The Crown's military forces, however, did not increase dramatically in size in his reign. Of the force with which Monck had restored the king, Charles retained an English-based army of only four standing regiments, excluding the small force based in the twenty-eight regional garrisons. The size of this army was temporarily increased at the time of the emergency levies for the French and Dutch wars, but by 1684 – after the return of the Tangier garrison – the number of troops totalled barely 6,000 men.[1] Monmouth's rebellion provided James II with the means and the justification for a more rapid military expansion. During his reign, the size of the navy almost doubled, and peace-time expenditure on the army more than doubled. The clearest manifestation of a permanent military presence in England at this time was the thousands of men gathered for training at the camp on Hounslow Heath in the summers of 1686, 1687 and 1688.[2] Yet it was not the militarism of James II that caused the sharpest increase in the size of the Army, but the wars fought by his successors. Immediately after war had been declared in 1689, 10,000 troops were raised, and in spite of the temporary reduction imposed by Parliament in 1697, the British Army had increased to at least 70,000 men by 1711, the number of regiments having almost quadrupled since the days of James II.[3] Almost as dramatic was the increase in the size of the Navy. Charles II and James II, had raised the number of first, second and third rate

---

1   Childs, pp. 13, 17, 29-30. Cf. Western, p. 125.

2   *Ibid.* pp. 125, 130 ff.

3   Plumb, *The Growth of Political Stability*, pp. 125-6; Fortescue, *History of the British Army*, I. 554 ff. The 70,000 figure does not include foreign regiments in British pay.

ships from thirty in 1660 to fifty-nine in 1688, and increased the total tonnage of the fleet from 62,594 to 101,032 tons in that time. The greatest growth in English naval power, however, again occurred in the 1689-1714 period. In 1689 the English fleet was second in size and quality to the French and not vastly superior to the Dutch, but by 1714 it was the largest in Europe. The fleet had increased in number from 173 to 247 ships, in tonnage from nearly 102,000 to over 167,000, and in fire-power from 6,930 to 10,603 cannon.[1] The number of men in constant service in the Navy throughout the later war period, was 40,000.[2]

Of more direct relevance to our study was the development of the services responsible for war administration. The attempt by Blathwayt, as secretary of war, to increase his authority over the Ordnance Office has already been mentioned.[3] This illuminates the extent of the secretary at war's power by the closing years of the seventeenth century. The secretary had developed from being the mere personal assistant to the chief of the forces, to a supremely important military executive officer, with direct control over recruitment, the granting of leave, the provision of quarters and the issue of clothing. By the early eighteenth century the secretary at war had even assumed responsibility for presenting estimates to Parliament. One of the key instruments in this transmutation was the warrant issued on 27 September 1676 which gave the secretary authority over appointments, convoys, and quartering. This warrant also changed his status from a military to a civil officer by making him answerable to the king rather than the commander of the forces. Another reason for the secretary's advance was William Blathwayt's long tenure in office from 1683 to 1704. The change is illustrated by the growth of a small retinue of officials into a substantial sub-department working under the secretary at war. It is also exemplified by the differing types of person holding the office in the period. The earlier secretaries at war, such as Sir William Clarke and Matthew Locke, were men of small stature in national affairs. By the end of the period both St. John and Walpole had held the office. It has by then clearly become an important acquisition for the aspiring politician, and a key appointment on the road of advancement to the highest positions in the

---

1 Western, p. 122; Plumb, *The Growth of Political Stability,* p. 123; Ehrman, pp. xv, xx.

2 This was the figure on which estimates were based (above, p. 171). In the peace years in between, the Navy was reduced to 15,000 men and the Army to 7,000. G. M. Trevelyan, *England under Queen Anne* (3 vols. 1930), I, 248.

3 See above, p. 40.

land.[1] The increase in importance of the secretaryship at war was mirrored by the creation in 1662 of the office of paymaster-general to act as banker for the Army, and the consequent growth of an independent secretariat under the paymaster responsible for all aspects of military finance.[2]

The evolution of the place of secretary to the Admiralty was closely related to the emergence of the office of secretary at war. The title, secretary to the Admiralty, only appeared at the Restoration and, like the early secretaries at war's position *vis à vis* the commander of the forces, the earliest occupants of the post of secretary to the Admiralty — Sir William Coventry, Matthew Wren and Sir John Werden — were the personal secretaries of the lord admiral rather than servants of the Crown. Pepys's career as secretary to the Admiralty, 1673-9, 1684-8, like Blathwayt's service at the War Office, did much to establish the departmental nature of the post, its public character being confirmed when Pepys was appointed by letters patent in 1684. The three great advances made during Pepys's tenure of office — the regulation of business, the classification of records and the accommodation of a permanent staff — ensured that there was a stable organisation to initiate and co-ordinate naval affairs. Indeed, as we have seen, Pepys's influence was such that he often acted as a third secretary of state.[3] The office was rapidly assuming a political character under Pepys, but its subsequent history, in contrast to the development of the secretary at war's position in the 1690s, ensured that the Admiralty secretaryship would retain its administrative functions within the Admiralty Office rather than the king's Court or Parliament.

Although the Admiralty Office was still subject to political pressures after 1689, as evidenced by the rapid turnover in appointments to the Admiralty commission and the dismissal of George Clarke as Admiralty secretary in 1705 for voting against the court in the 1705 election of the Speaker, the administrative developments within the Office ensured that a change in the nature of the commission would not necessarily mean a complete disruption of departmental

---

1   The best summary of the secretary at war's position in this period is contained in Childs, pp. 94-7 and Scouller's *Armies of Anne,* pp. 10ff. Also see Fortescue, I, 313 and Clode, I, 71. For Blathwayt and Walpole's careers as secretaries at war see Jacobsen, *Blathwayt, passim,* and J.H. Plumb, *Sir Robert Walpole: The Making of a Statesman* (1956) pp. 129-62.

2   Clode, I, 73. For other members of the Restoration Army staff, see Childs, pp. 102-4.

3   See above, pp. 41-2.

routine. The classification of Admiralty documents was continued on Pepysian lines. These documents, moreover, were bound and filed, thereby providing a continuous series of records to which reference could be made where there was doubt as to the correct procedure to be followed. Other aspects of departmental business were re-organised. As the 1689-97 war progressed Admiralty board meetings were regulated. A series of office rules drawn up in the autumn of 1693, required one of the chief clerks to distribute copies of all correspondence to each member of the board and to sort out each paper needing the board's signature. Letters from the secretaries of state were to be left on one side and be dealt with before all other business. In the following year two other domestic arrangements were made relating to the tabling of an agenda at the end of each office day and the establishment of a clearing day for all current business. These procedures had not existed earlier and were made in response to the vast increase of naval business in the war.

But perhaps the most important sign of the growth of a permanent Admiralty Office was the change in status of the Admiralty secretary and the clerical establishment. The transition in the secretary's position from personal assistant to public official occurred with the appointment of Burchett as joint secretary with Bridgeman in January 1695. Burchett was to continue as Admiralty secretary for a period of nearly fifty years, for unlike his predecessors he did not leave office with the dismissal of his patron. The year before Burchett's appointment, moreover, the Admiralty secretary had been granted a salary from the public funds in the place of a personal allowance from the lord admiral or Admiralty commission. Prior to 1694 the Admiralty clerks had also been paid by private arrangement, but from the midsummer of that year they were entered on the Navy treasurer's accounts as salaried officials. From this date the chief clerks enjoyed a recognisable status within the Admiralty Office, with defined duties and the opportunity of promotion to the Admiralty secretaryship. Junior clerks could also look forward to promotion within the Office or the naval hierarchy. The importance of the first post-Restoration public payment to officials within the Admiralty Office — making it more a department of state and less a coterie of officials dependent on personal connections — may hardly be over-emphasised. The erection of an Admiralty building in Whitehall, 1694-5, was a more obvious manifestation of the development of the Admiralty from the personal office of the lord admiral to a government body.[1]

1 The contract for the building was signed on 1 September 1694, shortly after the granting of salaries. Prior to this there had been no permanent base for the

The emergence of the Admiralty Office as a more public department of government post-dated by some years similar developments within the Navy Board. The development of the Navy Board affords a far closer comparison with the early history of the Ordnance Office than does the relatively late evolution of the Admiralty Office. The existence of Ordnance and Navy boards from the 1540s enabled a more settled routine of business to develop, which was aided by the firm establishment of both Offices within the vicinity of the Tower. The Restoration period witnessed a further development. Both Offices acquired a public status through the payment of salaries to its officials, the opening up of avenues of promotion, and the settling of instructions detailing the duties of each officer.

The genesis and composition of the boards of the Navy and Ordnance Offices were remarkably similar. By the mid 1540s the keeper of the ships, the keeper of the king's storehouses, the comptroller and treasurer of maritime causes, and the surveyor and rigger, were acting in concert as a board under the direction of the lieutenant of the Admiralty. These officers, with the exception of the lieutenant, were to form the nucleus of the Navy Board for almost three centuries, although under slightly different guises. At the Restoration the Navy Board was 're-established on an enlarged basis. The treasurer remained excluded from any share of general business, but the three remaining principal officers, the comptroller, the surveyor and the clerk of the acts, were re-inforced by three new members, who were styled commissioners of the Navy. In the succeeding years further commissioners with more specific duties were assigned to the board, so that by 1688 their number had increased to five — the comptrollers of victuallers' accounts and stores, and the resident commissioners at Chatham, Portsmouth, and Deptford with Woolwich.

The replacement of the Navy Board from 17 April 1686 to 13 October 1688 by a special commission of twelve members, whose duties were completely re-defined, was out of step with Ordnance practice. Three of the four former principal officers were assigned to pass and settle the old accounts, and another group, consisting of men eminent in the shipbuilding and naval world, were seconded to deal with current business, in an attempt to improve the efficiency of naval

conduct of Admiralty business. For the history of the Admiralty Office in this period see Ehrman, pp. 196 ff., 554 ff., O.A.R. Murray, 'The Admiralty', parts III-V, *Mariner's Mirror* 23 (1937), pp. 316-31, *Mariner's Mirror* 24 (1938), pp.101-4, 204-25; G.F. James and J.J. Sutherland Shaw, 'Admiralty Administration and Personnel, 1619-1714', *BHR* 14 (1936-7), 10-24, 166-83; J.C. Sainty, *Admiralty Officials, 1660-1870; Office Holders in Modern Britain* IV (1975), pp. 1-4.

administration. The Navy Office establishment, however, was unaffected by the change. This was itself indicative of the growth of a more permanent naval department of government, and contrasted sharply with the situation in the early seventeenth century, when the absorption of the Navy Board by a special commission usually meant that its business would be carried on in a different building by a new set of officials.

The detailed instructions for the Navy Office, promulgated by the Duke of York on 28 January 1662, were also a sign that naval administration was coming of age. Like the 1683 instructions for the Ordnance Office they were not completely original, but they were a marked improvement on those that had been issued by the lord admiral in 1640, and they remained the basis of subsequent orders for the Board until well into the following century. A further set of instructions in September 1671 re-defined the treasurer's duties. The fault with the Navy Office instructions, as with those of the Ordnance Office, was that they left very little room for individual initiative. They depended on every member of the board checking the duties of each other, and left no-one with ultimate responsibility for any action, as Pepys found after eight years experience in the Navy Board as clerk of the acts:

> The Office is spoiled by having so many persons in it, and so much work that is not made the work of any one man but of all and so is never done. . . . The best way to have it well done were to have the whole trust in one, as myself, to set whom I please to work in the several businesses of the Office, and me to be accountable for the whole.

The Navy Board instructions, then, did not necessarily improve the efficiency of naval administration. Their real function in the long-term history of government was to instill notions of loyalty and duty into each serving officer of the Navy Board.

From an early date the Navy Office, like the Ordnance Office, provided opportunities for advancement, as well as a salary from the public funds. There was no system of regular promotion within the Navy Office in this period, but men of ability had a good prospect of moving up the naval hierarchy. Resident commissioners were advanced from the smaller to the larger yards, and occasionally a resident commissioner might find his way onto the board, although promotions of this type were unusual. In the 1688-95 period the clerical staff of the Navy Office were as likely to be recruited for the board as the dockyard staff — the clerical staff graduating to such posts as the clerk of the acts and the comptroller of accounts and the dockyard men to the posts of surveyor and resident commissioner — but it was more usual for appointments to the board to be made from serving naval officers. After the Revolution, there was also a regular salaried Navy Office establishment working under the Navy Board.[1]

There were three naval sub-departments, concerned with victualling, sick and wounded, and transport, that were partly under the jurisdiction of the Navy Board. These departments, indeed, had grown out of the Navy Board, which Office held control over them by checking and, if necessary, modifying their instructions and supervising their accounts.

There were important developments in all three services in this period. In 1683 the direct contracting for victuals by the Navy Board was replaced by a commission, which was established in an attempt to tighten Admiralty control over the provision of victuals. Some of the former contractors were appointed as members of the commission and future commissions were largely recruited from outside the ranks of the naval hierarchy. The formation of the victualling commission, however, did not solve all the organisational problems at a stroke. The composition of the commission meant there was always the danger of a combination between a group of big contractors; the board's proceedings lacked order and method; the commission's accounting procedures left much to be desired; and there was also great inefficiency in the supply of provisions. Nevertheless, the formation of a distinct unit for the administration of sea victuals in the 1680s provided the framework on which to base future reforms. In 1700 instructions were formulated to help achieve a regular course of payment and uniformity in the organisation, by keeping the Victualling Board under the control of the Navy Board. Two extra Victualling commissioners were appointed and a regular compilation of records maintained from 1702. The yards at Portsmouth and Plymouth were rebuilt, the London office was re-organised, and the board started buying vessels to ease the problems of transport and storeroom. Despite these and other improvements a select committee of the House of Commons held an enquiry into victualling abuses in 1711 and produced much damaging evidence against the Office.[2]

The commissioners for Sick and Wounded, like the Victualling commissioners, were not generally naval officers. Unlike the victuallers,

---

1 For the above, see Davies, 'The Administration of the Royal Navy', p. 272; Murray, 'The Admiralty' part III, pp. 316 ff.; Ehrman, pp. 179 ff.

2 *Ibid.* p. 177; Watson, pp. 112 ff. For the early victualling arrangements before the 1683 commission see Ogg, *England in the Reign of Charles II* I, 262-3.

however, they were only appointed in wartime. Their responsibility was divided with the Navy Board, the latter Office taking charge of the service on board ship and the Sick and Wounded commissioners for the service ashore. Improvements to the service were made under the pressure of war in the early years of the eighteenth century by the fifth commission for Sick and Wounded: notably in the imposition of a new set of instructions in 1702. At the end of the 1702-13 war, the Sick and Wounded Commission was amalgamated with the Transport Board and this consolidation secured their position as a permanent department of state.[1]

The Transport Board itself was a comparatively new department. The Navy Board handled the transport of troops by sea until the appointment of the first Transport Commission on 20 March 1690. As we have seen, the early commissions do not appear to have been particularly efficient bodies. In the middle years of the 1702-13 war, however, the transport service began to work more smoothly. A treasurer was appointed in 1704, and in the following year a third commissioner, Thomas Colby, was added to the board. Colby seems to have been partly responsible for improving relations between the Victualling and Transport Boards and in raising the standard of the service. Financial instructions were devised in 1705, instituting a regular course of payment, and more detailed instructions were drawn up for the local agents.[2]

The changes that occurred in the war departments of state in this period may be briefly summarised. A secretary at war and paymaster-general emerged as the heads of a nascent War Office, and an Admiralty department, with a permanent office, secretary, and secretariat, took the place of the former *ad hoc* jurisdiction. The Ordnance Office and Navy Board became greater departments, with the vast increase in size of the sea and land forces, and three new organs of government were created to perform the work delegated by the Navy Office.

Closely allied to developments within the departments of state responsible for the Army and Navy was the growth of organs of government with jurisdiction over trade and diplomacy, for both these activities flourished under war conditions. The growth of a colonial system resulted in the emergence of a Board of Trade responsible for colonial administration, staffed by public servants

---

1 Ehrman, p. 176; Watson, pp. 193 ff.

2 *Ibid.* pp. 260 ff. Also above, pp. 150-1, for the relationship between the Transport and Ordnance boards.

accountable to the Crown. The diplomatic service also grew with the increase in status of England as a foreign power.[1] Changes in late-seventeenth century government, however, were not confined to the peripheral reaches of administration but to the heart of government itself, for the period witnessed the slow metamorphosis in the position of the Privy Council and the rise of the secretaries of state and Treasury offices.[2] As great a transformation occurred with the abolition of tax-farming and the formation of Treasury controlled revenue offices. The establishment of retinues of Ordnance officials at the outports was matched by the creation of an army of revenue officials, employed at ports throughout England and Wales, to administer the taxes.[3]

As important as the institutional changes were the crucial adjustments made to the character of government in the later Stuart epoch. Many of the conditions of a modern civil service, which had been tried out in the Commonwealth and Protectorate period, were gradually instituted after the Restoration. Salaries from the public funds were replacing fees, thereby freeing officials from dependence on any particular type of business for remuneration and making them more aware of their general responsibilities. The old tenures of office were also slowly changing. The demise of life and reversionary tenures among the senior office-holders made their places less secure. To compensate, the tenures of the more subordinate officials were becoming more secure, in order to preserve a continuity of expertise in government. This enabled a defined system of promotion among the clerical establishment to develop in a wide range of departments. The members of the lower echelons of government, responsible for the daily execution of administration, were becoming more like permanent public officials and less like temporary personal servants, whilst their seniors were losing their continuous contact with the departments because they were being increasingly subject to pressures from Parliament. Administration was not only becoming more professional but also more party political.

1　See J.C. Sainty, *Officials of the Board of Trade, 1660-1870 : Office Holders in Modern Britain* III (1974), *passim;* Plumb, *The Growth in Political Stability,* pp. 127-8; D.B. Horn, *The British Diplomatic Service, 1689-1789,* (Oxford, 1961), pp. 13, 15, 44.

2　See chapter 1. For the growth of the staffs of these Offices in this period see Sainty, *Officials of the Secretaries of State,* pp. 1-21, and *Treasury Officials,* pp. 1-6.

3　By 1675 there were 344 customs officials employed in the port of London, and 512 officials at forty-six ports in the rest of England and Wales. See University of London Library, MS. 672. 'An Establishment of the Offices of his Majesty's Customs in London and Outports . . . 1675'. I am grateful to Dr Paul Kelly for this reference.

Accompanying these changes was the emergence of a new type of administrator whose solution to problems was based on a rational judgement from a compilation of available evidence. Pepys is the most famous example of a royal official who adopted a more rational stance in the face of the practical problems of government, but he is by no means an isolated figure. Wren, Lowndes and Newton are three late seventeenth century administrators who were imbued with scientific ideas, and there were many others. Indeed, it would be useful to know how many civil servants of the period were also members of the Royal Society. This more intellectual and systematic approach to administration, based as it was on admiration for the French model and on current ideas of political arithmetic and natural philosophy, must inevitably have had a beneficial effect on governmental efficiency.[1]

How may we place the late seventeenth and early eighteenth centuries in the history of modern government?

One of the characteristics of any administrative system is that it constantly adapts to new situations. Some periods of change, however, are more meaningful than others, and it is the task of the administrative historian to select these critical moments and emphasise their significance. Professor Elton has recognised three such periods as being of 'revolutionary' importance in the history of government from medieval times to the nineteenth century: the Anglo-Norman creation of a centralised feudal state governed by the king in Household; the formation of bureaucratic departments and officers of state in the 1530s in the place of Household administration; and the nineteenth century establishment of a government, based on departments responsible to Parliament rather than the Crown.[2] In formulating this cyclical theory of administrative development, however, he has underestimated the importance of the late seventeenth century in the growth of modern government. Professor Elton himself has admitted this in an article written some ten years after the publication of *The Tudor Revolution in Government*. 'I now think', he writes, 'that I did not give enough weight to the reforms of the reigns of Charles II and William III, which assisted the system reformed by the Tudors to last another century'.[3] In this sense, the developments in this period only looked back to the Tudors. They shored up the old administrative system by making the necessary reforms in the light of the circumstances prevailing in the late seventeenth century. Such reforms

[1] For this see Plumb, *The Growth of Political Stability*, pp. 24-6.
[2] G.R. Elton, *The Tudor Revolution in Government*, (Cambridge, 1953), p. 424.
[3] G.R. Elton, 'The Tudor Revolution: A Reply', *Past and Present* 29 (1964), pp. 43-4.

as the gradual adoption of salaries instead of fees and the immunisation of departmental government from the disease of political interference were not to be completed until the nineteenth century. Yet simply viewing late seventeenth century government in the terms of the past ignores the far-reaching changes that took place in government in this period. As Professor Plumb has argued, 'in many ways the developments in administrative efficiency between 1660 and 1715 were far more fundamental in moulding both the nature of our constitution and our politics than the schemes of Thomas Cromwell'.[1] The rise of the Treasury and the later revolution in finance, the great expansion in departmental government, and the successful establishment of a more professional civil service were radically new departures in the history of administration.

The developments that took place within the Ordnance Office within this period were a microcosm of these general changes in government. Indeed, such developments were often in advance of other reforms, for, apart from the Treasury, it was the war departments that showed the most marked changes in this period, and felt the most need for informed government and rational administrators. As Professor Elton has conceded, 'the administration of naval and military matters remained very incomplete, occasional, and unbureaucratic, until the era of wars and imperial development after 1660 forced the government to attend to it'.[2] It is in the later Stuart period that the great reorganisations took place which forged the war departments that were to serve the fighting services throughout the eighteenth century and beyond.

Not all the developments that took place within the organisation of the Ordnance Office in the late seventeenth century were fundamental to its constitution. The decisive change in its structure occurred in the mid-sixteenth century, when a board of principal officers and a rudimentary accounting system were established, and although alterations were made to the Office's constitution in this period they were firmly based on the Tudor model. The separation of the functions of lieutenant and treasurer in 1670 was the logical step forward from the earlier position, and even the 1683 instructions for Ordnance officers may be looked on as an elaboration and re-codification of Tudor procedures. The resurrection of the old Ordnance board in 1660 was an indication that changes were to be made on the Tudor pattern, in opposition to the attempted reforms of the Commonwealth and

1 Plumb, *The Growth of Political Stability*, p. 25.
2 Elton, *Tudor Revolution* p. 422.

Protectorate eras. The influence of the Cromwellian epoch, however, was not completely lost on the post-Restoration Ordnance Office. The imposition of salaries rather than fees on Ordnance personnel was continued, thereby giving them a more public character than before the civil war period. Ordnance clerks, for instance, were ceasing to be the mere personal servants of the principal officers and were becoming servants of the state, the representatives of a permanent civil service who remained in office even when their principal officers were removed.

The later Stuart period, however, should not be simply dismissed as being of little importance in the history of the Ordnance Office. It is true that a number of changes may be seen as the climax of earlier reforms, but the extent and rate of the changes within the department in this period were entirely without precedent, and were of fundamental consequence to its future organisation. New instruments of credit and new methods of payment to Ordnance creditors were devised to cope with the ever-expanding amount of business necessary to be transacted. The increase of business resulted in a vast expansion in the size of the Ordnance establishment. Distinct military and civil branches of the service emerged, thereby changing the function of many of the existing officers. It was becoming increasingly less likely for principal officers, for instance, to serve on artillery trains and in naval actions. Jonas Moore's active engagement as assistant surveyor in the naval campaign of 1673[1] would not have been repeated by his eighteenth century counterpart. By the eighteenth century, moreover, it had ceased to be practicable for the Tower principal officers and their clerks to take remains and survey stores returned from ships, although they had been enjoined to do so in the 1683 instructions[2] This was a natural result of the great expansion of business at the major garrisons and outports, apart from the Tower. The dispersal of stores away from the Tower and the growth of other depots resulted in the formation of separate establishments of Ordnance personnel at these places. It also meant the erection of new fortifications to defend them.

It is not difficult to explain why such rapid progress should have been made in the Office's development in the late seventeenth and early eighteenth centuries. For almost half of the fifty-four years from the Restoration to 1714 England was at war, and many of the major developments in the Ordnance Office within that time were forged — directly or indirectly — by the demands of war. It was imperative for England's survival that the Ordnance service be refurbished in answer

1   See SP 30, case f, *A Just Vindication* . . .
2   See WO 47/33, pp. 238-9, regulations for the outports, 14 June 1720.

to the threats of the Dutch and the French. For the first time since the late sixteenth century England was threatened with invasion by a hostile power and was actively and continuously engaged — at least after the Revolution — in making war on the continent.

This book, however, has been concerned with the activities, as well as the organisation, of a department of government. What judgement, then, may finally be passed on the efficiency of Ordnance administration in this period?

A superficial survey of Ordnance administration from 1660 to 1714 would inevitably result in condemnations of its efficiency. Indeed, historians who have only taken a cursory glance at Ordnance records have almost universally agreed that the Office was hopelessly corrupt and inefficient.[1] Some of these charges cannot be ignored. There is little point denying that Ordnance officers accepted undue rewards. There is no point in contesting accusations of failures of supply, or insinuations against the poor quality of some Ordnance stores. There is no possibility of successfully defending the Office against the charge of being unable to maintain many garrisons in a suitable state of defence. Many of the reforms implemented with a view to ironing out these deficiencies were no more than piece-meal palliatives. The exception was the massive codification of Ordnance instructions in 1683, but even these new instructions were by no means uniformly successful, and in 1686 a number of the 1683 instructions were modified. The surveyor-general's order to keep check books on the treasurer's and storekeeper's accounts, for instance, was accepted as having 'rather impede[d] and hinder[ed] than be[en] of any use or advantage to our service' and was counter-manded.[2] Even with these modifications some instructions were unworkable.[3]

An historian dismissing evidence revealing inefficiencies and corruption in Ordnance administration, then, would be on perilous ground. It is important, however, not to end the story there without giving the Office a right to reply to the historians' damning judgements.

In any study of the workings of a government department it is the singular event that is highlighted. Documents illustrating the peculation of stores by an Ordnance officer or the failure of an expedition speak for themselves, but it may well have been unprofitable for the

1 See above, p. 144. Also see Childs, p. 87.
2 King's 70, fo. 48.
3 See D.1778/V 71, petition of T. Gardiner to Darmouth; WO 47/33, pp. 238-40, regulations for outports, 14 June 1720.

historian to have recorded evidence relating to an official's honest discharge of duty or a speedy supply to the forces. The weight of quoted evidence casting doubt on the Office's integrity or efficiency, must always be balanced against the far greater weight of material simply illustrating the routine discharge of a department's functions that the historian has found unprofitable to cite. The fact that the Ordnance Office was usually successful in maintaining supply and meeting the demands of its creditors throughout this period must not be ignored. The impression generally given from the mass of letters from the board is of an Office endeavouring to do its best within the limits of the administrative system of the time.[1] Some of these limitations must be emphasised if a fair picture is to emerge of Ordnance administration.

One of the keys to an understanding of the government of the Ordnance Office is an appreciation of the limitations of its finances. Invariably there was an insufficiency of ready money to meet its needs, and although it usually managed to maintain its credit, the lack of money meant a stringent guard had to be kept on the disposal of the available resources. This affected every aspect of Ordnance administration. Had sufficient monetary supplies been made available to the Office there need have been little resort to corruption, the tradesmen could have fulfilled all their contracts, and Ordnance facilities at the ports and garrisons could have been improved. As it was, only by diligent husbanding of supplies could the Office manage to keep the wheels of government turning. Yet even if all the board's demands were met by Parliament and Treasury there could have been no final solution to the problems of Ordnance administration. The lack of technological advance and the failure of co-ordination between the departments themselves would have inevitably resulted in delays in the manufacture and provision of stores. Such delays had occurred at the time of the Armada, such delays were to recur later in the eighteenth century. The regular payment of an increased salary, moreover, would not necessarily have curbed the cupidity of all Ordnance personnel.

So the final word about Ordnance administration in this period must necessarily be inconclusive. A damning indictment of its activities would be as warped as an overwhelmingly favourable appraisal. The truth does not lie in the clear red or violet ends of the historical spectrum, but in the hazy yellow and green bands in the middle. The Office may be said to have performed its functions adequately but not

1 See e.g. WO 46/3, pp. 2-3, O.b. to Sidney, 9 Aug. 1693; WO 55/339, pp. 138-9, O.b. to Nottingham, 2 Mar. 1692.

spectacularly. No final answer had been found to the problems of Ordnance administration which remained to confound the succeeding generations of Ordnance administrators until the final disbandment of the Office in 1855. Indeed, in the light of recent scandals over naval victualling, it is to be doubted whether there is any final solution to problems of government. Until government is in the hands of independent automatons devoid of human contact, it will be subject to the whims and vagaries of human behaviour. Early modern government as manifested in the Ordnance Office of the late seventeenth and early eighteenth centuries was no exception.

APPENDIX
A LIST OF ORDNANCE OFFICIALS, 1660-1714

It would be an impossible task to list all the officials of the Ordnance Office during this period, and the following lists are necessarily incomplete. Extraordinary clerks, artificers, labourers and ordinary gunners, engineers and military personnel have not been listed. The lists of storekeepers and miscellaneous officials, moreover, are less accurate and full than those of the other officials, as these officers were not generally entered on the quarter books. The majority of their names have been taken from the treasury ledgers, the bill books, and miscellaneous warrant books. (WO 48, 51, 55). The lists of principal officers have been compiled from the patent rolls (C.66. I am heavily indebted to Mr John Sainty for many of these references); other lists have largely been compiled from the quarter books (WO 54/20-72, Sept. 1660-Dec. 1714). In the latter case the dates listed are not usually the dates on which particular appointments were made, but the quarter from which time salaries were assigned.

Masters-General

Compton, Sir William	27 June 1660 - Oct. 1663 (death)
Berkeley, Lord John)	
Duncomb, Sir John)	31 Oct. 1664 - June 1670
Chicheley, Sir Thomas)	
Chicheley, Sir Thomas	4 June 1670 - June 1679
Chicheley, Sir John[1])	
Hickman, Sir William)	23 June 1679 - Jan. 1682
Musgrave, Sir Christopher)	
Legge, George, Lord Dartmouth	28 Jan. 1682 - Apr. 1689
Schomberg, Frederick, 1st Duke of	18 Apr. 1689 - July 1690 (death)
Sidney, Henry, 1st Earl of Romney	28 July 1693 - June 1702
Churchill, John, 1st Duke of Marlborough	29 June 1702 - Jan. 1712
Savage, Richard, 4th Earl of Rivers	10 Jan. 1712 - Aug. 1712 (death)
Douglas, James, 4th Duke of Hamilton	5 Sept. 1712 - Nov. 1712 (death)
Churchill, John, 1st Duke of Marlborough	from 4 Oct. 1714

Principal Officers

Lieutenants-General

Legge, William	28 June 1660 - Oct. 1670 (death)
Walter, David	15 Nov. 1670 - Apr. 1679 (death)

[1] Sir John Chicheley was granted the reversion to the mastership of the Ordnance in Nov. 1674 (C.66/3165; *Cal. Treas. Books 1672-5*, p. 618, 27 Nov. 1674; *Cal. SP Dom. 1673-5*, p. 411, 13 Nov. 1674; D.1778/V 27; *Bulstrode Papers*, p. 272, 7 Dec. 1674). In June 1675 a warrant empowered him, 'to sit at the board as assistant to his father', and he took his place at the board 'on the left hand of the master of the Ordnance' (WO 47/19b, 17 June 1675).

Legge, George[1]	Apr. 1679 - Jan. 1682
Musgrave, Sir Christopher	28 Jan. 1682 - Aug. 1687
Tichburne, Sir Henry	1 Aug. 1687 - Apr. 1689
Goodricke, Sir Henry	16 Apr. 1689 - June 1702
Granville, John, 1st Lord of	
Potheridge	29 June 1702 - May 1705
Erle, Thomas	2 May 1705 - June 1712
Hill, John	21 June 1712 - Sept. 1714
Erle, Thomas	from 29 Sept. 1714

Surveyors-General

Nicholls, Francis	22 June 1660 - Nov. 1669
Moore, Sir Jonas, senior	13 Nov. 1669 - Aug. 1679 (death)
Moore, Sir Jonas, junior[2]	Aug. 1679 - July 1682 (death)
De Gomme, Sir Bernard	29 July 1682 - Nov. 1685 (death)
Sheer, Sir Henry	2 Dec. 1685 - July 1689
Charlton, John	19 July 1689 - June 1702
Bridges, William	29 June 1702 - Dec. 1714
Richards, Michael	from 2 Dec. 1714

Clerks of the Ordnance

Sherburne, Sir Edward[3]	16 June 1660 - Aug. 1668
Swaddell, John[4]	Aug. 1689 - Mar. 1690

[1] Legge gained the reversion to the office on 7 Dec. 1672 (C.66/3142), but he did not succeed to the office until April 1679 (O.F.G. Hogg, 'Notes on the Board of Ordnance' (PRO typscript), p. 111). He was, however, admitted to the board, 'with full power to sit, advise and vote as a principal officer there', before that date (D.1778/V 27, warrant 23 Aug. 1671; *Cal SP Dom. 1671*, p. 475, 10 Sept. 1671).

2 Moore junior gained the reversion to the office on 8 Feb. 1675 (C.66/3171), and succeeded after the death of his father in Aug. 1679. The warrant granting the reversion to Moore was dated 30 Dec. 1674 *(Cal. SP Dom. 1673-5*, p. 486. Also see *Cal. Treas. Books 1672-5*, p. 668, 3 Feb. 1675).

3 Sherburne secured the reversion in 1638 (C. 66/2773) and succeeded as clerk of the Ordnance after the death of his father in 1641, but he was deprived of his place by order of the Lords, 17 Aug. 1642 *(DNB)*. Sherburne, with Marsh, shortly afterwards joined the king and continued in the king's service within the Royalist Ordnance Office at Oxford (Roy, thesis pp. 275 ff). On 17 May 1660 the Lords agreed to Sherburne's and Marsh's petition claiming their right of office, and ordered that they should be restored as clerk and storekeeper of the Ordnance. On 19 May, however, upon the counter petition of the parliamentary officers, Nicholls and Fawkner, the previous order was suspended and it was ordered that Nicholls and Fawkner were to execute the places until the king's pleasure was known *(LJ* XI, 31, 33-4). Charles II evidently restored Sherburne and Marsh again, after further petition, on 16 June 1660 *(Cal. SP Dom. 1659-60,* p. 447, 27 May 1660; Hogg, 'Notes', p. 164). In Dec. 1688 Sherburne, 'without cause shown, or being so much as nominated therewith', was forced out of his house in the Tower and dispossessed of the clerkship of the Ordnance, 'upon pretence of being a suspected Roman Catholic' (Sloane 1048, fo. 1, Sherburne's petition to William III, *c.* 1700).

4 Swaddell gained the reversion in 1673 (C. 66/3149). A Treasury warrant to the barons of the Exchéquer was made out to swear Swaddell into the place of clerk of the Ordnance 'forfeited' by Sherburne declaring himself a Roman Catholic and not taking the oath and declaration on 7 Aug. 1689 *(Cal. Treas. Books 1689-92*, p. 213, 7 Aug. 1689).

Littleton, Sir Thomas	26 Mar. 1690 - May 1696
Musgrave, Christopher (junior)	15 May 1696 - Dec. 1714
Ashe, Edward	from 2 Dec. 1714

Storekeepers

Marsh, Richard[1]	16 June 1660 - Mar. 1672 (death)
Marsh, George[2]	26 Mar. 1672 - Nov.? 1673 (death)
Conyers, Edward	1 Dec. 1673 - Aug. 1683
Bridges, William	1 Aug. 1683 - Apr. 1685
Gardiner, Thomas	2 Apr. 1685 - Mar.? 1691 (death)
Meesters, William	27 Mar. 1691 - Feb.? 1701 (death)
Lowther, James	15 Feb. 1701 - Sept. 1708
Lowther, Robert	27 Sept. 1708 - Apr. 1710
Ashe, Edward	26 Apr. 1710 - June 1712
Windsor, Dixie	from 28 June 1712

Clerks of deliveries

Clarke, George[3]	16 June 1660 - Apr. ? 1670 (death)
Wharton, George	15 Apr. 1670 - Nov. 1670
Fortrey, Samuel	25 Nov. 1670 - ? 1681
Bridges, William	2 Feb. 1682 - Aug. 1683
Gardiner, Thomas	1 Aug. 1683 - Apr. 1685
Trumbull, Sir William	2 Apr. 1685 - Dec. 1685
Musgrave, Philip	2 Dec. 1685 - ? 1689 (death)
Musgrave, Christopher, junior	27 July 1689 - May 1696
Lowther, James	15 May 1696 - Feb. 1701
Pulteney, John	15 Feb. 1701 - June 1703
Craggs, James	18 June 1703 - Mar. 1711
Ousley, Newdigate	1 Mar. 1711 - June 1713
King, Richard	30 June 1713 - Dec. 1714
Craggs, James	from 2 Dec. 1714

Treasurers

Wharton, George	25 Nov. 1670 - Aug. 1681 (death)
Bertie, Charles[4]	Aug. 1681 - June 1699
Mordaunt, Harry	8 June 1699 - June 1702

1 Marsh gained the reversion to the office on 2 Jan. 1643, but did not execute it after the Restoration until June 1660 (Grant recorded in W.H. Black, *Docquets for letters Patent, 1642-6*, (1837), p. 348. For Marsh also see above p. 224, n.3).

2 George Marsh gained the reversion on 7 Nov. 1648 (Hogg, 'Notes', p. 164). On 16 Mar. 1667 a warrant was drawn up appointing him as assistant to his father Richard Marsh at £200 p.a. (*Cal. SP Dom. 1666-7*, 16 Mar. 1667). He was admitted to the office after the death of his father on 26 Mar. 1672 (Hogg, 'Notes', p. 164).

3 Clarke gained the patent on 17 July 1640 with Thomas Eastbrooke (C.66/2879). He lost office in the Civil War, but was restored on 18 May 1660 by the House of Lords (*LJ* XI, 32). He was finally confirmed in office, 'from the execution of which you have had a long suspension by the late public interruptions', by the king's warrant of 16 June 1660 (Hogg, 'Notes', p. 176).

4 Bertie gained the reversion on 23 Jan. 1675 (C.66/3164).

Bertie, Charles	16 June 1702 - May 1705
Mordaunt, Harry	28 May 1705 - June 1712
Eversfield, Charles	30 June 1712 - 1714
Mordaunt, Harry	from 2 Dec. 1714

Assistant surveyors[1]

Moore, Sir Jonas, senior	from 19 June 1665
De Gomme, Sir Bernard	from 27 Oct. 1679
Rothwell, James	from 4 Dec. 1685
Townesend, Thomas	to Nov. 1689
Boulter, William	18 Nov. 1689 - 1702

Clerks in Ordinary [2]

Chief Clerks (secretaries) to the master-general

Baylie, Matthew	Sept. 1660 - Sept. 1663
Baylie, Matthew	Dec. 1664 - Mar. 1668
Bennett, Thomas	2 Nov. 1668 - Mar. 1670
Beck, Richard	23 June 1670 - June 1671
Beaumont, Charles	8 July 1671 - June 1679
Langley, Thomas	4 Oct. 1673 - Dec. 1681
Graham, Richard	28 Feb. 1682 - Sept. 1687
Musgrave, Philip	Dec. 1687 - Mar. 1689
Holford, William	June 1689 - Sept. 1689
Cardonnell, James	Dec. 1689 - Sept. 1690
Pulteney, John	Sept. 1693 - June 1702
Craggs, James	Dec. 1702 - Dec. 1711
Ousley, Newdigate	Mar. 1712 - June 1712
Mason, Gawin	from Dec. 1712

Clerks to the Lieutenant-General[3]

First Clerks

Wharton, George	Sept. 1660 - Mar. 1670
Hubbald, Edward	June 1670 - Sept. 1670

---

1 The assistant surveyor had power 'to sit and be present at all counsels and meetings, and to do all other thing and things to the said Office and place of surveyor . . . as the said surveyor himself doth' (WO 55/388, fo. 172). By 1689, however, the place was apparently a sinecure for it was represented to Schomberg that the assistant surveyorship was 'unneedful being more charge than use to the king' (WO 55/337, fo. 60, Schomberg to board, 6 Dec. 1689).

2 The quarter books do not make clear which clerk belonged to which officer and which clerk had seniority. However, an attempt, based on their differences in pay and their position in the list of quarter payments, has been made to distinguish between them.

3 Until 1670 the lieutenant-general had £160 p.a. for two clerks, as he acted as both lieutenant and treasurer of the Ordnance. It was ordered in Feb. 1665, however, that on the death of William Legge the offices of lieutenant and treasurer would be separated, that the lieutenant would only be allowed one clerk at £50 p.a., and that two clerks would be assigned to the treasurer at £60 p.a. each (S.P. 29/112, fo. 168). The lieutenant was not allowed a second permanent clerk until the 1683 alteration of the instructions of the Office (King's 70, fo. 43).

Petty, Robert	Dec. 1670 - June 1679
Graham, John	Sept. 1679 - Dec. 1681
Winteringham, Christopher	Mar. 1682 - Mar. 1687
Blake, John	June 1687 - Dec. 1714

Second Clerks

Martyn, John	Sept. 1660 - Dec. 1661
Hooper, John	June 1662 - Mar. 1666
	(salary discontinued)
	Mar. 1667 - June 1667
Leece, James	Mar. 1668 - Sept. 1670
Bindlosse, Christopher	Dec. 1683 - Mar. 1685
Blake, John	Sept. 1685 - Mar. 1687
Masters, Harcourt[1]	1687?
Sturgeon, Richard	June 1687 - June 1688
Hanway, Richard	Sept. 1688 - Mar. 1689
Williamson, Robert	June 1689 - Sept. 1694
Williamson, Henry	Mar. 1696 - June 1702
Griffith, James	Sept. 1702 - June 1705
De Lanion, John	Sept. 1705 - Dec. 1714 (still in office)

Clerks to the surveyor-general

First clerks

Fleet(e)wood, Jeffrey	Sept. 1660 - June 1665
Rothwell, James	Sept. 1665 - Dec. 1685
Criche, Samuel	Mar. 1686 - Sept. 1701
Woolrich, Samuel	Dec. 1701 - Sept. 1702
Mercator, David	Dec. 1702 - Dec. 1714 (still in office)

Second clerks

Rothwell, James	Sept. 1660 - June 1665
Moore, Jonas, junior	Mar. 1666 - Dec. 1669
Duxbury, John	Mar. 1671 - Sept. 1676
Stevenson, Nicholas	Dec. 1676 - Sept. 1678
Fleet(e)wood, Jeffrey, junior?	Dec. 1678 - Sept. 1679
Criche, Samuel	Dec. 1679 - Dec. 1685
Fist, Anthony	Mar. 1686 - Dec. 1714 (still in office)

Third clerks

Cockshott, John	Mar. 1666 - Mar. 1667
Duxbury, John)	June 1667 - Dec. 1669
Whiteing, John)	
Allis, James	June 1682 - Sept. 1682
Read(e), John	Dec. 1683 - Dec. 1689
Woolrich, Samuel	Mar. 1690 - Sept. 1701
Thomas, Leeson	Mar. 1702 - Dec. 1702
Ayres, Thomas	Mar. 1703 - Sept. 1704
Yonge, Francis	Dec. 1704 - June 1712

Clerks to the clerk of the Ordnance

First clerks

Francklyn, William	Sept. 1660 - Sept. 1661

---

1 Masters was second clerk according to the list made out by Eustace in the early eighteenth century. Blenheim B I 23.

Candland, Thomas	Sept. 1662 - Dec. 1669
Harrison, Richard	Mar. 1670
Whiteing, John	June 1670 - Sept. 1702
White, Thomas	Dec. 1702 - Dec. 1714 (still in office)

Second clerks

Townesend, Thomas	Sept. 1660 - June 1689
Hooper, John	Sept. 1689 - Dec. 1692
Phelps, William	Mar. 1693 - June 1703
Gardiner, Christopher	Sept. 1703 - Mar. 1705
Lister, Christopher	June 1705 - Dec. 1714 (still in office)

Third clerks

Harrison, Richard	28 Sept. 1664 - Dec. 1669
Pontie, Thomas	June 1670
Povey, Francis	Sept. 1670 - Mar. 1680
Hooper, John	Mar. 1681 - June 1689
Phelps, William	Sept. 1689 - Dec. 1692
Gardiner, Christopher	Mar. 1693 - June 1703
Lister, Christopher	Sept. 1703 - Mar. 1705
Gibson, Rowland	June 1705 - Dec. 1714 (still in office)

Fourth clerks

Nicholson, Humphry	Dec. 1673 - Mar. 1674
Lay, Augustine	Sept. 1674 - Mar. 1685
Phelps, William	June 1685 - June 1689
Cardonnell, James	Sept. 1689 - Dec. 1689
Purcell, Matthew	Mar. 1690
Gardiner, Christopher	June 1690 - Dec. 1692
Deere, Edward	Mar. 1693 - Dec. 1714 (still in office)

Clerks to the storekeeper

First clerks

Conyers, Edward	Sept. 1660 - Mar. 1666 (salary discontinued)
	Mar. 1667 - Dec. 1673
Goodhand, Charles	Mar. 1674 - Mar. 1676
Allen, John, senior	June 1676 - Dec. 1714 (still in office)

Second clerks

Aldham, Thomas	Sept. 1660 - Sept. 1661
Fowke, Roger	Sept. 1662 - Dec. 1664
Robson, Thomas	Mar. 1665 - Sept. 1665
Fowke, Roger	Mar. 1666 - Dec. 1672
Barton, Abell	Mar. 1673 - Sept. 1693
Bla(c)kler, John	Dec. 1693 - Sept. 1705
Eustace, Alexander	Dec. 1705 - Dec. 1714 (still in office)

Third clerks

Baron, Apsley[1]	Mar. 1666 - Dec. 1666
Pontie, Thomas	Dec. 1670 - Sept. 1671

---

1 One Thomas Ewen officiated for one of these quarters, but Marsh was unwilling that two clerks should be entered for two quarters, and ordered that Baron should be entered for both, and that he should pay Ewen for his quarter's salary when he received it. WO 49/112.

Billinghurst, George	Dec. 1671 - Mar. 1673
Allen, John, senior	June 1673 - Mar. 1676
Whittaker, Henry	June 1676 - Sept. 1678
Bla(c)kler, John	Mar. 1679 - Sept. 1693
Eustace, Alexander	Dec. 1693 - Sept. 1705
Allen, John, junior	Dec. 1705 - June 1713
Wright, Robert	Sept. 1713 - Dec. 1714 (still in office)

Clerks to clerk of deliveries

First clerks

Sparkes, Edward, senior	Sept. 1660 - Mar. 1671
Sparkes, Edward, junior?	June 1671 - Mar. 1674
Fortrey, William	June 1674 - Mar. 1682
Whittaker, Nicholas	June 1682 - Dec. 1714 (still in office)

Second clerks

Sparkes, Edward, junior	Dec. 1664 - Mar. 1671
Rogers, Thomas	June 1671 - Dec. 1675
Whittaker, Nicholas	June 1676 - Mar. 1682
Mercator, David	June 1682 - June 1684
Smith, Thomas	Sept. 1684 - Dec. 1696
Musgrave, William	Mar. 1697 - Dec. 1706
L(l)oyd(e), John	Mar. 1707 - Dec. 1714 (still in office)

Clerks to the treasurer

First clerks

Leece, James	Dec. 1670 - Mar. 1690
Hubbald, Edward	Sept. 1690 - Dec. 1699
Churchill, William	Mar. 1700 - June 1703
Leece, James, junior?	Sept. 1703 - Mar. 1705
Lansdell(e), John	Sept. 1705 - Dec. 1712
Lee, Joseph	Mar. 1713 - Dec. 1714 (still in office)

Second clerks

Hubbald, Edward	Dec. 1670 - June 1690
Mar(r)iott, Richard	Dec. 1691 - June 1699
Leece, James, junior?	Mar. 1700 - June 1703
Mar(r)iott, James	Sept. 1703 - Mar. 1705
Mar(r)iott, Richard	June 1705 - Sept. 1705
Pearce, John	Dec. 1705 - Mar. 1713
Middleton, Arthur	June 1713 - Dec. 1714 (still in office)

Third clerks

Hooper, John	Mar. 1678
Birkett, George	June 1678 - Dec. 1678
Scattergood, William	June 1679 - Sept. 1691
Leece, James, junior?	June 1690 - Dec. 1699
Purcell, Matthew	Mar. 1700 - June 1701
Pearce, John	Sept. 1701 - June 1705
Foster, Samuel	Sept. 1705 - Mar. 1706
Clifford, George	June 1706 - Dec. 1711
Burton, John	Mar. 1712 - Dec. 1714 (still in office)

Fourth clerk

Hooper, John	Sept. 1678 - Mar. 1680

Storekeepers of Rich Weapons,
Saltpetre and Small Guns

Keepers of rich weapons

Marsh, Richard	Sept. 1660 - Mar. 1672
Marsh, Sir George	June 1672 - Dec. 1673
Conyers, Edward	Mar. 1674 - Sept. 1683

Keepers of saltpetre

Baylis, (Baylie?), Matthew	from 24 Mar. 1662
Wharton, George	from Dec. 1663
Hubbald, Edward	Dec. 1683 - Dec. 1699 (at Woolwich)
Griffith, Jeffrey	Mar. 1700 - June 1712 (at Woolwich)
Farmer, Edward	Sept. 1712 - Dec. 1714 (at Woolwich, still in office)

Keepers of small guns

Hooker, John	Sept. 1660 - Sept. 1663
Baylie, Matthew [1]	14 Oct. 1663 - Feb. 1664
Batchler, Richard	Mar. 1664 - June 1678
Beaumont, Charles	Sept. 1678 - June 1691
Gardiner, Thomas, junior	June 1691 - Dec. 1714 (still in office)

Armoury Storekeepers

Deputy keepers of the armoury

Faireside, William	by Oct. 1670
Franklyn, George	7 Oct. 1682 - Mar. 1695
May, George	June 1695 - Sept. 1696
May, Charles	Dec. 1696 - Mar. 1699
Nicholas, William	18 May 1699 - Dec. 1714 (still in office)

Keepers of the armoury at St. James's

Nicholls, William	from 10 Aug. 1684
Jones, James	from 1 Apr. 1687
Marley, John	15 July 1689 - Apr. 1714

Keepers of the armoury at Whitehall

Houghton, Jeremiah	19 May 1671 - Sept. 1685
De Latre, Jean	from 25 Nov. 1685
Graham, John	from 18 Jan. 1689
Kemp, John [2]	c. 1689
Beaubuson, Peter Guanon	from 23 Jan. 1690
Kemp, William ?	by Nov. 1695

Keeper of the armoury at Hampton Court

Harris, John	from 30 Nov. 1699

---

1 Compton appointed Major Matthew Baylie to look after the office, in the place of Hooker, until the king could signify his pleasure by the signing of a patent (PRO 30 37/15, 22 Sept. 1663, Compton's warrant). A patent for the office was apparently procured by Baylie, but he was suspended from office as he had inserted in the patent a claim to repair all arms within the Office of Small Guns. The office was given to Batchler because Baylie refused to have the patent altered. WO 55/388, fo. 31, 16 Feb. 1664; WO 47/5, pp. 158-9, 203.

2 Kemp claimed that he had a grant of the office from Schomberg, though it is not clear whether he ever executed the office. *Cal. SP Dom. 1689-90.* p. 499.

Storekeepers at Garrisons and Outports

Barbados (Storekeeper and Engineer)

Lilly, Christian   by June 1713

Berwick

Jackson, Charles   Dec. 1683 - June 1689
Grieve, Thomas   Sept. 1689 - Mar. 1711
Sibett, John   1 July 1711 - Dec. 1714 (still in office)

Bridlington

Aslaby, Thomas   by Sept. 1685
Erett, Thomas   by Dec. 1692

Carlisle

Fielding, Basil   from 24 May 1686
Dalston, Christopher   from 20 Apr. 1689
Longstaffe, George   from 12 Dec. 1691
Welsh, Robert   3 Feb. 1700 - Apr. 1714 (still in office)

Chatham

Browne, John[1]   from *c.*1660 - *c.* 1665
Batchler, Richard[1]   29 June - 23 Dec. 1665
Gregory, Edward   )[2]   from 3 Mar. 1666
Robson, Thomas   )   from 27 Nov. 1666
Cheltenham, Nicholas   13 Mar. 1668 - Dec. 1696
Smith, Thomas   Mar. 1697 - June 1700
Goodricke, George   Sept. 1700 - Dec. 1714

Chepstow

Hughes, Charles   from 2 Mar. 1686
Hull, George   from 5 Feb. 1689
Lewis, Henry   from 15 July 1689

Chester

Shackerley, Peter)[3]
Fielding, William)   from 30 May 1686
Williams, Powell   from 15 June 1689
Brett, John   from 20 Jan. 1689
Brampton, Richard   from 24 Jan. 1691

Clifford's Fort (Storekeeper and Master Gunner)

Lupton, David   from 22 Oct. 1689

Dover

Hollingsbury, ?   by Feb. 1708

---

1 Batchler's appointment was probably only a temporary one. WO 49/111, Marsh to Batchler, 8 July 1665. A Captain Audley was sent to help him during the summer of 1665. WO 49/112, letter from Marsh, 1 Aug. [1665].

2 Thomas Robson executed the office jointly with Gregory during 1666, and on 27 Nov. of that year he was formally appointed joint storekeeper at £40 p.a. WO 55/332, p. 90.

3 From 3 Feb. 1688 Shackerley executed the office by himself. WO 55/472, p. 63.

Greenwich

Brockhurst, Francis	from 24 Jan. 1691
	Apr. 1714 (still in office)

Gibraltar

Gauden, Jonathan	from Oct./Nov. 1685
Clarke, ?	by Apr. 1708
Musgrave, Thomas	by Mar. 1713

Guernsey

le Merchant, William	17 Mar. 1691 - Apr. 1714 (still in office)

Harwich

Newby, Francis	from 6 Jan. 1666
Taylor, Sylas	4 Apr. 1667 - Dec. 1678

Hull

Watkinson, John	26 Jan. 1660 - June 1685
Duxbury, John	Sept. 1685 - June 1689
Idell, William	Sept. 1689 - Mar. 1708
Jackson, Ralph	18 Mar. 1708 - Dec. 1714 (still in office)

Hurst Castle and Yarmouth

Combes, John	by June 1705

Jamaica

Chester, Theodore	22 Feb. 1678 - Dec. 1682
Bell, Thomas	by 1 Jan. 1703
Baxter, John	by June 1707
Hawkyns, Francis (Storekeeper and Engineer)	by Apr. 1709

Jersey

Dumaresque, Charles	23 Dec. 1690 - Apr. 1714 (still in office)
Hardy, John	from 1 Oct. 1714

Kinsale

Penne, William	from 19 Mar. 1668
Walker, James	from 19 July 1694
Soulden, Gabriel	from 28 July 1697

Landguard Fort

Marbury, Richard	from Feb. 1665
Marshall, George	from Oct. 1710
Hunton, Nicholas	1 Jan. 1713 - Apr. 1714 (still in office)

Lisbon

Bowles, Phineas	*c*. Mar. 1685 - *c*. June 1687

Londonderry

Spurway, Samuel	from 27 Feb. 1689

Margate

Cooke, William	by Dec. 1692

Pendennis Castle

Halling, Thomas (Master Gunner in charge of stores)	by Dec. 1685

| Collins, George | from 30 May 1686 |
| Thorpe, John | 13 Nov. 1690 - Apr. 1714 (still in office) |

Plymouth

Blake, Richard	16 Sept. 1665 - *c.* Dec. 1681
Hooke, Henry (port and garrison storekeeper by Dec. 1692)	15 Mar. 1682 - Dec. 1714 (still in office)
Langford, William (garrison stores)	Oct. 1662 - Sept. 1667

Portsmouth

Newberry, Thomas	1660
Clarke, Henry	from Dec. 1660
Fleetwood, Thomas	from 23 Feb. 1665
Povey, William	from 10 Mar. 1666 - *c.* Sept. 1669
Bennett, Thomas	4 Aug. 1670 - May 1674
Perkins, Henry	7 Mar. 1674 - Sept. 1678
Perkins, Timothy	12 Nov. 1678 - Mar. 1681
Ridge, Richard	3 Feb. 1681 - June 1689
Felton, Francis	Sept. 1689 - *c.* Dec. 1691
Felton, Francis, junior	12 Dec. 1691 - June 1695
Hooper, John	Sept. 1695 - Dec. 1714 (still in office)
Williams, Samuel (garrison stores)	prior to June 1685
Holford, Matthew (garrison stores)	from 26 June 1685
Starkey, James (garrison stores)	from 19 Feb. 1686
Holford, Walter (garrison stores)	18 Apr. 1691 - Dec. 1714 (still in office)

Sheerness

Newby, Francis[1]	by 1668
Dye, Francis	16 Jan. 1675 - Sept. 1678
Thompson, Robert	16 Jan. 1675 - June 1678
Aynge, Charles	24 Dec. 1678 - June 1683
Crawford, Robert	24 May 1683 - Dec. 1706
Withers, Henry ?	Mar. 1707 - Dec. 1714 (still in office)

Tangier

| Bennett, Thomas | by Aug. 1675 |
| Povey, Francis | by Apr. 1680 |

Tilbury

Newby, Francis	from Nov. 1677
Povey, Francis	11 Feb. 1686 - June 1687
Legge, William	12 May 1687 - June 1689
Jordan(e), Francis	Sept. 1689 - Dec. 1699
White, Charles	Mar. 1700 - Dec. 1714 (still in office)

Tynemouth

| French, Edward | prior to Apr. 1690 |
| Sisson, Edward | 7 Apr. 1690 - Apr. 1714 (still in office) |

[1] Prior to Newby's appointment the stores were in the charge of Lewis Williams, a gunner of the fort. WO 47/19a, p. 273, 17 Apr. 1669.

Upnor Castle

Baylie, Matthew	*c.*Sept. 1668 - Mar. 1670
Fortescue, John	by Nov. 1670
Myners, Robert	by Sept. 1675 - June 1689
Brockhurst, Francis	8 June 1689 - Mar. 1691
Myners, Robert	26 Feb. 1691 - Mar. 1695
Taylor, Sir Thomas bt.	1 Jan. 1695 - Dec. 1696
Rouse, Edmund	1 Dec. 1696 - Sept. 1703
Hastings, Edward	2 Nov. 1703 - Mar. 1711
Webb, John	June 1711 - Dec. 1714 (still in office)

Windsor Castle

Batchler, Richard	from 7 Feb. 1663
Wise, Edward	13 May 1664 - June 1684
Graham, John	Sept. 1684 - June 1689
Holford, Thomas	Sept. 1689 - Dec. 1692
Carty, Daniel	1 Feb. 1703 - Dec. 1714 (still in office)

Woolwich

Linby, Paul	by Oct. 1669
Povey, William	by Aug. 1670
Chuseman, Francis	1 Feb. 1671 - Sept. 1677
Peach, Thomas	10 Oct. 1677 - Dec. 1692
Hooper, John (at Tower Place)	Mar. 1693 - June 1695
Felton, Francis (at Tower Place)	Sept. 1695 - Dec. 1714 (still in office)
Baxter, John (at Laboratory)	from 18 Apr. 1698

Yarmouth (Norfolk?)

Yeames, Edward	by Sept. 1695

Miscellaneous Officials

Armourers

Hoden, Richard	by Mar. 1688 - Sept. 1709
Hicks, John	by Mar. 1688 - June 1689
Wright, George	by Mar. 1688 - Dec. 1714 (still in office)
Crawford, Jeremiah	Sept. 1689 - Dec. 1713
Hoden, Henry	Mar. 1710 - Dec. 1714 (still in office)
Thwaites, Abraham	June 1714 - Dec. 1714 (still in office)

Astronomical Observator at Greenwich

Flamstead, John	by Dec. 1692

Captain of Office Yacht

Leake, Richard	by June 1677
Stradder, George	from 11 July 1677

Clerks of Check

Marbury, Richard	by mid 1661
Fiske, John	from 21 Dec. 1665
Barton, Abell	from 17 Apr. 1672
Blyton, Matthew	28 July 1673 - Mar. 1702
Wright, William	20 Mar. 1702 - Dec. 1714 (still in office)

Furbishers of Small Arms[1]

Steadman, Robert [2] (in Rich Weapon Office)	2 Aug. 1660 - Dec. 1664
Fisher, George (in Tower)	Sept. 1660 - Sept. 1664
Fisher, George, junior (in Tower)	Dec. 1664 - Dec. 1694
Cripps, Henry (in Tower)	Mar. 1695 - Mar. 1710
Woolridge, Richard (in Tower)	June 1711 - Dec. 1714 (still in office)
Richardson, Michael (at Portsmouth)	15 Nov. 1675 - Mar. 1686
Silvester, John (at Portsmouth)	June 1686 - Dec. 1714 (still in office)
Silvester, Edward (at Portsmouth)	from June 1712 - Dec. 1714 (still in office)

Gentlemen of the Ordnance

At Tower

Paslew, Richard	from Christmas 1669
Kelly, Hugh	from 31 Mar. 1670
Smith, Francis	from 21 Aug. 1686
Silvester, Edward	from 13 Mar. 1691
Silvester, Thomas	from 17 Feb. 1699

At Whitehall, St. James's Park

Lewen, John	from 21 Aug. 1686
Graham, John	from 15 Jan. 1689
De Cardonnel, James	from 20 May 1689
Whittaker, Nicholas	from Feb. 1692
White, Thomas	from 18 Jan. 1700
La Comb, René	by June 1703

At Outports

Mossom, Charles	from 21 Aug. 1686
Hubbald, William	from 20 Apr. 1689
Phelps, William	from 30 Nov. 1700
Aleman, John (Portsmouth)	from 1 Feb. 1703

Messengers

Ball, Adam	2 Aug. 1660 - Sept. 1687
Snapes, Edward	Dec. 1687 - Dec. 1703
Harrison, Francis[3]	Mar. 1704 - Dec. 1708
Watson, Thomas	Mar. 1709 - Mar. 1710
Parmer, Edward	Sept. 1712 - Dec. 1714 (still in office)

1 Only the major furbishers have been listed. By 1707 there were two furbishers of small arms at the Tower at £50 *per annum* each, one furbisher of swords and bayonets at the Tower at £35 *per annum*, one furbisher at St. James and Hampton Court, one at Windsor Castle, one at Chester, one at Hull, two at Berwick, and one at Plymouth, at £70, £50, 2s. (per day), £36. 10s., £20 (each) and £20 *per annum* respectively (WO 48/46, list 14 Aug. 1707, 16th payment). It is clear that there were also numerous other furbishers at the Tower, as in Mar. 1717 Gardiner reported to the board that there were 21 at work, 3 sick and 27 not at work (WO 47/30, p. 80).

2 This office was discontinued after the death of Steadman in Dec. 1664. WO 47/6, p. 82, minute 8 Dec. 1664.

3 Thomas White, clerk in ordinary under the clerk of the Ordnance, executed the messenger's place after the death of Snapes until Harrison was appointed. WO 48/42, list 30 June 1704, 66th payment.

Overseers of Fortifications

Riding Overseer of Forts in Great Britain

Ayres, Thomas	from 23 Nov. 1710
Smith, James (in North Britain)	from Jan. 1711

Overseers at Hull

Duxbury, John	by Mar. 1682
Raven, Edward	by Aug. 1707
Barrett, George	by 1712

Overseers at Portsmouth

Jackson, Ralph	by Aug. 1707
Bowerbank, Thomas	from 5 Mar. 1708

Overseers at Tilbury

Newby, Francis	from 1 July 1684
Henly, John	by Aug. 1707

Proofmasters

Francklyn, Richard	by July 1664
Bagnall, Richard	Sept. 1660 - Sept. 1673
Lanyon, John	Sept. 1660 - Sept. 1661
Baylie, Matthew	29 Sept. 1661 - Mar. 1668
Kelly, Hugh	18 Aug. 1668 - June 1679
Smith, Francis	3 Jan. 1674 - Dec. 1691
Piggott, John	Sept. 1679 - June 1681
Lloyd, Charles	Sept. 1680 - Mar. 1686
Hartup(p), Sir William	June 1686 - Dec. 1692
Littleton, Edward	Mar. 1692 - Sept. 1693
Blake, John	Mar. 1693 - Dec. 1714 (still in office)
Allen, John	Dec. 1693 - Mar. 1711
Allen, John, junior	June 1711 - June 1713
Mercator, David, junior?	Sept. 1713 - Dec. 1714 (still in office)
Rowney, Thomas (at Birmingham)	by Dec. 1692

Purveyors

Merry, John	by Dec. 1675 - Sept. 1683
Bennet(t), Robert	7 Mar. 1672 - Mar. 1698
Bennet(t), Isaac	June 1700 - Dec. 1714 (still in office)

Purveyors for Measuring Works

Hill, John	by July 1681
Willoughby, William	from 15 May 1689
Meads, William	from 30 Nov. 1693

Seizer of Embezzled Stores

Green, Edmund	from 4 Sept. 1677

Solicitor

Cowart, Charles	deceased June 1718

Surgeons

Seale, Thomas	from 4 Nov. 1676
Herriot, Andrew	4 Dec. 1693 - *c*. Oct. 1700
Gardner, John	from Nov. 1700

Waggon Masters[1]

Sherburne, Justinian	19 Mar. 1675 - June 1689
Bernard, George	Sept. 1689 - Sept. 1693
Ball, Charles	Dec. 1693 - Dec. 1714 (still in office)

Waterworker

Walford, Thomas	by Dec. 1692

Yeomen of Tents and Toils

Howard, Thomas	6 Feb. 1686 - Sept. 1701
Hayward, Thomas	Dec. 1701 - Mar. 1703
Trovilla, John	June 1703 - June 1710
Forstbrok(e), Thomas	Sept. 1710 - Mar. 1712
Howard, Thomas	June 1712 - June 1713
Howard, Charles	Sept. 1713 - Dec. 1714 (still in office)

Fireworkers

Comptroller of Fireworks

Beckman, Sir Martin[2]	11 Aug. 1688 - June 1702
Hop(c)ke(y), John Henry	1 May 1706 - Dec. 1714 (still in office)

Chief Firemasters

Circlebach(k), Matthias	by June 1667 - June 1669
De Rüis, Ernest Heinrich[3]	19 Oct. 1670 - Sept. 1677
	12 Apr. 1682 - Sept. 1685
Sleinsteine, Nicholas	Dec. 1685
Wo(o)llfermen(n), John Christopher	Mar. 1686 - Dec. 1689
Neilson, Isaac	Mar. 1690 - Dec. 1690
Schlundt, Johan Signum	Mar. 1691 - Dec. 1698
Hop(c)ke, Henry	Mar. 1699 - Mar. 1706
Pendlebury, James	June 1706 - Sept. 1710
Hara, Alexander	Dec. 1710 - Sept. 1712
Borgard, Albert	Dec. 1712 - Dec. 1714 (still in office)

1 Before the appointment of Sherburne the waggon master was only a temporary appointment (WO. 51/9, fo. 13, payment to Baylie employed as waggon master-general, 13 June - 30 Aug. 1667, at 5s. per day). By 1689 there was a deputy-master (WO 48/29, 17 Apr. 1691, payment to Bateman).

2 Beckman's salary was stopped on the accession of William, and the warrant was not renewed until Mar. 1693 (PC 2/74, p. 102, 2 Mar. 1693). His arrears of salary were ordered to be repaid (WO 55/340, fo. 206, king's warrant, 13 Dec. 1694).

3 De Rüis was given a pass to Sweden 'on his private occasions' in Sept. 1677, and to stay there until the following summer (*Cal. SP Dom. 1677-78*, p. 368, 21 Sept. 1677). He does not seem to have been re-appointed at the Ordnance office, however, until Apr. 1682.

Mates to Chief Firemaster

Fiefe, Frederick	Sept. 1682
Wo(o)llferman(n), John Christopher	5 Dec. 1682 - Dec. 1685 ?
Neilson, Isaac	23 Jan. 1683 - Dec. 1689
Hop(c)ke, John Henry	Mar. 1690 - Dec. 1698
Baxter, John	Mar. 1699 - Dec. 1714 (still in office)

Fireworkers

Browne, John	30 Nov. 1671 - Dec. 1678
Lingard, John	1 Feb. 1676 - Sept. 1679
De Rüis, Magnus Henry	12 Apr. 1682 - Sept. 1685
Neilson, Isaac	12 Apr. 1682 - Dec. 1682
Browne, George	12 Apr. 1682 - Dec. 1687
Gale, Thomas	12 Apr. 1682 - Mar. 1684
English, James (also Firemaster for the Fireships by Dec, 1692)	12 Apr. 1682 - Mar. 1700
Porteen, John	Dec. 1685 - June 1687
Wo(o)llferman(n), Hans Jacob	June 1684 - Dec. 1685
Blagwitz, Jacob	Sept. 1687 - Mar. 1703
Hoftman, Andrew	Mar. 1686 - Dec. 1690
Poolman, John	Mar. 1691 - Dec. 1698
Wood, William	Mar. 1699 - Dec. 1703
Baxter, John	June 1688 - Dec. 1698
Barker, Robert	Mar. 1699
Felton, James	June 1700 - Dec. 1714 (still in office)
Sims, Hugh	June 1699
Pendlebury, James	Sept. 1699 - Sept. 1710
Traherne, Thomas	June 1703 - Dec. 1714 (still in office)
Egerton, Joseph	Mar. 1705 - Dec. 1714 (still in office)
Hara, Alexander	Dec. 1710 - Sept. 1712
Spencer, George	Mar. 1713 - Dec. 1714 (still in office)

Chief Bombardiers

Moody, Daniel	Dec. 1686 - Mar. 1688
Browne, George	June 1688 - Sept. 1702 (not listed Sept. 1695)
Watson, Jonas	Sept. 1703 - Dec. 1714 (still in office)

Chief Petardiers

Fawcett, John	Dec. 1686 - Mar. 1711 (not listed Sept. 1695)
Musgrave, George	June 1711 - Dec. 1714 (still in office)

Gunners

Master Gunners

Woolaston, Richard	to June 1660
Weymes, James	Sept. 1660 - Sept. 1664
Pyne, Valentine	June 1666 - May ? 1677
Leake, Richard	21 May 1677 - Oct. ? 1696
Browne, George	30 Oct. 1696 - Sept. 1702
Silver, Thomas	16 Mar. 1703 - Sept. 1709
Pendlebury, James	30 Nov. 1710 - Dec. 1714 (still in office)

Mates to Master Gunner

Leake, John	12 Apr. 1682 - June 1700
Dodge, Thomas	12 Apr. 1682 - June 1703

Silver, Thomas	12 Apr. 1682 - Mar. 1703
Leake, Richard, junior	Sept. 1700 - Dec. 1714 (still in office)
Bousfield, William	June 1705 - Dec. 1714 (still in office)
Hall, Thomas	June 1705 - June 1708
Guybon, Robert	Mar. 1711 - Mar. 1714
Baxter, John	June 1714 - Dec. 1714 (still in office)

Engineers

Chief Engineers

Lloyd, Sir Charles[1]	1660 - 1661
Lloyd, Sir Godfrey	from 17 Jan. 1661
De Gomme, Sir Bernard	1 Apr. 1661 - Dec. 1685
Beckman, Sir Martin[2]	23 Dec. 1685 - June 1702
Richards, Michael	Dec. 1711 - Dec. 1714 (still in office)

2nd Engineers

Beckman, Martin	19 Oct. 1670 - Dec. 1685
Phillips, Thomas[3]	23 Dec. 1685 - Sept. 1689
	8 May 1691 - Dec. 1693
Blood, Holcraft	Feb. 1696 - Sept. 1707 (not listed Jan./Sept. 1702)
Edwards, Talbot	Feb. 1696 - Dec. 1714 (still in office)

3rd Engineers

Phillips, Thomas	Sept. 1683 - Dec. 1685
Richards, Jacob	6 June 1686 - June 1701
Lilly, Christian	June 1701 - Dec. 1714 (still in office)

1 Charles Lloyd was granted the reversion on 6 Apr. 1639, after the demise of Thomas Rudd or John Paperell. He came into the place upon the death of Paperell, and apparently held it for one year from the Restoration before his decease. T. 51/3, fo. 208-9, warrant 24 Mar. 1662.

2 Beckman gained the reversion in Mar. 1678. *Cal. Treas. Books 1676-9,* p.938; *Cal. SP Dom. 1678,* p. 40.

3 Phillips was suspended from office in 1689 by Schomberg. T. 1/18, fo. 294.

Note on Manuscript Sources

The major manuscript source for this study is to be found in the Public
Record Office, where there are several hundred volumes relating to the
late Stuart Ordnance Office in the following series: WO 44, WO 46-49
WO 51 and WO 54-55). The first class of these series, WO 44 (in-letters,
petitions etc. to the master-general and board) is not of great importance
for the department in this period. The first six volumes of the out-letters
series (WO 46) are of more interest. The first two volumes relate to Hull
garrison, and the next few to correspondence between the board and
master-general (mainly during the absences of Romney and
Marlborough). The minute books (WO 47/5-33, 1664-1720, various
series with gaps) are of crucial importance as they reflect the day to
day activities of the Ordnance Board. The early volumes of the series,
however, are not minute books as we would know them today, for
they are not solely confined to recording minutes of the board's
proceedings — the in-letter order, paper or warrant from which the
board's action arose is noted, together with the minute expressing the
board's decision, and the subsequent correspondence arising from that
decision. As the period progresses, however, this extraneous matter is
largely excluded and the minutes become more formalised (Compare,
for example, WO 47/8, minutes, 1666, with WO 47/16, minutes, 1685.
In the earlier volume there is little order about the minute entries,
which are intermingled with relating documents, whereas in the latter
volume the minutes are recorded on one side of the page, and a blank
side is then left for information as to whether the minutes have been
acted upon. The later volumes — minutes series II and III,
WO 47/22-25, 27-33, covering the years 1705-8 and 1714-20 — are even
more formalised copy books of the board's proceedings and include a
detailed index.) The Ordnance treasury ledgers and debenture, bill and
quarter books (WO 48-49, 51 and 54) may be taken together as they
are similar in content. They provide a detailed record of many aspects
of the department's work, including the names and activities
of Ordnance personnel, the nature of contracts and the size
of departmental receipts and expenditures. The treasury ledgers
(WO 48, complete 1660-1714) record under various heads all payments
made by the Ordnance treasury; they also give an account of the
Office's receipts. The earlier ledgers are arranged somewhat haphazardly
but, like the minute books, they become more ordered, so that the
last volume of the series for this period (WO 48/53, Charles Eversfield's
account, 30 June - 1 Dec. 1714) is meticulously drawn up. It is
divided into several parts. The first records the departmental receipts —
Exchequer charge, voluntary charge and vacated imprests; the second

and third parts are accounts, on various lists, of quarter book and debenture payments; and at the back of the volume is an abstract account of the receipts and payments for that year. The ledger books, therefore, largely duplicate the debenture payments books (WO 49, an incomplete record of debenture payments); bill books (WO 51, a continuous series which details all Ordnance bills, including those not paid by debenture — the earlier books also include accounts of the amounts and costs of stores received); and quarter books (completed list, Sept. 1660 - Dec. 1714, of the personnel officers on the Ordnance establishment with their quarterly salaries and allowances). WO 55 is an important miscellaneous class of Ordnance documents. This class includes entry books of letters patent and warrants from the king, Council, master-general, Admiralty etc.; the Ordnance instructions; accounts of store issues and receipts; store remains; contract registers; and a host of miscellaneous books and papers. All these series are listed in *Lists and Indexes,* XXVIII, War Office Records (HMSO, 1908), pp. 147-232. A useful guide to the records of the department has recently been compiled (PRO typescript, 26417).

The public archives also contain Ordnance material among the Admiralty records, the declared accounts (which largely duplicate the Ordnance treasury ledgers), the Privy Council registers, and the State and Treasury papers. The dates of appointment of the principal officers may be obtained from the patent rolls, and the wills of various officers are to be found among the probate records formerly in the custody of the Prerogative Court of Canterbury. The Pritchett MSS. (PRO 30/37) are the only relevant private collection for the department of this period within the Public Record Office. These papers all relate to the 1660s, or earlier, and include entry books of contracts, deliveries and receipts, and letter books of the master-general, lieutenant-general and master-general commissioners. The most important private collections for this study within the country at large are to be found at Stafford (Dartmouth MSS.), Carlisle (Lonsdale MSS. - Lowther papers), and Cambridge (Pepys Library and Erle MSS.). The only important Ordnance papers in the British Library are contained within the Marlborough MSS., which have recently been transferred there from Blenheim Palace. There are interesting individual items within other collections at the British Library and at the Bodleian Library, Oxford.

INDEX

(*Note:* Only the major references have been given under the heading ordnance office, board)

58-9, 63; patronage powers of, 73-5, 87, 96 (*see also* individual officers)

master-general's chief clerks or secretaries, 48 & n, 50, 53, 65, 82; allowances of, 89, 90n, 94, 96

master gunners, 3, 8n, 14, 47, 57, 65, 73, 77, 150n, 238; allowances of, 89, 90n, 96, 122

Masters, Harcourt, 86, 227 & n

May, Charles, 230

May, George, 230

Meads, William, 236

Medway raid, 147, 164

Meesters, William, 49, 60, 65, 66, 79, 99, 225

Merbury, Nicholas, 2

Mercator, David, the elder, 229

Mercator, David, the younger, 227, 236

Merry, John, 236

messengers, 47, 55-6, 77, 235 & n

Middleton, Arthur, 229

Middleton, Captain Charles, 66, 74

Mildenhall, Robert, 1

military manuals, 134

Minories, vi, 74, 88, 109, 118-19, 122, 127

mint, 1, 35, 41

Monck, General George, 1st Duke of Albemarle, 85, 208

Monmouth *see* Scott, James

Moody, Daniel, 238

Mordaunt, Charles, 3rd Earl of Peterborough, 73

Mordaunt, Harry, 67, 73, 80, 82, 85n, 97, 101, 225, 226

Moore, Sir Jonas, the elder, 47, 59, 60, 61, 79, 84, 85, 101, 115n, 117, 120, 219, 224 & n, 226

Moore, Sir Jonas, the younger, 60, 63, 71, 78, 79, 101, 224, 226, 227

Morris, Christopher, 3

Morris, John, 77

mortars, 57, 103, 107n, 122, 133, 150n, 207

Mossom, Charles, 235

Mountjoy, Blount, 1st Earl of Newport, 79

Musgrave, Sir Christopher, the elder, 59, 60, 66, 71, 75, 76, 79, 223, 224

Musgrave, Christopher, the younger, 60, 66, 68, 71, 72 & n, 76, 80, 85n, 101, 225

Musgrave, George, 238

Musgrave, Philip, 48, 66, 71, 79, 150n, 190, 225, 226

Musgrave, Thomas, 232

Musgrave, William, 229